The Federalist Papers:
Modern English Edition Two

Mary E. Webster

Translator/Editor

Website: http://Mary.Webster.org
Email: Mary.Webster.org

Table of Contents

Defense: Domestic

Taxation

Drafting Constitution

Constitutional Convention

Federal Powers

State Powers

"Separation of Powers" Within Government

Structure of Proposed Government

Legislative: House of Representatives

THE CONSTITUTION OF THE UNITED STATES OF AMERICA

September 17, 1787

We, the people of the United States, In Order to form a more perfect Union, establish Justice, insure domestic Tranquility, provide for the common defence, promote the general Welfare, and secure the Blessings of Liberty to ourselves and our Posterity, do ordain and establish this

Constitution for the United States of America.

Article One

Section 1. All legislative Powers herein granted shall be vested in a Congress of the United States, which shall consist of a Senate and House of Representatives.

Section 2. The House of Representatives shall be composed of Members chosen every second Year by the People of the several States, and the Electors in each State shall have the Qualifications requisite for Electors of the most numerous Branch of the State legislature.

No person shall be a Representative who shall not have attained to the Age of twenty five Years, and been seven Years a Citizen of the United States, and who shall not, when elected, be an Inhabitant to that State in which he shall be chosen.

[Representatives and direct Taxes shall be apportioned among the several States which may be included within this Union, according to their respective Numbers, which shall be determined by adding to the whole Number of free Persons, including those bound to Service for a Term of Years, and excluding Indians not taxed, three-fifths of all other persons.]* The actual Enumeration shall be made within three Years after the first Meeting of the Congress of the United States, and within every subsequent Term of ten Years, in such Manner as they shall by Law direct. The number of Representatives shall not exceed one for every thirty Thousand, but each State shall have at Least one Representative; and until such enumeration shall be made, the State of *New Hampshire* shall be entitled to choose three, *Massachusetts* eight, *Rhode Island and Providence Plantations* one, *Connecticut* five, *New York* six, *New Jersey* four, *Pennsylvania* eight, *Delaware* one, *Maryland* six, *Virginia* ten, *North Carolina* five, *South Carolina* five, and *Georgia* three.

When vacancies happen in the Representation from any State, the Executive Authority thereof shall issue Writs of Election to fill such Vacancies.

The House of Representatives shall chuse their Speaker and other Officers; and shall have the sole Power of **Impeachment.**

Section 3. The **Senate** of the United States shall be composed of **two** Senators from each **State**, [chosen by the legislature thereof,]* for **six years**; and each Senator shall have one vote.

Immediately after they shall be assembled in Consequence of the first Election, they shall be divided as equally as may be into three Classes. The Seats of the Senators of the first Class shall be vacated at the Expiration of the second Year, of the second Class, at the Expiration of the fourth Year, and of the third Class, at the Expiration of the sixth Year, so that one third may be chosen every second Year; [and if Vacancies happen by Resignation, or otherwise, during the Recess of the Legislature of any State, the Executive thereof may make temporary Appointments until the next Meeting of the Legislature, which shall then fill such Vacancies.]*

No person shall be a Senator who shall not have attained to the Age of **thirty Years**, and been **nine Years a Citizen** of the United States, and who shall not, when elected, be an **Inhabitant of that State** for which he shall be chosen.

The Vice President of the United States shall be President of the Senate, but shall have no Vote, unless they be equally divided.

The Senate shall choose their other Officers, and also a President *pro tempore,* in the absence of the Vice President, or when he shall exercise the office of President of the United States.

The Senate shall have the sole Power to try all **Impeachments**. When sitting for that Purpose, they shall be on Oath or Affirmation. When the President of the United States is tried, the Chief Justice shall preside: And no Person shall be convicted without the Concurrence

of two thirds of the Members present.

Judgment in Cases of **Impeachment** shall not extend further than to removal from Office, and disqualification to hold and enjoy any Office of honor, Trust or Profit under the United States: but the Party convicted shall, nevertheless, be liable and subject to Indictment, Trial, Judgment and Punishment, according to Law.

Section 4. The Times, Places and Manner of holding **Elections for Senators and Representatives,** shall be prescribed in each State by the Legislature thereof; but the Congress may at any time by Law make or alter such Regulations, except as to the Places of Chusing Senators.

The Congress shall assemble at least once in every Year, and such Meeting shall be [on the first Monday in December,]** unless they shall by Law appoint a different Day.

Section 5. Each House shall be the Judge of the Elections, Returns and Qualifications of its own Members, and a Majority of each shall constitute a Quorum to do Business; but a smaller Number may adjourn from day to day, and may be authorized to compel the Attendance of absent Members, in such manner, and under such Penalties, as each House may provide.

Each House may determine the **Rules** of its Proceedings, punish its Members for disorderly Behaviour, and, with the Concurrence of two thirds, expel a member.

Each House shall keep a **Journal** of its Proceedings, and from time to

2

time publish the same, excepting such Parts as may in their Judgment require Secrecy; and the Yeas and Nays of the Members of either House on any question shall, at the desire of one fifth of those Present, be entered on the Journal.

Neither House, during the Session of Congress, shall, without the Consent of the other, **adjourn** for more than three days, nor to any other Place than that in which the two Houses shall be sitting.

Section 6. The Senators and Representatives shall receive a **Compensation** for their Services, to be ascertained by Law, and paid out in the Treasury of the United States. They shall in all Cases, except Treason, Felony and Breach of the Peace, be privileged from Arrest during their Attendance at the Session of their respective Houses, and in going to and returning from the same; and for any Speech or Debate in either House, they shall not be questioned in any other Place.

No Senator or Representative shall, during the Time for which he was elected, be appointed to any civil Office under the Authority of the United States, which shall have been created, or the Emoluments whereof shall have been increased during such time; and no Person holding any Office under the United States, shall be a Member of either House during his Continuance in Office.

Section 7. All Bills for **raising Revenue** shall originate in the House of Representatives; but the Senate may propose or concur with Amendments as on other Bills.

Every Bill which shall have passed the House of Representatives and the Senate, shall, before it becomes a Law, be presented to the President of the United States; If he approve he shall sign it, but if not he shall return it, with his Objections to that House in which it shall have originated, who shall enter the Objections at large on their Journal, and proceed to reconsider it. If after such reconsideration two thirds of that House shall agree to pass the Bill, it shall be sent, together with the Objections, to the other House, by which it shall likewise be reconsidered, and if approved by two thirds of that House, it shall become a Law. But in all Cases the Votes of both Houses shall be determined by Yeas and Nays, and the Names of the Persons voting for and against the Bill shall be entered on the Journal of each House respectively.

If any Bill shall not be returned by the President within ten Days (Sundays excepted) after it shall have been presented to him, the Same shall be a Law, in like Manner as if he had signed it, unless the Congress by their Adjournment prevent its Return, in which Case it shall not be a Law.

Every Order, Resolution, or Vote to which the Concurrence of the Senate and House of Representatives may be necessary (except on a question of Adjournment) shall be presented to the President of the United States; and before the same shall take Effect, shall be approved by him, or being disapproved by him, shall be repassed by two thirds of the Senate and House of Representatives, according to the Rules and Limitations prescribed in the Case of a Bill.

Section 8. The Congress shall have Power To lay and collect **Taxes,** Duties, Imposts, and Excises, to pay the Debts and provide for the common **Defence** and general Welfare of the United States; but all Duties, Imposts, and Excises shall be uniform throughout the United States;

To **borrow money** on the credit of the United States;

To regulate **Commerce** with foreign Nations and among the several States, and with the Indian Tribes;

To establish an uniform Rule of **Naturalization**, and uniform Laws on the subject of **Bankruptcies** throughout the United States;

To **coin Money**, regulate the Value thereof, and of foreign Coin, and fix the Standard of **Weights and Measures**;

To provide for the Punishment of **counterfeiting** the Securities and current Coin of the United States;

To establish **Post Offices** and post Roads;

To promote the Progress of Science and useful Arts, by securing for limited Times to **Authors** and **Inventors** the exclusive Right to their respective Writings and Discoveries;

To constitute **Tribunals** inferior to the supreme Court;

To define and punish **Piracies** and Felonies committed on the high Seas, and Offenses against the **Law of Nations**;

To **declare War**, grant Letters of Marque and Reprisal, and make Rules concerning Captures on Land and Water;

To raise and support Armies, but no Appropriation of Money to that Use shall be for a longer Term than two Years;

To provide and maintain a Navy;

To make Rules for the Government and Regulation of the land and naval Forces;

To provide for calling forth the Militia to execute the Laws of the Union, suppress Insurrections, and repel Invasions;

To provide for organizing, arming, and disciplining the Militia, and for governing such Part of them as may be employed in the Service of the United States, reserving to the States respectively, the Appointment of the Officers, and the Authority of training the Militia according to the discipline prescribed by Congress;

To exercise exclusive Legislation in all Cases whatsoever, over such District (not exceeding ten Miles square) as may, by Cession of particular States and the Acceptance of Congress, become the Seat of the Government of the United States, and to exercise like Authority over all Places purchased by the Consent of the Legislature of the State in which the Same shall be, for the Erection of Forts, Magazines, Arsenals, dockyards, and other needful Buildings;—And

To make all Laws which shall be necessary and proper for carrying into Execution the foregoing Powers, and all other Powers vested by this Constitution in the Government of the United States, or in any Department or Officer thereof.

Section 9. The Migration or Importation of such Persons as any of the States now existing shall think

4

proper to admit, shall not be prohibited by the Congress prior to the Year one thousand eight hundred and eight, but a tax or duty may be imposed on such Importation, not exceeding ten dollars for each Person.

The privilege of the Writ of Habeas Corpus shall not be suspended, unless when in Cases of Rebellion or Invasion the public Safety may require it.

No Bill of Attainder or ex post facto Law shall be passed.

No Capitation, or other direct, Tax shall be laid, unless in Proportion to the Census or Enumeration herein before directed to be taken.

No Tax or Duty shall be laid on Articles exported from any State.

No Preference shall be given by any Regulation of Commerce or Revenue to the Ports of one State over those of another; nor shall Vessels, bound to, or from, one State, be obliged to enter, clear, or pay Duties in another.

No Money shall be drawn from the Treasury, but in Consequence of Appropriations made by Law; and a regular Statement and Account of the Receipts and Expenditures of all public Money shall be published from time to time.

No Title of Nobility shall be granted by the United States; And no Person holding any Office of Profit or Trust under them, shall, without the Consent of the Congress, accept of any present, Emolument, Office, or Title, of any kind whatever, from any King, Price, or foreign State.

Section 10. No State shall enter into any Treaty, Alliance, or Confederation; grant Letters of Marque and Reprisal; coin Money; emit Bills of Credit; make any Thing but gold and silver Coin a Tender in Payment of Debts; pass any Bill of Attainder, ex post facto Law, or Law impairing the Obligation of Contracts, or grant any Title of Nobility.

No State shall, without the Consent of Congress, lay any Imposts or Duties on Imports or Exports, except what may be absolutely necessary for executing its inspection Laws: and the net Produce of all Duties and Imposts, laid by any State on Imports or Exports, shall be for the Use of the Treasury of the United States; and all such Laws shall be subject to the Revision and Controul of the Congress.

No State shall, without the Consent of Congress, lay any duty of Tonnage, keep Troops, or Ships of War in time of Peace, enter into any Agreement or Compact with another State or with a foreign Power, or engage in War, unless actually invaded, or in such imminent Danger as will not admit of delay.

Article Two

Section 1 The executive Power shall be vested in a President of the United States of American. He shall hold his Office during the Term of four Years, and together with the Vice President, chosen for the same Term, be elected as follows:

Each State shall appoint, in such Manner as the Legislature thereof may direct, a Number of Electors, equal to the whole Number of Senators and Representatives to which the State may be entitled in Congress: but no Senator or Representative, or Person holding an Office of Trust or Profit under the United States, shall be appointed as Elector.

[The Electors shall meet in their respective States, and vote by Ballot for two Persons, of whom one at least shall not be an Inhabitant of the same State with themselves. And they shall make a List of all Persons voted for, and of the Number of Votes for each; which List they shall sign and certify, and transmit sealed to the Government of the United States. Directed to the President of the Senate. The President of the Senate shall, in the Presence of the Senate and House of Representatives, open all the Certificates, and the Votes shall then be counted. The Person having the greatest Number of Votes shall be the President, if such Number be a Majority of the whole Number of Electors appointed; and if there be more than one who have such Majority, and have an equal Number of Votes, then the House of Representatives shall immediately chuse by Ballot one of them for President; and if no person have a Majority, then from the five highest on the List the said House shall in like manner chuse the President. But in chusing the President, the Votes shall be taken by States, the Representation from each State having one Vote; a quorum for this Purpose shall consist of a Member or Members from two-thirds of the States, and a Majority of all the States shall be necessary to a Choice. In every

Case, after the Choice of the President, the Person having the greatest Number of Votes of the Electors shall be the Vice President. But if there should remain two or more who have equal Votes, the Senate shall chuse from them by Ballot the Vice President.]

The Congress may determine the Time of chusing the Electors, and the Day on which they shall give their Votes; which Day shall be the same throughout the United States.

No person except a natural born Citizen, or a Citizen of the United States at the time of the Adoption of this Constitution, shall be eligible to the Office of President; neither shall any Person be eligible to that Office who shall not have attained to the Age of thirty-five Years, and been fourteen Years a Resident within the United States.

[In Case of the Removal of the President from Office, or of his Death, Resignation, or Inability to discharge the Powers and Duties of the said Office, the same shall devolve on the Vice President, and the Congress may by Law provide for the Case of Removal, Death, Resignation, or Inability, both of the President and Vice President, declaring what Officer shall then act as President, and such Officer shall act accordingly until the Disability be removed, or a President shall be elected.]

The President shall, at stated Times, receive for his Services, a Compensation, which shall neither be increased nor diminished during the Period for which he shall have been elected, and he shall not receive within that Period any other Emolument from the United States, or any of them.

Before he enter on the execution of his Office, he shall take the following Oath or Affirmation:—

"I do solemnly swear (or affirm) that I will faithfully execute the Office of President of the United States, and will to the best of my Ability preserve, protect, and defend the Constitution of the United States."

Section 2 The **President** shall be **Commander in Chief** of the Army and Navy of the United States, and of the Militia of the several States, when called into the actual Service of the United States; he may require the Opinion, in writing, of the principal Officer in each of the executive Departments, upon any subject relating to the Duties of their respective Offices, and he shall have Power to Grant Reprieves and **Pardons** for Offenses against the United States, except in Cases of Impeachment.

He shall have Power, by and with the Advice and Consent of the Senate, to make **Treaties**, provided two-thirds of the Senators present concur; and shall nominate, and, by and with the Advice and Consent of the Senate, shall appoint **Ambassadors**, other public Ministers and Consuls, **Judges** of the supreme Court, and all other Officers of the United States, whose Appointments are not herein otherwise provided for, and which shall be established by Law; but the Congress may by Law vest the Appointment of such inferior Officers, as they think proper, in the President alone, in the Courts of Law, or in the Heads of Departments.

The President shall have Power to fill up all Vacancies that may happen during the Recess of the Senate, by granting Commissions which shall expire at the end of their next Session.

Section 3. He shall from time to time give to the Congress Information of the **State of the Union**, and recommend to their Consideration such Measures as he shall judge necessary and expedient; he may, on extraordinary Occasions, convene both Houses, or either of them, and in Case of Disagreement between them, with Respect to the Time of Adjournment, he may adjourn them to such Time as he shall think proper; he shall receive Ambassadors and other public Ministers; he shall take Care that the Laws be faithfully executed, and shall Commission all the Officers of the United States.

Section 4 The President, Vice President and all civil Officers of the United States. Shall be removed from Office on Impeachment for, and Conviction of, Treason, Bribery, or other high Crimes and Misdemeanors.

Article Three

Section 1 The judicial Power of the United States, shall be vested in one **supreme Court**, and in such **inferior Courts** as the Congress may from time to time ordain and establish.

The Judges, both of the supreme and inferior Courts, shall hold their

7

Offices during good Behaviour, and shall, at stated Times, receive for their Services, a Compensation, which shall not be diminished during their Continuance in Office.

Section 2 The judicial Power shall extend to all Cases, in Law and Equity, arising under this Constitution, the Laws of the United States, and Treaties made, or which shall be made, under their authority;—to all Cases affecting Ambassadors, other public Ministers and Consuls;—to all Cases of admiralty and maritime Jurisdiction;—to Controversies to which the United States shall be a Party;—to Controversies between two or more States;—[between a State and Citizens of another State;—]* between Citizens of different States;—between Citizens of the same State claiming Lands under Grants of different States, [and between a State, or the Citizens thereof, and foreign States, Citizens, of Subjects.]*

In all Cases affecting Ambassadors, other public Ministers and Consuls, and those in which a State shall be a Party, the supreme Court shall have original Jurisdiction. In all the other Cases before mentioned, the supreme Court shall have appellate Jurisdiction, both as to Law and Fact, with such Exceptions, and under such Regulations as the Congress shall make.

The Trial of all Crimes, except in Cases of Impeachment, shall be by Jury; and such Trial shall be held in the State where the said Crimes shall have been committed; but when not committed within any State, the Trial shall be at such Place or Places as the Congress may by Law have directed.

Section 3: Treason against the United States, shall consist only in levying War against them, or in adhering to their enemies, giving them Aid and Comfort. No Person shall be convicted of Treason unless on the Testimony of two Witnesses to the same overt Act, or on Confession in open Court.

The Congress shall have power to declare the Punishment of Treason, but no Attainder of Treason shall work Corruption of Blood, or Forfeiture except during the Life of the Person attained.

Article Four

Section 1 Full Faith and Credit shall be given in each State to the public Acts, Records, and judicial Proceedings of every other State. And the Congress may by general Laws prescribe the Manner in which such Acts, Records and Proceedings shall be proved, and the effect thereof.

Section 2 The Citizens of each State shall be entitled to all Privileges and Immunities of Citizens in the several States.

A Person charged in any State with Treason, Felony, or other Crime, who shall flee from Justice, and be found in another State, shall on Demand of the executive Authority of the State from which he fled, be delivered up, to be removed to the State having Jurisdiction of the Crime.

[No Person held to Service or Labour in one State, under the Laws thereof, escaping into another, shall, in Consequence of any Law or Regulation therein, be discharged from such Service or Labour, but shall be delivered up on Claim of the Party to whom such Service or Labour may be due.]

Section 3 New States may be admitted by the Congress into this Union; but no new State shall be formed or erected within the Jurisdiction of any other State; nor any State be formed by the Junction of two or more States, or parts of States, without the Consent of the Legislatures of the States concerned as well as of the Congress.

The Congress shall have Power to dispose of and make all needful Rules and Regulations respecting the **Territory** or other Property belonging to the United States; and nothing in this Constitution shall be so construed as to Prejudice any Claims of the United States, or of any particular State.

Section 4 The United States shall **guarantee** to every State in this Union a **Republican Form** of Government, and shall protect each of them against Invasion; and on Application of the Legislature, or of the Executive (when the Legislature cannot be convened) against **domestic Violence.**

Article Five

The Congress, whenever two-thirds of both Houses shall deem it necessary, shall propose **Amendments** to this Constitution, or, on the Application of the Legislatures of two thirds of the several States, shall call a Convention for proposing Amendments, which, in either Case, shall be valid to all Intents and Purposes, as Part of this Constitution, when ratified by the Legislatures of three-fourths of the several States, or by Conventions in three fourths thereof, as the one or the other Mode of Ratification may be proposed by the Congress; provided that no Amendment which may be made prior to the Year One thousand eight hundred and eight shall in any manner affect the first and fourth Clauses in the Ninth Section of the first Article; and that no State, without its Consent, shall be deprived of its equal Suffrage in the Senate.

Article Six

All Debts contracted and Engagements entered into, before the Adoption of this Constitution, shall be as valid against the United States under this Constitution, as under the Confederation.

This Constitution, and the Laws of the United States which shall be made in Pursuance thereof; and all Treaties made, or which shall be made, under the Authority of the United States, shall be the supreme Law of the Land; and the Judges in every State shall be bound thereby, any Thing in the Constitution or Laws of any State to the Contrary notwithstanding.

The Senators and Representatives before mentioned, and the Members of the several State Legislatures, and all executive and judicial Officers, both of the United States and of the several States, shall be bound by Oath or Affirmation, to support this Constitution; but no religious Test shall ever be required as a Qualification to any Office or public Trust under the United States.

Article Seven

The Ratification of the Conventions of nine States, shall be sufficient for the Establishment of this Constitution between the States so ratifying the Same.

Done in Convention by the unanimous Consent of the States present the Seventeenth day of September in the Year of our Lord one thousand seven hundred and Eighty seven and of the Independence of the United States of American the Twelfth In Witness whereof We have hereunto subscribed our Names,

G Washington—Presid
And deputy from Virginia Attest:
William Jackson Secretary

Amendments

Article One

Congress shall make no law respecting an establishment of religion, or prohibiting the free exercise thereof; or abridging the freedom of speech, or of the press; or the right of the people peaceably to assemble, and to petition the Government for a redress of grievances.

Article Two

A well-regulated Militia, being necessary to the security of a free State, the right of the people to keep and bear Arms shall not be infringed.

Article Three

No Soldier shall, in time of peace, be quartered in any house, without the consent of the Owner, nor in time of war, but in a manner to be prescribed by law.

Article Four

The right of the people to secure in their persons, houses, papers, and effects, against unreasonable searches and seizures, shall not be violated, and no Warrants shall issue, but upon probable cause, supported by Oath or affirmation, and particularly describing the place to be searched, and the persons or things to be seized.

Article Five

No person shall be held to answer for a capital, or otherwise infamous crime, unless on a presentment or indictment of a Grand Jury, except in cases arising in the land or naval forces, or in the Militia, when in actual service in time of War or public danger; nor shall any person be subject for the same offense to be twice put in jeopardy of life or limb; nor shall be compelled in any criminal case to be a witness against himself, nor be deprived of life, liberty, or property, without due process of law; nor shall private property be taken for public use, without just compensation.

Article Six

In all criminal prosecutions, the accused shall enjoy the right to a speedy and public trial, by an impartial jury of the State and district wherein the crime shall have been committed; which district shall have been previously ascertain law, and to be informed of the nature and cause of the accusation; to be confronted with the witnesses against him; to have compulsory process for obtaining witnesses in his favor, and to have the assistance of counsel for his defence.

Article Seven

In Suits at common law, where value of controversy shall exceed twenty dollars, the right of trial by jury shall preserved, and no fact tried by a jury shall be otherwise re-examined in any Court of the United States, than according to rules of the common law.

Article Eight

Excessive bail shall not be required, nor excessive fines imposed, nor cruel and unusual punishments inflicted.

Article Nine

The enumeration in the Constitution certain rights shall not be construed to deny or disparage others retained by the people.

Article Ten

The powers not delegated to the United States by the Constitution, nor prohibited by it to the States, are reserved to the States respectively or to the people.

Article Eleven

The judicial power of the United States shall not be construed to extend to any suit in law or equity, commenced or prosecuted against one of the United States by Citizens of another State, or by Citizens or Subjects of any Foreign State.

Article Twelve

The Electors shall meet in their respective states, and vote by ballot for President, and Vice President, one of whom, at least, shall not be an inhabitant of the same State with themselves; they shall name in their ballots the person voted for as President, and in distinct ballots the person voted for as Vice-President, and they shall make distinct lists of all persons voted for as President, and of all persons voted for as Vice-President, and of the number of votes for each, which lists they shall sign and certify, and transmit sealed to the seat of the government of the United States, directed to the President of the Senate;--The President of the Senate shall, in the presence of the Senate and House of Representatives, open all the certificates and the votes shall then be counted; The person having the greatest number of votes for President, shall be the President, if such number be a majority of the whole number of Electors appointed; and if no person have such majority, then from the persons having the highest numbers not exceeding three on the list of those voted for as President, the House of Representatives shall choose immediately, by ballot, the President. But in choosing the President, the votes shall be taken by states, the representation from each State having one vote; a quorum for this purpose shall consist of a member or members from two-thirds of the states, and a majority of all the states shall be necessary to a choice. [And if the House of Representatives shall not choose a President whenever the right of choice shall devolve upon them, before the fourth day of March next following, then the Vice-President shall act as President, as in the case of the death or other constitutional disability of the President---]* The person having the greatest number of votes as Vice-President, shall be the Vice-President, if such number be a majority of the whole number of Electors appointed, and if no person have a majority, then from the two highest numbers an the list, the Senate shall choose the Vice-President; a quorum for the purpose shall consist of two-thirds of the whale num-

---

* Superseded by section 3 of 20th Amendment.

ber of Senators, and a majority of the whale number shall be necessary to a choice, But no person constitutionally ineligible to the office of President shall be eligible to that of Vice-President of the United States.

Article Thirteen**

Section 1 . Neither slavery nor involuntary servitude, except as a punishment for crime whereof the party shall have been duly convicted, shall exist within the United States, or any place subject to their jurisdiction.

Section 2. Congress shall have power to enforce this article by appropriate legislation.

Article Fourteen*

Section 1. All persons born or naturalized in the United States, and subject to the jurisdiction thereof, are citizens of the United States and of the State wherein they reside. No State shall make or enforce any law which shall abridge the privileges or immunities of citizens of the United States; nor shall any State deprive any person of life, liberty, or property, without due process of law; nor deny to any person within its jurisdiction the equal protection of the laws.

Section 2. Representatives shall be apportioned among the several States according to their respective numbers, counting the whole number of persons in each State, excluding Indians not taxed. But when the right to vote at any election for the choice of Electors for President and Vice-President of the United States, Representatives in Congress, the executive and judicial officers of a State, or the members of the Legis-

lature thereof, is denied to any of the male inhabitants of such State, being twenty-one years of age, and citizens of the United States, or in any way abridged, except for participation in rebellion, or other crime, the basis of representation therein shall be reduced in the proportion which the number of such male citizens shall bear to the whole number of male citizens twenty-one years of age in such State.

Section 3. No person shall be a Senator or Representative in Congress, or elector of President and Vice-President, or hold any office, civil or military, under the United States, or under any State, 'who, having previously taken an oath, as a member of Congress, or as an officer of the United States, or as a member of any State Legislature, or as an executive or judicial officer of any State, to support the Constitution of the United States, shall have engaged in insurrection or rebellion against the same, or given aid or comfort to the enemies thereof. But Congress may by a vote of two-thirds of each house, remove such disability.

Section 4. The validity of the public debt of the United States, authorized by law, including debts incurred for payment of pensions and bounties for services in suppressing insurrection or rebellion, shall not be questioned. But neither the United States nor any State shall assume or pay any debt or obligation incurred in aid of insurrection or rebellion against the United States, or any claim for the loss or emancipation of any slave; but all such debts, obligations and claims shall be held illegal and void.

Section 5, The Congress shall have power to enforce, by appropriate legislation, the provisions of this article.

** Ratified 12/06/1865
* Ratified 07/09/1868.

Article Fifteen[**]

Section 1. The right of citizens of the United States to vote shall not be denied or abridged by the United States or by any State on account of race, color, or previous condition of servitude

Section 2. The Congress shall have power to enforce this article by appropriate legislation.

Article Sixteen[***]

The Congress shall have power to lay and collect taxes on incomes, from whatever source derived, without apportionment among the several States, and without regard to any census enumeration.

Article Seventeen[*]

The Senate of the United States shall be composed of two Senators from each State, elected by the people thereof, for six years; and each Senator shall have one vote. The electors in each State shall have the qualifications requisite for electors of the most numerous branch of the State legislatures.

When vacancies happen in the representation of any State in the Senate, the executive authority of such State shall issue writs of election to fill such vacancies: *Provided*, That the Legislature of any State may empower the executive thereof to make temporary appointments until the people fill the vacancies by election as the legislature may direct.

This amendment shall not be so construed as to affect the election or term of any Senator chosen before it becomes valid as part of the Constitution.

Article Eighteen[**]

[**Section 1.** After one year from the ratification of this article the manufacture, sale, or transportation of intoxicating liquors within, the importation thereof into, or the exportation thereof from the United States and all territory subject to the jurisdiction thereof for beverage purposes is hereby prohibited.

Section 2. The Congress and the several States shall have concurrent power to enforce this article by appropriate legislation.

Section 3 This article shall be inoperative unless it shall have been ratified as an amendment to the Constitution by the legislatures of the several States, as provided in the Constitution, within seven years from the date of the submission hereof to the States by the Congress.]

Article Nineteen[***]

The right of citizens of the United States to vote shall not be denied or abridged by the United States or by any State on account of sex.

Congress shall have power to enforce this article by appropriate legislation.

Article Twenty[*]

Section 1. The terms of the President and Vice-President shall end at noon on the 20th day of January, and the terms of Senators and Representatives at noon on the 3d day of January, of the years in which such terms would have ended if this article had not been ratified; and the terms of their successors shall then begin.

Section 2. The Congress shall assemble at least once in every year,

---

[**] Ratified 02/03/1870
[***] Ratified 02/03/1913
[*] Ratified 04/08/1913.

[**] Ratified 01/16/1919. It was repealed by the 21st Amendment, 12/05/1933.
[***] Ratified 08/18/1920.
[*] Ratified 01/23/1933.

and such meeting shall begin at noon on the 3d day of January, unless they shall by law appoint a different day.

Section 3. If, at the time fixed for the beginning of the term of the President, the President elect shall have died, the Vice-President elect shall become President. If a President shall not have been chosen before the time fixed for the beginning of his term, or if the President elect shall have failed to qualify, then the Vice-President elect shall act as President until a President shall have qualified; and the Congress may by law provide for the case wherein neither a President elect nor a Vice-President elect shall have qualified, declaring who shall then act as President, or the manner in which one who is to act shall be selected, and such person shall act accordingly until a President or Vice-President shall have qualified.

Section 4. The Congress may by law provide for the case of the death of any of the persons from whom the House of Representatives may choose a President whenever the right of choice shall have devolved upon them, and for the case of the death of any of the persons from whom the Senate may choose a Vice-President whenever the right of choice shall have devolved upon them.

Section 5. Sections 1 and 2 shall take effect on the 15th day of October following the ratification of this article.

Section 6. This article shall be inoperative unless it shall have been ratified as an amendment to the Constitution by the legislatures of three-fourths of the several States within seven years from the date of its submission.

Article Twenty-one[*]

Section 1 The eighteenth article of amendment to the Constitution of the United States is hereby repealed.

Section 2 The transportation or importation into any State, Territory, or possession of the United States for delivery or use therein of intoxicating liquors, in violation of the laws thereof, is hereby prohibited.

Section 3 This article shall be inoperative unless it shall have been ratified as an amendment to the Constitution by conventions in the several States, as provided in the Constitution, within seven years from the date of the submission hereof to the States by the Congress.

Article Twenty-two[**]

Section 1. No person shall be elected to the office of the President more than twice, and no person who has held the office of President, or acted as President, for more than two years of a term to which some other person was elected President shall be elected to the office of the President more than once. But this Article shall not apply to any person holding the office of President when this Article was proposed by the Congress, and shall not prevent any person who may be holding the office of President, or acting as President, during the term within which this Article becomes operative from holding the office of President or acting as President during the remainder of such term.

Section 2. This article shall be inoperative unless it shall have been ratified as an amendment to the Constitution by the legislatures of three-fourths of the several States within seven years from the date of

[*] Ratified 12/05/1933.
[**] Ratified 02/27/1951.

its submission to the States by the Congress.

Article Twenty-three***

Section 1. The District constituting the seat of Government of the United States shall appoint in such manner as the Congress may direct:

A number of electors of President and Vice-President equal to the whole number of Senators and Representatives in Congress to which the District would be entitled if it were a State, but in no event more than the least populous State; they shall be in addition to those appointed by the States, but they shall be considered, for the purposes of the election of President and Vice President, to be electors appointed by a State; and they shall meet in the District and perform such duties as provided by the twelfth article of amendment.

Section 2. The Congress shall have power to enforce this article by appropriate legislation.

Article Twenty-four*

Section 1. The right of citizens of the United States to vote in any primary or other election for President or Vice-President, for electors for President or Vice-President, or for Senator or Representative in Congress, shall not be denied or abridged by the United States or any State by reason of failure to pay any poll tax or other tax.

Section 2. The Congress shall have power to enforce this article by appropriate legislation.

Article Twenty-five**

Section 1. In case of the removal of the President from office or of his death or resignation, the Vice President shall become President.

*** Ratified 03/29/1961.
* Ratified 01/23/1964
** Ratified 02/10/1967.

Section 2. Whenever there is a vacancy in the office of the Vice President, the President shall nominate a Vice President who shall take office upon confirmation by a majority vote of both Houses of Congress.

Section 3. Whenever the President transmits to the President pro tempore of the Senate and the Speaker of the House of Representatives his written declaration that he is unable to discharge the powers and duties of his office, and until he transmits to them a written declaration to the contrary, such powers and duties shall be discharged by the Vice President as Acting President.

Section 4. Whenever the Vice President and a majority of either the principal officers of the executive departments or of such other body as Congress may by law provide, transmit to the President pro tempore of the Senate and the Speaker of the House of Representatives their written declaration that the President is unable to discharge the powers and duties of his office, the Vice President shall immediately assume the powers and duties of the office as Acting President.

Thereafter, when the President transmits to the President pro tempore of the Senate and the Speaker of the House of Representatives his written declaration that no inability exists, he shall resume the powers and duties of his office unless the Vice President and a majority of either the principal officers of the executive department or of such other body as Congress may by law provide, transmit within four days to the President pro temp ore of the Senate and the Speaker of the House of Representatives their written declaration that the President is unable to discharge the powers and duties of his office. Thereupon Congress shall decide the issue, assembling within forty-eight hours for that purpose if not in session. If the Congress, within twenty-one days after receipt of the latter written declaration, or, if Congress is not in session, within twenty-one days after Congress is required to assemble, determines by two-thirds vote of both Houses that the President is unable to discharge the powers and duties of his office, the Vice President shall continue to discharge the same as Acting President; otherwise, the President shall resume the powers and duties of his office.

Article Twenty-six[*]

Section 1. The right of citizens of the United States, who are eighteen years of age or older, to vote shall not be denied or abridged by the United States or by any State on account of age.

Section 2. The Congress shall have power to enforce this article by appropriate legislation.

Article Twenty-seven[**]

No law, varying the compensation for the services of the Senators and Representatives, shall take effect, until an election of Representatives shall have intervened.

---

[*] Ratified 07/1/1971

[**] Congress submitted the text of the 27th Amendment to the States as part of the proposed Bill of Rights on September 25, 1789. The Amendment was not ratified together with the first ten Amendments, which became effective on December 15, 1791. The 27th Amendment was ratified on -5/07/1992, by the vote of Michigan.

Introduction to Federalist Papers

Number 1: Call to Study New Constitution

You are asked to study and consider adopting a new Constitution for the United States of America to replace the current, ineffective federal government. This is a very important decision. Our country's existence depends on it. So does the safety and welfare of its people, communities, and States. We will decide the fate of a nation that is, in many respects, the most interesting in the world.

The people of this country will decide important questions: Can societies establish a good government by careful thought and choice? Or are people destined to be governed only by accident and force? The answers depend on our response to the current crisis. And the wrong decision will be unfortunate for all of mankind.

Special Interests will Influence Debate

2   Conscientious patriots understand the importance of deciding whether to adopt the new Constitution. And they know their decision will affect all human societies.

It would be wonderful if we based our decision only on the best interests of our society, unbiased by less noble interests not connected with the public good. Although we may sincerely wish this, it can't be expected. The Constitution affects many special interests and changes many local institutions. Subjects other than its merits will be discussed. The debate will include passions and prejudices unrelated to discovering the truth and meaning of the Constitution.

Politicians May Fear a Loss of Power

3   Many politicians will oppose the new Constitution. Some politicians are afraid that the Constitution will decrease the power and benefits of their current State offices. Others think that they can have more power if the country is in turmoil or is broken up into several small countries.

Moderation Urged

4   However, I don't plan to talk about political motives. I don't know if a person's opposition is due to self-interest or ambition even if their views seem suspicious. Even opponents of the new Constitution may be motivated by upright intentions. And much of the opposition will spring from blameless, if not valid, motivations. Jealousies and fears will lead arguments astray into honest errors in thinking.

A false bias can be created for a variety of good reasons. Wise and good men often argue on both the wrong and right side of society's most important questions. This fact should teach moderation to anyone who thinks they are always in the right in any argument.

There's a further reason for caution. People who support the right side of a question can also have ulterior motives like ambition, avarice, personal animosity, and party opposition.

Moderation is important. The mean spirit that characterizes political parties is awful. In politics, as in religion, it's absurd to try to persuade people with fire and sword. Bad ideas can rarely be defeated by persecution.

Constitution Called Thief of Liberty

5 Angry and malignant passions will be let loose about this subject, as in all former cases of great national debate. To get supporters, the opponents of the new Constitution will loudly and bitterly condemn it.

People supporting the energetic government proposed by the Constitution will be demonized as liking dictators and hating liberty. When supporters declare that the rights of the people must be very carefully protected, it will be called insincere and an obvious attempt to become popular while hurting the general public.

Dangers to the rights of people usually spring from the head rather than the heart. Enthusiasm for liberty is often infected with narrow-minded bigotry and distrust.

A healthy government is essential to secure liberty. A strong government and liberty can never be separated. Dangerous ambition is more often masked by a zeal for the rights of the people than the zeal for a firm and efficient government. History teaches us that most men who have overturned the liberties of republics began their career by proclaiming their devotion to the people. They gain position by arousing people's prejudices and end as tyrants.

I Support the New Constitution

6 My fellow citizens, guard against all attempts, from whatever side, to influence you. Your decision on the new Constitution, which is very important to your welfare, should be based on truth.

I'm sure you have noticed that I like the new Constitution. Yes, my countrymen, I admit that after giving it careful thought, I believe it is in your interest to adopt it. I am convinced that this is the safest course for your liberty, your dignity, and your happiness. The new Constitution has my full and unambiguous support.

I don't pretend that I am undecided about ratifying the Constitution. I have decided. And I will tell you why I think it is a good idea. I will try to make my arguments truthful. Everyone who reads them can judge for themselves whether I've succeeded.

Discussion of Constitutional Issues

7 I propose to discuss the following subjects in a series of papers:
- Why the UNION is important to our political life.
- Why the current Confederation can't preserve the UNION.
- Why we need an energetic federal government.
- How the proposed Constitution conforms to the principles of republican government.
- A comparison of the proposed Constitution to the New York constitution.
- How the Constitution will preserve liberty, property and the republican form of government.

As this discussion progresses, I will try to answer objections that arise.

Opponents Argue 13 States Too Many

8 It may seem like everyone agrees that remaining united is important. But some opponents of the new Constitution say thirteen States are too many. They argue that we must break into several separate confederacies.[*]

The alternative to adoption of the new Constitution is dismemberment of the Union. Therefore, I will examine the advantages of staying united, the probable dangers, and certain evils of dissolution. This will be the subject of my next editorial.

PUBLIUS

---

[*] The same idea, tracing the arguments to their consequences, is held out in several recent publications against the new Constitution. --PUBLIUS

19

Dangers Facing the United States: Foreign

Number 2: United America

1,2 Government is necessary. The people must cede some of their natural rights to the government to give it some powers. Will one federal government best serve the people of America? Or should they divide themselves into separate confederacies, giving each the powers of a national government?

Dividing America into Several Nations

3   Until recently, everyone agreed that America should remain united and that our prosperity depends on being one nation. Now some politicians say that looking for safety and happiness in one country is wrong. They want to divide the States into separate confederacies or nations. Before adopting this new idea, citizens should be sure that it is based on sound policy.

America is Geographically United

4   America is one connected, fertile, wide-spreading country. Providence blessed it with a variety of soils, watered with countless streams to delight and fulfill the needs of its inhabitants. As if to tie it together, navigable water forms a chain around its borders. The noblest rivers in the world form convenient highways for easy communication and transportation of commodities.

American is Culturally United

5   Providence gave this one connected country to one united people. The people speak the same language and profess the same religion. They believe in the same principles of government and have similar manners and customs. They fought side by side through a long and bloody war, establishing liberty and independence.

One Country, One People

6   This country and this people seem to have been made for each other. It appears like this inheritance was designed by Providence for a band of brethren united by the strongest ties. They should never split into a number of unsocial, jealous, and alien sovereignties.

States Have Acted as One Nation

7   Until recently, everyone agreed that we should remain united. We have acted as one people. Each individual citizen enjoys the same national rights, privileges, and protection. As a nation we made peace and war. As a nation we formed alliances and made treaties.

Current Government Hastily Formed

8   Very early, while their homes were in flames and citizens were bleeding, the people created a federal government. However, there wasn't time for the calm and mature reflections that must precede the formation of a wise and well-balanced government for free people. Therefore, it's not strange that the government has a lot of problems and is unable to serve its purpose.

Importance of Sound Union to Liberty

9   Being intelligent, the people saw the government's defects. They were attached to the union and loved liberty. They saw that the union was in immediate danger, a danger that would eventually jeopardize their liberty. The people knew that a more wisely framed national government could secure the union and personal liberty. They recently met in Philadelphia to consider this important subject.

Constitutional Convention

10   The men at the convention are respected. Many showed their patriotism, virtue, and wisdom during a time that tried the minds and hearts of men.

The convention undertook the difficult task. During a time of peace, they spent many months in cool, uninterrupted, daily discussions. They were neither awed by power nor influenced by any passion except love for their country. They unanimously recommended to the people their plan—the proposed Constitution.

1774 Congress: Wise Recommendations

11   This plan is only *recommended*, not imposed. It is neither recommended for *blind* approval nor *blind* rejection. This important subject demands calm and candid consideration. However, a thoughtful examination of the Constitution is more to be wished than expected. Experience teaches us not to be too optimistic.

Let's remember what happened in 1774. Americans felt that they were in imminent danger. They formed the Congress of 1774, which made some wise recommendations. However, the press wrote against them. Some people said the advice of that patriotic Congress should be rejected. Many politicians opposed them, putting self-interest before the good of the country. Others were unduly influenced by political allies or saw it as a threat to personal ambitions.

However, the majority of Americans saw through the deceit and decided judiciously. Reflecting back, they are happy they did so.

Respected Men Framed Constitution

12,13   Americans concluded that wise and experienced men composed the 1774 Congress. Each delegate was committed to public liberty and prosperity. It was their duty to recommend only wise measures. And Americans relied on the judgment and integrity of that Congress.

There are even more reasons to respect the judgment and advice of the recent convention. Members of the 1774 Congress have proved that they are patriotic and talented. They continued learning about politics and governments. Some of the most distinguished men from the 1774 Congress brought their accumulated knowledge and experience to this year's Constitutional Convention.

Remaining One Union Important

14 The prosperity of America depends on its Union. The Constitutional Convention wrote the proposed Constitution to preserve and perpetuate the Union. What are the real motives behind current attempts to depreciate the importance of the Union? Why do some people say that we should break into three or four confederacies?

I believe Americans have always thought right on this subject. Their attachment to the Union is based on great and important reasons, which I will try to explain in some ensuing papers.

The people who want to break up America into several separate confederacies know that if the Constitution is rejected, the Union will be in jeopardy. I sincerely wish that every good citizen realizes that, if the Union is dissolved, America will have reason to exclaim, in the words of the poet: "FAREWELL! A LONG FAREWELL TO ALL MY GREATNESS."

PUBLIUS

Number 3: Union Provides Safety Against Foreign Danger

People of any country (if, like Americans, they are intelligent and well informed) seldom hold erroneous beliefs about their best interests for many years. This is why Americans feel that the States should remain united with one federal government. And the federal government needs enough power to fulfill its responsibilities.

2   The more I study the reasons for this opinion, the more I'm convinced they are valid.

Safety: Government's First Objective

3,4 Wise and free people have several goals. *Safety* is first. The desire to be *safe* can mean many things. I will discuss two: safety against dangers from *foreign arms and influence* and dangers arising from domestic causes.

22

Danger from Foreign Nations

The first danger is from foreign nations. If we remain one nation, with an efficient national government, we will have the best security against *hostilities* from other nations.

5 Both *real* and *imagined* grievances *provoke* or *invite* wars. Will a *united* America or a *disunited* America find more *just* causes for war? If a united America will find fewer reasons, then if we remain one Union, it will tend to preserve a state of peace with other nations.

Relationships With Other Nations

6 Just causes for war include treaty violations and direct violence, attack or invasion. America already has treaties with at least six nations. All, except Prussia, have navies that could injure us. We have extensive commerce with Portugal, Spain, and Britain. Spain and Britain also have neighboring territory.

7 To stay at peace, America must observe the laws of nations. One national government can do this more easily than either thirteen separate States, or three or four confederacies.

Highly Qualified Men in National Government

8 When an efficient national government is established, usually the best men in the country will be appointed to manage it. A town or county can place men in State and local offices. However, to recommend men to national offices, a wider reputation for talents and qualifications is necessary. The public will choose from the widest field, never lacking qualified persons. Therefore, the administration, legislation, and judicial decisions of the national government will be more wise and judicious than those of individual States. Consequently, a Union will be *safer* with respect to other nations, as well as *safer* with respect to us.

Standard Treaties, Policies

9 One national government will always interpret treaties and laws of nations in one way. However, if thirteen States—or three or four confederacies—interpreted the same treaties and laws, they would sometimes come to different conclusions. Different local laws and interests would influence each government. Therefore, it is wise to have one judicial system appointed by and responsible to one national government to decide such questions.

10 The people governing one or two States may be tempted to swerve from trustworthiness and justice. But local temptations would have little or no influence on the national government, preserving good faith and justice. The peace treaty with Britain is a good example.

Fewer Temptations for National Officials

11 Individual States have specific interests that cause temptations. The governing party may not be able or willing to stop an injustice or punish the aggressors. Unaffected by local interests, national officials will not be tempted to commit such wrongs themselves. They will try to prevent it. And they will punish its commission by others.

Treaty Violations Lead to Just Causes for War

12 Both intentional and accidental violations of treaties and laws of nations provide *just* cause for war. They are less likely to happen under one general government than several lesser ones. Therefore, the people are *safer* under one national government.

States Provoke Wars

13, 14   Direct, unlawful violence also starts wars. Passions and interests of one or two States rather than the whole Union usually cause it. One good national government provides the greatest security against this.

For example, the federal government has never started an Indian war. But the improper conduct of individual States provoked several Indian wars. Those States were either unable or unwilling to stop or punish offenses that led to the slaughter of many innocent people.

15 Some States border Spanish and British territories. Only bordering States, because of an irritation or sense of injury, would be likely to use violence to start a war with these nations. Regional passions won't sway a wise and prudent national government. And the national government can block the danger.

Cool Heads Will Settle Disputes

16 A national government will have more power to settle hostilities. It will be more temperate and cool than the offending State. Pride makes both men and States justify their actions and oppose acknowledging or correcting their errors and offenses. Not affected by this pride, the national government will be more moderate. And it will work towards a solution for the threatening difficulties.

Apologies of Strong Nations Accepted

17, 18 Explanations and compensations from a strong nation are often accepted as satisfactory, when they would be rejected as unsatisfactory if offered by a State or confederacy of little power. In 1685, the state of Genoa offended Louis XIV. He demanded they send their chief magistrate to *France* to ask his pardon and receive his terms. To make peace, they had to obey. Would he have demanded or received the same humiliation from Spain, Britain or any other *powerful* nation? PUBLIUS

Number 4: Strong Union Provides Strong Defense

With only one national government, other nations would have fewer *just* causes for wars. And when problems developed, it would settle them more easily than either the State governments or the proposed small confederacies.

Just and Pretended Reasons for War

2   To remain safe, America must not give other nations *just* causes for war. *And* it must not get into situations that *invite* hostility. Nations start wars both for legitimate and illegitimate (pretended) reasons.

Kings Start Wars for No Logical Reason

3   It is a sad fact that nations, in general, will start a war whenever they think they can get something from it. In fact, dictators and kings often start wars when their nation gains nothing. Motives include: a desire for military glory, revenge for personal insults, ambition, and private agreements to promote families or friends. Personal motives lead dictators and kings to start wars that are neither just nor good for the people they govern.

But there are other reasons that both nations and kings use to start wars. And some of them grow out of situations like ours.

International Trade

4   France, England and America catch and sell fish. But America can sell fish in France and England at a cheaper price than their own fishermen. To try to stop us, their governments pay rewards to their fishermen and tax the American fish.

5   Our boats also compete with European nations in cargo transport. They don't want to see our transportation business increase because it decreases theirs. It's in their interest to limit our trade, not promote it.

6   Our trade with China and India has reduced the profits of several nations. We now directly import items that we used to purchase through a monopoly.

Regional Trade

7   Any nation with territories on or near this continent can't be happy about our commercial growth. Our products are cheap and excellent. Our convenient location gives our hard-working merchants and ships advantages in those territories, to the displeasure of Europe.

8   Spain doesn't allow our boats on the Mississippi river. Britain doesn't allow our ships on the Saint Lawrence River. And neither permits commercial ships on the other waterways that flow between them and us.

9   For these—and some other reasons—other nations may become jealous and afraid of us. They will worry about our advancement in union and power, land and sea.

One Government Safer Than Several

10   Americans know these circumstances may lead to war. As will other reasons, not currently obvious. When there is an opportunity, nations find an excuse to start a war. Therefore, if we remain united under a good national government, we will defensively discourage war instead of *inviting* it. The best defense depends on the government, the arms, and the resources of the country.

11   The safety of the whole is the interest of the whole. To be safe, we must have a government, either one or many. In this context, will one good government provide more safety than any other number?

12   One government can use the talents and experience of the very best men. It can have a uniform policy. It can look ahead, create standard policies for the whole nation, and protect the parts.

In drafting treaties, one government will think of both the whole nation and its parts. And when one part is attacked, it can use the resources and power of the whole to defend that part. The army will have one chain of command up to the President. One army is more efficient than thirteen, or three or four independent forces.

Example: Great Britain

13   Consider the British army. What if the English army obeyed the government of England, the Scot army obeyed the government of Scotland, and the Welsh army obeyed the government of Wales? If invaded, would those three governments (if they agreed at all) operate as effectively against the enemy as the single government of Great Britain?

14   The fleets of Britain have been praised. If we are wise, in time the fleets of America may also be praised. But if Britain's one national government hadn't regulated navigation, making it a place for seamen to learn—if one national government hadn't used national resources and materials to form fleets—their prowess and ability would not be praised.

Let England have its navigation and fleet—let Scotland have its navigation and fleet—let Wales have its navigation and fleet—let Ireland have its navigation and fleet—let the four parts of the British empire be under four independent governments and they would each dwindle into insignificance.

Divided America More Vulnerable

15 Apply these facts to our case. Divide America into thirteen or three or four independent confederacies. What armies could they raise and pay? What fleets could they hope to have? If one was attacked, would the others fly to its aid, spend blood and money in its defense? Or would foreign powers talk the other confederacies into remaining neutral by making false promises of peace? The confederacies would fear threatening their peace and safety for the sake of their neighbors—neighbors they may already envy.

Although such conduct is not smart, it is natural. The history of Greece and other countries has many examples. And under similar circumstances, it probably would happen again.

Better Defense Decisions

16 Let's say neighboring States are willing to help another State or confederacy that has been attacked. How, when, and what shall determine the amount of men and money? Who will command the allied armies? Who will settle terms of peace? Who will settle disputes and make the nations obey the decisions? There would be many difficulties.

But one government, watching over the interests and directing the powers and resources of the whole, would be free from these tricky questions.

Strong Nation Creates Strong Defense

17 Whatever our situation—one national government or several confederacies—foreign nations will know and will act towards us accordingly. If they see an efficient national government with regulated trade, a disciplined army, well-managed resources, good credit, and a free and united people, they will want to be our friends rather than our enemies.

However, if they find our government ineffectual (each State doing right or wrong, as its ruler finds convenient) or split into three or four independent republics or confederacies that probably don't get along—one a British ally, another an ally of France, a third to Spain, and perhaps played off each other by the three—America will be a poor, pitiful figure in their eyes! She'd become a target for their contempt and their outrage.

When a people or family divides, it never fails to be against themselves.

PUBLIUS

27

Number 5: Greatest Threat to American Confederacies: Each Other

Queen Anne wrote to the Scot Parliament on July 1, 1706. She talked about the importance of the *Union* then forming between England and Scotland. She said, "An entire and perfect union will be the solid foundation of lasting peace: It will secure your religion, liberty, and property; remove the animosities amongst yourselves, and the jealousies and differences betwixt our two kingdoms. It must increase your strength, riches and trade; and by this union the whole island, being joined in affection and free from all apprehensions of different interest, will be *enabled to resist all its enemies*. . ."

"We most earnestly recommend to you calmness and unanimity in this great and weighty affair, that the union may be brought to a happy conclusion, being the only *effectual* way to secure our present and future happiness, and disappoint the designs of our and your enemies, who will . . . *use their utmost endeavors to prevent or delay this union*."

Weak Nation Invites Foreign Danger

2   When a nation is weak and has many internal disagreements, it invites danger from other nations. Union, strength, and good government protect us. There is a lot to say about this subject.

Disputes Before Britain United

3   We may learn from the history of Great Britain without paying the price it cost them.

It seems obvious that the island should be only one nation. But for many, many years it was divided into three. They were almost always at war. Policies and jealousies kept them angry, despite their common interest in dealing with continental Europe. They hurt each other more than they helped each other.

Bordering Nations, Disputes Arise

4   If America divides into three or four nations, the same thing would happen. Instead of being "joined in affection," envy and jealousy would kill all affection. Each confederacy would pursue its own policies, not the general interests of all America. Like most *bordering* nations, they would always be either involved in disputes and war, or live with the constant fear of them.

Confederacies Won't Remain Equal

5   If created, the three or four American confederacies would not be equal in strength. No human plan can guarantee equality. Geography

and local resources will increase power in one confederacy and hurt progress in another. Better policy and good management would raise one government above the rest. This would destroy the relatively equal strength. Good policy, prudence, and foresight would not be uniform among the confederacies.

6   One confederacy would become more politically important than her neighbors, who would envy and fear her. The other confederacies would do anything to decrease her importance; they would not help her prosper. She would notice the unfriendly feelings, lose confidence in her neighbors, and feel equally unfavorable to them. Distrust creates distrust. Nothing changes goodwill more quickly than jealousies and insinuations, whether expressed or implied.

North Would Become Strongest

7   The North is generally the region of strength. In time, the most Northern confederacy would be the strongest. Then the southern parts of America would have the same feelings about the northern States as the southern parts of Europe felt towards the *Northern Hive*. And the northerners might be tempted to invade and exploit their luxurious and more delicate southern neighbors.

Confederacies Become Enemies

8   History shows that American confederacies would not become neighbors. They would neither love nor trust one another. Instead, they would suffer from discord, jealousy, and mutual injuries. We would be in the exact situation some nations wish to see us, which is *threatening only to each other*.

9   The confederacies would not become allies. They would not unite arms and resources in defense against foreign enemies.

Different Commercial Goals

10   Britain and Spain are independent states. When did they ever unite their forces against a foreign enemy?

The proposed American confederacies would be *distinct nations*. Each would have commerce with foreign nations, regulated by treaties. And since their products and commodities are different and targeted for different markets, the treaties would be different.

Different commercial concerns create different interests and different political alliances with different foreign nations. The *Southern* confederacy might be at war with an ally of the *Northern* confederacy. Therefore, an alliance between the confederacies would not be easy to form. Or, if formed, it wouldn't be easy to maintain.

Foreign Alliances against Neighbors

11 In America, as in Europe, neighboring nations, with opposite interests and unfriendly passions, would frequently take different sides.

Because of our distance from Europe, the confederacies would be more fearful of other American confederacies than distant nations. They would use foreign alliances to guard against each other, rather than guard against foreign dangers with alliances between themselves.

Don't forget, it is easier to receive foreign fleets into our ports and foreign armies into our country than it is to persuade or force them to leave. How many conquests did the Romans and other nations make under the guise of allies? What changes did they make in the governments they pretended to protect?

Separation Wouldn't Stop Foreign Influence

12 Let candid men judge whether dividing America into several independent sovereignties would secure us against the hostilities and improper interference of foreign nations.

PUBLIUS

Dangers Facing the United States: Domestic

Number 6: Hostilities Between Separated States or Confederacies

Disunion would expose us to worse dangers than those from foreign nations—the dangers from each other.

2   Only a dreamer would believe that if the States break apart they wouldn't frequently fight each other. Men are ambitious, vindictive, and greedy. If you expect harmony between neighboring countries, you have ignored both history and psychology.

Causes of Hostility Between Nations

3   There are many reasons that nations dislike each other. Some reasons are present in all large groups of people. These reasons include the love of power, the desire to control other people, jealousy, and the desire for equality and safety.

Other, more indirect, reasons also cause hostility between nations. These include competition between commercial nations.

Sometimes hostility between nations comes from the private passions of its leaders—friendships, hatreds, interests, hopes, and fears. Rulers often abuse their public office by using the excuse of doing something good for their citizens to start a war for personal gain or other selfish motives.

Rulers' Personal Reasons Start Wars

4   For example, Pericles, the ruler of Athens in ancient Greece, attacked and destroyed the city of the *Samnians* because he was angry with a prostitute. It was expensive and many of his countrymen died.

He also started the *Peloponnesian* war—which ruined the Athenian commonwealth—for one or more reasons: because he was annoyed with the *Megarensians* (another nation of Greece), to avoid prosecution as a coconspirator in the theft of a statue of Phidias, and/or to get rid of accusations of using state funds to purchase popularity.

5   In Britain, the ambitious Cardinal Wolsey, prime minister to Henry VIII, wanted to become pope. He hoped Emperor Charles V would help him. To gain his favor, Wolsey pushed England into war with France, putting the safety and independence of both England and Europe in danger. Charles V wanted to become universal monarch. Wolsey became both his instrument and dupe.

6   Current European policy and hostilities have been greatly influenced by Madame de Maintenon's bigotry, the Duchess of Marlborough's petty complaints and the secret plotting of Madame de Pompadour.

American Example: Shay's Rebellion

7 Throughout history, personal motives have influenced national events. People who know a little psychology need no examples. However, a recent event illustrates the general principle. If Shays had not been a *desperate debtor*, Massachusetts probably would not have been plunged into a civil war.

Some People: Republics are Peaceful

8 Despite history, some dreamers—or men who want to increase their personal power—make the false claim that if the States disunite, they will always be peaceful. They say republics are naturally peaceful. They claim that commerce softens men, extinguishing the hot emotions that so often start wars. They say commercial republics will not waste themselves in ruinous wars with each other, but will promote peaceful relationships.

Same Emotions Affect Republics

9 But isn't it in the interest of all nations to be peaceful? If this is in their best interest, have they pursued it?

No. Passions and self-interest have more control over human conduct than policy, usefulness, or justice. Republics love war as much as monarchies. Men administer both. Bigotry, rivalries, and desires to conquer land and people affect nations as well as kings. Legislatures also feel rage, resentment, jealousy, avarice, and other violent emotions.

A republic is influenced by the passions of the people governing it. Commerce only changes the objects of war. The love of wealth is as strong a passion as power and glory. Commercial motives have started as many wars as the desire for territory.

Historical Examples

10, 11   Athens and Carthage were commercial republics, yet they often fought wars. Sparta, another republic, was little more than an army camp. And the Roman republic never got tired of war and conquest.
12   More recently, Venice was in several wars of ambition. Finally, Pope Julius II founded the League of Cambray that defeated Venice.
13   Holland, until overwhelmed by debt and taxes, led and participated in European wars. They fought England for control of the sea. And they were opponents of Louis XIV.

House of Commons Encouraged Wars

14   Britain has been commercial for a long time. And one branch of the national legislature—the House of Commons—represent the people.

Nevertheless, few nations have been in more wars, frequently started by the people.

15 On various occasions, Britain's representatives have dragged their monarchs into war. Or they went against the monarch's desires and the best interests of their country and continued a war. The long struggle between *Austria* and *Bourbon* is an example. The English dislike of the French and the ambition and greed of the Duke of Marlborough lengthened the war well beyond sound policy and the opposition of the royal court.

16 The desire to protect or increase trade has influenced the wars of England and France.

17 A recent war between Britain and Spain started because British merchants were trading illegally with the Spanish Main. The Spaniards cruelly retaliated against British citizens. After a while, both the innocent and guilty were punished. English merchants complained, spreading the desire for violence through the nation, the House of Commons, and the ministry. Letters of reprisal were granted and war started. Consequently, the alliances formed only 20 years before, with hopes of long-term peace, were overthrown.

We Are a Long Way from Perfection

18 Why should we expect peace if the States separate? Imperfections, weaknesses, and evils are part of every society. Isn't it time to awake from the deceitful dream of a golden age? We, as well as all people in the world, are a long way from the happy empire of perfect wisdom and perfect virtue.

19 Let the extreme depression over our national dignity, the inconveniences felt everywhere from a lax and ill government, the revolt within North Carolina, the late menacing disturbances in Pennsylvania, and the actual insurrections and rebellions in Massachusetts, declare--!

20 Some people are trying to lull asleep our fears that if the States disunite, there will be discord and hostility. Generally, mankind behaves quite differently. History shows that nearness makes nations natural enemies.

Abbe de Mably says: NEIGHBORING NATIONS are naturally enemies of each other, unless their common weakness forces them to combine in a CONFEDERATE REPUBLIC and their constitution prevents the differences that closeness causes, extinguishing that secret jealousy that makes all states want to aggrandize themselves at the expense of their neighbors.

This passage both points out the EVIL and suggests the REMEDY.

PUBLIUS

Number 7: Potential Reasons for Wars Between Disunited States

Some people condescendingly ask: If the States disunite, what reasons would they have to make war on each other? A full answer is: The same reasons that have started the wars in other nations.

Unfortunately for us, however, the question has a more specific answer. Even under the restraints of a federal constitution, we have felt the effect of the differences between us. We can figure out what would happen if those restraints were removed.

Disputes Over Territory

2 Arguments over land cause the greatest number of wars between nations. The disunited States would fight over land.

A large amount of land within the United States remains unsettled. If the Union were dissolved, all the States would make claims on the land.

Some land was not granted at the time of the Revolution and remains the subject of serious disagreements. The States that controlled their colonial governments claim them as property; other States say that land rights granted by Britain no longer existed after the founding of the Union.

Great Britain gave up the Western territory in the peace treaty. To settle the disputes over it, Congress had the States give it to the United States. If the Confederacy broke up, States that had given up the property would probably want it back. The other States would insist on a part, arguing that the territory was acquired by joint efforts of the Confederacy.

Even if all the States agreed to share in this common territory, the question of how to divide it would remain. Agreement between the States would be difficult.

Recent Territorial Disputes

3 We should fear that sometimes war would decide the differences over western territory.

The dispute over Wyoming land reminds us not to expect easy answers. Under the Articles of Confederation, Connecticut and Pennsylvania asked a federal court to decide. The court decided in favor of Pennsylvania. But Connecticut was unhappy. After negotiation, some other land was given to Connecticut. I'm not saying that Connecticut did anything wrong. She thought she deserved the land. States, like people, don't like decisions where they lose something.

States Ally Against Each Other

4 When New York and Vermont disagreed, other States got involved. They were afraid that New York would become too powerful. If New

York had tried to assert its rights by force, a war between the States might have started.

Some States seemed to want to divide New York into smaller States. New Jersey and Rhode Island supported Vermont's independence; Maryland agreed until it looked like Canada and Vermont were allies. If the States disunited, there could be more disagreements like these.

Commerce Can Create Controversies

5   Commerce is another source of controversy. Each State or separate confederacy would have a unique commercial policy with different taxes and product incentives. Commerce in this country has always been based on equal privileges. The change would make some States unhappy.

Injuries are caused by legitimate and justifiable acts of independent sovereignties with different interests.

America's enterprising businesses use every opportunity to improve. If trade regulations are made that only benefit one State, the other States probably won't obey them, which would lead to arguments, new regulations aimed at hurting the other States, then wars.

Import Duties→Negativity towards NY

6   Some States would make commercial laws that make other States involuntarily subservient. The situation of New York, Connecticut, and New Jersey is an example.

New York put a tax on imports from Connecticut and New Jersey. Consumers in the two exporting States pay a large part of these taxes. New York will not voluntarily give up this advantage. How long would Connecticut and New Jersey pay taxes that only benefit New York? Would New York survive with the weight of Connecticut on one side and New Jersey on the other?

Conflict over National Debt

7   The Union's public debt would also cause conflict between the separate States or confederacies. Both the decision about how much each State should pay and paying the debt would produce anger. Some States either don't know the importance of national credit or they don't want to pay the nation's debt. In other States, the nation owes the citizens more than their State's proportion of the national debt.

States that owe money would procrastinate; citizens that are owed money in other States would become resentful. Arguments and excuses would delay making the decision about how much each State should pay. Foreign nations would demand the money owed to them. And the peace of the States would be in double jeopardy from external invasion and internal quarrels.

Hostilities over Paying National Debt

8 Suppose a decision about each State's debt payment was made. It would be difficult for some States to pay and they would want their share lowered. The other States would refuse to have their part of the debt increased. Their refusal would give the complaining States an excuse to withhold their contributions, creating bitter arguments.

Even if the division of the debt payment was equal in principle, some States would not pay for several reasons: lack of resources, financial mismanagement, governmental mismanagement, and the reluctance of men to postpone purchases by using money to pay debts.

Delinquencies, from whatever causes, produce complaints, recriminations, and quarrels. Mutual financial obligations that don't yield an equal benefit disturb the tranquility of nations. It is as true as it is trite: men differ over nothing so quickly as the payment of money.

Conflicts Between State Laws

9 Laws that violate private contracts and injure citizens of a State are another source of hostility. State codes have often been disgraced. If legislatures are unrestrained by a national government, they will not behave fairly.

For example, Connecticut wanted to retaliate against Rhode Island because of offenses by the Rhode Island legislature. Under other circumstances, a war, not of *paper* but of the sword, would punish breaches of moral obligation and social justice.

Alliances with European Nations

10 Preceding papers explained why States or confederacies would probably ally with different foreign nations and how such alliances would hurt the peace of the whole. If America is not connected at all or only by the feeble tie of a league, foreign alliances will gradually entangle it in all the harmful labyrinths of European politics and wars. And the arguments between the American States would be used by nations who are equally the enemies of them all. *Divide et impera* (Divide and command) must be the motto of every nation that either hates or fears us.

PUBLIUS

Number 8: Disunited States Threat to Each Other

Let us assume the States disunite and alliances are formed from the wreck of the Union. All neighboring nations face peace and war, friendship and enmity. We would face the same thing.

Armies and Forts Block Invasions

2   At first, war between the American States would cause more distress than in countries with long military establishments. Although they damage liberty and the economy, the presence of disciplined armies in Europe make sudden conquests difficult.

Fortifications also delay conquests. The nations of Europe are encircled by fortified places. Campaigns against armed forts waste invasion resources. Obstacles occur at every step. Their strength is exhausted. The invader's progress is delayed. Formerly, an invading army got to the heart of a country almost as quickly as news of its approach reached its rulers. Now, a small force of disciplined defensive troops block larger invasions.

In Europe, whole nations are no longer conquered. Instead, towns are taken and returned, battles decide nothing. There is much effort and little acquisition.

Disunited States →Conquests, Ruin

3   In this country, the opposite would happen. The separated States would postpone military spending. There are no forts, leaving State frontiers unguarded. Populous States would easily overrun less populous neighbors. However, conquests would be difficult to keep. Random wars would be followed by PLUNDER and devastation. Our military actions would create disasters for our citizens.

Military Bases Destroy Freedom

4   This is not an exaggeration. But the situation would soon change. Safety from external danger is the most powerful motivator of national conduct. After a time, even the deep love of liberty will diminish. War destroys life and property, and creates a continuous state of danger. For security, even nations that love liberty must build institutions that tend to destroy their civil and political rights. To be safer, they will risk being less free.

Arms Race Between Confederacies

5   If the Union dissolves, standing armies will be used. Frequent wars and constant fear require a trained military.

The weaker States or confederacies—those with a smaller population and less money—would build a stronger defense, including disciplined standing armies and military fortifications. Their executive branch of government would be strengthened, evolving towards a dictatorship. During war, executive power increases at the expense of legislative authority.

6 Small nations with less natural strength but vigorous governments and disciplined armies, often triumph over larger nations or nations with greater natural strength.

The other States or confederacies would quickly use military means to get back what they lost. In a little time, the same type of tyrannies that hurt Europe will be established in this country.

7 This is the way people and nations naturally act.

America Commercial Nation

8 The ancient republics of Greece frequently fought. Why didn't standing armies spring up? This question has several answers.

Greece was primarily a nation of soldiers. Today, people pursue profits and spend their time and money improving agriculture and commerce. This activity is incompatible with a nation of soldiers. The growth of revenue and industry has completely changed how a nation defends itself. Professional, disciplined armies, rather than citizen-armies (militias), are used when there are frequent wars.

Little Interior Defense

9 When a country is seldom exposed to military invasions, the rulers don't have any excuse to keep armies as large as in a nation that is easily invaded. And armies are rarely used for interior defense, so the people are in no danger of living under military rule. Citizens' rights and freedoms remain strong because there are few military emergencies. The civil state remains strong, not corrupted by the activities of a military state. The community is stronger than the small army.

Since the citizens don't need to be protected by the military and they don't live under oppressive military rule, they neither love nor fear soldiers. The citizens view soldiers as a necessary evil and are ready to resist any attempt to limit their civil rights.

The executive branch of government may use the army to suppress a small faction or an occasional insurrection. But it won't be able to stop a rebellion staged by the united efforts of all the citizens.

Large Military Decreases Civil Rights

10 In a country always afraid of war, the opposite happens. The government must always be prepared, needing armies large enough for instant defense. The constant need for their protection makes soldiers more important and reduces the citizens' freedoms. The military state becomes elevated above the civil.

Territories are often the theater of war. The inhabitants are subjected to frequent limitations on their rights, weakening their sense of those rights. Gradually, the people begin to consider soldiers not only as their protectors but also as their superiors. The transition to seeing them as masters is not difficult. Once it has happened, however, it's difficult to get the people to effectually resist usurpations.

Britain Doesn't Need Large Army

11 Great Britain is seldom exposed to internal invasions. Since it is an island and has a powerful navy it doesn't need a large army within the kingdom. It only needs a force large enough to hold invaders at bay until the militia can be raised. Neither national policy nor public opinion has tolerated a lot of domestic troops. And it has been a long time since an internal war has produced a military state.

Britain being an island has helped preserve its liberty, in spite of corruption. If Britain was on the continent, she would need internal military establishments as big as other European powers. She, like them, would probably be a victim of a dictator.

The island might be enslaved from other causes, but not from the small army that is usually kept within Britain.

United States Insulated from Danger

12 If we're wise enough to preserve the Union, we may enjoy the advantage of an insulated situation for a long time. Europe is a great distance from us. Her neighboring colonies will probably continue having so little strength that they won't be dangerous. Therefore, our security will not require extensive military establishments.

But if we disunite, our liberties would be at risk. We would need armies to defend against the ambition and jealousy of each other.
14 This concern is solid and weighty. It deserves serious and mature consideration by all men. If they think about it and look at all its consequences, they will give up trivial objections to a Constitution because if the Constitution is rejected, the Union will probably end. The ghosts that flit before the sick imaginations of some opponents of the Constitution would quickly be replaced by more substantial forms of dangers: real, certain, and formidable.

PUBLIUS

Number 9: Constitution Refines "Confederate Republic" Form

A strong Union will reduce domestic violence and revolts. This preserves the peace and liberty of the States.

Horror filled the republics of Greece and Italy. Revolutions produced the extremes of tyranny and anarchy. Short-lived calms were followed by bloody rebellions. People who seem to want a dictator use this historical example as an argument against both the republican form of government and the principles of civil liberty. They say a free government cannot be ordered. And they maliciously attack its supporters.

Fortunately, a few glorious governments were founded on liberty. They disprove the ugly lies. I hope America will be the solid foundation of other governments that are no less magnificent.

Republican Government Improved

3 Like most sciences, the science of politics has improved. We now understand important principles that ancient governments either didn't know about or didn't understand. We know that government's power needs to be divided into several separate parts or branches with legislative balances and checks. Judges need lifetime appointments and can only be removed for bad behavior. And the people elect legislative representation. These principles save the good parts of republican government and reduce its flaws.

Another improvement is enlarging the size, both of the country and the number of States in a confederacy. We will now study the latter. The country's size will be examined later.

Republic Doesn't Need to be Small

4 A confederacy guards the peace of states. It can suppress internal faction and increase external security.

Opponents of the Constitution claim that Montesquieu said that a republican government requires a small territory. But they have overlooked other things he said. And they don't see the consequence of their argument.

5 When Montesquieu recommends a small area for republics, he's referring to a size much smaller than almost every one of our States. If we adopt this view of Montesquieu's ideas, we would have to either become a monarchy or split ourselves into an infinity of little, jealous, clashing nations. And we would become the miserable objects of universal pity or contempt.

Some opponents of the Constitution take Montesquieu's idea and then suggest that the large states should be divided. Doing this would create a lot of political offices. Men who have no qualifications to hold office— beyond their narrow scope of personal intrigue—could have political positions. But it could never promote the greatness or happiness of the American people.

6 Montesquieu's theory only refers to the SIZE of the largest MEMBERS of the Union. It does not argue against them being joined under one confederate government.

Montesquieu: Confederate Republic

7 Montesquieu doesn't oppose a Union of the States. He says that a CONFEDERATE REPUBLIC is suitable. It combines the advantages of a monarchy with republicanism.

8 In the *Sprit of Laws*, book 9, he says mankind probably would have always lived under a monarch or dictator. Then a constitution was developed that incorporated the internal advantages of a republic and the external force of a monarchy, that is, a CONFEDERATE REPUBLIC.

9, 10 In a confederate republic, he continues, several *States* agree to become members of a large *one*. It can add new States until it is powerful enough to provide security for the entire nation. This kind of republic can withstand external force and internal corruption.

11 He explains that if one man attempted usurping supreme authority, he wouldn't have equal influence in all the States. If he had too much influence in one, it would alarm the rest. If he subdued a part, the rest would oppose and overpower him.

12, 13 A popular rebellion in one State would be stopped by the others. If abuses creep into one part, he argues, the other parts can reform it.

The State may be destroyed on one side and not on the other. The confederacy can be dissolved and the States remain sovereign. Since the government is composed of small republics, it has internal happiness. And it has the advantage of a large monarchy in external situations.

Union Represses Domestic Faction

14 This should explain how Montesquieu's writing supports our proposed Union. He also writes about how a Union tends to repress domestic faction and rebellion.

Confederate Republic Form

15 Some people say that a confederacy has limited authority. They say it only has authority over the member States in their collective capacities [legislation for States], without reaching the individual citizens. They think the national government should not be involved with any part of internal administration, and that the States have equal suffrage.

This is an arbitrary definition. Neither principle nor experience support it. Historically, many confederate governments had these characteristics, but there have been many exceptions. There is no absolute rule on the subject. On the other hand, where such strict limitations [legislation for States rather than individuals] have been tried, disorder and stupid consequences followed.

16 We define a *confederate republic* as "an assemblage of societies" or an association of two or more States into one nation. The extent and objects of federal authority are discretionary. The member States can re-

main separate, constitutionally existing for local purposes. They can even subordinate their authority to the authority of the union. It will be a confederacy.

The proposed Constitution doesn't abolish the State governments. It makes them part of the national government with direct representation in the Senate. They will have certain exclusive and important sovereign powers. This corresponds with the idea of a federal government.

17 The Lycian confederacy had 23 CITIES or republics. The largest had *three* votes in the COMMON COUNCIL, the middle *two*, and the smallest *one*. The COMMON COUNCIL appointed judges and executives of the CITIES. This was invasive control of the CITIES. If local jurisdictions have any exclusive authority, it should be the appointment of their own officers. Yet Montesquieu says, "Were I to give a model of an excellent Confederate Republic, it would be that of Lycia."

Therefore, we see that Montesquieu did not strictly limit the authority of confederacies as some erroneously suggest.

PUBLIUS

Number 10: Large Republic: Best Control of Effects of Faction

A well-constructed Union is the best way to control the violence of faction. Faction is a dangerous vice that occurs in popular governments. We welcome a plan that provides a cure for faction without violating the principles of liberty.

Unstable and unjust government agencies and departments kill popular governments. Opponents of the Constitution use this excuse in their most specious arguments.

The American State constitutions improve the popular governing models, both ancient and modern. They were expected to remove the danger, but they don't.

Our most virtuous citizens, men devoted to personal liberty, complain that our governments are too unstable. They say rival parties disregard the public good. An overbearing majority too often make decisions that should be based on justice and the rights of the minority party.

We may wish that these complaints had no foundation, but the evidence shows that they are in some degree true.

The government has been erroneously blamed for some of our problems. However, other causes, alone, don't account for our worst misfortunes. All across the continent, people worry about the nation's debt and they fear loss of their personal rights. This is largely the effect of distrusting the unjust, factious spirit that is part of our government administration.

Faction Defined

2   A faction is a group of citizens, either a majority or minority, whose actions are motivated by a passion or interest adverse to the rights of other citizens or to the permanent and aggregate interests of the community.

Faction Cure

3   Faction can be cured two ways: remove its causes or control its effects.

Remove Causes

4   To **remove its causes** either (1) liberty must be destroyed or (2) every citizen must have the same opinions, passions, and interests.

5   The first remedy is far worse than the disease. Liberty is to faction what air is to fire. Without the nourishment of liberty, faction instantly dies. But abolishing liberty because it nourishes faction is as silly as the wish to annihilate air because it gives fire its destructive energy.

6   The second cure is as impractical as the first is unwise. Men's abilities are diverse, creating another barrier to their agreeing on common interests. As long as a connection between reasoning and self-love exists, opinions and passions will influence each other. And passions will sway opinions.

Property rights originate from the people. But men's abilities are diverse, creating an insurmountable obstacle to equality of acquisitions. Protection of these abilities is government's primary function. Because government protects different and unequal abilities to acquire property, the people end up owning properties of varying value and kind. This diversity of property ownership divides society into groups with different interests and concerns.

Faction: Inherent in Human Nature

7   Therefore, faction is part of the very nature of man. People have different opinions about religion and government. Ambitious leaders, human passions and diverse interests divide mankind into parties and inflame animosities. People tend to oppress each other, not cooperate for their common good. Frivolous differences become excuses to kindle unfriendly passions and excite violent conflicts.

The most common source of factions is the unequal distribution of property. Property owners and people without property have different interests. Likewise, creditors and debtors.

Civilized nations have property owners, manufacturers, merchants, bankers and many less defined occupations. This creates different groups of people with different views and interests. Regulating these conflicting interests is the principal task of modern legislation. Therefore, factions are a part of the ordinary operations of government.

Legislators: Parties to Causes

8 No man is allowed to be a judge in his own cause. His interest would bias his judgment and probably corrupt his integrity.

For even greater reasons, a group of men are unfit to be both judges and litigants at the same time. Yet legislative acts are basically judicial determinations, not about the rights of individuals, but about the rights of groups of citizens. Yet legislators are both advocates and parties to the causes they determine.

If a proposed law concerns private debts, creditors and debtors are the parties. Justice should balance between them. Yet legislators, who are both creditors and debtors, are the judges. The most numerous group or, in other words, the most powerful faction will prevail.

Should foreign manufacturers be restricted to support domestic manufacturers? Landowners would say no; manufacturers would say yes. Neither would probably use justice and the public good as their only guide.

Determining the amount of taxes on different types of property requires impartiality. Yet no legislative act has a greater opportunity and temptation for the majority party to trample on the rules of justice. With every dollar they overburden the minority party, they save a dollar in their own pockets.

9 It is naïve to say that enlightened statesmen will adjust the different interests, making them all subservient to the public good. First, enlightened statesmen will not always be at the helm. Second, we must consider indirect and future effects. These less obvious consequences will rarely prevail over the immediate interest one party may have in disregarding the rights of another or the good of the whole.

Effect of Faction Must Be Controlled

10 Obviously, the *causes* of faction cannot be removed. Its *effects* must be controlled.

Downside of Majority Faction

11 If a faction isn't a majority, the majority can defeat its sinister views. The minority faction may clog the government and agitate society, but under the Constitution, it can't carry out its plans and hide its violence.

When a faction is a majority, it can sacrifice public good and the rights of other citizens to their passions and interests.

We want to secure the public good and private rights against the danger of a majority faction. At the same time, we want to preserve the popular government form. Our great task is to rescue the reputation of popular government so that it will be valued and adopted by mankind.

Majority Faction's *Passions* or *Actions*

12 To control the effects of a majority faction, either (1) the negative passions and interests in a majority faction must be prevented or (2) the majority faction must be unable to carry out plans of oppression.

If desire and opportunity coincide, neither moral nor religious values will control oppressive behavior. Morality doesn't control the injustice and violence of individuals. And its ability to control bad behavior decreases as the number of people involved increases. In other words, as the need for morality increases, its effectiveness decreases.

Pure Democracy Increases Violence

13 In a pure democracy, citizens assemble and administer the government in person. Democracy doesn't cure the harm caused by faction. Usually, the majority will feel a common passion. There is nothing to stop the desire to sacrifice the weaker party or obnoxious individual.

Therefore, pure democracies are always turbulent. They don't secure personal or property rights. They have short lives and violent deaths. Some political theorists think that after people become politically equal, their possessions, their opinions, and their passions will also be equal. This doesn't happen.

Republic vs. Pure Democracy

A republic—a government administered by representatives of the people—promises the cure we are seeking. We will examine the differences between a republic and a pure democracy. This will show both the cure and why the Union makes it more effective.

15 A republic and a democracy differ in two ways: First, in a republic, the citizens elect a small number of governmental delegates. Second, a republic can have more citizens living across a larger country.

16 Representation refines public views by passing them through the delegates. The representatives' wisdom may see their country's true interests. Their patriotism and love of justice will make them less likely to sacrifice their country. Representatives of the people may do a better job of looking out for the public good than if all the people gathered and spoke for themselves.

On the other hand, the opposite effect may happen. Men with local prejudices or sinister plans may use intrigue or corruption to be elected, and then betray the interests of the people.

Will small or large republics elect better guardians of the public good? For two reasons, large republics do.

Representative/Constituent Ratio

17 First, in a small republic there still must be enough representatives to guard against the plots of a few. In a large republic, the number must be limited to guard against the confusion of a multitude. The proportion of representatives to their constituents is larger in the small republic. If the proportion of qualified people is the same in a large as a small republic, the large republic will have more options and a greater probability of a good choice.

18 In a large republic, each representative is chosen by a greater number of citizens. It will be more difficult for unworthy candidates to successfully win through vicious election practices. And with wide voter freedom, elections will more likely center on men who possess the most merit and highest character.

19 When a representative has too many constituents, it will be difficult for him to know all the local issues. When a representative has too few constituents, his worry about local issues will make him unfit to understand and pursue national issues. The federal Constitution forms a good combination. The national issues are referred to the national government; local issues are referred to State legislatures.

Large Area: Conspiracy Harder

20 Second, a republic can have more citizens and a larger territory than a democracy. This makes raising a damaging amount of support for a faction more difficult.

A small society has fewer people, parties and interests. In a small community, it is easy for a faction to become a majority and execute oppressive plans.

A large society has a variety of people, parties and interests. It is less likely that a majority will invade the rights of other citizens. Even if a common motive exists, it will be more difficult for those holding it to discover their combined strength and act in unison with each other. When unjust or dishonorable purposes exist, communication is limited by distrust in proportion to the number whose concurrence is necessary.

Union as Control of Effects of Faction

21 Hence, a republic controls the effects of faction better than a democracy. And a large republic controls it better than a small republic. It may have more enlightened, virtuous representatives who are above local prejudices and schemes of injustice. There will be a greater variety of parties, so one party can't outnumber and oppress the rest. An increased variety of parties increases the Union's security. A large republic has more obstacles to the secret wishes of an unjust majority.

Factious Passions: Effect on Union

22 Factious leaders may kindle a flame within their States, while not able to spread a conflagration through the other States. A religious sect may degenerate into a political faction in a part of the Confederacy. But the variety of sects dispersed over the entire country secures the national councils against this danger. A rage for paper money, for an abolition of debts, for an equal division of property, or for any other improper or wicked project, will be less able to pervade the whole Union, just like a malady is more likely to taint a specific county or district than an entire State.

Positive Effects of Size, Structure of Government

23 In the size and proper structure, therefore, we see that our Union cures the most common diseases of republican government. And according to the degree of pride we feel in being a republic, we will cherish and support the character of federalists.

PUBLIUS

Advantages of Staying United

Number 11: Benefits of Strong Union to American Commerce

Everyone who has considered the subject, believes that staying united is important to our commerce. The benefits apply to both trade with foreign countries and trade among the States.

European Policies Restrain Our Trade

2   America's adventurous commercial spirit worries several naval powers in Europe. They worry that we will cut into their shipping trade, which supports their naval strength.

Some nations have colonies in North America. Those nations worry about our abilities. If we stay united and have the resources to create a powerful navy, we will be a threat to their American colonies.

Europe will encourage disagreements between States. This could deprive us of an ACTIVE COMMERCE in our own ships. Therefore, we could not interfere in European navigation, Europe would get the major profits from our trade and keep us from being a dangerously powerful nation. We would probably be able to trace Europe's policy of limiting our commerce to its governments.

Uniform Commercial Regulations

3   If we remain united, we can counteract policies that hurt our prosperity. National regulations may force foreign countries to bid against each other for our markets. Our market of three million people—with a fast growing population of farmers—is important to any manufacturing nation. Our trade and shipping will be very different if we use our own ships rather than be forced to use the ships of another country to bring products to and from America.

For example: We currently have no commerce treaty with Great Britain. Suppose the American government could exclude Great Britain from all our ports. How would this affect her politics? Couldn't we negotiate valuable commercial rights from her?

Some people say that prohibitions would not change our trade with Britain because she could use the Dutch to continue trading with us. Holland would buy and transport British goods to our markets. But British navigation would be seriously hurt and the Dutch would get the primary profits. Paying for freight would reduce Britain's profit. The British circuitous supply line would encourage competition among other nations, increasing the price of British commodities in our markets.

4   This would hurt Britain. And since Britain trades with America and the West India Islands, Britain would relax her present system.

Navy Will Help Commerce

5   A federal navy would influence European commerce. If the Union continues, it will create a navy. It might not be a great navy but it could change the outcome of a struggle if it allied with either side of a conflict, especially in the West Indies. A few ships, helping either side, could decide the fate of a campaign that had halted trade. We could bargain for commercial privileges and sell supplies. We could become the arbiter of Europe in America.

6   But if we disunite, the rivalries between us will produce a stalemate, frustrating our great natural advantages. Warring nations will meddle with our commerce. They'll plunder our property. Neutrality is respected only when defended by adequate power; a weak nation forfeits even the privilege of being neutral.

7   European alliances could restrain our growth. However, if we have a strong national government, they would be less successful. Europe would be less likely to make the alliances. We would create an active commerce, extensive navigation, and a flourishing navy.

Disunited, Europe Dominate Commerce

8   If we disunite, European alliances might be successful. Nations with a powerful navy could dictate the conditions of our political existence.

They would want to carry our products and prevent us from becoming their shipper. They'd probably form alliances, destroy our navigation, and confine us to PASSIVE COMMERCE. We would have to accept the first price for our commodities. Our profits would be snatched from us to enrich our enemies and persecutors would get our profits. American merchants and navigators have an unequaled spirit of enterprise and an inexhaustible mine of national wealth. It would be stifled and lost. Poverty and disgrace would spread across a country that could have been the envy of the world.

9   Our Union has some very important trade rights, especially the fisheries and the navigation of Western lakes and the Mississippi. If the Union dissolved, the future of these rights would come into question. Spain's attitude towards the Mississippi needs no comment. France and Britain view our fisheries as important to their navigation. Since we can undersell those nations in their own markets, they would ban our dangerous competition.

Commerce Improves Navigation

10   Commerce will improve our navigation. This resource will help when we build a navy.

11 A NAVY. Staying united will support this great national objective. Every institution grows and flourishes in proportion to the amount of resources put towards its formation and support.

It will be easier for the United States to create a navy than any single State or small confederacy. Different areas of the country have different resources. The southern States have naval stores—tar, pitch, and turpentine. Their wood is more solid and lasting. Some southern and middle States have high quality iron. The northern States will supply most of the seamen.

Naval protection of our commerce is important; maritime commerce will help our navy.

Union Promotes Commerce

12 Unrestrained commerce between the States will advance trade. The free circulation of commodities will replenish the veins of commerce. The States will have a diversity of products. When the staple of one State fails from a bad harvest, it can get the staple of another.

Both the variety and value of export products contribute to an active foreign commerce. Trade competitions and market fluctuations are a part of foreign commerce. Our commerce will be more profitable if we have a large variety of products of a given value than a small number of the same value. Some products may be in great demand at certain periods and unwanted at others. But if there were a variety of products, rarely would they all be unwanted.
Speculative traders understand that this analysis is valid. The total commerce of the United States would be better than that of 13 separate States or several small confederacies.

Disunity Creates Commercial Barriers

13 Some people may argue that whether the States are united or disunited, interstate commerce would achieve the same ends. But disunity would hurt commerce. Unified commercial and political interests can only be achieved through a unified government.

Union Eliminates European Domination

14 We should aim for a position of dominance in American affairs.

The world is politically and geographically divided into four parts. Each part has a distinct set of interests. Unhappily for the other three, Europe, using arms and negotiations, by force and fraud, has extended her dominion, to varying degrees, over them all. Africa, Asia and America have successively felt her domination. Europe's superiority has tempted her to crown herself Mistress of the World, considering the rest of mankind as created for her benefit.

Some philosophers say Europeans are physically superior. And they have gravely asserted that all animals, including humans, degenerate in America. They say that even dogs cease to bark after breathing our air for a while.

For too long, facts have supported these European pretensions. We must save the honor of the human race and teach Europe moderation. As a Union, we can do it. Disunion will add another victim to Europe's triumphants.

Let Americans refuse to be European pawns! Let the 13 States, as a Union, erect one great American system that controls all transatlantic force or influence, and dictate how the old and new world will be connected.

PUBLIUS

Number 12: Union Promotes Revenue

Staying united will promote American prosperity and wealth.

Commerce Benefits Agriculture

2   Commerce produces the most national wealth. Therefore, it's an important political concern.

The desire to make money, the object of human avarice and enterprise, energizes industry. The hard-working merchant, farmer, mechanic, and manufacturer look forward to this reward for their work.

Farmers and merchants used to be rivals but now their interests are interwoven. Commerce increases land values, improves the movement of agricultural products, stimulates the cultivation of land, and increases the quantity of money in a State. Therefore, commerce helps agriculture, and agriculture creates many commercial products. It's astonishing that some people didn't agree with this simple truth. Jealousy can lead men astray from the plainest truths.

Commerce Increases Taxes

3   A country's ability to pay taxes is related to the quantity and turnover of money in circulation. Commerce contributes to these objectives, making payment of taxes easier.

Germany is fertile, cultivated and populous. And it has the best gold and silver mines in Europe. But the monarch's revenues are limited because the country doesn't support commerce. Several times he's been compelled to borrow money from other nations. And he is unable, using his own resources, to sustain a long war.

4   In America, direct taxation is impractical. Despite new tax laws and new collection methods, the States' treasuries remain empty. When trade decreases, money becomes scarce. Extensive tax collections have been impossible. And the State legislatures have learned the folly of attempting them.

5   Similar situations happen in other countries. In Britain, a rich nation, direct taxes are easier to collect. And the vigorous British government makes it more practical than in America. Yet most of Britain's national revenue comes from indirect taxes, imposts and excises like import duties.

6   Clearly, America must depend on revenue from import duties for a long time. The people find excise taxes intrusive and dictatorial. Farmers will pay only very limited taxes on their houses and lands. Personal property is such an invisible asset, it can be taxed only through the imperceptible agency of taxes on consumption.

Union Improves Tax System

7   We must adopt a government that will improve and extend our valuable resources. Without a doubt, a general Union is the best system. As this helps commerce, State revenues will increase. A Union simplifies regulations and makes collecting duties easier. All States would charge the same amount of duties. And the government would increase the rate without prejudice to trade.

Illicit Trade Between States Easy

8, 9 The closeness of the States, the intersecting rivers, the bays, the ease of communication in every direction, the same language and manners, and similar commercial habits make illicit trade easy. The commercial regulations of each State are frequently evaded.

If the States separated, duties would have to be low to avoid the temptations of illicit trade. European nations guard the land and water avenues into their countries. France uses more than twenty thousand army troops to enforce their commercial regulations against contraband. Yet people still find ways to smuggle goods.

Preventing illicit trade over an inland border is very difficult. If the States disunited, it would be difficult to collect duties. Border patrols would need more powers, powers that are intolerable in a free country.

Easy to Guard Atlantic Coast

10   Most of our foreign commercial transactions are only on ONE SIDE—the ATLANTIC COAST. If the States remain united, there would be only one side to guard. When vessels filled with valuable cargoes arrive from foreign countries, they would rarely choose the danger of unloading prior

to coming into port. They would fear the dangers of both the coastal waters and being discovered by government officials. Normal vigilance would prevent most tax evasion. At a small expense, a few armed vessels could be stationed at our ports. And since the national government is interested in preventing violations everywhere, each State would tend to cooperate and make them effective.

In this respect, too, the Union has an advantage over separated States. The United States are a great distance from Europe and all other places with extensive foreign trade. If the States became separate nations, international shipping time would be reduced to a few hours or overnight, as between France and Britain. This would eliminate our natural security against direct contraband with foreign countries. Contraband could easily and safely travel through one State to another. The difference between direct importation and indirect, through a neighboring State in small parcels, is obvious.

National Duties could be Increased

11 One national government could have higher duties on imports than separate States or partial confederacies. Until now, I believe duties have averaged about 3%. In France, they are estimated to be 15% and in Britain, the proportion is still greater.

This country could triple import duties. Under federal regulation, alcohol could be heavily taxed, increasing the government's revenue. The United States imports about four million gallons. A shilling per gallon would produce 200,000 pounds. Alcohol would easily bear this rate. However, if the tax decreased alcohol consumption, it would be equally favorable, favorable to agriculture, the economy, the morals, and the health of society. There is, perhaps, no national extravagance like alcohol.

12 What will happen if we can't fully use import duties? A nation needs revenue to exist. Without taxes, it must give up its independence and sink into the degraded condition of a province. Therefore, revenue is necessary.

In this country, if commerce isn't taxed, land must be. The people are largely opposed to internal taxation. With agriculture almost the only employment in the States, there are few objects for excise taxes and collections would be limited. Personal property is difficult to trace, so large tax contributions can only be achieved through consumption taxes. In populous cities, people would probably have to pay oppressive personal taxes and little benefit would go to the State. Outside these cities, most assets escape the eye and hand of the tax collector.

Nevertheless, funds must be gathered to pay the government's expenses. When they can't be obtained from any other source, landowners must carry the majority of the burden.

On the other hand, unless all tax sources are available when needed for government finances, the community won't have the money to remain respectable and secure. So we won't even have the consolation of a full treasury to make up for the oppression of farmers. Public and private distress will be equal. And everyone will deplore the foolishness that led to disunion.

PUBLIUS

Number 13: One Government Cheaper Than Several

While discussing tax revenue, it is proper to consider the smaller cost of having one national government. If the States remain united, they will need less total tax revenue. The federal government can apply money saved in one area to another area. And we will support only one national government. If the States divide into several confederacies, each confederacy will have a full national bureaucracy.

Few people have suggested that the States should divide into thirteen unconnected sovereignties. It would be expensive and dangerous. The men who want the States to disunite usually suggest three confederacies: the four Northern States, four Middle States, and five Southern States. A greater number of confederacies is improbable.

Each confederacy would need a government as large as the one in the proposed Constitution. When a nation reaches a certain size, its government needs to be the same size as much larger nations. This cannot be proven, but consider this: each proposed confederacy is approximately the size of the British island, which has a population of eight million. And the British government is probably large enough for a much larger population. Properly organized, civil power can become very large and wide spread. Using subordinate institutions, it can reproduce itself in every part of a great empire.

2 The government of each confederation of States would be as large as the one proposed in the Constitution.

If the States disunite, they will probably league themselves under two governments.

The four Eastern States (New Hampshire, Massachusetts, Connecticut, and Rhode Island) would unite. New York and New Jersey would probably join them. Pennsylvania would join the Northern group of States because her foreign commerce is similar. For various reasons, the Southern States may not want to encourage shipping, allowing all nations to be both carriers and purchasers of their commodities. Pennsylvania may not want to join the Southern States because of their commercial policies.

No matter what happens, Pennsylvania will be a frontier. She may decide it is safest to have her exposed side turned towards the weaker power of the Southern Confederacy, rather than towards the stronger Northern power. This would give her the best chance to avoid being the Flanders of America.

Whatever Pennsylvania decides, if New Jersey joins the Northern Confederacy, there will be only one confederacy south of that State.

3   Thirteen States will be able to support a national government better than one-half, or one-third, or any number less than the whole. Yet people object to the Constitution based on its expense. This objection appears to be a mistake.

4   There are expenses in addition to having several civil bureaucracies. People must be employed to guard the inland borders against illicit trade. Conflicts between the divided States would make military forts necessary. Separation would injure the economy, tranquility, commerce, revenue, and liberty of every part.

PUBLIUS

Summary of Issues Covered

Number 14: Republic: Best for American People

We have seen that we need a Union:
- to **protect us from foreign danger** [Numbers 3, 4, 5],
- to keep the **peace among ourselves** [Numbers 5, 6, 7, 8],
- to **guard our commerce** [Number 11] and other common interests,
- as the only **substitute for those military establishments** that have subverted the liberties of the Old World [Number 8].
- as the antidote to **diseases of faction** that have destroyed other popular governments. Alarming symptoms of them have already appeared in ours. [Number 10].

The last objection to discuss is based on the **size** of the Union. Some people fear that a republic isn't practical in such a large geographic area. Opponents of the new Constitution use this prejudice to invent problems because they can't find solid objections.

Democracy Must be Small

2   A republic does not have to be limited to a small area (as discussed in paper Number 9). A republic has been confused with a democracy. Opponents have applied democracy theories to a republic.

In a democracy, the people meet and administer the government in person. In a republic, representatives and agents assemble and administer it. Consequently, a democracy must be small. But a republic may be large.

Monarchy vs. Democracy or Republic

3   This is an unintentional error. Some famous authors influence modern public opinions. Since the authors lived in monarchies, they are biased. They stress the advantages or rationalize the evils of monarchies by comparing them to the vice and defects of a republic. To prove their points, they cite the turbulent democracies of ancient Greece and modern Italy.

The terms "democracy" and "republic" are misused. Observations made about a "democracy" are erroneously transferred to a "republic." One is that a republic must have a small number of people, living within a small territory.

4   Most ancient popular governments were democracies. Modern Europe developed the great principle of representation. However, it has no example of a completely popular and republican government.

America developed representation as the basis of large republics. It is sad that some people want to block America from adopting the Constitution and showing how well the system works.

Democracy Limits Area, Population

5   A democracy must be small with a limited population. All citizens must be able to assemble and administer the government.

The natural limit of a republic is the distance from the capital that allows representatives to meet and administer public affairs. Is the United States too big? During the last thirteen years, representatives of the States have been almost continually assembled. The attendance records of members from distant States have been no worse than those from the States in the neighborhood of Congress.

6   Let's look at the actual dimensions of the Union. According to the peace treaty, the eastern boundary is the Atlantic, the southern is the latitude of 31 degrees, the western is the Mississippi, and the northern is an irregular line running between 42 degrees and 45 degrees. The average north-south distance is 868¾ miles. The average distance between the Atlantic and the Mississippi probably doesn't exceed 750 miles.

Let's compare this size to European countries and we'll see that a republic is practical. Our territory is not much larger than Germany, where representatives continually assemble. Until the national assembly was recently ended in Poland, it was the center of supreme power. Although Great Britain is smaller, representatives from the northern most part of the island travel as far to their national council as required of those from the most remote parts of our Union.

Other Advantages of Republic:

Federal Government: Defined, Limited Jurisdiction

7   More observations will place the subject in a still better light.

8   First, the federal government will not have the whole power of making and administering laws. Its jurisdiction is limited to specific objectives. The State and local governments will keep their authority to care for all other concerns. If the new Constitution abolished the State governments, there would be a reason to object. In fact, if they were abolished, self-preservation would force the national government to reinstate them.

Constitution: Union, Adding States

9   Second, the immediate goal of the federal Constitution is to secure the union of the thirteen original States and adding new States. But how will the territory on our northwestern frontier be handled? This is best left to people whose experience, at the time, will make them equal to the task.

Improves Commerce, Communication

10 Third, national infrastructure improvements will make commerce easier throughout the Union. Roads will be shortened and better maintained. Places for travelers to eat and sleep will increase and improve. River navigation will extend through most of the thirteen States. Communication will become easier. Nature gave our country many rivers; engineers find them easy to connect with canals.

States Benefit from Union's Defense

11 A fourth and most important consideration is safety.

Almost every State will be a frontier. For general protection, some sacrifices will be required. States furthest from the heart of the Union may receive fewer ordinary benefits from the Union but they share a border with foreign nations. Sometimes they will have the greatest need for the Union's strength and resources. Sending representatives to the capital may be inconvenient. However, it would be harder for them to struggle alone against an invading enemy or carry the full expense of defensive precautions. So, if they get fewer benefits in some respects than less distant States, they will get greater benefits in other respects. Thus, the proper balance will be maintained throughout.

American Spirit Unique in History

12 I know you will objectively evaluate these observations. You will never automatically allow predictions of catastrophe to drive you into despair, even if they appear formidable.

Affection binds America together. Don't listen to people who say we can no longer live together as members of the same family and guardians of our mutual happiness. Or that we can no longer be citizens of one great, respectable, and flourishing empire. Do not listen to the voice that says the government framed by the Constitution is so unusual that it has no place in even the wildest political theories and that it is impossible to establish.

No, my countrymen, shut your ears against this unhallowed language. Shut your hearts against its poison. Kindred blood flows in the veins of Americans. They shed blood to defend their sacred rights and consecrate their Union. We should be horrified at the idea of their becoming aliens, rivals, enemies.

If we are to shun new concepts, the rashest new concept is the idea that breaking apart will preserve our liberties and promote our happiness.

Why should the idea of a large republic be rejected just because it is a new concept? Americans study and respect opinions of former times and other nations. But, to their glory, they do not suffer from blind devotion for antiquity or custom. They overrule suggestions that go against their

58

good sense, the knowledge of their situation, and the lessons of their experience.

Posterity will be indebted to the American spirit for its many innovations that improve private rights and public happiness. The Revolutionary leaders took unprecedented steps. They established a unique model of government. If they hadn't, the people of the United States might currently be laboring under the weight of some form of government that has crushed the liberties of the rest of mankind.

Happily for America. Happily, we trust, for the whole human race, they pursued a new and more noble course. Their revolution has no parallel in the annals of human society. They designed a great Confederacy. Their successors must improve and perpetuate it. If their works have imperfections, we wonder at how few.

If they erred most in the structure of the Union [Articles of Confederation], this was their most difficult work. Your Constitutional Convention has made a new model. And it is that act on which you are now to deliberate and decide.

PUBLIUS

No Federal Authority Over Individual Citizens

Number 15: Confederation Near Total Collapse

I have tried to show that remaining united is important to your political safety and happiness. A sacred knot binds the American people. I've showed the dangers if the knot is severed by ambition or avarice, by jealousy or misrepresentation.

I next discuss truths that have not been mentioned. This may seem tedious, but this is the most important subject to free people. There's a lot of information, and sophistry has increased the difficulties. I want to both simplify and thoroughly discuss the issues.

Current Confederacy Can't Save Union

2 I will next discuss why the present Confederation cannot preserve the Union.

Both opponents and supporters of the new Constitution agree this is true. Our national system has significant imperfections. We need to be rescued from impending anarchy.

Facts—not speculation—support this opinion. Even the people whose bad policies have made our dangerous situation even worse reluctantly agree that there are defects in the organization of our federal government. Intelligent friends of the Union point out and regret these defects.

Nation Faces Total Humiliation

3 We are close to total national humiliation. We have experienced nearly everything that can wound the pride or degrade the character of an independent nation:

We violate our commitments. During the war, we borrowed money from foreigners and our own citizens, but we don't have a plan to repay them.

We are entitled by nature and treaty to navigate the Mississippi, but Spain bans us. This should have been corrected a long time ago. But the Union has no troops, nor treasury, nor government to repel an aggressor. We can't even protest with dignity.

During dangerous times, public credit is absolutely necessary. But we seem to have decided it's impossible.

Commerce is important to our national wealth; ours has totally deteriorated.

Our government is so weak that foreign governments don't need to negotiate with us. Our ambassadors only imitate representatives of a sovereign nation.

A dramatic decrease in land value is a symptom of national distress. The price of improved land is much lower than can be accounted for by the quantity of wasteland on the market. Lack of private and public confidence has depreciated property.

Private credit supports industry. But credit is at its lowest because of insecurity, not a scarcity of money.

Is there any type of national disorder, poverty, and insignificance that does not form a part of the dark list of our public misfortunes? Yet we are blessed with many natural advantages.

People Who Created Problems Oppose Const

4   The people who now oppose the proposed Constitution brought us to this sad situation. After leading us to the brink of a precipice, they seem resolved to plunge us into the abyss.

Let us make a firm stand for our safety, our tranquility, our dignity, our reputation. Let us break the fatal charm that has seduced us from the paths of felicity and prosperity.

Amendments Can't Correct Flaws

5   Our national system is defective. A remedy based on the only principles with a chance of success has been proposed. But adversaries of the federal system are very opposed to it. They admit the United States government has no energy, then fight against giving it the powers necessary to supply that energy.

They have disgusting and mutually exclusive goals. They want to increase federal authority without reducing State authority. They want a sovereign Union with completely independent members.

The defects and basic flaws of the Confederation must be listed. It cannot be amended but must be completely rebuilt.

Problem: Legislation for States

6   The basic defect of the Confederation is the principle of LEGISLATION for STATES in their COLLECTIVE CAPACITIES rather than for the INDIVIDUALS living in the States.

This principle doesn't apply to all the federal government's powers. However, it is such an important part of our current system that it leaves the Union virtually powerless. For example, the United States can requisition men and money, but it has no authority to directly raise either from individual citizens. In theory, federal resolutions are constitutionally binding on the States; but in practice, they are merely recommendations that the States observe or disregard.

Legislation for States Ruined Confederation

7   This shows how fickle people are. Some men object to the new Constitution because it doesn't include the principle [legislation for States] that ruined the old, a principle that can only be enforced with the violence of the sword. Courts and judges will do the enforcement under the new Constitution.

Treaties: Very Limited Effectiveness

8   A **treaty** creates a league or alliance of nations. Treaties depend on the good faith of the signature nations. Treaties can change or be ignored during peace and war, they can be observed or not observed, as the interests or passions of the signature nations dictate.

Earlier this century, treaties were very popular in Europe. Politicians hoped for benefits that never appeared. Alliances were formed then quickly broken, showing how little reliance should be placed on treaties.

States as Nations: Both Allies, Enemies

9   If the States become separate nations then form alliances, it would be ruinous. We'd make offensive and defensive alliances, which would change as jealousies and rivalries changed. Foreign nations would promote hostile relationships between the States. And the States would be alternately friends then enemies.

Federal Authority Extends to Citizens

10 But if we are unwilling to be in this dangerous situation and want a national government, our plan must establish a government, not a league. Union authority must extend to the citizens—the only proper objects of government.

Laws Enforced By Courts or Armies

11 A government has the power to make laws. A law needs a sanction— a punishment or penalty for disobedience. If no penalty is tied to disobedience, resolutions that pretend to be laws are nothing more than advice or recommendations.

A penalty can be only inflicted in two ways: by the courts or by military force—by COERCION of the judiciary or by COERCION of arms. The first can apply only to individual people; the last must be employed against politic groups, communities, or states.

Of course, courts have no way to directly enforce laws. Sentences may be pronounced against violators. But sentences can only be executed by the sword. If the authority is based on an alliance, every breach of the law must involve a state of war—punishment by the military. Such a situation doesn't deserve to be called a government. And no prudent man would depend on it for his happiness.

Government: Control over Passions

12 We were told that States wouldn't violate federal regulations. Some people said that States would comply because of our common interests. Today, this sounds ludicrous. It betrayed an ignorance of psychology and contradicted the original reason for establishing civil power. Current pronouncements will sound just as wild after we receive more lessons from that best oracle of wisdom, experience.

Why should we have a government? Because the passions of men won't conform to the dictates of reason and justice without constraint. Do groups of men act with more virtue than individuals? Observers of human behavior know that the opposite happens. An individual worries more about his reputation than that of his group, because blame for the detestable action of a group is divided among a number of people. A group of people is often poisoned by faction, pushing it into improper and excessive behavior that would embarrass the individuals.

Sovereignties Hate Outside Control

13 By its very nature, sovereign power hates control and it hates any external attempt to restrain or direct its operations. Because of this, when a group of small sovereign states unites in a league or alliance, the smaller units tend to fly off from the common center. The origin of this tendency is the love of power. Power controlled or restrained is almost always the enemy of that power doing the controlling. Administrators of individual states in an alliance will not be always ready to execute the decrees of the general authority. So predicts the psychology of human nature.

Allies Can't Be Forced to Comply

14 Therefore, if the alliance's resolutions can only be enforced by each member state, they probably won't be implemented at all. The rulers of the member states, whether they have a constitutional right to do it or not, will try to judge each resolution. They will consider whether the resolution is important to their immediate interests. They will then decide if enforcing the resolution will be inconvenient. These judgments will be made without knowing the national situation or the reasons for the resolution, both essential information.

And local plans and objectives will also influence the decision. Every member of the alliance will repeat this process. Some states will comply and others won't, depending on the information, lack of information and prejudiced opinions of each state. The distant legislatures of the states that make up the alliance will discuss the resolution at different times.

Each will have different views on the subject and they can't be forced to cooperate.

States Not Supporting Confederation

15 Under the current Confederation, the thirteen sovereign States must agree to enforce every important resolution and law proposed by the Union. What happened was expected. The measures have not been executed. State delinquencies have grown, stopping the wheels of the national government. Congress is barely able to keep some kind of administration until the States can agree on a functioning replacement for the present shadow of a federal government.

Our current awful situation didn't happen overnight. At first, a few States didn't fulfill the Union's requisitions. When they didn't pay, the least delinquent States were tempted not to pay, feeling that they shouldn't pay proportionately more than other States in the Union. Why should they pay more than their share of the common burden? Each State has successively withdrawn its support. Now the frail and tottering national confederation seems ready to fall on our heads and crush us beneath its ruins. PUBLIUS

Number 16: Legislation for States → Civil War Inevitable

Legislation for States or communities hurts all confederate governments. It has hurt our government. Historically, the negative effects of legislation for States increase as it is used in more areas of the government.

State Noncompliance Leads to Civil War

2 Legislation for states is the parent of anarchy. It is very easy for States to not fulfill their requisitions. Some States are delinquent. When States are delinquent, the only constitutional remedy is force. The national government must send troops to the State to the State to fulfill its requisitions. The consequence of using force is a civil war.

3 Our government might not even be able to enforce the legislation. If the national government doesn't have a standing army, it can't use force. And if it could use force, violations by the States would start wars between different parts of the Confederacy. The strongest force would prevail, whether it supported or defied the national authority.

A delinquency would rarely be confined to a single State. If more than one neglected their duty, they probably would unite for common defense.

If a large, influential State were delinquent, some non-delinquent States would support its cause. The delinquent State would create excuses for their delinquencies. They would use specious arguments like warning of the danger to liberty.

Excuses for deficiencies would be invented to increase fears, inflame passions, and win over the good will of some non-delinquent States. For example, the ambitious rulers of a large State might not want the federal government to control them. They would not pay their requisitions to advance their plans for personal aggrandizement. They probably would encourage the leaders of adjacent States to join them. If other States didn't become allies, they would ask a foreign nation for aid. Foreign powers would promote disagreements within the Confederacy because if it is firmly united, they will have much to fear.

Once the sword is drawn, men's passions rule over their objectivity. If the Union used force against delinquent States, resentment and wounded pride would push those States to avenge the insult to avoid the disgrace of submission. The first war of this kind would probably dissolve the Union.

More States will be Delinquent

4　The Confederacy could die violently. Currently, we are close to a more natural death. We must quickly and substantially renovate the federal system.

Our history suggests that complying States would rarely support the Union's authority by going to war against non-complying States. Instead, they would identify with the delinquent states and imitate their example. Their common guilt would become their common security. Our experience has shown this.

In fact, it would be difficult to decide when to use force. A State might not send funds because they didn't want to pay. Or it might not be able to pay, an excuse they could always use. And the deception must be obvious to justify forced compulsion. Every delinquency would produce factious views, partiality, and oppression by the majority in the national congress.

Military Coercion Never Works

5　The States shouldn't want a national Constitution that needs a standing army to enforce ordinary laws. Yet this must happen if the Constitution doesn't extend to individuals. If practical at all, it would instantly degenerate into a military tyranny.

But it is, in every way, impractical. The Union won't be able to afford to create and maintain an army capable of forcing the larger States to do their duty.

6 Even in confederacies with members smaller than our States, the principle of legislation for sovereign states, enforced by the military, has never worked. It has only been enforced against the weaker states. And it usually produced bloody civil wars.

Judiciary Enforces Legislation

7 If a federal government is supposed to regulate common concerns and preserve tranquility, it must have authority over the citizens. It must not need approval from the State legislatures. The judiciary must have the authority to enforce its resolutions. The federal government, like each State, must be able to focus on the hopes and fears of individuals and attract support from the strong passions of the human heart. In short, it must have the ability and the right to execute its powers as the State governments do.

States Could Still Block Union's Laws

8 An objection to this reasoning could be raised. If any State becomes disloyal to the Union's authority, it could still use force to obstruct the execution of the Union's laws.

Non-Compliance vs. Active Resistance

9 However, there is an important difference between NON-COMPLIANCE, and DIRECT and ACTIVE RESISTANCE. If every federal law must be approved by each State legislature, if a State just doesn't ACT (NON-COMPLIANCE) they defeat the law. A State could make up an excuse for neglecting its duty. State leaders might even create a temporary convenience, exemption, or advantage. It would be easy to convince the people that they were not defying the federal Constitution or ignoring a federal law.

Blocking Laws Requires Conspiracy

10 But how could a State block a national law that applies directly to citizens? The State government would have to use violent, unconstitutional power to block them. Ignoring the law would not be enough. They would be forced to act. Everyone could see the encroachment on national rights. With a constitution able to defend itself, this action would be hazardous. Enlightened citizens would know the difference between legal authority and illegal usurpation of authority.

Blocking a national law would require a factious majority in the State legislature, the courts, and the citizens. If judges didn't conspire with the legislature, they would rule that the State law was contrary to the supreme law of the land, unconstitutional, and void. The people are the natural guardians of the Constitution. If they didn't agree with the State legislature, they would support the national government. Because of the danger to them, State leaders would not lightly or rashly attempt this, except when the federal government uses its authority tyrannically.

Nat'l, Local Laws Enforced Same Way

11 If rebellious individuals opposed national laws, the judiciary would guard the laws from illegal or immoral behavior. The federal government could suppress a faction within a single State.

Deadly feuds sometimes spread violence through a whole nation or a large part of it. Discontent with the government would spread the violent feuds. We can't estimate how far the violent feuds would spread. When they happen, they usually become revolutions that dismember an empire. No form of government can always either avoid or control them. It is impossible to guard against events that are impossible to predict. It is stupid to object to a government because it could not perform impossibilities.

PUBLIUS

Number 17: Authority Over Individual Citizens: Would National Government Usurp State Authority?

Some people argue that if the federal government's laws are binding on individual citizens, the national government will become too powerful. And the Union might assume some of the State's authority. But even the greatest love of power won't tempt national administrators to take over State authorities. Even ambitious people will not find the regulation of State police very attractive. People who want power are more interested in commerce, finance, negotiation, and war. And the national government should have all these powers.

Local laws concern agriculture, the administration of justice between citizens of the same State, and similar concerns. These issues are not attractive to a national government. Therefore, federal politicians probably would not usurp these powers. The attempt would be difficult and the increase in power would be tiny. They contribute nothing to the dignity and importance of the national government.

State Encroaches National Authorities

2 But let's say, for argument's sake, that maliciousness and lust for power make some people to want control over State issues. But the national House of Representatives, representing the people of all the States, would control this huge appetite.

It is always easier for State governments to gradually take over the national powers, than for the national government to take over State powers. If the State governments are honest and wise, they will usually have more influence over the people. Therefore, federal constitutions are always weak. They must be carefully structured to give them all the power that is compatible with the principles of liberty.

3 Local governments have more influence over citizens because the national government deals with issues that are rarely a part of their daily lives. State administrations deal with more common issues.

Nearness Promotes Affection

4, 5 The depth of loyalty that people feel depends on distance and how much the people or organization effects their lives. Man is more attached to his family than his neighborhood, to his neighborhood than the community at large. People of a State feel more loyal to their local governments than towards the Union, unless their loyalty is destroyed by a much better administration of the latter.

Local Governments: Small, Vital Issues

6 Local governments will supervise a large variety of important issues that are part of the people's everyday life. A list of the issues that State, county and city governments will regulate would be tedious and we would learn very little.

Justice Systems Give States Power

7 The States administrator criminal and civil justice. This is the most powerful source of local obedience and attachment. It guards life and property, and everyone can see its benefits and its terrors. Its decisions were important to personal interests and everyday life. More than anything else, this influences the people's affection, esteem, and reverence towards the government. This, alone, will make the States very powerful; they could even become dangerous rivals to the power of the Union.

National Focus: More Esoteric Issues

8 Most of the citizens won't see the national government's functions. The benefits derived from it will chiefly be watched and perceived by speculative men. Since they relate to more general interests, they will be less in touch with the feelings of people at home and less likely to inspire obligation and loyalty.

Historical Proof

9 All historical federal systems have examples of this.

10 Although the ancient feudal systems were not confederacies, they were similar. The sovereign's authority extended over the whole nation. A number of barons or lords supervised large areas of land. And numerous *inferior* vassals occupied and cultivated that land. Each supervising baron was like a sovereign or governor within his territory. The barons constantly opposed the national sovereign's authority and fought each other. The nation was usually too weak to preserve the public peace or protect the people against the oppressions of their immediate lords. Historians call this European era a time of feudal anarchy.

Barons More Powerful than Sovereign

11 Sometimes the sovereign was vigorous and could successfully rule. But in general, the barons triumphed over the prince. And in many instances, the sovereign's rule was entirely thrown off and the barons created independent principalities or states.

When the king prevailed, it was usually because the barons abused their citizens. The barons were both enemies of the sovereign and oppressors of the common people. They were dreaded and hated by both. Eventually, the king and the common people united to defeat the aristocracy. If the nobles had been loyal to the common people and treated them with clemency and justice, they would have won their contests with the monarch and the royal authority would have been weakened.

Scot Clans More Power than Monarch

12 This assertion isn't based in speculation. Scotland will furnish an example. Early on, clanship was introduced into that kingdom. The nobles and their dependents were united by ties like those within an extended family. This made the aristocracy more powerful than the monarch, until the incorporation with England subdued its fierce and ungovernable spirit with the civility already established in England.

State Government like Feudal Baron

13 The State government in a confederacy is like the feudal barons. With this advantage, they will usually have the confidence and goodwill of the people. With this support, they will effectively oppose encroachments by the national government. It's good that they will not be able to counteract the national government's legitimate and necessary authority.

Study of Historical Confederacies

14 We will review other confederate governments. This will further illustrate this important doctrine. Inattention to history has been the source of our political mistakes and allowed jealousy to point us in the wrong direction.   PUBLIUS

Weaknesses in Other Confederacies

Number 18: Weaknesses Doomed Ancient Greek Confederacies

The most important ancient confederacy was the association of Greek republics under the Amphictyonic federal council. It has instructive analogies to our Confederation of the American States.

Federal Powers, Responsibilities

2 The Greek city-states were independent, sovereign states with representatives (Amphictyons) and equal votes in the federal council. The council could propose and resolve whatever was necessary for the common welfare of Greece. It declared and waged war, acted as the last court of appeals in controversies between states, used force against disobedient members, and admitted new members. The federal council guarded the religion and immense riches of the temple of Delphos. It had jurisdiction in controversies between inhabitants and people who came to consult the oracle. Council members took an oath to defend and protect the united cities, punish violators of this oath, and inflict vengeance on sacrilegious despoilers of the temple.

In Theory, Council's Power Sufficient

3 In theory, these powers seem sufficient. In several ways, they exceed the powers in the Articles of Confederation. For example, they could use coercion against disobedient cities. And they pledged to use this authority when necessary.

In Reality, Not Enough Power

4 The reality was very different than the theory. Deputies appointed by the city-states administered the powers. The confederacy was weak. Disorders were followed by the destruction of the confederacy. The more powerful cities tyrannized the rest. Athens ruled Greece for 73 years. Sparta next governed it for 29 years. After the battle of Leuctra, Thebes ruled.

Stronger States Tyrannized Weaker

5 The representatives of the strongest cities often threatened and corrupted those of the weaker, and judgment favored the most powerful party.

Wars Didn't Even Unite City-States

6   Even during dangerous wars with Persia and Macedon, the city-states never acted as a unit. They were, more or less, the dupes of their common enemy. The time between foreign wars was filled with domestic convulsions and carnage.

7   After the war with Persia, Sparta demanded some cities be expelled from the confederacy for being unfaithful. However, the Athenians decided they would lose more partisans than Sparta, giving the latter a majority. So, Athens opposed and defeated the attempt.

This shows the inefficiency of the confederacy. Ambition and jealousy motivated its most powerful members. The rest were degraded, becoming dependent. In theory, the smaller members were entitled to equal pride and majesty; in fact, they became satellites of the larger members.

Weakness: Danger from Other States

8   Abbe' Milot says that if the Greeks had been as wise as they were courageous, experience would have taught them the necessity of a closer union. And they would have used the peace following their success against Persia for reforms. Instead, Athens and Sparta, inflated by victories and glory, became rivals and then enemies. They inflicted more mischief against each other than they had suffered from Persia. Their mutual jealousies, fears, and hatreds ended in the famous Peloponnesian war, which ended in the ruin and slavery of Athens, who had started it.

Enter as Ally; Stay as Conqueror

9   When a weak government is not at war, disagreements within the nation bring new dangers from other nations. After the Phocians plowed up consecrated ground at the temple of Apollo, the Amphictyonic council fined the sacrilegious offenders. The Phocians, aided by Athens and Sparta, refused to submit to the decree. On the other side, the Thebans, with some other cities, supported the Amphictyons' authority to avenge the violated god.

Philip of Macedon was invited to help the Thebans. However, he'd secretly started the feud. He gladly seized the opportunity to execute his plans against the liberties of Greece. By his intrigues and bribes, he won over the popular leaders of several cities. Their influence and votes gained his admission into the Amphictyonic council. And by his intrigues and his arms, Philip made himself master of the confederacy.

10   If Greece had been united by a stricter confederation and fought to stay unified, she never would have worn the chains of Macedon. And she might have been a barrier to Rome.

Achaean League

11 The Achaean league, another society of Grecian republics, supplies valuable instruction.

12 This union was far more intimate and organized more wisely than the preceding one. Although not exempt from a similar catastrophe, it did not equally deserve it.

Division of Governmental Authorities

13 The cities in the league had municipal jurisdiction, appointed their own officers, and were perfectly equal. They were represented in the senate. The senate had the exclusive rights to make peace and war, send and receive ambassadors, enter into treaties and alliances, and appoint a chief magistrate or praetor.

The praetor commanded their armies and, with the advice and consent of ten senators, administered the government during the senate recess and shared in its deliberations when assembled. Their constitution called for two administrative praetors but in practice one was preferred.

14 The cities had the same laws and customs, the same weights and measures, and the same money. But it's uncertain whether this was a federal decree. The only mandate was that cities have the same laws and usages.

As a member of the Amphictyonic confederacy, Sparta fully exercised her government and her legislation. However, when Sparta became part of the Achaean league, her ancient laws and institutions were abolished and those of the Achaeans adopted. This shows the major difference between the two systems.

15 It's too bad that a better historical record of these interesting political systems doesn't exist. If their internal structure could be studied, we would probably learn a lot about the science of a federal government.

Achaean Government More Just

16 Historians agree that after Aratus renovated the Achaean league and before its dissolution by Macedon, its government was more moderate and just than any of the sovereign cities. Abbe' Mably says that the popular government, so tempestuous elsewhere, caused no disorders in the members of the Achaean republic, *because it was tempered by the laws of the confederacy.*

Faction Caused Problems

17 However, we shouldn't hastily conclude that faction did not agitate the cities, or that subordination and harmony reigned. The contrary is shown in the vicissitudes and fate of the republic.

18 When the Achaean cities fell to Macedon, Philip II and his son, Alexander the Great, saved Greece. Their successors followed a different policy. Each city had separate interests and the union was dissolved. Some fell under the tyranny of Macedonian garrisons; others fell to usurpers within Greece.

Before long, shame and oppression awakened their love of liberty. Cities reunited when opportunities to cut off their tyrants were found. Soon the league embraced almost the whole Peloponnesus [southern peninsula of Greece]. Macedon saw its progress but internal dissensions hindered her from stopping it.

All Greece seemed ready to unite in one confederacy until jealousy and envy in Sparta and Athens, over the rising glory of the Achaeans, threw a fatal wrench into the enterprise. The dread of Macedonian power induced the league to court an alliance with the kings of Egypt and Syria who, as successors of Alexander, were rivals of the Macedonian king.

Ambition led Cleomenes, king of Sparta, to make an unprovoked attack on the Achaeans. As an enemy of Ma-cedon, Cleomenes got the Egyptian and Syrian princes to breach their treaty with the league. The Achaeans were reduced to the dilemma of submitting to Cleomenes or requesting the aid of Macedon, its former oppressor.

The Achaeans chose the aid of Macedon. A Macedonian army quickly appeared and took possession of Sparta. Cleomenes was vanquished to Egypt. But the Achaeans soon learned that a victorious and powerful ally is often just another name for a master.

The tyrannies of Philip, the king of Macedon, provoked new alliances among the Greeks. The Achaeans were weakened by internal dissensions and by the revolt of one of its members, Messene, but they joined the Aetolians and Athenians in opposition. But they weren't strong enough and had to resort to the dangerous expedient of help from foreign arms. The Romans were invited and eagerly accepted. Philip was conquered. Macedon was subdued.

The league faced a new crisis. Rome promoted hostilities between its members. Popular leaders manipulated their countrymen. To nourish discord and disorder, Rome suggested members leave the league; Rome appealed to their pride, saying the league violated their sovereignty. This union, the last hope of Greece and the last hope of ancient liberty, was torn into pieces. Such imbecility and distraction reigned that the Roman army easily completed the ruin that their intrigues began. The Achaeans were cut to pieces and Achaia loaded with chains under which it groans at this hour.

Federal Government Tends Towards Anarchy

19 This history teaches several things. And it shows the tendency of federal bodies more towards anarchy among the members than to tyranny in the head.

PUBLIUS

Number 19: Current Confederacies: German, Polish, Swiss

We will study some existing governments. The first is Germany.

History of Germany

2 In the early days of Christianity, seven nations occupied Germany. After conquering the Gauls, the Franks established a kingdom. In the ninth century, Germany became part of Charlemagne's vast empire.

Charlemagne and his descendants had imperial power. Charlemagne didn't abolish the national assembly, which slowly moved towards independence. The emperor could not preserve the unity and tranquility of the empire. Different princes and states fought wars. The emperor's authority declined. Anarchy reigned between the death of the last emperor of the German province of Swabia and the first emperor of Austria.

In the 11th century the emperors held full sovereignty; by the 15th century they were only symbols of power.

Legislative, Executive, Judiciary

3 In many ways, the feudal system was similar to a confederacy. Germany's federal system grew from it.

A legislature, the diet, represents the states in the confederacy. The emperor can veto legislation. The two judiciary courts—the imperial chamber and the aulic council—have final jurisdiction in controversies concerning the empire or among its states.

Legislative Authorities

4 The legislature (the diet) has the power to make war and peace, make alliances, assess quotas for troops and money, construct forts, regulate coins, admit new states, and punish disobedient states. States of the confederacy can't make treaties that could hurt the empire, impose duties on interstate commerce without the consent of the emperor and legislature, alter the value of money, or assist internal rebellions. Violators may be punished.

Emperor: Duties, Rights

5 The emperor has exclusive right to propose and veto legislation, name ambassadors, confer titles, fill vacant electorates, found universities, grant privileges not injurious to the states, receive and send public reve-

nues, and watch over the public safety. The emperor has no special land, housing, or income. But his personal income and lands make him one of the most powerful princes in Europe.

6   These constitutional powers suggest that the German government's character is different than similar systems. Nothing could be further from the reality. It rests on the fundamental principle that the empire is a community of sovereigns, that the legislature represents sovereign states, and that the laws are addressed to sovereign states. This renders the empire powerless. It can't regulate its members or build a defense against external dangers. The German states are constantly fighting each other.

Internal Battles, Invasions, Misery

7   Germany has a history of wars. The emperor and the states fight. The weak are oppressed. Foreign nations have invaded and developed conspiracies. The states ignored requisitions for money and men. Either the requisitions were not enforced or they were enforced by the military, which killed the innocent and the guilty. It's a history of stupidity, confusion, and misery.

8   In the 16th century, the emperor, supported by part of the empire, fought the other states. The emperor had to flee from one conflict after nearly being made prisoner. The late king of Prussia fought his imperial sovereign more than once, usually defeating him.

Before the peace of Westphalia (1648), thirty years of war desolated Germany. The emperor and one half the empire opposed Sweden and the other half. Foreign powers finally negotiated and dictated the peace. The peace treaty became a fundamental part of the German constitution.

Emergencies and Internal Conflict

9   Even if the nation tries to unite for self-defense during an emergency, its situation is still awful. Jealousies, differing views, and clashing pride of sovereign bodies inflame their legislative discussions, stalling any military preparations. An enemy can invade the country before the legislature decides on a military defense. And the enemy is settling into winter quarters before federal troops are prepared to fight.

Army Inadequate, Underpaid

10, 11   Germany's small, peacetime army was poorly maintained, badly paid, and infected with local prejudices. Maintaining order and dispensing justice was impossible. The empire was divided into nine or ten circles (states). The military enforced laws against delinquent and disobedient states.

This demonstrates the flaws of their constitution. Each state has the deformities of this political monster. They either fail to do their duties or are forced with all the devastation of civil war. Sometimes whole states default, increasing the problems they were established to remedy.

12 Citizens of Donawerth, a free city within the Swabian circle (state), committed outrages on Abbe de St. Croix. In consequence, the city was put under the ban of the empire. The Duke of Bavaria was appointed to enforce it. He arrived in the city with 10,000 troops, then claimed the city had been stolen from his ancestors' territory. He took possession of it, disarmed and punished the inhabitants, and reannexed the city to his domain.

Danger Promotes Status Quo

13 This disjointed country doesn't completely fall apart because most states are weak and unwilling to expose themselves to foreign powers. The emperor has great influence from the land and wealth he inherited. And he wants to save a country that is part of his family pride and makes him the first prince of Europe.

It is a feeble and precarious Union. By their nature, sovereign states don't want to consolidate. But even if the districts decided to consolidate, neighboring nations wouldn't allow it; the empire would be too strong and powerful. Foreign nations want Germany to remain in turmoil.

Poland: Government Over Sovereigns

14 Poland is a government over local sovereigns. It is incapable of self-government and self-defense. Poland is at the mercy of its powerful neighbors who recently took one-third of its people and territories.

Swiss States Not Confederacy

15, 16 Sometimes people use the Swiss states as an example of a stable confederacy. But the connection between the Swiss states can't be called a confederacy. They have no common treasury, no common armies even in war, no common coin, no common judicatory, nor any other common mark of a sovereignty.

17 The Swiss states are kept together for several reasons: their geographic location, their individual weakness and insignificance, the fear of powerful neighbors (one formerly ruled them), their joint interest in Swiss territories, mutual aid for suppressing insurrections and rebellions, and a system that is supposed to solve disputes among the states. To settle disputes, each party involved chooses four judges from neutral states. This tribunal pronounces a sentence that all the states are bound to enforce. However, this regulation hasn't been effective.

Controversies Easily Severed League

18, 19   Comparing their case to the United States confirms our opinion. However effective the union may be in ordinary cases, it failed as soon as severe differences appeared. In three instances, religious controversies have severed the league. And that separation has produced opposing alliances with foreign powers.   PUBLIUS

Number 20: United Netherlands: Failure of Legislation for States

The United Netherlands is a confederacy of aristocrats. It confirms the lessons we have discussed.

Equal States; Equal, Independent Cities

2   The United Netherlands has seven equal, sovereign provinces. Each province is composed of equal, independent cities. Both the provinces and the cities must unanimously approve important issues.

3   The States-General represents the union. The provinces appoint the deputies, who serve different terms, decided by the provinces.

4   The States-General can enter into treaties and alliances, establish duties, make war and peace, raise armies and equip fleets, determine tax quotas, and demand contributions. However, all the provinces and cities must agree.

They appoint and receive ambassadors, execute treaties, collect taxes, regulate the mint, and govern the dependent territories.

Stadholder: National/Provincial Ruler

5   The chief executive of the union is a hereditary prince. Most of his influence comes from his independent title, his family connections within Europe, and, most of all, his also being stadholder (governor) in several provinces in addition to being the chief executive of the union.

As a governor, he appoints town officials, enforces local laws, is the local judge, and has the power of pardon.

6-9 As chief executive of the union, he has many exclusive duties. He settles disputes between provinces. He assists at the deliberations of the States-General. He meets with foreign ambassadors and appoints ambassadors. He commands the federal troops, provides for forts and garrisons, confers military ranks, and he is admiral-general.

10 His revenue, exclusive of his private income, is 300,000 florins. He commands a standing army of about 40,000 men.

Theoretical Organization; Chaos Reality

11 This is how the confederacy is organized on paper. How has it functioned in reality? Imbecility in the government. Discord among prov-

inces. Foreign influence and indignities. Precarious existence in peace and calamities during war.

12, 13 Grotius has said that the only thing that has saved his country from being ruined by the vices of their constitution is their hatred of Austria. Another respected writer says the States-General has the authority to secure harmony, but jealousy in each province makes reality very different from theory.

Inland Provinces Can't Pay Taxes

14-16 Each province is supposed to pay contributions, but inland provinces have little commerce and cannot pay an equal quota. The provinces that are able to pay must pay, and then use any method to get money from the other provinces. More than once, money was collected at bayonet point. This is an awful solution when one member of a confederacy is much stronger than the rest. And this solution won't work in a confederacy composed of several members of equal strength, resources, and defenses.

Foreign Ministers Overstep Authority

17 Former foreign minister Sir William Temple says foreign ministers avoid matters taken *ad referendum* by tampering with the provinces and cities. In 1726, the treaty of Hanover was delayed this way for a year. Examples like this are numerous and notorious.

Weak Constitution Leads to Tyranny

18 In emergencies, the States-General oversteps its constitutional bounds. It has agreed to several treaties without the consent of all the provinces.

A weak constitution ends up being ignored. Then it dissolves either from a lack of power or government officials usurp the powers necessary for the public safety. The usurpation may stop at a healthy point or go forward to a dangerous extreme. Tyranny more frequently grows out of the assumptions of unconstitutional power that is needed in an emergency but is not included in a defective constitution, than out of the full exercise of the largest constitutional authorities.

Stadholder

19 Without the stadholder, the confederacy would have dissolved long ago. Abbe Mably says the Union could not have survived without a motivator from within the provinces. This motivator is the stadholder.

Other Nations Influence Corruption

20 Other factors also control the tendency to anarchy and dissolution. The surrounding foreign powers make union absolutely necessary. At the same time, foreign intrigues nourish the constitutional vices. To some degree, the republic is always at their mercy.

Can't Agree How to Fix Problems

21 Patriots have convened four *conventions* to find a remedy to these potentially fatal vices. But they haven't been able to convince a majority of the people that the existing constitution needs to be corrected before it completely fails.

Let us pause for one moment, my fellow citizens, over this sad history lesson. Let's shed a tear for the calamities that result from mankind's adverse opinions and selfish passions. Then let our praise of gratitude for the amity distinguishing our political counsels rise to Heaven.

Federal Tax Plan Failed

22 A tax system administered by the federal government was conceived. It also failed.

Maybe Crises Will Form Stronger Union

23 This unhappy people currently suffer from popular revolts, conflicts between states, and foreign invasion. These emergencies will determine their destiny. All nations are watching the awful spectacle.

Hopefully, their severe problems will create a revolution that will establish their union, making it the parent of tranquility, freedom, and happiness. If not, we hope that as they see how quickly our country secures these blessings they will be encouraged to do the same thing.

Fatal Flaw: Government Governing Government

24 The study of these federal precedents is important. Experience is the oracle of truth. When its lessons are unambiguous, they should be regarded as conclusive.

A sovereignty over sovereigns, a government over governments, legislation for communities—rather than a government over individuals—is illogical in theory. In practice it takes away order and ends civility by substituting *violence* in place of *law*. In it, laws must be enforced by the destructive *coercion* of the *sword* instead of the mild and solitary *coercion* of the *magistracy*.

PUBLIUS

Problems in Articles of Confederation

Number 21: Defects of United States Articles of Confederation

I will now list the most important defects in our system. To decide a safe and satisfactory remedy, we must know the extent and harmfulness of the disease.

No Power to Enforce Federal Laws

2   The existing Confederation has no SANCTION—no way to enforce—its laws. Currently, the federal government doesn't have the power to demand obedience or the authority to use force against delinquent members. We might say that the nature of the social compact between the States includes the right to enforce federal laws. But this assumption is contrary to the *States' rights* clause, Article Two, Articles of Confederation: "that each State shall retain every power, jurisdiction, and right, not *expressly* delegated to the United States in Congress assembled." This leaves us two options: either accept the crazy idea that the federal government has no power to enforce federal laws or violate the States' rights clause in Article Two.

The new Constitution has no States' rights clause. It has been severely criticized for this. However, if we don't weaken the States' rights provision, the United States will become the weird spectacle—a government without any constitutional power to enforce its own laws.

No Federal, State Mutual Guaranty

3   The Articles say nothing about a mutual guaranty of the State governments. A guaranty would be useful and we might suggest that it exists, but it would flagrantly violate the States' rights clause. Although not having a guaranty may endanger the Union, it isn't as dangerous as the federal government not having the constitutional power to enforce federal laws.

U. S. Can't Defend State Constitutions

4   Without a guaranty, the Union cannot help fight domestic threats to State constitutions. Usurpations could trample State liberties and the national government could legally do nothing but watch in anger and sorrow. A successful faction could erect a tyranny within a State and the Union could not constitutionally help supporters of the State's constitutional government.

Massachusetts barely survived the recent turmoil. What if someone like Caesar or a Cromwell had led the malcontents? If despotism had been established in Massachusetts, how would it have changed liberty in New Hampshire, Rhode Island, Connecticut, or New York?

Mutual Guaranty: Advantage of Unity

5 Some people object to a federal government guaranty. They say that the federal government should not interfere in internal State issues. But they misunderstand the provision. And they want to deprive us of advantages expected from union. A majority of the people could still legally and peacefully reform a State's constitution. The guaranty could only operate when violence was used to force changes.

People Hold Governmental Authority

The people hold the whole power of the government. When disagreements appear, the people will have fewer excuses to use violence. In a representative government, the natural cure for poor administration is changing men. A national guaranty would be used against both tyrannical rulers and community factions.

Taxation by State Quotas

6 Currently, State contributions to the national treasury are regulated by QUOTAS, which haven't been met. There is no one standard to measure the degrees of national wealth. Land values and population numbers have been suggested as ways to determine each State's quota. But neither truly represents the State's wealth.

For example, let's compare the wealth of the United Netherlands to Russia, Germany, or France. There is no relationship between their wealth and their land value and population. The United Netherlands has the higher wealth; the three other nations have immense land and much larger populations.

We can compare American States in the same way and get a similar result. Compare Virginia with North Carolina, Pennsylvania with Connecticut, or Maryland with New Jersey. Their comparative wealth has little relationship to their lands and populations. Counties within New York State illustrate the same thing. If either land value or population is the criterion, the active wealth of King's County is much greater than that of Montgomery County.

No Measurement of Wealth Accurate

7 An infinite variety of causes create a nation's wealth. They include location, soil, climate, products, the type of government, the genius of its citizens, knowledge, commerce, arts, and industry. And there are many more causes that are too complex to quantify. These combine to create differences in the relative wealth of different countries. There is no common measure of national wealth. And there is no way to measure a State's ability to pay taxes. Therefore, trying to calculate each State's

quota by using a rule based on land or population would be glaringly unequal and extremely oppressive.

Quotas/Requisitions, States Unequal

8   Even if federal requisitions could be enforced, the inequality between
States' wealth alone would eventually destroy the American Union.
Public burdens would be unequally distributed. Some States would be
impoverished and oppressed while citizens of others would scarcely notice their small tax burden. Suffering States would secede. The principle
of quotas and requisitions creates this evil.

National Government Needs Revenue

9   To avoid this problem, the national government must be able to raise
its own revenue.

Like fluid, taxes on articles of consumption will, in time, find their
level with the means of paying them. To a degree, each citizen's contribution will be his own option, determined by his resources. The rich
may be extravagant. The poor can be frugal. And private oppression
may be avoided by judiciously selecting the objects to be taxed. If inequalities arise in some States from duties on specific objects, these probably will be counterbalanced by proportional inequalities in other States
from duties on other objects. In time, an equilibrium, as far as it is at-
tainable in so complicated a subject, will be established everywhere. Or,
if inequalities continue to exist, they will not be as odious as those that
come from using quotas.

Tax Revenue Limits Federal Authority

10 Consumption taxes tend to block excess taxation. They prescribe
their own limit. If they are too high, they defeat their purpose—
increasing government's revenue.

Excessive Taxes Decrease Revenue

When applied to taxation policy, it is true that "in political arithmetic,
2 and 2 do not always make 4." If duties are too high, people make fewer purchases, less tax is collected, and the government's revenue is less
than if taxes were confined within proper and moderate bounds. This
forms a complete barrier against any significant oppression of citizens by
taxes of this kind. And it naturally limits the power of the imposing authority.

Indirect vs. Direct Federal Taxes

11 For a long time, most of the government's revenue must be raised by
indirect taxes.

Direct taxes principally relate to land and buildings, and they may be
appropriate for the rule of apportionment. Either the land value or the

number of people may serve as a standard. Agriculture and population density are co-related. For taxation, numbers are usually preferred because of their simplicity and certainty.

Land valuation is a herculean task. In a country only partly settled and constantly being improved, the difficulties make it nearly impossible. And the expense of an accurate valuation is a major objection. There are no natural limits to direct taxes. Therefore the establishment of a fixed rule, compatible with its purpose, might be a better idea than leaving the discretion unbound.   PUBLIUS

Number 22: Defects in Articles of Confederation

The existing federal system is unfit to administer the Union and it has several more defects.

No Federal Regulation of Commerce

2   Currently, the federal government has no power to regulate commerce. But we must have federal regulation of commerce. We haven't been able to have good commercial treaties with other nations. Since the States have been arguing about commerce, no nation will sign a commercial treaty with the United States. They know that individual States could violate the treaty at any time. Besides, they already have every advantage in our markets without giving us any in return except when it is convenient.

In England, Mr. Jenkinson introduced a bill in the British House of Commons to temporarily regulate commerce between our two countries. He declared that earlier bills with similar provisions answered Great Britain's commercial needs. He said that they shouldn't change their policies until the American government became more consistent.[1]

Uniform Foreign Commerce Authority

3   Some States have tried to change Great Britain's commercial policies by limiting or prohibiting some British products. But different States have different restrictions. We won't be able to influence Great Britain's commercial conduct until we have one federal authority and one commercial policy.

Uniform Interstate Commerce Laws

4   Contrary to the true spirit of the Union, some State regulations hurt the commerce in other States. Without national control, there will be

---

[1] As nearly as I can recollect, this was the sense of his speech on introducing the bill.

more of these policies and anger between the States will grow, further damaging commerce.

The Encyclopaedia[2] ("Empire") describes Germany's commercial situation. Each German prince taxes the merchandise that travels through his state. The wide variety of taxes within Germany has put commerce in constant turmoil. And shippers have to stop and pay taxes so many times along the commercial routes that they don't even bother using Germany's navigable rivers.

This description may never completely apply to us. But as each State makes different commercial regulations, citizens of one State will treat citizens of other States no better than foreigners and aliens.

Quotas, Requisitions to Raise Armies

5   Under the Articles of Confederation, when the federal government needs to raise troops it must requisition quotas from the States. During the recent war, the requisition system made a vigorous and economical defense very difficult. To fill their quotas, States competed against each other, offering enormous rewards. Men who wanted to serve put off enlisting, hoping to get a larger bonus.

The result? During emergencies, enlistments were few, slow, short-term and very expensive. The constantly changing troops ruined discipline and the soldiers who had mustered out threatened public safety. The occasional forced enlistment only worked because of enthusiasm for liberty.

Unfair, States Not Compensated

6   Using State quotas to raise troops doesn't work. The enlistment bonuses hurt the economy. And only some of the States filled their quotas. The States near the heart of the war, influenced by self-preservation, furnished the required number of men. Usually, the States that were not in immediate danger didn't fulfill their quotas. Of course, if a State falls behind paying their money quota, it can be made up. It's impossible to supply delinquent deficiencies of men. However, States probably won't pay for their monetary failures. Whether it is used to raise men or money, the quota system is unequal and unjust.

Problems from States' Equal Suffrage

7   Currently, each State has an equal vote in the national congress. This is another problem. Every rule of fair representation condemns the principle that gives Rhode Island equal power with Massachusetts or Con-

---

[2] The article title is "Empire."

necticut or New York. This goes against the basic principle of republican government: the will of the majority should prevail.

Some people may say that each State in the Union is a sovereign and sovereigns are equal. Therefore a majority of the votes of States will be a majority of confederate America. But this logical sleight-of-hand doesn't remove the dictates of justice and common sense. A majority of States can be a small minority of American citizens.[3]

Two thirds of the people will not allow one third to manage their interests. After a while, the larger States will revolt. Giving up majority rights is contrary to the love of power and it sacrifices equality. It is not rational to expect the first, nor just to require the second. Since the smaller States depend on union for their safety and welfare, they should readily renounce a pretension that, if not relinquished, would be fatal to that union.

2/3 of States Doesn't Assure Majority

8   It may be proposed that two-thirds of the States (9) must consent to pass important resolutions. But an equal vote between States of unequal dimensions and populations is improper. Besides, nine States can have less than a majority of the people.[4] A bare majority might still decide significant issues. Additionally, the number of States will probably increase and there is no provision for increasing the ratio of votes.

2/3 Majority = Minority Control

9   But this is not all. A two-thirds majority may look like a solution. In reality it makes the problem worse. When more than a majority is needed to make a decision, the minority gets a negative over the majority. It subordinates the feelings of the majority to the minority. Because a few States have been absent from our current Congress, a single VOTE—one-sixtieth part of the union—has frequently stopped all business.

A two-thirds majority is supposed to provide security. In practice, it does the opposite. It becomes nearly impossible to administer the government. And it substitutes the desires or schemes of a tiny or corrupt group of politicians for the decisions of a majority.

During national emergencies, the government needs to be strong and it must often take an action. Public business must, one way or another,

---

[3] New Hampshire, Rhode Island, New Jersey, Delaware, Georgia, South Carolina and Maryland are a majority of the whole number of States but they do not contain one third of the people. –PUBLIUS

[4] Add New York and Connecticut to the foregoing seven and they will be less than a majority. –PUBLIUS

go forward. If a stubborn minority is in control, to accomplish anything, the majority must accept the decisions of the minority. Delays, negotiations, and intrigue would hurt the public good. Sometimes compromises won't be possible and the legislature will be unable to act. This would create a government that is weak and sometimes bordering on anarchy.

Foreign, Domestic Corruption Easier

10 If a two-third majority is required, both foreign corruption and domestic faction will be easier. If a large number is needed to pass a national act, nothing improper is likely *to be done*. However, good legislation may be prevented and bad things might happen because the Congress is unable to act.

Simple Majority Harder to Corrupt

11 For instance, suppose a foreign ally wants a war with a third nation but we want a peace treaty. It would be easier for our ally to use bribes or threats to tie the hands of our government from making peace if a vote of two-thirds were required rather than a simple majority. In the first case, a smaller number (34%) would need to be corrupted; in the latter, a greater number (51%). By the same principle, a foreign power at war with us could stop our congress from functioning and embarrass us.

We may also suffer commercial inconveniences. We might have a commerce treaty with a nation, who could easily block a treaty with her trade competitor, even though it would be beneficial to us.

Republics and Foreign Corruption

12 These evils are not imaginary. A weak side to republics is that foreign corruption is easy. A king or dictator often sacrifices his subjects to his ambition but it is difficult for a foreign power to make a bribe large enough for him to sacrifice his state.

Foreign Corruption of Republics

13 In a republic, people are elected to important offices and have great power. They may be offered bribes that only the most virtuous can refuse. Other officials may be more motivated by ambition or personal interests than their obligations to duty.

History has many horrible examples of foreign corruption in republican governments: It helped ruin the ancient republics. Neighboring nations have bought the officials of the United Provinces. And France and England alternately bought officials in Sweden.

Lack of Federal Supreme Court

14 The Confederation's worst defect is the lack of a judiciary power. Laws are pointless without courts to interpret and define their true meaning and operation.

Treaties must be considered as part of the law of the land. Their effect on individuals must, like all laws, be defined by judicial decisions. To have uniform decisions, as a last resort they should be submitted to one SUPREME TRIBUNAL that is created under the same authority that signs the treaties.

If each State has a court of final jurisdiction, there may be as many different final decisions on an issue as there are courts. Men hold a limitless variety of opinions. We often see not only different courts, but also judges of the same court, differing from each other. Contradictory decisions create confusion. To avoid this, all nations have established one court of last resort, authorized to settle a uniform rule of civil justice.

State Courts Will Not Always Agree

15 This is more important when the laws of the whole country are in danger of being contradicted by the laws of the States or regions. If State or regional courts have the final opinions, a bias based on local views and local regulations would produce contradictions. People might prefer a local law over a federal law. Men in office naturally yield to the authority to which they owe their job.

16 Currently, thirteen different legislatures and thirteen different supreme courts can interpret or misinterpret every treaty signed by the United States. Therefore, the reputation and peace of the whole country are at the mercy of the prejudices, passions, and interests of each State. Can foreign nations either respect or trust such a government? How long will Americans entrust their honor, happiness, and safety to this unstable foundation?

Amendments Won't Cure Flaws

17 I have mentioned the Confederation's most significant defects, passing over the imperfections that make its power largely impotent. All unbiased men must realize that the system is radically vicious and unsound. It cannot be cured by amendments. It requires an entire change in its important features and character.

One Congress: Inadequate/Dangerous

18 Currently, Congress does not have the powers that the federal government needs. The federal government has limited authority. Therefore, a single congress may be proper. But even rational adversaries of the proposed Constitution say that the federal government needs more

power. And a single assembly cannot be trusted with the additional powers.

If the new Constitution is not adopted, the country will either fall apart or Congress will be given tyrannical powers. A weak federal government and the schemes of ambitious men who expect to increase their personal power will push the Union towards dissolution. If the country doesn't fall apart, a single "congress" will accumulate all the sovereign powers, creating the tyranny that adversaries of the new Constitution say they don't want.

People Didn't Ratify Articles

19 The PEOPLE never ratified the Articles of Confederation. Instead, the State legislatures approved it. Now some people are questioning whether it is valid, which has led to the outrageous doctrine of legislative repeal—since it was ratified by the State, the State can repeal it. This is the same as saying that a *party* to a *contract* has a right to revoke that *contract*. As silly as it sounds, some respectable people support the doctrine.

The foundation of our national government must be laid deeper than just the approval of the people's representatives. The American empire should rest on THE CONSENT OF THE PEOPLE. The streams of national power should flow from that pure, original fountain of all legitimate authority.

PUBLIUS

Defense: Foreign

Number 23: Federal Responsibilities, Powers, Organization

An energetic Constitution is necessary to preserve the Union.
Our inquiry covers four topics:
- The reasons for having a federal government.
- The amount of power the federal government needs to fulfill its purposes.
- The people who should control that power.
- The organization of the federal government.

The most important reasons for a union and federal government are:
- Defense.
- To keep the peace against both internal turmoil and external attacks.
- To regulate commerce with other nations and between the States.
- To supervise our political and commercial interests with foreign countries.

Powers Essential for Defense

4   To defend the country, the federal government needs the power to raise armies, build and equip fleets, direct army and navy operations and provide support for both. These powers should not be limited *because it is impossible to predict future national emergencies or the size and type of force that may be necessary to solve them.*

An infinite number of things can endanger the nation's safety. Therefore, constitutional limits on the power to protect the nation are unwise. Defensive power should equal the strength of all possible emergencies.

5   This truth carries its own evidence. It rests on universal axioms. The *means* should be proportionate to the *end*; the persons charged with attaining the *end* should possess the *means* for attaining it.

6   Should a federal government be entrusted with the common defense? If the answer is yes, the government needs the power to execute that trust. Authority to provide for defense cannot be limited. Any matter essential to the *formation, direction,* or *support* of the NATIONAL FORCES should not be limited.

Defense: States Requisitioned

7   The people who wrote the Articles of Confederation apparently understood this principle. But they didn't provide a way to do it. Congress can requisition (demand that each State send a specific amount) men and money and control the army and navy. Congressional requisitions are constitutionally binding on the States; the States have a legal duty to furnish the required supplies. The Articles of Confederation authorized the federal government to command all resources that are necessary for the "common

defense and general welfare." The authors of the Articles assumed that the States would be aware of their best interests and duty to the Union and they would fill the federal requisitions.

Direct Authority Over Citizens

8   However, this was a mistaken assumption. If we really want to give the Union energy and a long life, we must stop making laws that States are supposed to obey. Federal laws must extend to individual citizens. Quotas and requisitions are impractical and unjust. They must be discarded.

The Union should have the power and money to draft troops, support an army, and build and equip a navy in the same way as other governments.

Powers to Fulfill Responsibilities

9   We need a compound or confederate government instead of a simple, single government. The RESPONSIBILITIES of each branch of power must be determined. And each branch must have enough authority to fulfill its responsibilities.

Should the Union guard the common safety? Are fleets, armies and money necessary? The Union must have the power to pass all laws and regulations that relate to them. The same is true for commerce and every other area under its jurisdiction.

Is the administration of justice between citizens of the same State a responsibility of local government? The local governments must have the authority to fulfill their responsibilities.

It is unwise to not give each part of government the amount of power that it needs to fulfill its duties. And it would put the future national needs in disabled hands.

10   The federal government is charged with public safety and defense. It will have the most information needed to understand the extent and urgency of threats. Representing the WHOLE, it will want to protect every part. With authority throughout the States, it can establish uniform plans to secure the common safety.

Isn't it illogical to make the federal government responsible for national defense, but leave the *effective* power of providing for defense with the State governments?

The States won't always cooperate. There will be weakness and disorder. Some States will face more of the horrors of war and the intolerable increase of expense that accompanies it. We saw these effects during the revolution.

Proposed Powers = Federal Goals

11 We should not entrust our NATIONAL INTERESTS to a government that doesn't have all the powers a free people *should give to any government*.

The government that is supposed to take care of these interests must have the power to do it.

Adversaries of the Constitution would seem more sincere if they limited their arguments to showing that the people can't trust the internal structure of the proposed government. They shouldn't have wandered into pointless discussions about how much power the national government will have.

The POWERS are not too extensive for the OBJECTIVES of a federal government; or, in other words, for the management of our NATIONAL INTERESTS. And there are no good arguments that show it has excess powers. If the federal government has too much power, then the difficulty stems from the nature of government. If it is unsafe to give the country all of the powers it needs, then we should downsize our ideas and simply form smaller, separate confederacies.

It is absurd to entrust national interests to a government that doesn't have the authority to properly manage them.

12   I don't believe that anyone can prove that one general system is impractical. This is a large country; only an energetic government can preserve the Union. The people who oppose the proposed Constitution predict that a national system spread across the entire area of the present Confederacy is impractical.

PUBLIUS

Number 24: Standing Armies During Times of Peace

There has been only one specific objection to the federal government creating and directing the national military: the Constitution does not ban standing armies during times of peace.

2   No logical argument supports this objection. And this is not how most Americans feel. Nor is it the practice of other free nations. Some people want to limit the LEGISLATURE'S authority to establish national military bases.

Armies Not Mandatory

3   Current newspaper articles give the impression that either the Constitution says that standing armies should be kept up in time of peace or it gives the PRESIDENT the whole power of raising troops without any legislative control.

Only Legislature Can Raise Army

4   However, neither provision is in the Constitution. The *legislature*, not the *president*, has the power to raise armies. And the legislature's power is limited. Money to support an army can only be appropriated for

two years. This precaution becomes security against keeping troops when they are unnecessary.

States Allow Peacetime Armies

5, 6   Do all the State constitutions prohibit standing armies in peacetime? Only *two* State constitutions prohibit them. The other eleven either say nothing on the subject or allow the legislature to authorize their existence.[*]

No Ban of Peacetime Armies

7   Are the opponents of the Constitution deliberately lying? Is there a logical reason for the outcry? Do the Articles of Confederation explicitly prohibit a peacetime military?

8   After a careful study of the Articles of Confederation, his astonishment would increase. It doesn't prohibit a peacetime military. The Articles restrict the authority of States on this subject but there is no restraint on the United States.

A rational man would start believing that a sinister opposition is lying. Why else would they harshly criticize a part of the Constitution that reflects the feelings of America as seen in the Articles of Confederation and State constitutions? The proposed Constitution even has a new, powerful guard that is not in any of the State constitutions.

He would sigh at the weakness of human nature. The opposition seems to want to mislead the people by alarming their passions rather than convince them with arguments addressed to their reason.

Ban Wouldn't Be Observed

9   Putting a clause in the Constitution that prohibits the legislature from establishing a peacetime military would be improper. And even if society demands it, it probably would not be observed.

Europe, Indians Potential Dangers

10   Although an ocean separates the United States from Europe, we should not be over-confident of our security. British and Spanish settlements surround us. These two powers own the West India Islands, which creates a common interest. The savage tribes on our Western frontier are

---

[*] This is taken from the printed collection of State constitutions. Pennsylvania and North Carolina constitutions say: "As standing armies in time of peace are dangerous to liberty, THEY OUGHT NOT to be kept up." This is a CAUTION not a PROHIBITION. New Hampshire, Massachusetts, Delaware, and Maryland each have a clause in their bills of rights, to this effect: "Standing armies are dangerous to liberty, and ought not to be raised or kept up WITHOUT THE CONSENT OF THE LEGISLATURE," which admits that the legislature has the authority. New York has no bill of rights and her constitution says nothing about the matter. The other States have no bill of rights and their constitutions are silent. I am told, however, that one or two States have bills of rights that are not in this collection and they recognize the legislative authority in this respect. –PUBLIUS

our enemies, and England and Spain's allies because they have the most to fear from us and the most to hope from them.

Improved navigation has improved communication. Many distant nations seem like neighbors. Britain and Spain are maritime powers in Europe. A future agreement between them seems probable. The family compacts between France and Spain are becoming weaker every day. We must not be over confident, thinking we are entirely out of the reach of danger.

Protection Needed on Borders

11   Since before the Revolution, small military forts on our Western frontier have been necessary. They are indispensable, if only for protection against the plundering of the Indians. Occasionally, the forts must get more military personnel either militia or federal army soldiers.

Using militia members is impractical and dangerous. Citizens would eventually refuse to leave their jobs and families to perform the most disagreeable duty in times of peace. Even if they could be forced, frequently calling up the militia would be expensive. And losing the commercial and farm labor force would injure both the public and private citizens.

A permanent army paid by the government amounts to a standing army in peacetime–a small one, indeed, but no less real for being small. A constitutional prohibition to a standing army is improper. The legislature should decide when an army is needed.

Border Needs Will Increase

12   As our strength increases, Britain and Spain will increase their military strength around us. If we don't want to be defenseless, we will need to increase our frontier garrisons as our Western settlements increase. Some military posts will serve large districts of territory. Some posts will also be important to trade with the Indian nations. Leaving them vulnerable to seizure by such powerful neighbors would be imprudent.

Navy will Replace Some Garrisons

13   We must form a navy. It is necessary for our commerce and safety along our Atlantic coast. We will need forts and soldiers to defend our dockyards and arsenals. A powerful navy can protect its dockyards without additional soldiers. Until our navy is fully established, moderate garrisons will be an indispensable security against destructive attacks on arsenals and dockyards, and sometimes the fleet itself.

PUBLIUS

Number 25: Defense: Federal, Not State, Responsibility

Some people say the States should provide armies, under the direction of the federal government. However, the primary purpose of our combining to form a confederacy under a federal government is defense. If States held the military power, it would oppress some States, be dangerous to all, and harmful to the Confederacy.

Danger of Making Defense State Duty

2   The territories of Britain, Spain, and the Indian nations do not border specific States. They encircle the Union. To differing degrees, all of the States are in danger. Therefore, the national government and treasury should be responsible for defense.

Some States are exposed to more danger, including New York. If the States had to provide for their own defense, New York would carry the whole burden of her immediate safety and, ultimately, the protection of her neighbors. This would not be fair to New York or safe for other States.

The States who need military posts won't be willing or able to support a military for a long time. Therefore, national security would depend on the stinginess, lack of foresight, or inability of one State.

On the other hand, if a State had the men and money, it would increase its military spending proportionately. If two or three powerful States held the whole military force of the Union, the other States would be alarmed. They would take counter measures. Military establishments, nourished by mutual jealousy, would swell. The State armies would destroy the national authority.

State Military a Danger to Liberty

3   State and federal governments are rivals because all governments love power. In a dispute between the federal government and a State, people will probably support their local government. If the State had military forces, it would be tempted to challenge and subvert the constitutional authority of the Union.

The people's liberty would be less safe. An army is a dangerous weapon of power; it is better if the targets of envy control it. History proves that people are in the most danger when a group or individual they least suspect have the ability to injure their rights.

State Military Would Be Dangerous

4   Separate State military forces are dangerous to the Union. Under the Articles of Confederation, Congress must approve State ships or troops. Both federal and State governments cannot have armies.

Can't Enforce Peace Military Ban

5   Improper restraints on the national legislature create problems. Some people object to standing armies during peacetime. But how far should the prohibition extend? Will it ban raising armies, as well as, to *keeping them up* in time of tranquility?

A prohibition that only limits keeping armies isn't specific and will not fulfill the purpose intended. Once armies are raised, what does the constitution mean by "keeping them up?" How much time would be a violation? A week, a month, a year? Or may they continue as long as there is a danger?

This means they can be kept up *in time of peace*, if there are threats or impending danger. This is different than the literal meaning of the prohibition. Who will judge that the danger continues? The national government can first raise troops, then keep them as long as the peace or safety of the community is in jeopardy. The provision could be easily ignored.

Excuses to Fortify Military

6   Some people want a constitutional ban of peacetime armies. They believe it would stop executive and legislature conspiracies to use the military to take over the government. However, even if the constitution banned peacetime armies, the conspirators could claim there is an approaching danger! Indian hostilities would always be an excuse. Or they could provoke a foreign power into looking like a threat, and then appease it with concessions. If such a conspiracy happened, the army could be raised—using any pretext—and used in the usurpation scheme.

Peacetime Army Ban, Union Defenseless

7   If the constitution prohibits the *raising* of armies in time of peace, the United States would be in the strangest situation ever seen—a nation that cannot prepare for its defense before it was actually invaded. The government couldn't begin drafting men until an enemy was physically within our borders. The nation couldn't prepare for a danger. Our property and liberty would be exposed to foreign invaders. They could capture us because we were afraid that rulers—elected by us and ruling according to our will—might endanger our liberty by abusing the power necessary to defend us.

Militia Insufficient National Defense

8   Depending on the country's militia—armed citizens—to defend the nation nearly lost us our independence. And it cost our country millions that could have been saved. The militia can't be our only defense. We must have a regular, disciplined army to defend against other disciplined armies.

The militia's valor during the recent war erected eternal monuments to their fame. But the bravest of them know that they could not have established the liberty of their country alone. Like most things, war is a science that is perfected by diligence, perseverance, time, and practice.

Penn, Mass Peacetime Military

9   All distorted policies defeat themselves because they don't follow the way people behave. Pennsylvania is a current example. Its Bill of Rights says that standing armies are dangerous to liberty and should not be kept up in peacetime. Nevertheless, during this time of peace, Pennsylvania has used disorders in one or two counties as an excuse to raise troops. And the troops will probably remain as long as there is any appearance of danger to the public peace.

Massachusetts is another example. Under the Articles, States are supposed to get Congressional approval before raising troops. Massachusetts didn't wait for that approval. It raised troops to put down a domestic rebellion. And it keeps a corps to prevent a revival of the revolt. This is instructive. Every government has similar problems and might need the military for internal security. Therefore, legislative discretion to raise and keep armies should not be controlled.

The Massachusetts example teaches us that States do not respect the rights of a weak government. And it teaches us that when there is a choice between written provisions and public necessity, public necessity wins.

Ignoring Laws Weakens Government

10   It was a basic maxim of the ancient Lacedaemonian commonwealth that no one could serve as their navy's commander-in-chief twice. Lysander had served, and then stepped down. However, after an ally was defeated at sea by the Athenians, Athens demanded that Lysander command the combined fleets. The Lacedaemonians wanted to fulfill their ally's wish and also obey their own law. They gave Lysander the power of the naval commander-in-chief but called him a sub-commander-in-chief.

I could give many examples confirming this truth. Nations ignore rules and maxims that, in their very nature, run counter to the necessities of society.

Wise politicians don't want to create constitutional restrictions that might need to be ignored. Every time a constitution is disobeyed, even if necessary, decreases the reverence that rulers should maintain towards it. And it creates a precedent for other breaches when a necessity does not exist or is less urgent.

PUBLIUS

Number 26: Legislative Military Authority

During a popular revolution men can't be expected to stop at the proper boundary between POWER and PRIVILEGE. That is, the balance between a strong government and secure private rights. We failed, which created our present problems. As we correct and improve our system, we must not repeat this error. Otherwise, we may go from one unrealistically utopian plan to another. We may try change after change. But we will probably never make any material change for the better.

Balancing Liberty, Public Safety

2   The legislature will authorize national defense. Some people want to limit this authority. This idea comes from false beliefs about liberty rather than knowledge.

Pennsylvania and North Carolina have tried to limit the legislature's power to authorize armed forces. The other States refuse to consider it. The people delegate power to the government. Therefore, the people must place their confidence in that government. It is better to take the chance that their confidence will be abused than endanger the public safety with impractical limits on the legislature's authority. Unlike the opponents of the proposed Constitution, the majority of Americans agree that the legislature must have full authority to authorize military forces.

We can safely correct the imbalances in our governmental system. But opponents of the Constitution want more dangerous imbalances. If the principles they support became accepted, the people of this country would be utterly unfit for any type of government whatever. But Americans are too intelligent to be persuaded into anarchy. The public firmly believes that greater government energy is essential to the welfare and prosperity of the community.

Origin of No Peacetime Military

3   Where did the idea of excluding military establishments during peacetime start? Probably England, the country of origin of most Americans.

4   For a long time after the Norman Conquest [1066], the English monarch's authority was almost unlimited. Gradually, liberty made inroads into the monarch's power, first by barons and later by the people, until the monarch lost most of his power and importance.

King Charles II [1661-1685] kept a body of 5,000 troops during peacetime. King James II [1685-1688] increased the number to 30,000. Finally, after the revolution in 1688, Prince William of Orange became king of Great Britain and English liberty triumphanted. The Bill of Rights limited his authority. It said "the raising or keeping a standing army within the Kingdom in time of peace, *unless with the consent of Parliament*, was against the law."

Power Must Equal Possible Emergencies

5   Liberty was at its highest peak in Britain. But the only security against the danger of standing armies was the prohibition against the monarch raising and keeping them.

The revolutionary patriots were well informed. They didn't want to restrain the legislature's discretion. They knew that a certain number of troops are indispensable. National emergencies can't be limited. A power equal to every possible scenario must exist somewhere in the government. By giving the legislature this power, they found the balancing point between precaution and the safety of the community.

States: Legislatures Raise Military

6   From this history, the people of America learned that standing armies in peacetime could endanger liberty. The revolution made us zealous protectors of our liberty. In some cases, our desire to protect our civil rights went further than is practical. Two States tried to restrict legislative authority over military establishments. A monarch's power must be feared. However, the over-reaction by these States extended this fear to the people's representatives. Some States didn't make this error but they have unnecessarily declared that standing armies are not to be kept up in peacetime WITHOUT THE CONSENT OF THE LEGISLATURE. There is a similar provision in the English Bill of Rights. But the States don't have the same reason for the provision. Under the State constitutions, only the legislatures have the power to raise armies. So, it was superfluous to declare that it should not be done without the consent of a body, which alone had the power of doing it. The other State constitutions are silent on the subject.

No State Prohibits Military in Peacetime

7   Two State constitutions seem to prohibit the military. However, they say an army *ought not* be kept up, not that armies *shall not be* kept up in time of peace. This ambiguity seems to result from the conflict between totally excluding them and the belief that an absolute exclusion would be unsafe.

8   When a situation arises, the legislature will interpret the clause as only an admonition and yield to the real or imagined needs of the State. Pennsylvania is an example. The provision is useless if the legislature can just ignore it whenever they want to.

Ban v. 2-Year Appropriations

9   Some people want to ban all military during times of peace. The proposed Constitution limits military appropriations to a two-year period. A peacetime military ban tries to do too much and will not be obeyed; a two-year appropriation provides for emergencies and will be a powerful remedy.

Politicians, States Guard Against Abuse

10   At least once in every two years the United States legislature will be *forced* to decide whether to keep a military force and declare their position by a formal, public vote. They cannot give the president unlimited funds for an army.

A partisan spirit infects all political bodies. Funding a military force will always be a favorite topic to denounce. As often as the question arises, the opposition party will publicly argue about it. If the majority party wants to appropriate more money than seems proper to support the military for two years, the community will be warned and be able to take measures to guard against it.

People will debate the issue. State legislatures will jealously guard the citizens' rights against encroachments from the federal government. If national rulers act improperly, they will sound the alarm. State legislatures will be the VOICE and, if necessary, the ARM of the people's discontent.

Subvert Liberty: Executive, Legislative Collusion

11   Schemes to subvert liberty *require time* to develop before taking action. A large army would be needed to threaten our liberties. The legislature and executive would have to conspire for a long time.

Would this happen? Would every man elected to the national Senate or House of Representatives instantly become a traitor to his constituents and his country? Would not one man be able to see the atrocious conspiracy, or bold or honest enough to tell his constituents of their danger?

If we assume that this could happen, there should be no more delegated authority. The people should take back the powers already given the government and divide themselves into as many States as there are counties so they can manage their government in person.

Military Expansion in Peace

12   Concealing such a conspiracy for long would be impractical. People would see a fast growing army during peacetime. Following the discovery, the people would quickly destroy the project and its sponsors.

Reason Needed to Build Military Force

13   Some people say limiting military appropriations to the period of two years won't be safe. They say that once the president has a large enough military to force the people into submission, it would also be large enough to get supplies without help from the legislature.

But what pretense could the President use to build a big military force in peacetime? If it was created in response to a domestic insurrection or foreign war, it can't be called a peacetime military buildup. Military forces should be raised to stop a rebellion or resist an invasion. If defense of the community makes it necessary to have an army large enough to threaten its liberty, this is one of those calamities that can't be prevented or cured. No form of government can provide against this. It might even happen in a simple league, if the allies need to form an army for common defense.

Military Expands If States Separate

14   However, this evil is infinitely less likely to happen to us if we are united than if we are disunited. It is hard to imagine dangers formidable enough to attack the whole nation, demanding a force large enough to place our liberties in jeopardy, especially when we remember that the militia should always be counted on as a valuable and powerful addition to the military. But in a state of disunion, the contrary of this supposition would be almost unavoidable.

PUBLIUS

Defense: Domestic

Number 27: Federal Authority Over Individual Citizens
Military Not Needed to Enforce Federal Laws

Some people argue that a military force will be needed to enforce the proposed Constitution. However, like most of the opposition's arguments, no logical reason supports it. It assumes that people dislike the use of federal authority in any internal matter. Let's look at this assumption.

Unless we presume that the federal government will be administered worse than State governments, there is no reason to assume that the people will oppose it. As a rule, the people accept and obey a government in proportion to the goodness or badness of its administration. The exceptions to this rule depend entirely on accidental causes, not the intrinsic merits or demerits of a constitution. Constitutions can only be judged by general principles and maxims.

Quality of Federal Administration

2   Under the proposed Constitution, the national government will probably be better administered than the State governments. The larger area will give voters more choices.

Usually the elected State legislators will carefully select national Senators. This method promises great knowledge and information in the national Senate. It is less likely that faction will taint the national Senate. And they will have fewer prejudices. In smaller societies, prejudices frequently contaminate public agencies and assemblies. They produce injustice and oppression. And prejudices often fuel plots that might fulfill a momentary desire, but end up causing general distress, dissatisfaction, and disgust.

A serious, objective study of the proposed government will strengthen this position. Federal laws will be accepted and enforced like State laws.

State Factions More Successful

3   While the dread of punishment discourages sedition, the hope of immunity encourages it. If it has enough power, sedition factions will fear *punishment* by the national government. And the national government will do a better job repressing *tendencies toward sedition* than a single State. A turbulent faction in a State may think it can make deals with friends in the State government. But it won't be foolish enough to think it can stand up against the entire Union. If this conclusion is reasonable, dangerous conspiracies are less possible in the federal government than in a single State.

Federal Government Will Seem Normal

4   As the federal government becomes more involved in ordinary governmental operations, the local community's attachment and respect for it will grow. As it becomes a familiar part of their daily lives, citizens will grow accustomed to it.

Man is a creature of habit. If he only rarely notices something, it has only a little influence on his mind. The people have little interest in a remote government. But as the federal government effects internal matters, the citizens' affections will be strengthened, not weakened.   At the same time, as the citizens become familiar with the federal government's functions, the union will have fewer reasons to use force. The more it touches the citizens' everyday lives, the less it will need the aid of violent and dangerous punishments.

Legislation for States: Dangerous

5   In any event, one thing must be evident. The proposed government will have fewer reasons to use force than the type of government promoted by its opponents. Legislation for States operates on the States in their collective capacities; it encourages delinquencies by the States, which can only be collected, if at all, by war and violence.

Constitution: Courts Enforce Laws

6   The new Constitution extends federal authority to the citizens of the States. It allows the government to use State courts to execute its laws. The federal government will use the same methods to secure obedience as the State governments. In addition, States can call on the whole Union for assistance and support, which will influence public opinion.

The Constitution lists the Union's jurisdiction. A *legitimate* Union law will become the SUPREME LAW of the land. All State officers—legislative, executive, and judicial—will be bound by an oath. Thus the State legislatures, courts, and executives will be part of the national government *as far as its just and constitutional authority extends* and will help enforce its laws. If the Union is administered prudently, the Union laws will be peacefully obeyed.

If we arbitrarily suppose the contrary, we can deduce anything we want. Any authority that is used unwisely can provoke people into the wildest excesses. But even if the adversaries of the proposed Constitution presume that the national rulers will ignore the motives of public good or the obligations of duty, I still ask: How would it aid ambition or encroachment?

PUBLIUS

Number 28: National/State Resources Counter Threats

Sometimes the national government may need to use force. Emergencies happen. Sadly, revolts and rebellions are as much a part of the political body as diseases are part of the natural body.

Some political pundits say that republican governments can only use the force of law to govern. This daydream ignores the warnings of experience.

Local Danger→ Local Force

2   Some emergencies require that the national government use force. The force must be proportionate to the size of the problem.

A small revolt in part of a State can be suppressed by the militia from other parts of the State. And the militia would be ready to serve. A revolt eventually endangers all government. To keep the peace, citizens would oppose the insurgents. And if the national government promotes the prosperity and happiness of the people, the people will support it.

More than Militia Might Be Needed

3   If the revolt spreads throughout a whole State or a majority of it, a larger force might be needed. Massachusetts needed to raise troops to repress disorders. Pennsylvania did the same thing.

Suppose New York decided to reestablish control over Vermont. Could she have been successful using the militia alone? She would have needed a regular army.

The States need a force other than the militia during severe problems. The national government may need to use an army during some emergencies. Some men who say they like the Union use this issue to object to the Constitution. But under the plan they support, armies will be needed even more frequently. Who would not prefer the use of force to the rebellions and revolutions that harm petty republics?

Confederacies May Need Force

4   Let's look at this in a different way. Suppose that two, three, or even four American confederacies were formed. Each confederacy would have the same problems. And each one would use the same methods to uphold their authority.

Continuing this assumption, would the militia support the confederate authority? Whether we have one government for all the States or several governments, sometimes a force other than the militia may be necessary to keep the peace and maintain the lawful authority against revolts and rebellions.

People Control Government, Military

5 Remember, the whole power of the proposed government will be in the hands of the representatives of the people. In civil society, this is the only effective security for the rights and privileges of the people.

Hard to Block Usurpation in 1 State

6 If the elected representatives betray their constituents, self-defense is the only option. Self-defense against national usurpations will be more successful than against rulers of a State.

If the rulers of a single State usurp power, county governments don't have the resources to defend the people. The citizens won't have a plan or resources except their courage and despair. Because the State usurpers are cloaked in legal authority, they can often crush the opposition while it is tiny. Organizing the opposition in a small State will be more difficult and more easily defeated. The State usurpers will see their preparation and rapidly deploy the military against the opposition. In this situation, only luck will make the popular resistance successful.

Obstacles to Usurpation

7 If the citizens understand their rights and want to defend them, the ability to stop usurpation increases with the increased size of the state. The people in a large community have a natural strength. And that strength is greater than the artificial strength of the government and more able to stop an attempt to establish a tyranny.

In a confederacy, the people are the masters of their own fate. Since power is usually the rival of power, the national government will always stand ready to check State usurpations. And the States will be in the same position towards the national government.

Whichever side [State or national government] the people support will be the stronger. If their rights are invaded by either, they can use the other as the instrument of redress. The people will cherish the Union, preserving to themselves an advantage that can never be too highly prized!

States Protect Citizen's Liberty

8 It is an axiom in our political system that the State governments will, in all situations, provide complete security against invasions of liberty by the national authority.

Usurpation cannot be hidden by pretenses; the people and their representatives will see them. The legislatures can discover the danger in its infancy. They have civil power and the confidence of the people. They can immediately oppose them, using all the resources of the community. The States can unite their forces to protect their liberty.

Large Size Blocks Nat'l Usurpation

9 The large size of the country is further security. We have seen how it protects against attacks from a foreign power. It would also be protection against usurpation by the ambitious national rulers.

When citizens rebelled against the usurpation and the federal army stopped them in one State, distant States would raise fresh forces. The usurpers would abandon their advantage in the first State to subdue the opposition in others. The moment they left the first State, the resistance would revive.

State Forces Better Than National

10 Military force can be only as strong as the resources of the country permit. For a long time to come, maintaining a large army will be impossible. As we are able to strengthen our military, the population and community strength will also increase. Therefore, when will the federal government be able to raise and maintain an army capable of erecting a tyranny over all the people of an immense empire? The people can, by using their State governments, defend themselves with the swiftness and organization of independent nations.

This worry is like a disease that can't be cured with logic and reasoning. PUBLIUS

Number 29: Militia Not Threat to Liberty

During an internal revolt or an invasion by a foreign nation, the militia helps keep peace and defends the Confederacy.

National Control Leads to Uniformity

2 All members of the militia must have the same organization and discipline to get the best results. And uniformity requires national regulation of the militia. Therefore, the Constitution properly says that the Union will "provide for organizing, arming, and disciplining the militia, and for governing such part of them as may be employed in the service of the United States, *reserving to the States respectively the appointment of the officers, and the authority of training the militia according to the discipline prescribed by Congress.*"

Militia Can Replace Standing Army

3 Some opponents of the Constitution attack this provision. This wasn't expected. A disciplined militia is the natural defense of a free country. The federal government is responsible for guarding national security. Therefore, it should regulate the militia.

Standing armies can endanger liberty. The national government won't have any reason to keep a standing army if it controls the militia. If the federal government can command the militia during emergencies, it won't use the army. However, if it can't use the militia, it will have to use the army. If we don't want a permanent army, making it unnecessary works better than a thousand prohibitions on paper.

No Ban of Posse Comitatus

4 Opponents say the Constitution has no provision for calling out the POSSE COMITATUS to help the chief executive enforce the law, suggesting that military force will be the only alternative.

This shows how illogical the objections to the Constitution have been. Opponents first say the federal government's power will be despotic and unlimited and then say it doesn't even have the authority to call out the POSSE COMITATUS. Fortunately, neither statement is true.

The government can pass all laws *necessary and proper* to execute its powers. Therefore, it can require citizens to assist those officers who must enforce those laws. And even if the government is allowed to use the military when necessary, it is not the only way to enforce laws.

Illogical Fear of Militia

5 We are told to fear the militia, if the federal government regulates it. It is said that a young, eager corps may be formed and used by a tyrant. We don't know how the national government will regulate the militia. But I don't see it as dangerous. If the Constitution is ratified, my feelings about a militia would be as follows:

Citizen-Soldiers: Productivity Lost

6 It would be impossible to train the entire militia of the United States. Becoming an expert in military movements requires time and practice. A day or a week isn't enough. Making citizens go through military exercises often enough to become a well-disciplined militia would be a hardship on the people and a serious public loss. Annually, the country would lose nearly as much productive labor as the whole expense of all the State governments.

Spending the time and money to train the entire militia would injure labor and industry. And if tried, it couldn't succeed. Citizens would refuse to do it. Instead, we can only attempt to arm and equip the general population. And to do this, they will need to assemble once or twice every year.

Militia v. Standing Army

7 Disciplining the whole nation is impractical. However, we should adopt a well-formed plan to create a militia as soon as possible. The gov-

ernment should form a small army that is fit for service in case of need. With a clear plan, a trained militia will be ready whenever the defense of the States requires it. We will need fewer military forts and bases. And if circumstances ever force the government to form a large army, it will never be a big threat to the liberties of the people. There will be a large body of citizens who are members of the militia. They will be disciplined and trained in the use of arms. They will be ready to defend their own rights and those of their fellow citizens. This is the only substitute for a standing army. And it is the best security against a standing army, if it exists.

8   However, I don't know how the national legislature may reason on this subject.

How Can Militia Endanger Liberty?

9   The idea that the militia will endanger liberty is far-fetched. Where are our fears to end if we can't trust our sons, brothers, neighbors, and fellow citizens? We all share the same feelings, sentiments, habits, and interests.

The States have the *sole and exclusive power to appoint officers*. Since they appoint the militia's officers, the States will have the greatest influence over the militia. This should remove our fears about a militia under the federal government.

Constitution Distorted into Monster

10   If a man who knows nothing about the proposed Constitution read the articles written against it, he might think he is reading a horror story. He might think that it will transform the government into a monster.

Outrageous Uses of Militia

11   Exaggerations about the militia are examples: The articles make it sound like the New Hampshire militia will be marched to Georgia, the Georgia militia to New Hampshire, the New York militia to Kentucky, and the Kentucky militia to Lake Champlain. And that we plan to pay our debts to France and Holland with militiamen instead of money.

First they say a large army will ruin the liberties of the people. Then they say Virginia's militia will be dragged 500 or 600 miles to tame rebels in Massachusetts, and Massachusetts's militia will travel an equal distance to subdue aristocratic Virginians. Do the people who make these wild claims think that their eloquence can convince the people of America that any absurd statement is true?

Tyrannical Use of Militia Illogical

12   If a tyrant were going to use the army to take over the country, why would he need a militia? If there was no army, he would try to use the militia, sending them great distances to enslave follow countrymen. But

the militia would become irritated, march to the seat of the tyrant, and crush him.

Rulers do not usually start their career with evil acts of power that do not fulfill any goal and that draw universal hatred on themselves. Arguments that the army or militia will be used despotically are made by people who like to stir up trouble. Even if the national rulers were very ambitious, it is impossible to believe they would use such a preposterous way to accomplish their designs.

Insurrections, Invasions

13 During an internal revolt or an invasion by a foreign nation, the militia can be marched into a neighboring State to defend against an invader or guard the republic against the violence of faction or sedition. This happened during the recent war. And this mutual security is an important goal of our political association. If direction of the militia was left to the States, one State could easily ignore an invasion or revolt in a neighboring State. The nation will be more secure if the Union directs the militia.

PUBLIUS

Taxation

Number 30: Taxation: Revenue for National Government

The federal government should have the ability to support the national army. This includes the expenses of recruiting troops, building and equipping fleets, and all other military expenses. And the Union must raise revenue for other reasons. It must pay the national government's employees, current and future debts, and other appropriate expenses. Therefore, the government must have the power of taxation.

Inability to Tax Leads to Pillaging/Decay

2 Government needs money to fulfill its duties. Therefore, the power to raise money, as far as community resources will permit, is an essential part of every constitution.

Two evils result if a government doesn't have enough money. Either the people will be plundered, as a substitute for legitimate taxation, or the government will sink into a fatal atrophy and perish.

3 The emperor of Turkey [Ottoman Empire] has no right to impose a new tax. Consequently, the local governors [bashaws] pillage the people without mercy, squeezing from them the money the emperor needs to satisfy his needs and those of the state.

The American Union has gradually decayed for the same reason. In both countries, if they could legally tax, it would promote the people's happiness.

State Requisitions Create Bad Situation

4 Under the Articles of Confederation, the United States was supposed to have unlimited power to provide for the financial needs of the Union. But the system of requisitions hasn't worked. Congress asks the States for money [requisitions the States] to administer the United States. The States have no right to question whether the demand is appropriate. The States' only discretion is how to furnish the money demanded.

Different Papers have explained the consequences of the requisition system. Because of this system, we have embarrassed ourselves and helped our enemies feel triumphant.

Remedy: Directly Raise Revenues

5 The illogical system of quotas and requisitions must be changed. The national government must be able to raise revenues by taxation, as authorized in every well-ordered constitution. It will rescue us from the inconveniences and embarrassments resulting from limited money in the public treasury.

Opponents: Tax Only Imports

6   Opponents of the new Constitution agree. But they say the State governments should have exclusive power to collect *internal* taxes. They want the federal government to use *external* taxation—duties on imported articles.

Power Proportionate to Objective

Prohibiting the federal government from using internal taxation violates the maxim of good sense and sound policy. Every POWER ought to be in proportion to its OBJECTIVE. Commercial imports will never provide enough revenue for the Union's present and future needs. It is important to public justice and public credit that we pay the current foreign and domestic debt. And everyone agrees that some federal agencies are necessary. Import duties alone would never even meet the federal government's current needs. We cannot know its future needs. Therefore, they can't be limited. It must have the unlimited power to provide for them.

I believe history proves that, the necessities of a nation, in every stage of its existence, will be found at least equal to its resources.

Banning Internal Tax Leads to Weak Union

7   Some people say that State requisitions will make up the money the federal government will need. This shows why federal revenue can't be raised through import taxes alone. It acknowledges that deficiencies will occur. And whenever requisitions are used, it will make the Union weak, create conflict between the federal government and the States, and between the States.

In the future, will the States fulfill their requisitions any better than they do now? If less is required from the States, they will be proportionately less able to answer the demand. At some point, the States would say: this is the limit of where public happiness will be promoted by supplying the government money and everything beyond this point is unworthy of our care or anxiety.

How can a government, half supplied and always in need, provide for the security, advance the prosperity, or support the reputation of the nation? How can it possess energy or stability, dignity or credit, confidence at home or respect from other nations? How will it avoid sacrificing commitments to immediate necessity? How can it undertake large plans for pubic good?

War Funding Nearly Impossible

8   Let's look at what will happen during our next war. Let's assume, for argument's sake, that import duties will be enough to pay our debt and fund the peacetime federal government. Then a war breaks out. We can't

depend on State requisitions. The federal government would have to take appropriated funds from their proper objects to defend the States.

During a modern war, even the wealthiest nations need large loans. For a country as poor as ours, loans are necessities. But who would lend to a government that has no reliable method of raising repayment funds? The loans it could get would be the same that loan sharks commonly lend to bankrupt and fraudulent debtors—very small with an enormous interest rate.

Internal Taxes: Emergencies Met

9   Because the country has few resources, some people might fear that allocated funds will be diverted during such a crisis, even if the national government has the unrestrained power of taxation. But two considerations will quiet these fears: (1) during a crisis the full resources of the community will be used for the benefit of the Union and (2) deficiencies can be supplied by loans.

Taxes Protect Union's Credit

10   If the national government had the authority to raise money through new taxes, it could borrow as much as it might require. Both Americans and foreigners could confidently lend to it.

But to depend on a government that must, itself, depend on thirteen other governments to fulfill its contracts would require a credulity rarely seen in the monetary transactions of mankind and unreconcilable with the usual sharp-sightedness of avarice.

Taxation Issue Needs Attention

11   This discussion may seem unimportant to men who envision a poetic, utopian America. But to those who believe we will experience our share of the changes and calamities that have fallen to other nations, they are entitled to serious attention. Such men see the actual situation. They understand that ambition or revenge too easily inflicts evils upon a country.

PUBLIUS

Number 31: Federal Won't Usurp State Powers

Every subject has certain basic truths. People who don't see the truth either are incapable of understanding it or are influenced by a strong personal interest or prejudice.

Geometry maxims are of this nature: "the whole is greater than any of its parts; things equal to the same are equal to one another; two straight lines cannot enclose a space; all right angles are equal to each other."

Ethics and politics also have basic maxims: Every effect has a cause. The means ought to be proportional to the end. Every power ought to be equal to its objective. There should be no limitation of a power meant to fulfill a purpose that can't be limited.

Other truths in ethics and politics are not scientific axioms. However, they are so obvious—such common sense—they challenge a sound and unbiased mind to agree.

Theorems versus Common Sense

2   Although all geometry theorems can be proven, they don't all conform to common sense. But geometry doesn't stir up human passions. Therefore, people accept geometric theorems. They even accept the paradoxes. For example, mathematicians agree on the infinite divisibility of matter. In other words, a finite thing can be divided an infinite number of times, down to even the minutest atom. Yet this is no more comprehensible to common sense than religious mysteries that non-believers work so hard to debunk.

Objective Morals, Ethics Exist

3   But in the behavioral and social sciences of morals and politics, men are less easily convinced. To a degree, this is useful. We should be cautious. And we should investigate claims made by social science "experts." But caution can deteriorate into obstinacy, perverseness, or disingenuity.

Moral and political principles are not as objective as those of mathematics. But they are more objective than we might think. The obscurity usually exists in the passions and prejudices of the reasoner, not in the subject. Too often, men do not use their common sense. They yield to a bias and they entangle themselves in words and subtleties.

Biased Opposition to Taxation

4 If we assume the critics are sincere, how else can we explain their position against the Union needing the general power of taxation?

I will again summarize the positions before we examine the objections.

Power Must Equal Responsibility

5 Government is created to accomplish specific objectives. It should have every power required to fully accomplish its objectives and fulfill its responsibilities. The only control should be regard for the public good and the will of the people.

National Defense Can't Be Limited

6 The Union government has a duty to supervise the national defense and secure the public peace against foreign and domestic violence. Only two things can limit defense: the needs of the nation and the resources o the community.

7, 8   Revenue is essential. The government must have the power to get this revenue. State requisitions don't work. The federal government must have the unlimited power of ordinary taxation.

Opposition to Union Tax

9   But opponents of the proposed Constitution argue against this part of the plan. Therefore, it may be a good idea to analyze their arguments.
10 The opponents seem to be saying: "Just because the financial needs of the Union may not be limited, doesn't mean its power to tax ought to be unlimited. Local governments require revenue. And local governments are as important to the people's happiness as the national government. But if the *national government* has an unlimited power to tax, in time the *States* would probably not be able to raise revenues. The States would be at the mercy of the national legislature.

"Union laws will be the supreme law of the land and the Union will have the power to pass all the laws that may be necessary to execute its constitutional duties. Therefore, the national government might abolish State taxes on the pretense that they interfere with national taxes. Eventually, all tax resources may become a federal monopoly, excluding and destroying the State governments."

"Usurpation" Poor Argument

11 Sometimes this argument seems based on the assumption that the national government will usurp State powers. At other times, they seem to be saying that this will happen from the constitutional operation of the national government's powers.

Only the latter has any pretensions to fairness. If we start worrying about usurpations by the federal government, we fall into a bottomless abyss. No matter how the powers of the Union may be limited or modified, it's easy to imagine an endless number of possible dangers. And by indulging in excesses of jealousy and worry, we may bring ourselves to a state of absolute skepticism and irresolution.

All arguments based on the danger of usurpation of power should refer to the structure of government, not to the nature or extent of its powers. The State constitutions give the States complete sovereignty. Our security against State usurpation is their structure and the dependence of State administrators on the people. If the proposed federal government has the same type of security, all fears of usurpation should be discarded.

States Might Encroach On Union

12 States encroaching on the rights of the Union is as probable as the Union encroaching on the rights of the State governments. The winning side in such a conflict depends on what means the contending parties employ towards insuring success. In republics, strength is always on the side of

the people. And the State governments will usually possess the most influence over them. Therefore, such contests will probably end to the disadvantage of the Union. There is greater probability of encroachments by the States on the federal government, than by the federal government on the States.

However, these conjectures are vague and fallible. The safest course is to lay them aside. We should study the nature and extent of the powers as they are delineated in the Constitution. Everything beyond this must be left to the prudence and firmness of the people. They hold the scales and, it is hoped, they will always take care to preserve the constitutional equilibrium between the federal and the State governments. On this ground, the objections to an indefinite power of taxation in the United States can be anticipated and countered.

PUBLIUS

Number 32: Union Tax Doesn't Limit State Authority

Giving the Union the power to tax will not create the dangerous consequences feared by the State governments. Several things will block the oppressive use of taxation: the people's good sense, the danger of resentments from the States, and the need for local governments to fulfill local objectives.

The States need an independent authority to raise revenues that the federal government can't control. With the sole exception of taxes on imports and exports, under the Constitution the States keep that authority. If the national government tries to control State taxation, it would be a violent assumption of power that is not in the proposed Constitution.

Only 3 Exceptions to States' Sovereignty

2   An entire consolidation of the States into one national sovereignty would imply an entire subordination of the parts; State powers would be completely dependent on the federal government. But the Constitution is only a partial union or consolidation. The States retain all the rights of sovereignty they had before except those that are not *exclusively* delegated to the United States by the Constitution. State sovereignty is transferred to the Union in three cases:

(1) where the Constitution expressly grants exclusive authority to the Union;

(2) where it grants a specific authority to the Union and prohibits the States from exercising the same authority;

(3) and where it grants an authority to the Union, to which similar authority in the States would be absolutely and totally *contradictory* and *repugnant*.

This last case is different from concurrent jurisdiction. When there is a concurrent jurisdiction, national and State *policies* may overlap occasionally, but there won't be any direct contradiction of constitutional authority.

The three cases of exclusive federal jurisdiction may be exemplified by the following:

(1) The next-to-the-last clause of article one, section eight, says Congress will exercise *"exclusive legislation"* over the capital district. This answers the first case.

(2) The first clause of article one, section eight empowers Congress *"to lay and collect taxes, duties, imposts, and excises;"* and the second clause of article one, section ten declares that, *"no State shall,* without the consent of Congress, *lay any imposts or duties on imports or exports*, except for the purpose of executing its inspection laws."

Therefore, the Union would have exclusive power to lay duties on imports and exports, with the specific exception mentioned. But this power is limited to *duties on imports*. Another clause declares that no tax or duty shall be laid on articles exported from any State. This answers the second case.

(3) The third is the clause that declares Congress will "establish a uniform rule of naturalization throughout the United States." This must be an exclusive power because if each State had power to prescribe a distinct rule, there could not be a uniform rule.

Opposition Arguments Illogical

3   The federal government and the individual States have concurrent and coequal authority to impose taxes on all articles other than exports and imports.

The clause does not give the Union *exclusive* power. And no clause prohibits States from the power to tax. On the contrary, the State ban on taxing imports and exports implies that the States have the power to tax. And it also implies that State authority remains undiminished. In all cases not restricted, the States would have a concurrent power of taxation with the Union.

The clause that bans State import and export taxes is called a negative pregnant—that is, a *negation* of one thing and an *affirmation* of another. States **cannot** impose taxes on imports and exports and **can** impose them on all other articles. It is sophistry to argue that it excludes States *absolutely* from duties and allows them to lay other taxes *subject to the control* of the national legislature.

Union, States May Tax Same Objects

4   If a State taxes a specific article, it may be *inexpedient* for the Union to tax the same article. But another tax isn't unconstitutional. The size of the

tax is a question of prudence, but there is no direct contradiction of power. National and State tax policies may sometimes conflict. One or the other may need to change their policy. However, an inconvenience in the exercise of powers does not imply a constitutional ban of a preexisting right of sovereignty.

Tax Clause: Constitutional Interpretation

5   In some cases, joint jurisdiction is necessary. It results from dividing sovereign power. All authorities, except those the States explicitly relinquished to the Union, remain fully with the States. This is the clear meaning of the proposed Constitution. The Constitution has negative clauses prohibiting the States from exercising the authorities that are exclusively the Union's.

Article one, section ten contains such provisions. This clearly shows the convention's intentions. And it furnishes a rule for interpreting the Constitution—within the Constitution—that justifies my position and refutes every hypothesis to the contrary.   PUBLIUS

Number 33: Union's Power to Tax:

"Necessary and Proper," "Supreme Law of the Land"

The "necessary and proper" clause of the Constitution is the last clause of Article 1, Section 8. It authorizes the national legislature "to make all laws which shall be *necessary* and *proper* for carrying into execution the foregoing *powers*, and all other powers vested by this Constitution in the government of the United States, or in any department or officer thereof."

Article 6 says that "the Constitution and the laws of the United States which shall be made *in pursuance thereof* and all treaties made, or which shall be made, under the authority of the United States, shall be the *supreme law* of the land*; . . . anything in the constitution or laws of any State to the contrary notwithstanding."

Federal Power to Make Federal Law

2   These two clauses have been vehemently denounced. Using exaggeration and misrepresentation, opponents say these clauses will destroy both local governments and individual liberties. They are seen as monsters that will devour everyone.

However, they only declare a truth. The act of creating a federal government and giving it specific powers implies these clauses. The constitutional operation of the proposed government would be precisely the same if the clauses were removed or if they were repeated in every article.

Legislature's Job: Make Laws

3   The term "power" means having the ability to do something. "Legislative power" means that the legislature will have the power to make laws.

Article One, Section 8 says, "Congress shall have power to lay and collect taxes." Therefore, it is a legislative power. In other words, a power to make **necessary and proper** laws about taxes.

Federal Taxation Needs Tax Laws

4   By following this simple reasoning, we can judge the true meaning of the controversial clause. The truth is obvious: the power to lay and collect taxes includes all laws *necessary* and *proper* to execute that power. The "necessary and proper" clause in the Constitution only restates this obvious conclusion. (This clause is sometimes called the "sweeping clause.")

I'm using the taxation example because taxation is our current subject and taxation is the government's most important authority. But the same reasoning applies to every power in the Constitution. The "necessary and proper" clause authorizes the national legislature to pass those laws that are necessary and proper to execute the powers listed in the Constitution.

Any objection must be to the specific powers, not the general declaration. The declaration may be redundant, but it is harmless.

Clause Affirms Federal Authority

5   But suspicious people may ask why the "necessary and proper" clause was added to the Constitution. It could have been put in the Constitution to guard against attempts to limit and evade the legitimate authorities of the Union. The greatest threat to our political welfare is the State governments sapping the foundations of the Union. Therefore, on this important point, perhaps the convention wanted to leave nothing to interpretation.

Laws Judged Against Constitution

6   Who judges whether federal laws are necessary and proper?

First, if we removed the "necessary and proper" clause, we can still ask the question about the powers themselves. Second, the national government, the States and the citizens must judge the proper exercise of its powers.

If the federal government overreaches its authority and uses its power tyrannically, the people, who created it, must go to the Constitution. They must correct the injury done to the Constitution. To determine if a law is constitutional, we must look at whether the law is based on Constitutional powers.

Suppose the federal legislature attempts to change the law of descent in a State. Clearly, this is outside the federal government's jurisdiction and would trespass on the State's authority.

Or suppose that the federal government tries to abolish a State's property tax, saying it interferes with federal revenues. This would be an invasion of the concurrent tax jurisdiction.

National Law Supreme

7   The laws of the Union are to be the *supreme law* of the land. What does this mean? What if federal laws were not supreme? Clearly, they would amount to nothing. A law, by definition, includes supremacy. A law is a rule that those to whom it applies are bound to observe.

If individuals form a governed society, the laws of that society must be the supreme regulator of their conduct. If a number of political societies combine into a larger political society, the laws enacted by the larger society, if they are within its constitutional powers, must be supreme over the small societies and the individuals in them. Otherwise it would be a mere treaty—a treaty is dependent on the good faith of the parties—and not a government, which is only another word for political power and supremacy.

But this doctrine does not mean that acts of the larger society that are *not among* its constitutional powers, acts that invade the authority of smaller societies, will become the supreme law of the land. These will be acts of usurpation and deserve to be treated as such.

Hence, the clause that declares the supremacy of Union laws only repeats a truth. When a federal government is instituted, its laws are supreme. But it *expressly* confines this supremacy to laws made *pursuant to the Constitution.* This is an example of caution by the convention; the limitation would have been understood even if it had not been expressed.

State, Federal Taxation

8   Therefore, a United States tax law would be supreme in its nature and couldn't be legally opposed or controlled. However, a federal law abolishing or preventing collection of State taxes (unless on imports and exports) would not be the supreme law of the land. It would be a usurpation of power not granted by the Constitution.

If the State and federal governments taxed the same object and collection became difficult, this would be inconvenient for both. Neither has superior power. The federal government, the State government, or both using their power in a disadvantageous way would cause the problem. Presumably, the federal and State governments would cooperate and change their tax policies until they were more convenient.

The States will be able to raise revenue from any kind of taxation, except duties on imports and exports. The federal government will not have the authority to control States' taxes. The next paper discusses this concurrent jurisdiction in taxation.   PUBLIUS

Number 34: Union, States Concurrent Taxation Jurisdiction

Under the proposed Constitution, the States and the Union will have coequal taxing authority, except duties on imports. The majority of community resources will be available to the States. The States will have many taxation methods but will be responsible for only a small share of the public expenses. Therefore, they will have sufficient resources.

Existence Trumps Theory

2   Some people have said that this shared authority cannot exist. This is a theoretical argument that is contrary to fact and reality. Arguments that show something *ought not to exist* should be completely rejected when evidence proves that it does exist.

For example, the Roman republic had two legislatures, which had different opposite interests: the patrician and the plebian. Each had the power to *annul* or *repeal* the acts of the other. People may try to prove that having two contradictory authorities won't work. But if a Roman citizen tried to disprove their existence, he would have been called insane.

In the Roman legislature that was called the comitta centuriata, only people who had a specific amount of property could vote and the patrician interest was superior. In the conittia tribuia, all citizens could vote, so the plebeian interest predominated. These two legislatures coexisted for ages and Rome was a great republic.

Coequal Authority Less Contradictory

3   The coequal taxation authority is not as contradictory as the Roman example. Neither side can annul the acts of the other. And soon the States' needs will be very limited. Until then, the United States will probably not tax the objects that States want to tax.

Union Revenue Needs Unlimited

4   What expenses will the federal and State governments have? Federal expenses are unlimited and State expenses are limited.

We must look into the remote future. A civil government's constitution tries to combine existing needs with probable future needs. We cannot infer from an estimate of immediate needs, the extent of power it is proper to give the national government. It is unsafe to limit the national government's capacity to provide for future emergencies. The federal government must provide the national defense. It must protect the nation against foreign war and domestic violence. We can not predict the possibility of internal attacks. We must be able to defend our commerce. And we must be able to support a navy and pay for naval wars.

Revenue Needed for Defense

5   Even if we agree to try the novel and absurd political experiment of tying the hands of government from offensive war, the government must be able guard the community against the ambition or hatred of other nations. If war breaks out in Europe, will we feel some of its fury? Or will another cause or country disturb our tranquility? Peace or war will not always be left to our option. We might be moderate or unambitious but we can't count on the moderation or hope to extinguish the ambition of others. History shows us that the fiery and destructive passions of war are more powerful motivators of human behavior than the mild and beneficent sentiments of peace. Modeling our political systems on speculations of lasting tranquility is to depend on the weaker springs of the human character.

Defense Largest Expense

6   What are the chief sources of expense in every government? Wars and rebellions. We must guard against these two mortal diseases of society.

The expenses for domestic police, the legislative, executive, and judicial branches of government, and the encouragement of agriculture and manufacturing (in other words, almost all State expenditures), are insignificant when compared with the expense for national defense.

England: Defense vs. Executive

7   In the kingdom of Great Britain, only 7% of the nation's annual expenses support the ostentatious monarchy. The other 93% goes to national defense.

Someone could say that we can't compare the possible expenses of a republic with the expense of supporting a monarchy. But consider this—Britain is a wealthy kingdom with an extravagant monarchy. Our frugal republic will have a modest executive branch. If we balance a proper deduction from one side against what ought to be deducted from the other, the proportion may still stand.

Union vs. States Revenue Needs

8   If we look at the large debt from a single war, we see that there will always be an immense disproportion between federal and State expenditures. Currently, several States have excessive debts because of the war. But if the proposed system is adopted, this cannot happen again. After these debts are paid, State governments will only need revenue to support their civil lists.

Future Revenue Needs Unlimitable

9   In framing a government for both the present and the future, we should figure out how much the offices and departments will cost. The

State governments will need an annual sum of about 200,000 pounds. But the Union's requirements cannot be limited, even in imagination. Why should State and local governments be given an exclusive source of revenue for any sum beyond 200,000 pounds? If the States are given sources of tax revenue that the Union is excluded from using, funding sources that are needed for national defense will be given to local governments that have no just or proper use for them.

Current State Debts/Future Needs

10   Suppose the convention had tried to distribute revenue sources between the Union and the States in *proportion* to their needs. What amount would not be too little or too much for the States—too little for their present needs, too much for their future needs?

Let's say the federal government was limited to external taxation (taxes on imports) and only the States and local government could use internal taxes. 66% of the country's resources would be available to States to pay 5-10% of its expenses. The federal government would have 33% of the country's resources to pay from 90-95% of its expenses.

What if we give the States an exclusive power of taxing houses and lands? There would still be a great disproportion between the *means* and the *end.* The States would possess 33% of the country's resources to supply, at most, 10% of its wants.

If the States had a revenue source that was only large enough to meet the futures needs of the State, they would not be able to raise enough money to pay their current debts. The Union would have to make a provision for this purpose.

Concurrent Tax Jurisdiction

11   Therefore, a concurrent jurisdiction for taxation was the only admissible substitute for an entire subordination, in respect to taxation, of State authority to that of the Union. Separating objects of taxation would have sacrificed the great interests of the Union to the power of the individual States. A few other points about this important subject of taxation deserve further consideration.

PUBLIUS

Number 35: Representatives Understand Tax Policy Effects

If the national government is restricted and can only tax a few specific objects, those objects would carry too much of the public burden. This creates two evils: the industries that create and sell those objects would be oppressed, and States and citizens involved with that industry would be responsible for an unequal part of the tax burden.

High Taxes Make Severe Problems

2   Some people argue that the federal taxation power should be limited to import duties. If import taxes were the federal government's only source of revenue, it would frequently want to increase these taxes, which would be injurious. Some people think that import taxes can never be too high because high import taxes discourage extravagant consumption, produce a favorable balance of trade, and promote domestic manufactures. But all extremes cause harm.

Very high taxes on imported articles would increase smuggling. Smuggling hurts honest traders and merchants. And it decreases tax revenue.

High duties also tend to give people who manufacture goods within the country a premature market monopoly. Import taxes creates higher price. Domestic manufactures will be able to charge higher prices than in an open market.

High import taxes can force industry out of its more natural channels into less advantageous areas.

They also oppress merchants that sell imported goods. The merchant, especially in a country with small commercial capital, often must keep prices down to promote sales. To do this, the seller can't raise his price to cover the entire cost of the duty. This reduces or eliminates the merchant's profits and can eat into his business capital.

High Duties Affect States

3   Usually, the consumer pays the tax duties. Therefore, duties on imports should go into the national treasury rather than be used exclusively by the importing States. But it is not fair that duties should form the only national fund.

When the merchant pays duties, they become an additional tax on the importing State, whose citizens, as consumers, pay the duties. They would produce an inequality among the States that would increase as duties increased.

If import duties were the only source of national revenues, non-manufacturing States would have an unequal tax burden. Citizens in manufacturing States will buy fewer imported articles than non-manufacturing States. Excise taxes would be needed to increase the manufacturing States' contribution to the public treasury. And specific manufactures would be targeted.

The citizens of New York who want to limit the Union to external taxation may not understand the importance of this subject. New York is an importing State. Since New York has a small population in a large territory, the growth of manufacturing will be slow. New York would suffer if the Union were limited to only commercial taxes.

Increased Tax Rate Doesn't Increase Revenue

4   These are some of the reasons for limiting import duties. As mentioned in another paper, there is another reason: if we want the government to be able to collect tax revenue, import taxes must be limited. And import taxes would be limited as long as the government has other resources. But if other taxation avenues were closed, when the government needed more revenue it would increase import taxes and try other experiments like adding penalties. For a while tax revenues would increase—until people found ways to elude the new taxes. Government officials would get the false impression that raising taxes also raises the amount of money going into the federal treasury. This false impression would take a long time to correct. Necessity, especially in politics, often occasions false hopes, false reasoning, and a system of measures correspondingly erroneous.

Let us now return to the examination of objections to the Constitution.

Critics: Too Few Representatives

5   Critics of the Constitution often say that the House of Representatives is too small. They say more members are needed to represent all different classes of citizens, the interests of every part of the community, and to produce sympathy between the representative body and its constituents. This is a specious and seducing argument. And it is impractical and unnecessary to accomplish the goal it supposedly supports.

I will discuss whether there is a sufficient number of members in the House of Representatives in another place. I will examine the issue here as it relates to the subject of this paper.

Mechanics, Manufacturers Elect Merchants

6   The idea that every class of people have representatives from their class is a Utopian fantasy. Unless the Constitution expressly says that each occupation should send one or more members, it will never happen.

Mechanics and manufacturers will probably vote for merchants rather than persons in their own professions. Mechanics and manufactures furnish the materials of commerce. The merchant is their natural patron and friend. They may feel confident in their own good sense but they know that the merchant can more effectively promote their interests. They know that their life experiences haven't given them the skills needed in a legislative assembly. The merchants' influence, status, and talents can better oppose attitudes unfriendly to the manufacturing and trading interests in public councils. Artisans and manufacturers will usually vote for merchants or the people who merchants recommend. So merchants are the natural representatives of all of these classes of people.

Elect Learned Professionals

7   With regard to the learned professions, little need be said. They truly form no distinct interest in society. According to their situation and talents, they will be indiscriminately the objects of the confidence and choice of each other and of other parts of the community.

Property Owners'

8   Lastly, the landed interest. This group includes the wealthiest landlord down to the poorest tenant. Their political views, particularly in relation to taxes, are perfectly united. Property taxes affect the owner of millions of acres as well as the owner of a single acre. Every landholder will want to keep the taxes on land as low as possible. And common interests always create bonds of sympathy.

But even if the rich landholder and the small farmer had different interests, why would we think that the rich landholder would stand a better chance of being elected to the national legislature than the farmer? In fact, small landowners prevail in the New York senate and assembly. Where voters' qualifications are the same, their votes will go to men in whom they have the most confidence, whether they happen to have large fortunes, moderate property, or no property at all.

Group Usually Elected Representatives

9   Some people say that every class of citizen should have a member of their class in the representative body, so that their feelings and interests are better understood and attended to. However, if the people are free to vote for anyone, this will never happen. In open and free elections, the representative body will be composed mostly of landlords, merchants, and learned professions.

Won't the interests and feelings of the different classes of citizens be understood by men in these professions? The landlord will understand and promote the interests of property owners. Since he owns property, he will probably resist every attempt to prejudice or encumber it.

The interests of the merchant are tied to the interests of mechanic and manufacturer. The merchant will understand their interests and, as far as proper, promote them.

The learned professionals will be neutral towards the rivalships between different branches of industry. They will be impartial arbiters between them. And they will be ready to promote either, as it seems to promote the general interests of the society.

Elected Officials Inform Themselves

10   Wise administrators pay attention to the current feelings or desires in the different parts of society. A candidate depends on the votes of his fellow citizens to continue his public job. He will learn their dispositions and

inclinations. And they will influence his conduct to a proper degree. The representative feels dependent on the citizens. He knows that he will be judged by the laws he approves.

Knowledge Needed For Good Tax Policy

11   Taxation policy requires extensive information and a thorough knowledge of political economic principles. Anyone who understands these principles will not want oppressive taxes nor will they want to sacrifice any group of citizens to get more tax revenue.

The most productive system of obtaining governmental revenue will always be the least burdensome. In order to tax judiciously, the person with the power to tax should understand the general characteristics, habits, and thinking of the people, and the country's resources. Let every thinking citizen judge for himself who has the required qualifications.

PUBLIUS

Number 36: Internal Taxation by Federal Government

The previous paper explained why representatives will usually be property owners, merchants, and members of the learned professions. They will represent all the community's different interests and views.

There will be exceptions to this rule. Occasionally, people will rise above the disadvantages of their situation and their merit will be recognized by society. The door should be equally open to all. To the credit of human nature, such people will be in both the federal and State legislatures.

2   Mechanics, manufacturers, and labor can be great rivals. But to have representatives of every occupation, the legislature would be too big to have wise deliberations. I refuse to continue discussing this rather vague objection.

Representatives Bring Local Knowledge

3   It has been said that a national power of internal taxation will never be successful for two reasons: 1. There isn't enough knowledge of local circumstances. 2. The revenue laws of the Union and specific States will conflict.

The federal government will have the information. State legislatures learn about a specific county from citizens of that county. The national legislature will get similar information from the representatives of each State.

When discussing taxation, does "local" knowledge mean being topographically familiar with every mountain, river, stream, highway, and road in each State? No. It means a general understanding of its situation and resources, the state of its agriculture, commerce, manufacturers, the nature of its products and consumption, the amount and kinds of wealth, property, and industry.

Small Committees Prepare Tax Plans

4 In nations, a small group of men usually prepare taxation plans. The sovereign or legislature then turns the plans into laws.

5 Inquisitive, enlightened statesmen are best qualified to make a judicious selection of the proper objects of taxation. This is the type of "local" knowledge required for taxation.

Local Knowledge Affects Indirect, Direct Taxes

6 Internal taxes may be either *direct* or *indirect* taxes. Objections based on a "lack of local knowledge" have been made against both types of internal taxes.

When the federal government considers whether it should tax an article, it will look at the nature of the article. [i.e. home heating oil will be used more in northern States than southern States] Well-informed men, especially merchants, will supply more information. [i.e. perhaps an article is more expensive in some States because of shipping costs] If an article is already taxed by a State, the federal government shouldn't add another tax. Understanding an article's different situation in different States is easy.

7 Does the objection apply to direct taxes on real property, houses or land? No.

Land taxes are determined either by *actual* valuations or *occasional* assessments. In either case, local knowledge is only needed in the execution of the duty by commissioners or assessors. The law can only prescribe the manner the persons will be elected or appointed, fix their numbers and qualifications, and outline their powers and duties.

Either the national legislature or a State legislature can regulate the general principles. Local details must be referred to those who execute the plan.

State Collection System May Be Used

8 This can be further simplified. Each State's method of laying and collecting tax can be adopted and employed by the federal government.

Taxes Uniform Throughout Nation

9 Remember, the national legislature will not decide how much the people of each State must pay. That will be determined by each State's population, as described in Article one, Section two. The population will be determined by a census. Therefore, the national government can't be partial or oppressive to some States. It would be difficult to abuse the taxa-

tion power. There is also a provision that "all duties, imposts, and excises shall be uniform throughout the United States."

State Requisitions Still Possible

10 Remember, if internal taxation by the Union is really inconvenient, the federal government may stop using it and use State requisitions instead. It has been asked, why not just omit the ambiguous power and rely on State requisitions?

Two answers may be given: First, if it works, internal taxation will be more effective. Second, if the Union returns to using State requisitions, the constitutional power of direct taxation will have a strong influence. When the States know that the Union can go directly to the people, they will be motivated to fulfill their requisitions.

Federal, States Tax Differently

11 Legally, Union and State revenue laws cannot interfere with each other. However, Union and State policies do sometimes conflict. A solution will be to not tax those objects that the other side is already taxing. The federal and State governments can't *control* each other. Therefore, each will have an interest in this reciprocal forbearance. And when the current State debts are paid off, their expenses will decrease and the possibility of interference will almost vanish. A small land-tax will fulfill State needs.

Fears about Internal Taxation

12 The power of internal taxation has raised many fears: double sets of revenue officers, double taxation, and odious, oppressive poll taxes.

Double Sets of Revenue Officers

13 There won't be double sets of officers in two cases: The first is when the Union has exclusive right to impose the tax, for instance, duties on imports. And second, when the object to be taxed hasn't fallen under a State regulation or provision.

In other cases, the United States probably will either not tax objects the local government taxes or will use State officers and State regulations for collecting the additional tax. This will save collection expense and avoid problems with the State governments and the people.

The predicted evils do not necessarily result from the plan.

States Influences Nation

14 If a spirit of influence should infest the national councils, State officers could be employed, attaching them to the Union through their compensation. State influence would flow towards the national government, instead of federal influence flowing to the States.

Federal or State, Total Taxes Same

15 The answer to the worry about double taxation is plain. The wants of the Union are to be supplied in one way or another. If fulfilled by the federal government, the State government will not do them. The quantity of taxes paid by the community must be the same in either case.

If the federal government supplies the provision, it can use commercial taxes. The federal government can improve this revenue source better than the States, making other taxes less necessary.

There is another advantage. If there is a problem with internal taxation, the federal government will be careful about what it taxes. The national tax policy will make the rich pay as much as is practical and diminish the taxes paid by the more numerous, poorer people. It is fortunate when the government's interest in self-preservation coincides with a proper distribution of public burdens and tends to guard the least wealthy part of the community from oppression!

Poll Taxes Bad, May Be Needed

16 I strongly disapprove of poll taxes. Although they have been used in New England, States that have always promoted citizens' rights, I would hate to see the national government use them.

However, just because there is a power to use them, will they actually be used? Every State in the Union has the power to impose poll taxes. Yet several States have never used them. Are the State governments tyrannies because they have this power? If they are not, how can a similar power justify such a charge against the national government? Or be used as an obstacle to adopting of the Constitution? I hate poll taxes but emergencies are possible. The government should have the option of using them.

This country has few objects that can be used as sources of revenue. This is a reason for not limiting the discretion of the national councils. Nothing exempts this part of the globe from the calamities that have befallen other parts of it. I am averse to everything that disarms the government of a single weapon that might be employed for defense and security.

Essential Powers of Federal Government

17 The powers proposed for the United States that relate to the energy of government have been examined. And the principal objections answered. I have passed over some minor authorities that have not been attacked by opponents of the Constitution either because they are so small or so clearly proper to be controversial.

Judicial power might have been investigated under this topic. But its organization and authority are more advantageously considered together. They will be discussed later.   PUBLIUS

Constitutional Convention

Number 37: Difficulties Faced by Constitutional Convention

We have studied the Confederation's defects. To correct the defects, we need an energetic government as proposed in the new Constitution. And we have studied some important principles of the new Constitution.

The objective of these papers is to determine the quality of this Constitution and whether it is a good idea to adopt it. We will now study the Constitution, compare all its parts, and figure out how it will affect our country.

Papers' Target Audience

2   We should study a proposed public policy objectively. Will it advance or block the public good? Unfortunately, because of human nature, people are rarely objective when they discuss public policy. And people actually become less objective as the issues become more important.

The Constitution has important changes and innovations. It touches passions and interests on both sides of the issues. Therefore, many people have not judged its merits objectively. Some people condemned the proposed Constitution before they read it. Other people have an opposite bias, making their opinions unimportant. However, the people predetermined to praise the new Constitution may have purer intentions than those predetermined to condemn it.

Everyone admits our situation is critical and something must be done. Therefore, the person who wants the Constitution might be biased because of these considerations, as well as from sinister motives. On the other hand, the predetermined adversary has no venial motive whatever. The intentions of the first may be upright while also being culpable. The views of the last cannot be upright and must be culpable.

But these papers are not addressed to people in either category. They solicit the attention of people who can objectively judge how to promote the happiness of their country.

Constitution Not Faultless

3,4 These people will not magnify the Constitution's faults. They didn't expect a faultless plan. The convention was fallible. They will keep in mind that they, themselves, are only men. They will not assume infallibility as they judge the fallible opinions of others. And they will make allowances for the difficulties the convention faced.

Precedents Show Errors to Avoid

5   This was a novel undertaking. The existing Confederation is founded on fallacious principles. Consequently, we must change both the foundation and the building resting on it.

Other confederacies had the same problems. They show us what not to do but don't point us in the right direction. The Convention could only avoid the errors made by our Confederation and other countries, and provide an amendment process to correct the convention's errors, as future experience exposes them.

Balance Stability, Liberty

6   Combining government **energy and stability** with **liberty and the republican form** was difficult. But this was their task.

A government must have **energy** to protect the country from external and internal danger, and enforce its laws.

A **stable** government gets respect. It gives the people confidence, a blessing of civil society. Irregular and changing legislation is not particularly evil but the people hate it. People want the uncertainties within the State administrations corrected.

However, it is difficult to combine **energy** and **stability** with the principles of **liberty**. Inherently, **republican liberty** seems to demand that all power comes from the people. Government officials should depend on the people by having short terms. And the trust should be placed not in a few but a large number of hands.

However, to be **stable** government officials must continue in office for a longer time. Frequent elections create a frequent change in men and a frequent change of policies. **Energy** in government requires both long terms in office and only one person.

7   Did the convention create the right balance? It will become clearer as we study the Constitution. It was a difficult task.

State v. Federal Authority

8   Deciding the proper boundary between federal and State authorities was also a complicated task. Scientists and philosophers have tried to classify the abilities of the mind but no one has completed the task. The boundaries between the mental activities of sense, perception, judgment, desire, choice, memory, and imagination elude the subtlest investigations and are a source of controversy.

The boundaries between the various genuses and species in nature are another example of the same truth. Naturalists have not perfectly defined the line separating vegetable life from non-organic matter, or the line separating vegetable and animal life. There is an even greater obscurity between the objects in each category of nature.

Politics Inexact Science

9   Objective boundaries do exist in nature. They are unclear only because we are unable to make perfect observations. When we study man-made organizations, two things make it difficult to define the lines of authority: the subject and the imperfections of the humans who study it.

Political science hasn't been able to define the exact boundaries between the legislative, executive, and judiciary branches of government. Or even the powers of the different legislative houses. These obscure subjects puzzle the greatest political science experts.

Three Sources of Ambiguity

10   Brilliant legislators and jurists have tried to define the objectives and limits of different laws and courts of justice. This subject has been extensively studied in Great Britain. But the line between the different types of laws—common law, statute law, maritime law, ecclesiastical law, corporate law, and local laws and customs—still isn't clearly defined. The jurisdiction of Great Britain's different courts is frequently discussed, but it still isn't perfectly clear.

New laws are written with the greatest technical skill and passed after long deliberations. Yet they are considered as more or less obscure and equivocal until their meaning is ascertained by a series of discussions and adjudications.

Obscurity comes from (1) the complexity of the subjects, (2) human imperfections, and (3) the medium [i.e. words, sentences] used to convey men's ideas.

Humans use words to express ideas. Clear expression requires well-formed ideas and the appropriate words. But no language has words and phrases for every complex idea. And many words have several meanings. Therefore, the definition of even a precise subject can be inaccurate because words are inaccurate. This unavoidable inaccuracy grows worse as the subject becomes more complex or novel.

When God himself talks to mankind in our language, his meaning—brilliant as it must be—is made dim and doubtful by the cloudy medium through which it is communicated.

11   There are three sources of vague and incorrect definitions: (1) indistinctness of the subject, (2) the brain's imperfections, and (3) the language's inadequacies. When the constitutional convention worked to define the boundary between federal and State jurisdictions, it must have experienced all three problems.

States: Conflicting Interests

12   Additionally, large and small States had conflicting demands. Larger States wanted power matching their superior wealth and importance. Smaller States wanted equality. They had to compromise.

After compromising on the ratio of representation, a fresh struggle probably started. Each State wanted to organize the government and distribute its powers so they got the greatest share of influence.

13 Every State is divided into districts. Citizens have competing interests and feel local jealousies. Different States have different policies. And the different parts of the United States have competing interests. This variety of interests may have a healthy influence on the administration of the government once it is formed. However, as they wrote the Constitution, they must have experienced many conflicting interests. Features in the Constitution suggest these assumptions. The convention had to sacrifice theoretical perfection to other considerations.

Drafting Constitution

14 Sitting at home, alone, a person could write a "perfect" constitution. But the constitutional convention felt pressure from all sides; it couldn't be "perfect." It's amazing that so many difficulties were surmounted. The convention's ability to reach agreements was unprecedented. Any honest man must find this amazing. Any pious man must see the finger of that Almighty hand that has so frequently come to our relief at critical times of the revolution.

Opinions Sacrificed

15 The United Netherlands repeatedly and unsuccessfully tried to reform the ruinous and notorious vices of their constitution. [See #20] Factions disrupted the councils that tried to reconcile discordant opinions, assuage jealousies, and compromise. They are dark and degraded pictures. They show the infirmities and depravities of the human character. The few scattered instances of cooperation only serve as exceptions to caution us about the general truth.

After studying history, we are led to two important conclusions. First, the convention must have been free from the destructive influence of party animosities—the disease of deliberative bodies that contaminates their proceedings. Second, the delegations composing the convention were either satisfied by the Constitution or they agreed to it because they felt it was important to sacrifice their private opinions and interests to the public good or they feared the consequences of delays or new experiments.

PUBLIUS

Number 38: Ancient Republics Structured by Individuals

Ancient structured governments were framed by a wise individual rather than groups of men.

Authors of Ancient Republics

- Minos founded the government of Crete.

- Zaleucus founded Locrians.
- Theseus, then Draco and Solon, instituted the government of Athens.
- Lycurgus wrote Sparta's laws.
- Romulus founded the first Roman government. Two of his elective successors, Numa and Tulius Hostilius, completed the work. Brutus abolished royalty, substituting a reform that was prepared by Tulius Hostilius. The senate and people ratified the change.

This also applies to confederate governments. Amphictyon founded the league that bore his name. The Achaean league received its first birth from Achaeus and its second from Aratus.

Some Governmental Architects Authorized by Citizens

3 We don't know how much each of these men were responsible for their respective governments, or if the people gave them the authority. We do know that some were given the authority.

Athenians gave Draco the power to reform its government and laws. And Plutarch says Solon was elected to remodel the constitution. Fewer people gave Lycurgus of Sparta his authority. A small group of people asked him to reform the government.

Protection of Liberty vs. Reforms

4 The Greeks jealously guarded their liberty. To protect their liberty, the citizens of Athens demanded that a minimum of ten generals command an army. And they felt that if a fellow-citizen became famous, it was a danger to their liberties. So why did they place their fortunes and their posterity in the hands of one illustrious citizen? Why did they abandon caution and place their destiny in the hands of a single citizen rather than a group of citizens? We might expect more wisdom and safety from a group. Citizens must have feared discord even more than they feared treachery by a single individual.

Solon wrote a compromise policy. He confessed he had not given his countrymen the government best suited to their happiness, but most tolerable to their prejudices. And Lycurgus, more true to his objective, mixed some violence with the authority of superstition. Then he voluntarily renounced his country, then his life, to secure his final success.

On the one hand, we can admire America's improvement on the ancient method of creating a constitutional government. On the other hand, it warns us that such experiments are inherently difficult and we shouldn't unnecessarily multiply the difficulties.

U. S. Constitution Historically Unique

5 Writing a new Constitution is complicated and difficult. In areas with little historical experience, there will be errors even if the subject is care-

fully researched. And the errors will not be found until actual trial points them out.

Both logical reasoning and our experience with the Articles of Confederation suggest this. During the ratification of the Articles of Confederation, many objections were made and amendments were suggested. But no one mentioned the great error that actual trial uncovered. Although the objections proved immaterial, some States would have clung to them with dangerous inflexibility if their zeal for their opinions and interests had not been stifled by the more powerful sentiment of self-preservation. Although the enemy was within our country, one State refused to ratify the Articles for several years. She finally complied out of fear of being charged with protracting the public calamities and endangering the outcome of the war.

Medical Allegory

6 Let's study the case of a person who grows sicker every day. He finally decides that if he waits any longer to get help, he will be in extreme danger. He evaluates the reputations of different physicians, then calls the doctors that he thinks are the best and that are entitled to his confidence. The doctors arrive and carefully examine the patient. The doctors consult. They all agree that the symptoms are critical but that with proper and timely care the patient can actually have improved health. And they all agree on what must be done to produce this happy effect.

As the prescription is written, however, a number of other people arrive. They agree that the patient is in real danger. Then they tell the patient that the prescription will poison him and forbid him, under pain of certain death, to make use of it.

Before he followed the second suggestion, won't the patient demand that the group should agree on some other remedy? If the second group can't agree on a remedy, wouldn't he try the remedy that the first group of doctors unanimously recommended?

Criticisms: Irreconcilable Wide Variety

7 This patient mirrors America's current situation. She realizes she is sick. She has obtained unanimous advice from men of her own choice. Now other people warn her against following this advice under the pain of fatal consequences.

Does the new group say there is no danger? No.

Do they deny that a speedy and powerful remedy is needed? No.

Do even *two* critics agree on what is wrong with the proposed remedy or the proper substitution? Let them speak for themselves:

One says we should reject the proposed Constitution because it's not a confederation of the States, but a government over individuals.

Another admits it should be a government over individuals, but **not to the extent proposed.**

A third doesn't object to the government over individuals but wants a **bill of rights.**

A fourth says a bill of rights is necessary but it should not declare the personal rights of individuals, but the **rights reserved to the States**.

A fifth believe that a bill of rights would be superfluous, but the Constitution has the fatal power of **regulating the times and places of election.**

An objector from a large State exclaims loudly against the unreasonable **equality** in the **Senate**. An objector from a small State is equally loud against the dangerous **inequality** in the **House of Representatives.**

One group is alarmed with the **huge expense** because a large number of people will be needed to administer the new government. Another group—and even some of the people in the first group at a different time—cry out that Congress is too small and the government would be **less objectionable if** the number and the **expense were doubled.**

A patriot in a State, which doesn't import or export, objects to **direct taxation.** The patriot in an exporting and importing State is dissatisfied because the whole burden of **taxes** may be thrown **on consumption**.

One politician says the Constitution promotes a **monarchy**. Another is equally sure it will end in **aristocracy**. Another is puzzled over which of these shapes it will ultimately assume but sees clearly it must be one or the other. A fourth fears the opposite: the Constitution is not energetic enough to keep it upright and firm against **anarchy.**

Another group of adversaries to the Constitution says the **legislative, executive, and judiciary are intertwined**, which contradicts all the ideas of regular government and all the required precautions in favor of liberty. This is a vague objection with few supporters.

Two people rarely agree on one objection.

One says the Senate should not have to approve **presidential appointments**. Another says that House of Representatives should also approve appointments. Another person says that giving the **President** any **power** is always dangerous.

Some people say that the **trial of impeachments** by the Senate is wrong: they believe the judiciary should have this power.

Others reply that the **judiciary** already has too much power.

People who want an **executive council** can't agree on how it would be formed. Some people want a small council appointed by the House of Representatives. Others think the President should appoint a large council.

If Critics Wrote Constitution, Never Agree

8   Let's look at the situation in a different way. Let's assume the critics of the Constitution are brilliant and they can write a better constitution. Let's

further assume the country agrees and a second convention is formed to revise the work of the first.

You've read some of their opinions. And know how hostile they have been towards the Constitution Convention. Wouldn't their deliberations be full of discord?

If the current, proposed Constitution was ratified and used, not until a BETTER but until this new group of lawgivers agrees on ANOTHER, wouldn't it have a good chance of becoming immortal?

New Constitution Better than Articles

9   People who object to the new Constitution never talk about the defects in the Articles of Confederation. The Constitution doesn't need to be perfect; it just has to be better than the Articles. No man would refuse to leave a shattered, tottering house for a large, solid building because the latter had no porch, or because some of the rooms might be a little larger or smaller, or the ceiling a little higher or lower than his fancy would have planned them. The primary objections to the new Constitution lie with tenfold weight against the existing Confederation.

Is it dangerous for the federal government to have an **indefinite power to raise money**? The present Congress can requisition any amount of money from the States and the States are constitutionally bound to furnish it. It can emit bills of credit as long as it can pay for the paper. It can borrow both abroad and at home.

If an indefinite power to **raise troops** is dangerous, Congress currently has that power and it has already begun to make use of it.

Is it improper and unsafe to **intermix** the different **powers** of government? Currently Congress, a single body of men, is the sole depository of all the federal powers.

Is it dangerous to give the keys of the **treasury and** command of the **army** into the same hands? The Confederation places them both in the hands of Congress.

Is a **bill of rights** essential to liberty? The Articles has no bill of rights.

Is there an objection because the new Constitution empowers the Senate with the concurrence of the President to make **treaties** that **are** to be the **laws** of the land? Without any control, the existing Congress makes treaties that most States recognize as the supreme laws of the land.

Is the **importation of slaves** permitted by the new Constitution for 20 years? By the old, it is permitted forever.

Congress Wielding Unauthorized Powers

10   I will be told: The Confederation's powers may appear dangerous. But they are harmless because Congress is dependent on the States to use them. However large the Confederation's total power may appear to be, it is lifeless.

Then I say: we can charge the Confederation with the greater folly of declaring that certain federal powers are necessary and, at the same time, making them worthless. And if the Union is to continue under the Articles of Confederation, effective powers must either be granted to, or assumed by, the existing Congress.

But this is not all. The Confederation has already greatly increased its power. All the dangers from a defectively constructed national government seem to be realized.

The Western territory is a mine of vast wealth to the United States. It won't produce any regular revenue for public expenses for some time to come. But eventually, under proper management, it will help discharge the domestic public debt and furnish, for a certain period, liberal tributes to the federal treasury. Therefore, a rich, fertile territory, equal in size to the inhabited area of the United States, will soon become part of the nation. Congress has assumed its administration, formed new States, erected temporary governments, appointed officers for them, and prescribed the condition by which the States will be admitted into the Confederacy. All this has been done without the least constitutional authority. Yet no blame has been whispered; no alarm has been sounded.

Under the Articles of Confederation, a GREAT AND INDEPENDENT fund of revenue is passing into the hands of a SINGLE BODY of men [Congress]. The same group can RAISE TROOPS to an INDEFINITE NUMBER, and appropriate money to support them for an INDEFINITE PERIOD OF TIME. Yet some of the same men who have watched and advocated for this system have objected to the new system using the arguments presented here. Shouldn't they urge the adoption of the new Constitution as necessary to guard the Union against future powers and resources of a body constructed like the existing Congress?

Must Have Powers to Achieve Objectives

11 I don't mean, by anything said here, to criticize the current Congress. I know they had to act. They had to overstep their constitutional limits. But doesn't this prove that it is dangerous when a government doesn't have the necessary powers to fulfill its responsibilities? It is continually exposed to the dangers of dissolution or usurpation. PUBLIUS

Number 39: National vs. Federal Republic

The last paper concluded the introductory comments. We will now study the proposed Constitution

Is Proposed Government a Republic?

2 Is the proposed government a republic? The American people want a republic. Everyone who loves freedom wants self-government. We

fought the Revolution to attempt this political experiment. Therefore, we cannot defend the proposed Constitution—and must abandon it—if it does not create a republic.

Countries Called "Republic" In Error

3   What are the unique characteristics of a republic? We call several countries "republics," but they are not:

In Holland, none of its supreme authority comes from the people. In Venice, hereditary nobles exercise the absolute power over the people. Poland has a bad mixture of aristocracy and monarchy. England has one republican branch plus an aristocracy and a monarch.

The term "republic" is often inaccurately used in political discussions.

Republic = *All* Power from People

4   We define a republic as a government that gets all its powers—directly or indirectly—from the people. The people elect some of a republic's administrators, who appoint other officials. And government officials remain in office either for a limited term or during good behavior.

A republican government *must* come from all citizens, not just a favored class. If this is not true, a tyrant or a few tyrannical nobles could say they were creating a republic.

It is *enough* that the people appoint government officials either directly or indirectly. And government officials stay in office for a specific term or during good behavior. The people indirectly appoint many State officers. The governors and most State legislators have a specific term in office. Most State judges have lifetime appointments, during good behavior.

Constitution: Republic Form

5   The Constitution follows the republican form. The people elect the House of Representatives and indirectly appoint the Senate. The people indirectly elect the President. As in the States, even the judges and other officers of the Union will be the choice, though a remote choice, of the people.

The term in office also follows the republican form. Representatives serve two years. Senators serve six years. The President's term in office is four years. And he is impeachable at any time during his time in office. Judges have a lifetime appointment and can be impeached and removed from office. Congress will create laws to regulate the term in office for other ministers and administers.

Absolute Prohibition of Nobility Titles

6   The Constitution prohibits titles of nobility and guarantees the republican form of government.

Constitutional Convention: Number 39

Convention's Authority, Objective

7 Opponents of the Constitution say, "But it was not enough that the Convention followed the republican form. They should have kept the *federal* form; the Union should be a *confederacy* of sovereign States. Instead, they have created a *national* government; the Union will become a *consolidation* of the States." And they ask, "What authority did the Convention have to make this change?"

Analyzing Convention's Work

8 We will study this objection and (1) determine if the proposed government is federal or national, (2) ask if the convention was authorized to propose such a government, and (3) determine whether the delegates' duty to their country replaced their lack of regular authority.

Character of Proposed Government

9 We will determine the real character of the government through studying:
- the **foundation** on which the government is to be established,
- the **sources** of its ordinary powers,
- the **operation** of those powers,
- the **extent** of the government's powers,
- and the **authority** to make future changes in the government.

Foundation: Ratification: Federal Form

10, 11   The Constitution's **foundation** refers to the ratification process. It could have been set up several ways. If ratification required that a *majority* of the people of the entire nation accept the Constitution, then ratification would be a *national* act. However, this is not how the Constitution will be ratified. Nor will a *majority* of the States make the decision.

Instead, the people of each State will vote to ratify the Constitution. They will be acting as citizens of independent States, not as citizens of one nation. And the States must *unanimously* ratify the Constitution. The people—not the legislature—must accept the Constitution.

As they vote to ratify the Constitution, each State is a sovereign body. Each State will act independently and be bound only by its own voluntary act. In its **foundation**, the new government will be *federal*, not *national*.

Power Source: Both Federal, National

12 Next we'll look at the **source** of the ordinary powers of government. [Do the people (national) or the States (federal) elect/appoint the nation's officials?]

The people will elect the House of Representatives and will be represented proportionately. In this, the government is *national*, not *federal*.

The Senate, on the other hand, will derive its powers from the States as equal societies. In this, the government is *federal*, not *national*.

The executive power will come from a compound source. The States, as political units, will elect the President. The number of votes each State gets is based on a compound ratio. Each State has the same number of votes as their number of members in the US Congress: an equal number (two Senators) and a proportional number (number of Representatives). If no one wins that election, the national House of Representatives will pick the President; each State will have one vote, making the States distinct, equal political bodies.

As to its **source of powers**, the government structure appears mixed. It has as many *federal* as *national* features.

Government *Operation*: National Form

13 Opponents of the proposed Constitution say that a *federal* government operates on the political bodies [States] within the Confederacy and a *national* government operates on the nation's individual citizens. Using this criterion, the Constitution falls under a **national**, not *federal*, character. However, when there is a controversy between States, States will be viewed in their collective, political capacities only.

The government's operation most resembles a **national** government.

Extent of Powers: Federal Form

14 The **extent of** the proposed governments' **powers** has the *federal* form.

A *national* government has authority over individual citizens with an indefinite supremacy over all persons, things, and issues that can be objects of lawful government. A *federal* government vests some supremacy in the united body and some in the local legislatures.

A *national* legislature can control, direct, or abolish local authority at any time. In a *federal* system, local governments have areas of supreme power. The areas of local authority are no more subject to the federal authority than the federal authority is subject to State and local governments.

In the **extent of its powers**, the proposed government is not *national*. Federal jurisdiction extends to specific objectives only. The States will have a total sovereignty over all other issues.

The Supreme Court will ultimately decide boundary disputes between two jurisdictions. The federal government will establish the Supreme Court. But this doesn't change the principle. Such a tribunal is essential to prevent armed conflict between States and dissolution of the Union. Few people would argue against the national government creating the Supreme Court.

Amending: Federal, National Features

15 The Constitution's **amendment** process is neither totally *national* nor totally *federal*.

If it was totally *national*, a *majority* of the people of the Union could vote to ratify the Constitution. And a majority of people could alter or abolish the Union's government at any time.

On the other hand, if it were totally *federal*, every State in the Union would have to agree to constitutional amendments.

The amendment process in the Constitution doesn't follow either principle. By requiring more than a majority of *States*, not *citizens*, it has a *federal* character. By requiring less than the total number of States agree, it is less *federal* and more **national**.

Neither Strictly National nor Federal

16 Therefore, the proposed Constitution is not completely *national* or *federal*, but a composition of both:

- Its **foundation** is *federal*.
- Its **source** of governmental powers is part *federal* and part **national**.
- In the **operation** of these powers, it is **national**.
- In the **extent** of these powers, it is *federal*.
- And the **amendment** process is both *federal* and **national**.

PUBLIUS

Number 40: Was Convention Authorized to Draft Constitution?

[This paper continues the discussion started in Number 39, paragraph 8.]

The *second* question: Was the convention authorized to create and propose this mixed [with both national and federal features] Constitution?

Convention's Mission Defined

2 Why did the States send delegates to the Convention? The meeting in Annapolis in September 1786 and the congressional meeting in February 1787 defined their mission.

Annapolis Meeting, September 1786

3 The Annapolis meeting in September, 1786, recommended that the States appoint delegates to meet and consider "the situation of the United States; to devise *such further provisions* as shall appear to them necessary to render [make] the Constitution of the federal government *adequate to the exigencies of the Union;* and to report such an act for that purpose to the United States in Congress assembled, as when agreed to by them, and afterwards confirmed by the legislature of every State, will effectually provide for the same."

Congress Recommendation, Feb 1787

4 In February, 1787, Congress recommended: "Whereas there is provision in the Articles of Confederation and perpetual Union for making alterations therein, by the assent of Congress of the United States and the

legislatures of the several States; and whereas experience has evinced that there are defects in the present Confederation; as a means to remedy which, several States, and *particularly the State of New York,* by express instructions to their delegates in Congress, have suggested a convention for the purposes expressed in the following resolution; and such convention appearing to be the most probable means of establishing in these States a *firm national government*:

5 *"Resolved,* —That in the opinion of Congress it is expedient that on the second Monday in May next a convention of delegates, who shall have been appointed by the several States, be held at Philadelphia for the sole and express purpose *of revising the Articles of Confederation,* and reporting to Congress and all the legislatures the *alterations and provisions therein* as shall, when agreed to in Congress and confirmed by the States, render [make] the federal Constitution *adequate to meet the exigencies of government and the preservation of the Union"*

Convention's Objectives/Tasks

6 These two acts seem to say:

1) The convention's objective was to establish a firm national government that is adequate for the needs of the government and the preservation of the Union.

2) This goal could be met either by "revising the Articles of Confederation [with] alterations and provisions" (from act of Congress) or by "such further provision as should appear necessary" (Annapolis).

3) To take effect, Congress and the States must agree to the changes.

Convention's Mission Statement

7 We can summarize the convention's authority: (1) Frame a *national government* that can (2) meet the needs of government and the Union, and (3) change the Articles of Confederation into a form that accomplishes these purposes.

Conflicting Goals: Sacrifice Less Important

8 To analyze this mission statement, logic and legal axioms have two rules:

First, if possible, every part of the mission statement should have meaning and made to reach some common goal.

Second, if parts of the mission statement conflict, the less important should give way to the more important part. The means should be sacrificed to the goal, rather than the goal to the means.

Change Articles vs. New Constitution

9 What if the convention felt that they could not form a *national government that meets the Union's needs* [#1 and 2 in paragraph 6 above] . . . by *alterations* of the *Articles of Confederation* [#3 in paragraph 6 above].

Which part of the mission should be pursued and which part should be rejected? Which is more important—forming an adequate government or preserving the Articles of Confederation?

The people who object to the convention's work should answer this question: What was the purpose of government reform? To preserve the Articles? Or to establish an adequate government, even if the Articles have to be sacrificed?

Maybe Goals Are Not Irreconcilable

10 But are these goals irreconcilable? Perhaps the convention did alter the *Articles of the Confederation* to form a national and adequate government.

Alteration vs. Transmutation

11 The convention was authorized to *alter* and add *new provisions* to the **Articles of Confederation**. Therefore, changing the **title** to "**Constitution**" is not an exercise of ungranted power.

Where is the line between authorized and unauthorized changes? What degree of change is an *alteration*? How much change is actually a *transmutation* of the government? The States solemnly appointed a convention with big objectives. They must have expected some *substantial* reforms.

Did the convention change the *fundamental principles* of the Confederation?

Both the Articles and the proposed Constitution regard the States as independent sovereigns.

Under the Articles of Confederation, the people, not the State legislatures, may elect the delegates to Congress—a trait of a **national** government.

Some opponents say that the national government's power must act on States rather than individuals. Sometimes the new government will act on the States. And sometimes the existing confederation acts on individuals.

Do these fundamental principles require that States must play a role in all taxation? The current Confederation has a direct tax on the post office. And Congress says the power of coinage is a tax.

Besides these examples, one of the convention objectives—and the people expected—that the national government would regulate trade so it would be an immediate source of general revenue. Congress said that federal trade regulations are consistent with the fundamental principles of the Confederacy. And twelve States have already complied with the plan of Congress.

Should the federal government's powers be limited? Beyond this limit, should the States have sovereign and independent jurisdiction? In the new government—as in the old—the national powers are limited. And the States have sovereign, independent jurisdiction over all powers not specifically stated in the Constitution.

12 The important principles in the proposed Constitution are not new. They expand the principles found in the Articles of Confederation. The Constitution only looks like a new system because the Articles needed so much clarification.

Ratification Process Changed

13 In one area, the convention departed from their specific commission. *Nine States* need to ratify the Constitution, instead of *all the States.*

Although this could be an objection to the Constitution, it is rarely mentioned. This is probably because it would be absurd to subject the fate of twelve States to the perverseness or corruption of the thirteenth. Therefore, it has received little criticism. I dismiss it without further comment.

Did Duty Override Authority?

14 The *third* question is: How much did the delegates' feelings of duty to their country supply any lack of regular authority?

Convention Only Recommends Plan

15 Up to this point, we have rigorously analyzed the convention's work as if it had the authority to establish a Constitution for the United States. It has held up to scrutiny.

The convention was only authorized to advise and recommend. And the proposed Constitution is nothing more than pieces of paper, unless the people approve it.

Convention Delegates: Considerations

16 From the convention notes, the delegates seemed deeply concerned about the crisis in their country. Almost with one voice, they created the solemn Constitution to correct the errors that produced this crisis. They all agreed that the proposed reform is necessary to meet the convention's goals.

Citizens throughout this great empire anxiously watched their deliberations. And delegates believed that every external and internal foe of liberty and prosperity of the United States hoped they would fail.

Virginia offered an amendment to the Confederacy, which the delegates studied. The Annapolis convention—with *very few* deputies from a *very few* of the States—had recommended an important change that was not part of their commission; however, the public accepted it and twelve of the thirteen States made the change. And Congress has assumed powers to solve problems, problems far less urgent than those faced by the convention.

Delegates knew that when an established government needs great changes, form must give way to substance. The people have the right to "abolish or alter their governments as to them shall seem most likely to effect their safety and happiness."[*] Rigidly holding onto a specific form would make this nearly impossible. People don't spontaneously and universally move together towards their objectives. Therefore, some *informal and unauthorized proposals* made by some patriotic, respectable citizens start changes.

The States first united against danger because people believe that they could plan for their safety and happiness. Committees and congresses worked hard, defending the people's rights. *Conventions* established the *State* constitutions. The only people who demanded that existing forms be followed were people who secretly wanted to block delegates from creating the constitutions.

As they wrote the new Constitution, delegates knew that it would be submitted *to the people themselves*. If the people reject the plan, it will be destroyed forever. Likewise, approval by the people overrides any irregularities in its formation.

The delegates might have realized that once trivial objections are settled, the question of whether they exceeded their authority would not be criticized, particularly if their recommendation met the national needs.

Judging the Delegates

17 What if the convention hadn't created a system that they felt could secure the country's happiness? What if they had coldly decided to disappoint the country's deep hopes and sacrificed substance to form? Their country would have faced the uncertainties of delay and the hazard of events. Let me ask the rational patriot—how would the impartial world judge the convention? How would the friends of mankind and every virtuous citizen judge the conduct and character of this assembly?

If there is a man who wants to condemn the delegates and the convention, how does he plan to punish the twelve States who *usurped power* by sending deputies to the convention? How will he punish Congress, who recommended the appointment of this body? Or punish the State of New York, which first urged and then complied with this unauthorized intervention?

Source of Good Advice Unimportant

18 To disarm the objectors, let's agree for a moment that the convention was neither authorized by their commission nor justified by circumstances to propose a Constitution for their country. Does it follow that the Constitution, for that reason alone, should be rejected?

If it is lawful to accept good advice from an enemy, shall we refuse advice when our friends offer it? In all cases, the prudent inquiry shouldn't be *from whom* the advice comes but whether the advice is *good*.

---

[*] Declaration of Independence--PUBLIUS

Convention Didn't Exceed Authority

19 Opponents of the proposed Constitution say that the convention exceeded its power. The only change was the ratification process, which is rarely mentioned by the objectors. Otherwise, the charge has no foundation.

And if they did exceed their powers, they were not only justified but also required. They were servants of their country, who used their liberty to fulfill their mission.

And finally, even if they violated both their powers and their duty in proposing a Constitution, it should be ratified, if it seems to meet the goals and promote the happiness of the people of America. We are investigating whether this describes the Constitution.

PUBLIUS

Federal Powers

Number 41: Constitutionally Vested Federal Power

We may study the proposed Constitution in two ways:
FIRST: the federal government's power, including restraints on the States
SECOND: structure of the government and distribution of power among its
branches.

Federal Power

2   Regarding federal powers, two important questions arise:

(a) Are any of the powers given to the federal government unnecessary
or improper?

(b) Will the total federal powers be dangerous to the States?

Is Federal Power Too Extensive?

3   Is the federal government's total power greater than it should be?

4   Some people say the new Constitution gives the federal government
too much power. They rarely consider whether these powers are necessary. Instead, they talk about the inconveniences and how the power might
be abused. They may inflame the passions of the unthinking and confirm
the prejudice of the misthinking.

But cool and candid people know that even the purest of human blessings are part alloy. The choice must always be made, if not of the lesser
evil, at least of the GREATER, not the PERFECT, good. All political power
may be misapplied and abused. Therefore, whenever power is to be conferred, it must first be decided whether such a power is necessary for the
public good. If the Constitution is ratified, we will need an effective guard
against the misuse of power.

Six Categories of Federal Power

5   To judge this subject, we will review the powers given the federal government. The classes of federal power relate to the following issues:

1. Security against foreign danger.
2. Regulation of interactions with foreign nations.
3. Maintain harmony and interactions among the States.
4. Miscellaneous objects of general utility.
5. Restraint of the States from certain injurious acts.
6. Provisions giving effectiveness to these powers.

1. Security Against Foreign Danger

6   The powers within the *first* class are: declaring war, granting letters of
marque, providing armies and fleets, regulating and using the militia, levying and borrowing money.

7 Security against foreign danger is a primary objective of civil society. It is an essential objective of the American Union. Therefore, the federal government must have the powers to keep the nation safe.

Declare War

8 Everyone agrees that the power to declare war is necessary. It doesn't need to be proved. The existing Confederation has this power.

Power to Raise Armies

9 Is the power to raise armies and equip fleets necessary? This is part of self-defense.

10, 11 But is an INDEFINITE POWER of raising TROOPS and fleets necessary? Should troops and fleets be maintained in PEACE? This is discussed in another place. The answer seems obvious. How can we limit the U.S. defensive force when the offensive force of other nations cannot be limited? If a federal Constitution could block the ambition of all other nations, then it might prudently limit its own government's defense.

In Peacetime, Military Prevents War

12 How can readiness for war during peacetime be safely prohibited unless we can also prohibit the preparations of every hostile nation?

Security can only be regulated by the means and danger of attack. It will always be determined by these rules and no others. It is vain to oppose constitutional barriers to self-preservation. If one nation keeps a disciplined army, ready to serve ambition or revenge, the peaceful nations within its reach must take corresponding precautions.

During the 15th century, Charles VII of France created a peacetime army. If the other European nations hadn't built up their defenses, long ago all of Europe would have worn the chains of one king. Now, if every nation except France disbanded its peacetime armies, the same thing might happen. The veteran Roman army was an overmatch for the undisciplined valor of all other nations, making her the mistress of the world.

Military Endangers Liberty

13 The liberties of Rome became the final victim of her military triumphs. And Europe has lost the few liberties it once had because of military establishments. Therefore, a standing army is dangerous, even if it is necessary. At its best, a peacetime military is inconvenient. At worst, it may be fatal. Therefore, it deserves extreme caution.

A wise nation doesn't rashly prohibit any resource that may become essential to its safety. At the same time, it will limit a resource that may damage liberties.

Union: Protects Against Foreign Army

14 The proposed Constitution is prudent. It keeps the States united. And dangerous military establishments won't be needed. America united—without a single soldier—does a better job of blocking foreign ambition than America disunited with a hundred thousand veterans ready for combat.

Geography and a great navy insulate Great Britain, which has saved its liberties. British rulers have never been able to create a large peacetime military establishment. The distance of the United States from the powerful nations of the world gives us the same security. As long as the States are united, a dangerous peacetime military will not be necessary.

However, the moment the Union breaks apart, things will change. The fears of the weaker States or ambition of the stronger States or Confederacies will set the same example in the New World as Charles VII did in the Old World. Instead of using our advantage as Great Britain has used hers, America would become a copy of the European continent. Standing armies and perpetual taxes would crush liberty.

The fortunes of a disunited America would be more disastrous than those of Europe. The sources of evil in Europe are confined by geography. No superior powers from other parts of the globe will ally with her rival nations, inflaming their mutual animosities. However, internal jealousies and wars would form only part of the problem in America. Another source of evil is the unique relationship between Europe and this part of the earth.

15 The consequences of disunion cannot be too strongly or too often stated. Every man who loves peace, every man who loves his country, every man who loves liberty, should always have it before his eyes. He should cherish the Union of America and highly value preserving it.

Military Expenses: British v. US

16 Limiting the term for military appropriations is a second precaution against the danger from standing armies. The Constitution has this precaution.

Opponents of the Constitution say Great Britain requires an annual vote of the legislature for military appropriations and the American Constitution has lengthened this critical period to two years. [Article 1, Section 8] Is this a fair comparison? Does the British Constitution limit military appropriations to one year? Does the American require two-year Congressional appropriations? No. The British Constitution has no limit on military appropriations. And the American Constitution limits military appropriations to no more than two years.

17 Although the British Constitution doesn't have a term limit for appropriating supplies to the army, in practice the parliament has limited it to one year. In Great Britain, the House of Commons has seven-year terms.

A small proportion of the people elect a great proportion of the members. The representatives corrupt the voters; the Crown corrupts the representatives. The representative body has the power to make appropriations to the army for any period of time beyond one year.

The House of Representatives will be elected FREELY by ALL CITIZENS every second year. Military appropriations are limited to TWO YEARS. Shouldn't we be suspicious of people who pretend that our representatives can't be trusted?

Union Prevents Multiple Armies

18 A bad cause seldom fails to betray itself. The opposition to the federal government is an example of this truth. And their most striking blunder is their attempt to enlist the support of people who have sincere concerns about a standing army.

This is an important subject. The Constitution is the best guard against this danger. If the States disunite, each separate State or Confederacy will have a standing army. These armies will endanger properties and liberties more than the size of the military necessary under a united and efficient government. A strong Constitution will preserve the Union and support national defense.

Navy Has Avoided Censure

19 A navy is necessary. As in Great Britain, a navy will be our primary security against danger from other countries. And, happily, while a navy will repel foreign invaders, usurpers in government can never turn it against our liberties.

New York Seacoast Vulnerable

20 People living along the Atlantic coast want naval protection. Until now, they have felt safe and their property has been safe from hostile adventurers. Their safety is not the result of the existing government's ability to protect its citizens. So far, they've just been lucky.

Virginia and Maryland are vulnerable. So is New York. Her seacoast is extensive. A very important part of the State is an island. A large navigable river penetrates the State for more than 50 leagues. [A league is about 3 miles.] It could easily become a hostage to a foreign enemy or the greedy demands of pirates and barbarians.

If a war breaks out in Europe, it will be a miracle if we escape attacks and plundering from Europe. In America's present condition, vulnerable States have no hope of help from the current phantom national government. And if the States used their resources for defense, the object to be protected would be almost totally consumed by the means of protecting it.

Regulating, Calling Forth Militia

21 Regulating and calling forth the militia has already been discussed and justified.

Import Duties Will Decline

22 The power to levy taxes and borrow money—the financial support for national defense—has also been examined. The extent and form in the Constitution is necessary.

Some people believe that the power of federal taxation should be limited to external taxation—taxes on articles imported from other countries. Of course, this will always be a valuable source of revenue. For a long time, in fact, it must be the primary source. And at this moment, it is essential.

However, import tax revenue will vary as the amount and the kind of imports vary. And these variations won't correspond with the growth of our population, which is the general measure of how much money the government will need. As long as agriculture continues to be the only field of labor, as the population increases, the importation of manufactured goods will increase. As the population grows, American manufacturers will employ hands not needed for agriculture and imported manufactured goods will decrease. Eventually, manufacturers may import raw materials that will be made into articles for exportation. As raw material importation overtakes the importation of finished goods, the government will want to encourage imports, not discourage them with import taxes. A good government should remember these cycles and be able to handle them.

Tax Clause Not Unlimited Power

23 The proposed Constitution defines the federal government's taxation power. It says: "The Congress shall have the power to lay and collect taxes, duties, imposts, and excises, to pay the debts, and provide for the common defense and general welfare of the United States." [Article 1, Section 8] Some people have attacked the language that defines the taxation power, saying it amounts to an unlimited license to use any and every power that may be alleged to be necessary for the common defense or general welfare.

Stooping to such a misconstruction proves how far these writers will reach to find objections to the Constitution.

24, 25 If "to raise money for the general welfare" was the only definition of Congressional powers in the Constitution, the critics might have a reason for the objection. However, the specific congressional powers are listed after the general phrase. Nothing is more natural than to first use a general phrase and then to explain and qualify it by a recital of particulars.

Constitution Copies "Articles"

26 The objection seems even odder because the language in the Constitution appears to be a copy of the Articles of Confederation. The objective of forming a Union among the States, as described in Article Three, is

"their common defense, security of their liberties, and mutual and general welfare." Article eight says: "All charges of war and all other expenses that shall be incurred for the common defense or general welfare, and allowed by the United States in Congress, shall be defrayed out of a common treasury," etc. Similar language again occurs in Article Nine.

If we interpret these articles in the Articles of Confederation by the rules objectors have used on the new Constitution, the existing Congress has the power to legislate about everything. But what if Congress disregarded the specifications that define and limit the general expressions and exercised an unlimited power of providing for the common defense and general welfare? Would the people making the objections have employed the same reasoning in justification of Congress as they now make against the Convention. How difficult it is for error to escape its own condemnation! PUBLIUS

Number 42: 2. Regulate International Relationships

3. Provide Harmony, Relationships Among States

The federal government's *second* class of powers regulates how the country deals with foreign nations. The federal government will:
- make treaties
- send and receive ambassadors, ministers, and consuls
- define and punish piracies, felonies on the high seas and against the law of nations
- regulate foreign commerce (after 1808, it may prohibit the importation of slaves; until then, it will charge a duty of ten dollars per head to discourage such importations)

2   It is essential that the federal government have this class of powers. If we are to be one nation, other nations must see us as one nation.

Treaties, Ambassadors, Consuls

3   The federal government needs the powers to make treaties, send and receive ambassadors. Both are in the Articles of Confederation, with two differences. States cannot block treaties. And the Articles only mentions "ambassadors," the highest rank of public ministers; but Congress has used lower levels of ministers, including sending and receiving consuls.

4   Under the Articles, admitting foreign consuls into the United States may be part of the power of making commercial treaties. When no commercial treaties exist, putting American consuls in foreign countries *may* be covered under the authority of article nine of the Confederation "to appoint... such...civil officers necessary for managing the general affairs of the United States."

However, the Articles of Confederation do not mention admitting consuls into the United States, when no treaty mentions them. The new Constitution corrects this omission. It is a small change. However, the tiniest provisions become important when they prevent the need or pretext for gradual, unobserved usurpations of power.

Defects in the Articles have forced Congress to violate its authorities. The new Constitution corrects both small and large defects in the Articles of Confederation.

Piracies, Felonies on High Seas

5   Another improvement is the national government's power to define and punish piracies and felonies committed on the high seas, and offenses against the law of nations.

The Articles do not mention the law of nations. Consequently, actions by one State could draw the entire Confederation into problems with foreign nations.

On the subject of piracies and felonies, the Articles only creates courts to try these offenses. The definition of "piracies" might be left to the law of nations, even though most municipal codes define them.

A definition of "felonies on the high seas" is required. The term "felony" has many definitions. The common law and statute law of England give it various meanings. And no two States define it in the same way. For uniformity, therefore, the power to define "felonies" is absolutely necessary and proper.

Commerce, Federal Jurisdiction

6   We have already discussed why the regulation of foreign commerce is a federal responsibility.

Slave Trade Abolished in 1808

7   We wish that the Constitution banned the importation of slaves. Instead, the power to ban it is postponed until 1808.

For a long time, this traffic has been called barbarous. It is a great point in favor of humanity that in 20 years it might be banned forever within these States. During that period, the federal government will discourage it. The majority of the Union already prohibits it. And it can be totally abolished if the few States that allow the unnatural traffic agree to prohibit it. It would be happy for the unfortunate Africans if Europe also had a plan to prohibit it in twenty years!

8   Some opponents use this clause to object to the Constitution. One side says it is a criminal toleration of an illicit practice. The other says it was put in to prevent voluntary and beneficial emigrations from Europe to America. I mention these misconstructions only to show the manner and spirit of some people opposing the proposed government.

3. Provide Harmony Among States

9 The *third* class of powers provide for harmony among the States.
10 This classification could include the restraints on State authority and some judicial power. But the limits on State authority are a separate class and judicial powers will be examined when we discuss the structure and organization of the government. I will confine myself to a brief review of the remaining powers under this third description:

- regulate commerce among the States and the Indian tribes,
- coin and regulate the value of money,
- punish counterfeiting coins and securities of the United States,
- fix the standard of weights and measures,
- make a uniform rule of naturalization and uniform laws of bankruptcy,
- prescribe the way that public acts, records, and judicial proceedings of each State will be proved and the effect they will have in other States,
- establish post offices and post roads.

Regulate Commerce among States

11 The existing Confederacy doesn't have the power to regulate commerce between the States. Without this provision, the power to regulate foreign commerce is pointless.

Some noncommercial States must import and export through other States. If they could, States would charge import and export taxes on merchandise and material passing through their State. This would create animosities and probably end in violence.

Commercial States' desire to collect indirect taxes from their uncommercial neighbors must seem both unfair and politically inexpedient. It would be a poor political decision. Resentment and self-interest would make the people who have to pay the State duties find longer routes without the added taxes for their trade. However, as a State makes the decision to tax goods that travel through it, the people who want immediate revenue will drown out the people who rationally argue that it is a bad political decision. The mild voice of reason, pleading the cause of a larger interest, is drowned out by the clamors of impatient avarice for immediate and immoderate gain.

12 The experience in other countries shows that the federal government needs to be able to regulate trade between the States.

In Switzerland, each canton [state] must allow merchandise passage through its jurisdiction into other cantons without additional tolls.

A law in Germany forbids the princes and states from charging tolls or customs on bridges, rivers, or passages without the consent of the emperor and the diet [legislature]. However, this law, like many others in the Germany, hasn't been followed, producing the problems predicted here.

In the Union of the Netherlands, states must get permission to charge imposts that are disadvantageous to neighboring states.

Regulate Commerce: Indian Tribes

13 The provision in the Articles of Confederation for regulating commerce with the Indian tribes is obscure and contradictory. It says that the federal power to regulate trade is limited to Indians who are not members of any State, without violating the rights of any State within its own borders. But federal councils haven't determined which Indians are members of a State and which are not. And how can an external authority regulate trade with Indians, who live in a State but are not members of the State, without intruding on the internal rights of a State?

In several areas, the Articles of Confederation tries to do impossible things. One is giving the Union partial sovereignty while giving the States complete sovereignty. This subverts a mathematical axiom: it takes away a part, yet lets the whole remain.

Coin Money, Regulate Value of Currency, Punish Counterfeiters

14 The federal government will coin money, regulate its value, and regulate the value of foreign coin. The Articles of Confederation doesn't mention the regulation of foreign currency. Currently, Congress only regulates the value of coin *struck* by its own authority or the States. If the different States valued foreign currency differently, uniformity in the *value* of the currency might be destroyed.

15 The federal government determines the value of currency and public securities. Therefore, it should have the authority to punish counterfeiters.

Regulate Weights and Measures

16 The regulation of weight and measures is transferred from the Articles of Confederation and is based on similar reasons as the power of regulating coin.

National Naturalization Rule

17 Our current naturalization rules are confusing. The fourth Article of the Confederacy declares "that the *free inhabitants* of each of these States, paupers, vagabonds, and fugitives from justice excepted, shall be entitled to all privileges and immunities of *free citizens* in the several States; and *the people* of each State shall, in every other, enjoy all the privileges of trade and commerce," etc.

Why were the terms *free inhabitants* used in one part, *free citizens* in another, and *people* in another? And the meaning of the phrase "all the privileges of trade and commerce" is not clear.

It also seems to say that when people defined as *free inhabitants* of one State—but who are not citizens of that State—travel to a different State, they have all the privileges of *free citizens*. In other words, they may have greater privileges than in their home State. If the term "inhabitants" was changed to "citizens," the difficulty would only be diminished, not removed. Each State would retain the very improper power to naturalize aliens in every other State.

For example, let's say that in one State a short-term resident has all criteria for citizenship but another State requires more qualifications. An alien, therefore, only has to first reside in the former to elude the greater qualifications in the latter. Thus, preposterously, the law of the first State is dominant to the law of the second, within the jurisdiction of the second State.

We have escaped embarrassment on this subject only by good luck. Several States prohibit resident aliens from both the rights of citizenship and the privileges of residence. What would have happened if such persons had become citizens under the laws of another State, then demanded their rights to both residency and citizenship within the State that prohibit it? The consequences would probably have been very serious.

The new Constitution corrects this problem. The federal government will establish a uniform rule of naturalization throughout the United States.

Uniform Bankruptcy Laws

18 The power to establish uniform bankruptcy laws is closely connected with the regulation of commerce. It will prevent many frauds, where people or property may go into different States. Its importance will probably not be questioned.

Validity of Public Records

19 The federal power to determine how public acts, records, and judicial proceedings of each State will be proved, and the effect they will have in other States, is clearly a valuable improvement on the Articles of Confederation. This Constitutional power will be most beneficial on the borders of contiguous States where the effects liable to justice may be suddenly and secretly changed, in any stage of the process, within a foreign jurisdiction.

Post Roads Help Commerce in States

20 The power of establishing post-roads is a harmless power and if managed well it may produce a great public convenience, helping interstate commerce.

PUBLIUS

Number 43: 4. Miscellaneous Federal Powers

The *fourth* class of powers includes:

Copyrights, Patents

2   A power "to promote the progress of science and useful arts by securing for limited times to authors and inventors the exclusive right to their writings and discoveries." [Article 1, Sec 8]

3   This is a useful power. In Great Britain, the copyright of authors is a right of common law. The right to benefit from their inventions seems to belong to inventors. In both cases, the public good coincides with the claims of individuals. The States cannot effectively provide for either of these cases.

Federal Capital

4   "To exercise exclusive legislation in all cases whatsoever over such district (not exceeding ten miles square) as may, by cession of particular States and the acceptance of Congress, become the seat of the Government of the United States, and to exercise like authority over all places purchased by the consent of the legislature of the State in which the same shall be, for the erection of forts, magazines, arsenals, dockyards, and other needful buildings." [Article 1, Sec 8]

5   The seat of government must be independent. If it was located in a State, that State might influence national councils. Federal money will improve the capital. This public trust should not be left in the hands of a single State. And it would be nearly impossible to ever move the capital, which would further limit its independence.

The size of this federal district is limited. The State ceding the land for this use must consent. The State will make a compact with the federal government, assuring the rights of the citizens of the district. The inhabitants will have enough inducements to become willing parties to the cession. An elected municipal legislature will exercise authority over them. The legislature of the State and the people who live in the ceded part will agree to the cession and ratify the Constitution. Therefore, this seems to cover every objection.

Other Federal Property

6   The federal government must have authority over forts, military depots, arsenals, dockyards, etc. Public money will be spent on such places. The property and equipment stored there should not be under State authority. These are important to the security of the entire Union and shouldn't depend on one State. However, each State where they are located must agree.

Treason: Definition, Punishment

7 "Treason against the United States shall consist only in levying war against them, or in adhering to their enemies, giving them aid and comfort. No person shall be convicted of treason unless on the testimony of two witnesses to the same overt act, or on confession in open court.

"The Congress shall have power to declare the punishment of treason, but no attainder of treason shall work corruption of blood or forfeiture except during the life of the person attainted." [Article 3, Section 3]

8 Since treason may be committed against the United States, the United States should have the authority to punish it. However, some people have created new, artificial treasons, and used them as an excuse for malicious vengeance. The Constitution erects a barrier against this danger. It defines treason. It states the proof necessary for conviction. And Congress may not extend the punishment beyond the guilty person.

Creation of New States

9 "New States may be admitted by the Congress into this Union; but no new State shall be formed or erected within the jurisdiction of any other State; nor any State be formed by the junction of two or more States or parts of States, without the consent of the legislatures of the States concerned as well as of the Congress." [Article 4, Sec 3]

10 The Articles of Confederation doesn't mention the formation of new States. Canada was to be admitted. And other *colonies*, which probably means other British colonies, could be admitted at the discretion of nine States. [Article Eleven] This omission had been inconvenient. And it has led Congress into an assumption of power. The new system corrects the defect.

The federal authority and the States concerned must approve the formation of new States. This is an appropriate precaution. New States may not be formed by dividing a State without its consent; this quiets the jealousy of the larger States. There is a similar precaution against joining States without their consent.

Congress Regulates U. S. Territory

11 "The Congress shall have the power to dispose of and make all needful rules and regulations respecting the territory or other property belonging to the United States; and nothing in this Constitution shall be so construed as to prejudice any claims of the United States or of any particular State." [Article 4, Section 3]

12 This provision is probably necessary because of jealousies and questions about the Western territory.

Republican Government in Each State

13 "The United States shall guarantee to every State in this Union a republican form of government, and shall protect each of them against invasions, and on application of the legislature, or of the executive (when the legislature cannot be convened) against domestic violence." [Article 4, Section 4]

14 In a republican confederacy, the federal government needs the authority to defend against aristocrats, monarchs or dictators taking over any part of it. The Union has the right to insist that a republican government be *substantially* maintained.

A federal coalition of States is more successful if the State governments are founded on the same principles. Montesquieu says that "the confederate republic of Germany" has both "free cities and petty states, subject to different princes..." He says Germany is "more imperfect than Holland and Switzerland . . . Greece was undone," he adds, "as soon as the king of Macedon obtained a seat among the Amphictyons." In the latter case, a large army and the king of the new confederacy influenced events.

Is this precaution needed? If the federal government's intervention isn't needed, this Constitutional provision will be superfluous. But who can say what the States might try doing, or how ambitious State leaders or foreign powers may influence them?

Can the federal government change the State governments without the States agreeing? The national government only *guarantees* the republican form of government; this assumes a preexisting republican form. Therefore, the existing republican forms are guaranteed by the federal Constitution. If the States choose to substitute a different republican form, they have the right to do so and to claim the federal guarantee. The only restriction is that they shall not exchange a republican for an anti-republican Constitution.

States Protected Against Invasion

15 Every part of a society should be protected against invasion. The Constitution protects each State against the ambitious and vindictive actions of more powerful States. The weaker States will like this clause.

Union Protection: Internal Violence

16 Protection against internal violence is also proper. Even among the Swiss cantons, which are not really under one government, provision is made for this. And mutual aid is frequently requested and given. A recent, well-known event here has warned us to be prepared for similar emergencies.

17 At first glance, it might not seem right that in a republic, a minority can over-throw a majority government. But we must look at reality, not a theory. Couldn't a majority of a State, especially a small State, form a con-

spiracy and take over a State, just as it could happen in a county or city within a State? If the State authority should protect the local officials in the latter case, then shouldn't the federal authority, in the former, support the State authority?

Besides, parts of the State constitutions are interwoven with the federal Constitution. A violent blow to one will wound the other.

The federal government will rarely intervene in States, unless a very large number of people are involved. In such cases, it is better if federal power stops the violence than to have a bloody contest. The right to intervene will generally prevent the necessity of using it.

Strength May Not be on Ethical Side

18 Are force and right always on the same side in a republic? Could a minority of people have more money, talents and experience—or secret aid from foreign powers—to make it a superior military force? In actual battles, the larger number of citizens doesn't assure victory. A minority of CITIZENS can become a majority of PEOPLE by adding alien residents, mercenaries, or people in the State without voting rights.

I have not mentioned the unhappy group of people in some of the States who are considered below the level of men. During times of civil violence, they may become men and give superior strength to the side they join.

Other States Act as Impartial Judges

19 Let's say two violent factions are tearing a State to pieces. Would representatives of States not heated by the local battles make good umpires? They could act as impartial judges and friends. It would be wonderful if all free governments enjoyed such a remedy for its problems. And if an equally effective project could be established for universal peace!
21 Montesquieu says that if "a popular insurrection happens in one of the States, the others are able to stop it. Should abuses creep into one part, they are reformed by those that remain sound."
20 What if an insurrection arises in all the States? What if it has a superior force but not a constitutional right? This will probably not happen. And if it does, it's something that we can't plan for in advance. The federal Constitution reduces the risk of a calamity for which no possible constitution can provide a cure.

Confederacy Debts Valid

22 "All debts contracted and engagements entered into, before the adoption of this Constitution, shall be as valid against the United States under this Constitution, as under the Confederation." [Article 6]
23 This statement may have been put into the Constitution to satisfy foreign creditors of the United States. Some creditors might worry that a

change in our political system has the magical effect of dissolving our moral obligations.

24 One criticism of the Constitution is that the money owed to the United States should be included, as well as the country's debts. And in the spirit that usually characterizes little critics, the omission has been magnified into a plot against national rights. Most people know that, by their nature, debts are reciprocal. If they are valid on one side, they are valid on the other side. The article is a declaration. By establishing the principle in one case, it applies to every case.

Amending the Constitution

25 Article Five says that three fourths of the States are needed to ratify amendments with two exceptions only.

26 Experience will suggest how the Constitution should be altered. An extremely easy amendment process would make the Constitution too mutable. An extremely difficult process would preserve the faults discovered within it. Either the federal or the State governments can originate the amendment process.

One exception, referring to equality in the Senate, is probably a safeguard to the remaining sovereignty of the States, which have equal representation in one branch of the legislature. The States that worried about equality probably insisted on it.

The other exception must have been admitted on the same considerations that produced the privilege defended by it.

Ratification by Nine States

27 "The ratification of the Conventions of nine States shall be sufficient for the establishment of this constitution between the States so ratifying the same." [Article 7]

28 Only the people can validate the Constitution. If all thirteen States had to ratify the Constitution, the essential interests of the entire Union would be exposed to the caprice or corruption of a single State.

29 Two questions present themselves:

1. What is the principle that allows the new Constitution to replace the Articles of Confederation without the consent of all thirteen States?

2. What relationship will exist between the nine or more States ratifying the Constitution and the remaining few who do not ratify it?

30 The first question is answered by saying that it is absolutely necessary. Self-preservation is a primary law of nature and God. All political institutions are created to keep people safe and able to pursue happiness. When a political system fails to fulfill those goals, it must be sacrificed.

We may also find an answer within the compact itself. In many of the States, only the legislature ratified the Articles. This is one of its defects.

Reciprocity requires that its obligation on the other States should be reduced to the same standard.

When a legislature makes a compact with another sovereign state, the agreement has no more validity than a treaty between the parties. Treaties are only mutual conditions of each other. A breach of any one article in a treaty is a breach of the whole treaty. A breach committed by either party releases the others. They may pronounce the compact violated and void. And the Articles of Confederation have been violated in many ways.

Hopeful Relationships Will Remain Good

31 The second question is also delicate. We hope that all States ratify the Constitution.

No political relationship will continue to exist between the assenting and dissenting States. But the moral relationships will remain. Claims of justice on both sides must be fulfilled. The rights of humanity must always be duly and mutually respected. Hopefully, considerations of a common interest and, above all, the remembrance of the endearing scenes past, will urge moderation on one side and prudence on the other.

PUBLIUS

Number 44:   5. Provisions Restricting State Authority

6. Provisions Giving Efficacy to All the Rest

The *fifth* class of provisions restricts State authority:

2 "No State shall enter into any treaty, alliance, or confederation; grant letters of marque and reprisal; coin money; emit bills of credit; make anything but gold and silver coin a tender in payment of debts; pass any bill of attainder, ex post facto law, or law impairing the obligation of contracts, or grant any title of nobility." [Article 1, section 10]

Treaties, Alliances,

3 The Articles of Confederation also prohibits treaties, alliances, and confederations.

Letters of Marque

Under the Articles, States could grant letters of marque after war is declared. In the new Constitution, they must be obtained from the federal government. Uniformity in foreign policy justifies this change. The States are responsible to the nation; the nation is responsible for the conduct of every State.

States Can't Coin Money

4 The States cannot coin money. The federal government regulates the alloy and value of coins. Allowing States to manufacture coins has created two problems: many expensive mints and a diversity of shape, size, and

weight of coins. State mints prevented the inconvenience of transporting gold and silver to the central mint. Establishing local mints under the national authority can solve this problem.

No State Bills of Credit

5 Prohibiting State bills of credit [paper money] is just and promotes public prosperity. Since the peace, paper money has eroded the confidence so necessary between man and man, in public councils, in industry, and in the republican government. It has become an enormous debt that the issuing States will not be able to pay off for a long time.

States are denied the power to regulate coin for good reasons. For the same reasons, they should not create paper money. If every State could regulate the value of its coin, every State could have a different currency, hurting interstate commerce. If a State retroactively changed the relative value of its money, it would injure the citizens of other States, kindling animosities among the States themselves. The citizens of foreign nations might also suffer, discrediting and embroiling the Union by the indiscretion of a single State could discredit the entire Union.

Bills of Attainder, *Ex Post Facto* Laws

6 Bills of attainder, *ex post facto* laws, and laws impairing the obligation of contracts contradict the social compact and every principle of sound legislation. Some State constitutions expressly prohibit bills of attainder and *ex post facto* laws; the spirit of the State constitutions prohibits them all.

However, experience teaches us to create additional barriers against these dangers. Therefore, the Constitution adds this protection of personal security and private rights. Fluctuating policy often directs public councils. Americans are angry with laws that affect personal rights and laws that profit speculators while snaring the less-informed citizens. One improper law is just the first link of a long chain of improper laws. Each one grows out of the effects of the preceding. Reform is needed. Speculations about public measures must end. General prudence and industry must be encouraged.

Nobility Titles

The prohibition against titles of nobility is copied from the Articles of Confederation and needs no comment.

Taxes, Troops, Foreign Compacts

7 "No State shall, without the consent of Congress, lay any imposts or duties on imports or exports, except what may be absolutely necessary for executing its inspection laws; and the net produce of all duties and imposts, laid by any State on imports or exports, shall be for the use of the

Treasury of the United States; and all such laws shall be subject to the revision and control of the Congress.

"No State shall, without the consent of Congress, lay any duty of tonnage, keep troops or ships of war in time of peace, enter into any agreement or compact with another State or with a foreign power, or engage in war, unless actually invaded or in such imminent danger as will not admit of delay." [Article 1, section 10]

8 The federal government should regulate trade. The States may charge a reasonable inspection fee but the federal government can block any abuse of this discretion.

The remaining items in this clause are either obvious or have been previously discussed. Nothing else needs to be said about them.

6. Provisions Giving Efficacy to All the Other Powers

9 The *sixth* and last class consists of the powers and provisions that give efficacy to all the rest. These fall into four categories:

A. Make necessary and proper laws
B. Federal laws supreme
C. Oath to support Constitution
D. Executive, judicial federal powers

A. Make Necessary and Proper Laws

10 "To make all laws which shall be necessary and proper for carrying into execution the foregoing powers, and all other powers vested by this Constitution in the Government of the United States, or in any department or officer thereof." [Article 1, section 8]

11 This clause has been vigorously attacked. Yet on objective investigation, no part appears more invulnerable. Without the *substance* of this power, the whole Constitution would be a dead letter. Therefore, people who object to it must mean that the *form* is improper. Is there a better way to phrase it?

12 The Constitution could have approached this subject four ways:

1) Copy Article Two of the Articles; prohibit any power not expressly mentioned.
2) Try to list every power that is "necessary and proper."
3) Try to list every power that is not "necessary and proper."
4) Remain silent on the subject; leave the definition of "necessary and proper" powers to interpretation and inference.

1) Adopting Article Two of Confederation

[Articles of Confederation, Article Two: "Each State retains its sovereignty, freedom, and independence, and every power, jurisdiction, and right, which is not by this Confederation expressly delegated to the United States in Congress assembled."]

13 If the convention had copied the Second Article of the Confederation, the new Congress would have the same problem as the current Congress. Should the term *"expressly"* be interpreted strictly or loosely? A strict interpretation would strip the federal government authority and Congress could betray the public interests by doing nothing. A loose interpretation would destroy the restriction: Congress could violate the Constitution by using powers that are necessary and proper but are not *expressly* granted.

2) List All Necessary & Proper Powers

14 If the convention had tried to list every necessary and proper power, it would have meant listing every law on every subject in the Constitution, including future laws.

3) List Powers *Not* Necessary & Proper

15 Trying to list every power not necessary or proper to execute the general powers is also unrealistic. And would create another objection— every defect in the list would be the same as granting an authority. If they had listed only a few exceptions, the unnecessary and improper powers not included in the list would be less forcibly excepted than if no partial list existed.

4) No "Necessary And Proper" Clause

16 What if the Constitution had no "necessary and proper" clause? The federal government would still have all the powers that are required to execute the general powers. It is an axiom of law and reason that whatever the goal, the means are authorized: Wherever a general power is authorized, the specific powers needed to reach the goal are included. Therefore, every current objection to the clause would remain. And it would create a real problem: The "necessary and proper" clause can be used on critical occasions to raise doubt about the essential powers of the Union.

If Congress Oversteps Its Authority

17 What will happen if Congress misconstrues the "necessary and proper" clause and exercises powers not warranted by its true meaning? I answer, the same thing will happen as will occur if they misconstrue or enlarge any power vested in them. The same thing as if the State legislatures violated their respective constitutional authorities.

First, the power usurpation will only succeed if the executive and judiciary departments, which execute and interpret legislative acts, support it.

And in the last resort, the people will remedy the problem; they can elect more faithful representatives, who can annul the acts of the usurpers. This remedy may work better against the unconstitutional acts of the federal than the State legislatures, simply because every federal usurpation will invade the rights of a State. The States will notice deviations, sound the alarm, and use their influence to change federal representatives. There is no such intermediate body between the State legislatures and the people. Violations of the State constitutions are more likely to remain unnoticed and unredressed.

B. Federal Laws Supreme

18 "This Constitution and the laws of the United States which shall be made in pursuance thereof and all treaties made, or which shall be made, under the authority of the United States, shall be the supreme law of the land; and the judges in every State shall be bound thereby, anything in the Constitution or laws of any State to the contrary notwithstanding." [Article 6]

19 Adversaries of the Constitution attack this provision. But without it, the Constitution would have been very defective. What would happen if the federal Constitution confirmed the supremacy of the State constitutions by a saving clause in their favor?

20 First. Any authorities contained in the proposed Constitution that exceed those listed in the Articles of Confederation would be annulled. The new Congress would be as impotent as its predecessors.

21 Second. Some of the State constitutions do not expressly recognize the Confederacy's existing powers. A statement in the Constitution of the States' supremacy could create challenges of every power in the proposed Constitution.

22 Third. The State constitutions differ from each other. A treaty or national law important to all the States might contradict some State constitutions. Consequently, it would be valid in some States and have no effect in others.

23 In the end, the world would have seen a system of government founded on an inversion of the fundamental principles of all government. The authority of the whole Union would have been subordinate to the States, like a monster whose individual parts with different goals directing its head.

C. Oath to Support Constitution

24 "The Senators and Representatives before mentioned, and the members of the several State Legislatures, and all executive and judicial officers, both of the United States and of the several States, shall be bound by oath or affirmation, to support this Constitution; but no religious test shall ever be required as a qualification to any office or public trust under the United States." [Article 6]

25 Why must State officials support the federal Constitution? Officers of the United States don't take a similar oath in favor of the State constitutions.

26 There are several reasons. I'll give one. Federal officials will not be agents of State constitutions. However, State officials will be essential

agents of the federal Constitution. The election of the President and Senate will depend on the State legislatures. State officers will probably conduct the election of the House of Representatives, according to the laws of the States.

D. Executive, Judicial Federal Powers

27 The federal executive and judiciary might be discussed here as constitutional provisions that give efficacy to the federal powers. However, they will be examined in another place.

All Federal Powers *Are* Necessary/Proper

28 We have studied all the power given to the federal government by the proposed Constitution. No part of the power is unnecessary or improper for accomplishing the necessary objectives of the Union.

The question of whether this amount of power should be granted or not evolves into another question: whether or not a government that meets the needs of the Union should be established. Or, in other words, whether the Union itself should be preserved.

PUBLIUS

State Powers

Number 45: Federal Powers Not Dangerous to States

None of the powers transferred to the federal government is unnecessary or improper. But will the whole group of powers be dangerous to State authority?

Union Benefits vs. State Powers

2 To fulfill its duties, the federal government needs a certain amount of power. Opponents of the Constitution haven't talked about whether the federal government has the right amount of power. Instead, they say the amount of federal power in the Constitution may hurt the State governments.

Is the Union essential for the security of the American people? Does it protect us from foreign danger? Does it protect us from wars among the States? Does it guard against violent and oppressive factions that threaten liberty and the poisoning effect of military bases? In a word, is the Union essential to the happiness of the American people? The proposed federal powers are needed to meet the Union's objectives. It is preposterous to argue against a federal government by saying it may make the State governments less important.

We fought the American Revolution. We formed the American Confederacy. Thousands of people spilled their precious blood. And we spent the hard-earned money of millions. Did we do this so Americans can enjoy peace, liberty, and safety? Or did we do it for the State governments, so they can have power and sovereignty? The Old World doctrine said that people were made to serve kings, not kings to serve the people. Should we follow the same doctrine—in another shape—in the New World? Should we sacrifice the people's happiness to the States?

No form of government has any intrinsic value. A government's value is judged by how it fulfills the public good and meets the needs of the people. If the Constitution harmed public happiness, I would say: Reject the plan. If the Union hurt public happiness, I would say: Abolish the Union. In a similar manner, when State sovereignty is incompatible with the happiness of the people, every good citizen should cry out: Let the former be sacrificed to the latter.

No Danger from Federal Government

3,4 These Papers show that the federal government will not be fatal to the State governments. It is more likely that the large number of State governments will disturb the balance. The history of confederacies shows that states tend to plunder the federal government's authority. And federal governments are unable to defend themselves.

Most historical governments were very different from our proposed government. Therefore, we cannot learn much about the relationship between a federal government and state governments. However, the States keep much of their sovereignty under the Constitution. Let's look at some historical examples:

In the Achaean league and Lycia Confederacy, the federal governments had power similar to the proposed Constitution. But neither degenerated into one consolidated government. On the contrary, one of them was ruined because the federal authority couldn't prevent the discord and, eventually, disunion. And in both cases, the external pressures pushing the parts together were more powerful than in our case.

Feudal System: Local Bonds

5 In the feudal system, the people felt hostility for the local sovereigns [barons] and were often sympathetic to the general sovereign [monarch]. Yet the local sovereigns usually prevailed when the monarch tried to take more power. If external dangers hadn't forced national harmony and, more importantly, if the people had liked their local sovereigns, today there would be as many independent countries as there were formerly feudatory barons instead of a few great European kingdoms.

State Governments' Advantages

6 The State governments will have several advantages over the federal government. They will need to depend on one another. Local politicians will have personal influence. The States retain many powers. The people will be more likely to support their local government. And the States will watch each other and want to limit the powers and actions of other States.

7 The State governments are essential parts of the federal government. The federal government is not essential to the operation of the State governments.

The State legislatures are an essential part of the presidential election. The State legislatures will elect federal Senators. Even though the people elect the House of Representatives, the State legislators will influence their decision. Thus, each elected federal official will owe his political existence, more or less, to the State governments. Consequently, they will feel dependent towards them.

On the other side, the federal government will not appointment State officials. And federal officials will have little, if any, local influence.

More People Work for States

8 Under the Constitution, the State governments will have more employees than the federal government. Consequently, federal employees will have less personal influence.

State and local officials—State legislators, governors, judges, militia officers, county and city officers—will know all types of people. They will have more influence than the people employed by the federal government. If we compare the number of State-appointed militia officers with the military and navy officers in a permanent federal military, the States have a decisive advantage.

Both the federal and State governments will have tax collectors but there will be fewer federal tax collectors. State tax collectors will be spread throughout the country. And State officers will often collect federal taxes. However, if the federal government appoints separate tax collectors, every district with one federal collector will have no less than thirty or more State officers.

Indeed, it is extremely probable that State officers, especially judges, will also serve under the authority of the Union.

Federal Powers Limited; States Unlimited

9 The Constitution gives the federal government a few defined powers. The remaining State powers are numerous and indefinite.

Federal powers will be largely external: war, peace, negotiation, and foreign commerce. (Taxation will be the primary federal power over foreign commerce.) The State powers extend to the daily concerns of the people: their lives, liberties, property, internal order, improvement, and the prosperity of the State.

War vs. Peacetime Influence

10 The federal government's operations will be most extensive and important in times of war and danger. The State governments will be most important in times of peace. Since times of war will probably be small compared to peacetime, the State governments will enjoy another advantage over the federal government. Indeed, as the national defense improves, there will be less danger that the federal government will become more important than the State governments.

Invigorates Powers in Articles

11 The new Constitution adds few NEW POWERS to the Union. Instead, it invigorates its ORIGINAL POWERS.

The regulation of commerce is a new power. But few people seem to oppose it.

The Articles of Confederation gives Congress the powers relating to war and peace, armies and fleets, treaties and finance. The proposed Constitution doesn't enlarge these powers. It substitutes a more effective way to administer them.

The taxation method is changed. Currently, Congress may REQUIRE MONEY from the States for the common defense and general welfare. Under the Constitution, the future Congress will require the same amount from individual citizens. And the citizens will be no more bound than the States have been to pay their taxes.

If the States had paid or could have been forced to pay with as peaceable a means as may be used with success towards a single person, the State governments would have kept their constitutional powers and not consolidated. To maintain that this would have happened is the same as saying that State governments cannot exist within any system that accomplishes the essential purposes of the Union.

PUBLIUS

Number 46: Federal vs. State Government Authority

Will the people prefer and support the federal government or the State governments? Both will depend on the citizens of the United States. (I will prove this at another time.).

The federal and State governments are agents and trustees of the people. They have different powers to fulfill different purposes. Opponents of the Constitution seem to have forgotten the people. They view the federal and State governments as rivals and enemies that will want to usurp each other's authorities.

These gentlemen are making an error. The ultimate authority resides in the people alone. Whether either side increases its area of power at the expense of the other will depend on the sentiments and sanction of their common constituents, not which is more ambitious or where it is located.

Attachment of People to States

2   The people's first and most natural attachment will be to their State governments. More people in the State will be employees of the State governments than the federal government. The States will regulate most domestic issues and provide most personal services. The people will be more familiar with State issues. More people will have friendship, family, and party ties with State officials, strengthening the popular bias towards the State.

3   Experience confirms this bias. Up until now, administration of the federal government has been very defective. During the war, the federal government was as important as it will ever be in the future. It was protecting and acquiring everything important to the people. Nevertheless, the people were only enthusiastic about the early Congress for only a short time. Then their attention and attachment returned to their own State government. The federal administration never became a popular idol .

Some people oppose enlarging the federal government's powers. Many of them are men who want to use their fellow citizens' natural tendency to support local politicians to increase their power.

Federal Powers Limited

4   In the future, people may prefer the federal government over the State governments. However, the federal government must prove it is better administered than the State governments for this to happen. The people should place their confidence where they discover it is most appropriate. But even in that case, the State governments would have little to fear. The small group of federal powers is limited to powers that the federal government can do a better job administrating.

Resources: Federal vs. States

5   How will the federal and State governments be able to resist and frustrate the measures of each other?

States Influence Congress

6   The federal government will depend more on the States then the State governments will depend on the federal. Both the State and federal governments will depend on the people, who tend to be more loyal to the State governments. The State governments clearly have the advantage.

The State governments will have another important advantage. Because federal officials come from the States, they will generally favor the States. But State officials will rarely feel a bias in favor of the federal government. The federal Congress will feel the effect of State loyalties more often than a national spirit will prevail in State legislatures.

When State legislatures make errors, it is often because members make their decisions based on the best interests of their home county or district instead of best interests of the entire State. If State legislators don't focus on the collective welfare of their State, how can we imagine that federal legislators will focus on the prosperity of the entire Union and the dignity of the national government? Instead, federal legislators will probably focus on local objectives. Prejudices, interests, and pursuits within the individual States will often influence decisions, rather than national prosperity and happiness. Members of Congress have often acted like State partisans rather than impartial guardians of a common interest. National interests have suffered on a hundred occasions from inappropriate attention to State prejudices, interests, and views.

I believe the new federal government will embrace a more enlarged policy than the existing government has pursued. However, it will be disinclined to invade the rights of the individual State governments. States will not have the same attitude towards the federal government.

State Powers: Number 46

States can Block Encroachments

7   The States can defeat encroachments by the federal government. However, if the federal government doesn't like a State law, the State law goes into effect. If the federal government opposes the law or sends federal officers to stop it, the federal response would inflame the zeal of all parties on the side of the State. The evil couldn't be prevented or repaired, if at all, without using force, a method that must always be resorted to with reluctance and difficulty.

On the other hand, States can easily oppose unpopular federal laws. The people may refuse to cooperate with federal officials. State courts and legislatures would expose the difficulties. Large States could effectively block the law from going into effect. Adjoining States could present obstructions that the federal government would not be willing to confront.

States Fight Federal Usurpations

8   Many States would oppose federal encroachments on States. Every State government would support the common cause. Resistance plans would be made. One spirit would animate and lead the States. Fear of the federal yoke would produce the same resistance as the dread of a foreign yoke. And if the federal government did not voluntarily renounce its proposed changes, force would be used as it was before. But what degree of madness could ever drive the federal government to take such extreme actions?

In our war with Great Britain, England—the part of the empire with a large population—invaded the rights of the American colonies, which had a much smaller population. Great Britain's actions were unjust and unwise, but its goal of defeating the American colonies wasn't impossible.

But what if a State went to war against the federal government? Who would be the parties? A few representatives of the people [federal officials] would be opposed by the people themselves. Or one set of federal representatives would be contending against thirteen sets of State representatives, with all of their common constituents on the side of the latter.

Military Force to Usurp State Power

9   Military force is the only other way that the federal government could usurp State power. And it would take a very large military force. The federal government would have to build up the military. Over a long period of time the people and the States would have to elect men ready to betray them both. The traitors would have to systematically enlarge the military. The State governments and the people would have to silently watch the gathering storm and continue to fund the military until it was prepared to burst on their own heads.

This series of events is more like the incoherent dreams of jealousy or the exaggerations of a counterfeit zeal than like the sober fears of genuine patriotism.

Let's say an army devoted to the federal government was formed. The State governments—with the people on their side—could repel the danger. According to the best computations, the size of a country's standing army cannot exceed 1% of the total population or 4% of the number able to bear arms. In the United States, the army could be no bigger than 25,000 or 30,000 men. The militia with nearly half a million armed citizens and officers appointed by the States would oppose the federal army. The militia would fight for their common liberties. Local governments would lead the militia. And the militia would be loyal to the State governments.

Such a small federal army probably couldn't conquer the militia, just as we successfully resisted the British army. Americans, unlike the people of almost every other nation, have the advantage of being armed. And the people are attached to the State governments, which appoint the militia officers. This forms a barrier against federal ambition.

Several European kingdoms have large military establishments. Yet they are afraid to trust the people with arms. Citizen arms alone might not be powerful enough to defeat a monarchy. But if the people had the additional advantage of local elected governments, who could direct the national attacks and appoint militia officers, the throne of every tyranny in Europe would be speedily overturned in spite of the legions that surround it.

Let's not insult the free and gallant citizens of America. They can defend their rights more easily than the debased subjects of a tyrant can rescue their rights from their oppressors. And let's not insult the American people with the supposition that they will ever allow the long series of insidious measures that would necessitate the use of armed force.

People Will Stop Federal Usurpation

10 The federal government's construction will either make it sufficiently dependent on the people or it will not. If it is dependent on the people, that dependence will restrain schemes obnoxious to their constituents. Or if not, it will not possess the confidence of the people and the State governments—supported by the people—will easily defeat its usurpation scheme.

Federal Powers Won't Hurt States

11 Let's sum up the ideas in Papers 45 and 46. They show that the powers proposed for the federal government are not threats to the States' power. And they are necessary to accomplish the purposes of the Union. The fear that the State governments will be abolished is imaginary. PUBLIUS

"Separation of Powers" Within Government

Number 47: Separation of Legislative, Executive, Judicial Power

I will now examine the structure of the proposed government and the distribution of its power.

Critics: Violates Separation Rule

2   There is an important political rule. It says the legislative, executive, and judiciary departments should be separate.

Some opponents of the Constitution say the Constitution violates this rule. They say the separation-of-powers rule is an essential precaution to preserve liberty. And that some parts of the proposed federal government are exposed to the danger of being crushed by the greater power of other parts.

Separation of Powers Maintains Liberty

3   This objection is based on a political truth. A government becomes a tyranny when one person or a group of people holds all of government's powers—legislative, executive, and judiciary. It doesn't matter if the government is a monarchy, dictatorship, or a democratic republic. Therefore, if the new Constitution mixes powers in a way that could lead to one branch taking over the powers of the other branches, it should be rejected.

However, the Constitution does not violate this rule. Opponents are using the rule incorrectly. To understand this important subject, we will look at why the three types of power should be separate to preserve liberty.

Montesquieu: Separation of Power

4,5   The famous Montesquieu is the expert on this rule. And he said the British Constitution mirrors political liberty.

Powers Mixed in British Constitution

6   However, the British legislative, executive, and judiciary departments are not totally separate from each other.

The chief executive has some legislative authority. He makes treaties with foreign nations that sometimes have the force of legislative acts. The monarch appoints all judges; and he can petition the two Houses of Parliament to remove them. And if he wants to consult legislators, they can become one of his constitutional councils.

One legislative house is the monarch's constitutional council. It also has judicial power in cases of impeachment and is the supreme court of appeals in all other cases.

Judges often participate in the legislature's discussions, though they cannot vote.

No One Has *Total* Power of 2 Branches

7   Montesquieu said, "There can be no liberty where the legislative and executive powers are united in the same person, or body of magistrates," and "if the power of judging be not separated from the legislative and executive powers."

He didn't mean that the government's branches should have no *partial agency* in or no *control* over the acts of each other. His words and examples make his meaning clear.   If one person or one group holds all the power of two branches of government, the basic principles of a free constitution are subverted. For example, this would be true if the British king, the sole executive, also held all the legislative power. Or if the king acted as the country's supreme court. Or if the entire legislature was also the supreme court or held all executive authority.

The king cannot make law, though he can veto laws. He doesn't personally administer justice, though he appoints the judges.

The judges have no executive power, though the executive chooses them. And judges don't make laws, although they can advise legislative councils.

The entire legislature doesn't act as a court, but it can remove a judge from office, and one house has the judicial power of final appeal. The entire legislature, again, has no executive powers, though one house acts as the supreme executive magistracy. And the other house, after an impeachment vote, can try and condemn all the subordinate officers in the executive department.

Liberty Demands "Separation" Rule

8   Montesquieu's reasons for the separation rule clarify his meaning.

"When the legislative and executive powers are united in the same person or body," says he, "there can be no liberty, because apprehensions may arise lest *the same* monarch or senate *enact* tyrannical laws then *execute* them in a tyrannical manner."

And: "Were the power of judging joined with the legislative, the life and liberty of the subject would be exposed to arbitrary control, for *the judge* would then be *the legislator*. Were it joined to the executive power, *the judge* might behave with all the violence of *an oppressor*."

Some of the reasons are more fully explained in other places. But even these brief comments establish the meaning of the rule.

Separation of Powers: New Hampshire

9   The State constitutions have the "separation" rule. However, no State makes the departments of power absolutely separate.

New Hampshire has the newest constitution. It qualifies the rule. It says "that the legislative, executive, and judiciary powers ought to be kept as separate from, and independent of, each other *as the nature of a free government will admit; or as is consistent with that chain of connection that binds the whole fabric of the constitution in one indissoluble bond of unity and amity.*"

The New Hampshire constitution mixes the three departments in several ways. The Senate acts as a court for impeachment trials. The chief executive, the president, heads the Senate; he has an equal vote and the casting vote in cases of tie votes. The legislature elects the chief executive yearly; the executive council is chosen from the members of the legislature. The legislature appoints several State officials. And the executive appoints judges.

Massachusetts Constitution

10   The Massachusetts constitution says "that the legislative department shall never exercise the executive and judicial powers, or either of them; the executive shall never exercise the legislative and judicial powers, or either of them; the judicial shall never exercise the legislative and executive powers, or either of them."

This follows Montesquieu's rule. It prohibits any branch from having all the powers of another branch, like the proposed Constitution. The Massachusetts Constitution has a few overlapping powers. The chief executive has a qualified veto. The Senate is the impeachment court for members of the executive and judiciary. The executive appoints judges; the two legislative houses can remove them. And the legislature appoints a number of government officials.

Rhode Island, Connecticut, New York

11   The Rhode Island and Connecticut constitutions were written before the Revolution. At the time, few people were even aware of the separation of powers principle.

12   New York's constitution doesn't mention this subject. However, the framers understood the danger of improperly blending the different departments. Yet the chief executive and the judiciary have partial control over the legislature. And the legislative and the executive have roles in the appointment of executive officers and judges. One house of the legislature and the State's highest judges are its court for appeals and impeachment trials.

New Jersey, Pennsylvania Constitution

13   New Jersey's constitution blends the powers of government even more. The legislature appoints the governor. The governor judges some cases, is one of the supreme court judges, and is president —with a casting vote—of one of the legislative houses. The same legislative house is the governor's executive council and, with him, they are the Court of Appeals.

The legislature appoints judges, who can be impeached and removed by the legislature.

14   In Pennsylvania, the legislature has the primary role in electing the chief executive. The chief executive and his council appoint judges and form an impeachment court for trial of officers, judiciary and executive. The legislature may remove supreme court judges and justices of the peace. The legislature has some power to pardon, normally an executive power. The members of the executive council are EX OFFICIO [automatically] justices of peace in the State.

Delaware Constitution, New York

15   In Delaware, the legislature elects the chief executive every year. The speakers of the two legislative houses are vice-presidents in the executive branch. The chief executive with three people appointed by each legislative house is the Supreme Court of Appeals. The chief executive joins with the legislature to appoint other judges.

In all the States, it appears that legislators may also be justices of the peace. In New York, the members of one house are justices of the peace, as are the members of the executive council. The legislature appoints most executive officers. And one legislative house is the impeachment court. All officers may be removed by formal legislative petition.

Maryland, Virginia Constitution

16   The Maryland constitution declares that the legislative, executive, and judicial powers of government should always be separate. However, the legislature appoints the chief executive. And the executive appoints judges.

17   Virginia's Constitution declares, "that the legislative, executive, and judiciary departments shall be separate and distinct; so that neither exercise the powers properly belonging to the other; nor shall any person exercise the powers of more than one of them at the same time, except that the justices of county courts shall be eligible to either House of Assembly."

County judges may serve in the legislature. And the legislature appoints the chief executive and his council. Every three years, the legislature removes two members of the executive council. The legislature appoint all principal offices, both executive and judiciary. Also, in one case, the legislature has the executive power of pardon.

North Carolina, South Carolina, Georgia

18   North Carolina's constitution declares, "that the legislative, executive, and supreme judicial powers of government ought to be forever separate and distinct from each other." Yet the legislature appoints the chief executive and all the principal officers within both the executive and the judiciary.

19   The South Carolina legislature appoints all State officers, including the chief executive, judges, justices of the peace, sheriffs, and captains in the army and navy of the State.

20   The constitution of Georgia declares "that the legislative, executive, and judiciary departments shall be separate and distinct, so that neither exercises the powers properly belonging to the other." However, the legislature appoints all members of the executive and it has the executive power of pardon. The legislature even appoints justices of the peace.

New Constitution Doesn't Violate Maxim

21   In the State constitutions, the legislative, executive, and judiciary departments aren't kept totally separate. I am not supporting the organization of these State governments. They show many excellent principles. However, they also show the haste and inexperience under which they were framed. Some of the State constitutions violate the separation of powers rule. Some mix the powers too much. Some combine powers. And none of them provide a way to maintain the separation called for by their constitutions.

Opponents of the proposed Constitution say that it violates the separation of powers rule. This charge is not warranted. It doesn't violate the true meaning of the rule as it is understood in America.

The next paper will further discuss this interesting subject.

PUBLIUS

Number 48: Separation of Government's Powers, continued

In the last paper I showed that the three branches of government do not have to be totally unconnected to each other. I will now show that each branch must have some constitutional control over the others. Without it, the separation of powers can never be effectively maintained.

Encroaching Nature of Power

2   Everyone agrees that one branch of government should never directly administer either of the other branches. However, power has an encroaching nature and must be stopped from overstepping its authority. First government's power is divided into three branches. Then there must be a way for each branch to block invasions by the other branches. This is a more difficult task. What will this security be?

Written Barriers Inadequate

3   The Constitution defines the boundaries between the branches, but paper barriers do not stop the encroaching spirit of power. The State constitutions have not stopped the State legislatures from expanding their

power beyond their constitutional limits. Therefore, the weaker branches of government need a stronger defense against the more powerful legislative branch.

Danger from Legislative Usurpations

4 The founders of our republic knew that an all-grasping hereditary monarch, supported by a hereditary legislature, jeopardizes liberty. Legislative usurpations lead to the same tyranny as executive usurpations.

Protect Liberty from Legislature

5 In a monarchy, the executive branch is dangerous to liberty.

In a democracy, all the citizens gather to exercise the legislative functions. However, this huge number of people cannot regularly meet to discuss and make laws. Therefore, the executive can easily declare an emergency and assume tyrannical powers.

In a representative republic, the chief executive's power and term in office are limited. But legislators assume they have influence over the people and they fearlessly use their power. The people should take precautions against the ambition of the legislature.

Legislative Limits Imprecise

6 The legislative branch has many constitutional powers with imprecise limits. It can surreptitiously encroach on the other branches.

Executive power is better defined and less extensive. The judiciary is even more limited. People could immediately see and stop usurpation attempts by the executive or judiciary.

Nor is this all. The legislature both imposes taxes and sets the wages of the executive and judiciary branches. Therefore, all government officials are dependent on the legislature, making legislative encroachments even easier.

State Legislatures Usurping Power

7 Every State has an example of legislative power encroachments. I will give examples from two States.

Virginia Legislature Usurped Powers

8 The first example is Virginia. Its constitution says that the three government branches should not be intermixed. Mr. Jefferson is the governor.

In *Notes on the State of Virginia*, page 195, Mr. Jefferson says that all of government's powers—legislative, executive, judiciary—revert to the legislative body. In a despotic government, the same people hold all of the government's powers. Having a group of people hold all the power is no better than if a single person holds it. One hundred and seventy-three despots are as oppressive as one. For proof, look at the republic of Venice.

It is no consolation that we elect the representatives. We did not fight for an *elective despotism*. We fought for a government founded on free principles with powers divided and balanced among the government branches so that no one branch can use powers beyond their legal limits without being effectually checked by the others.

"For this reason, the convention that organized [Virginia's] government made the legislative, executive, and judiciary separate and distinct, so that no person should exercise the powers of more than one of them at the same time. *But no barrier was provided between these several powers.* The judiciary and executive branches were left dependent on the legislative for their subsistence in office, and some of them for their continuance in it. If, therefore, the legislature assumes executive and judiciary powers, no opposition is likely to be made; nor, if made, can be effectual because" they can create "acts of Assembly", which the other branches must okay. The legislature has often "*decided rights* which should have been left to *judiciary controversy*, and *the direction of the executive, during the whole time of their session, is becoming habitual and familiar.*"

Pennsylvania Violated Constitution

9   The Council of Censors in Pennsylvania assembled in 1783 and 1784 "to inquire whether the constitution had been preserved inviolate in every part; and whether the legislative and executive branches of government had performed their duty as guardians of the people, or assumed to themselves, or exercised, other or greater powers than they are entitled to by the constitution."

The council compared the actual legislative and executive acts with the constitutional powers of these branches. Most of the council agreed that the legislature flagrantly violated the constitution in a variety of important instances:

10   As a precaution, the Pennsylvania constitution requires that all bills of a public nature be previously printed for the people to consider. Yet many laws were passed without public notification.

11   The constitutional trial by jury has been violated and powers not delegated by the constitution have been assumed.

12   Executive powers have been usurped.

13   The Pennsylvania constitution requires that the salaries of judges must be fixed, but the legislature has occasionally changed them. And the legislature has frequently heard and judged cases belonging to the judiciary.

14   The Pennsylvania Council of Censors journals have more specifics. The war may have caused some of the problems. But the majority are the result of a poorly formed government.

Executive Violated Constitution

15   It appears that Pennsylvania's executive branch has also violated the constitution. However, three observations should be made:

1) Most were either necessary because of the war or they were recommended by national Congress or the commander-in-chief.

2) Most conformed to the sentiments of the legislature.

3) Pennsylvania's executive council has more members than the other States, so it's similar to a legislative assembly. And a council doesn't feel the same restraint as an individual, who is personally responsible for his acts. Members get confidence from each other and are influenced by each other so that unauthorized measures are more easily tried than where the executive branch is administered by a single hand or a few hands.

Words, Alone, Don't Block Tyranny

16   Defining the limits of each branch in the Constitution is not enough. Encroachments can lead to a tyrannical concentration of all the powers of government in the same hands.   PUBLIUS

Number 49: Jefferson: Constitution Convention to Correct Power

Paper number 48 quoted *Notes of the State of Virginia* by Mr. Jefferson. He also wrote a State constitution because the Virginia legislature planned to have a convention in 1783 to create a constitution.

Like everything by Mr. Jefferson, the plan is original, comprehensive, and accurate. It shows Mr. Jefferson wants a republic. And he suggests precautions against some dangers. One precaution safeguards the weaker branch of power against the invasions of the stronger. This may be his original idea.

2   He suggests that when the constitution needs to be altered or when the government takes unconstitutional actions, two of the three branches of government may call a convention.

Citizens Source of Power

3   People are the source of all government power. Government gets all its power from the constitution, which gets its power from the people. If government's powers need to be changed or one branch of government encroaches on the authorities of another branch, republican theory says that the people—the original authority—should make the corrections. Therefore, only the people can declare the constitution's true meaning and enforce it.

4   It seems reasonable to return to the people to keep the branches of government within their constitutional limits, but there are some insurmountable problems.

Two Branches Usurp Authority of Third

5   This proposal doesn't address the problem of two branches usurping the authority of the third. The legislature can easily influence the other branches. If either the executive or judicial branch supports the legislature, this provision wouldn't help the other branch.

I won't dwell on this objection. I object to the entire proposal, not its specific details.

Numbers Strengthen Opinions

6   The next objection comes from the basic nature of the proposal. Every call for a convention would imply the government is defective. Time gives people and organizations respect. If frequent conventions were held, the government would lose respect. Without respect, the wisest and freest government would not be stable.

Governments are only as strong as the people think they are. And the strength of each individual's opinion and its influence on his conduct depends on the number of people he thinks have the same opinion. When one man has an opinion, he is generally timid and cautious. As more people agree with him, he gains confidence. When *ancient* and *numerous* examples support an opinion, they have a double effect.

A nation of philosophers would not have to worry about this problem. Enlightened men would respect laws. But we cannot expect to have a nation of philosophers. Therefore, a rational government knows the advantage of having the prejudices of the community on its side.

Danger of Destructive Passions

7   There is a more serious objection. If the whole society has to decide constitutional questions, passions will be strong. This is a danger to public tranquility.

So far, our governmental reforms have been successful. We can credit the virtue and intelligence of the American people for this success. However, experimenting with the government's structure can be dangerous and should not be done lightly. The State constitutions were framed during a time of danger, which repressed many destructive passions. The people felt an enthusiastic confidence in their patriotic leaders. Because of the danger, there was less diversity of opinions, a diversity that we normally hear on great national questions. No party partisanship inflamed passions about the changes needed to reform abuses. Future situations will not have a similar security against the anticipated danger.

Legislature Most Influential Branch

8 Remember, we are looking for a way to keep the branches of government constitutionally equal. A constitutional convention could not achieve this goal.

In a republic, the legislative is the most powerful branch. Therefore, the executive and judiciary branches would usually request a convention. But would each branch have an equal voice at a convention?

The executive and judiciary branches have fewer members than the legislative. Therefore, fewer people personally know them. And politicians not in the executive are usually jealous of it. Therefore, negative propaganda can make members of the executive branch unpopular. And judges have a lifetime appointment, so they are less in touch with the everyday concerns of citizens.

On the other hand, legislative members are numerous. They live among the people. They have relatives, friends, and acquaintances in the most influential part of society. The fact that they were elected to the legislature implies that they have personal influence among the people and they are seen to be the guardians of the rights and liberties of the people. With these advantages, the branches seeking the correction would not have an equal chance for a favorable outcome.

Congressmen Majority of Delegates

9 Members of Congress could successfully plead their cause to the people, and they would probably also judge the issues. Members of Congress, especially congressional leaders, would be elected to the convention, just as they got elected to the legislature. In short, most members of the convention either would be past, current or future members of the branch whose conduct was being questioned. Consequently, parties to the question would be deciding the question.

Passions would Judge

10 Sometimes appeals would favor the executive and judicial branches. Legislative usurpations might be so outrageous and rapid that there is no time for a specious spin. A strong party might agree with the executive or judiciary. Or the president might be such a favorite of the people that members of the legislature have less influence on citizens. However, a convention's decision still would not be objective. The same prominent people who have argued for and against the measures debated at the convention will also make the decisions at the convention. Inevitably, the decision would reflect the spirit of pre-existing parties or of parties springing out of the question itself.

Public *passions*, therefore, not *reason*, would sit in judgment. But public reason, alone, should control and regulate government. And passions should be controlled and regulated by the government.

Convention Can't Enforce Words

11 We found in the last paper that just writing limitations into the Constitution is not sufficient to keep the branches within their legal rights. From the arguments in this paper, it appears that having an occasional convention would not be a proper or effective way to fulfill the goal.

I will not examine other parts of the Virginia constitution. Some are unquestionably founded on sound political principles, and all are framed with singular ingenuity and precision. PUBLIUS

Number 50: Periodic Conventions to Correct Infractions

The last Paper listed the objections to *occasional* conventions. What if conventions were scheduled? Would they prevent *and correct infractions of the Constitution?*

Scheduled Conventions Ineffective

2 I am examining ways to *enforce* the Constitution and keep the branches of power within their limits. I am not discussing having conventions to *alter* the Constitution.

Scheduled conventions will not be any more helpful than conventions held when problems come up. If the time period between conventions is short, the same circumstances will exist that tend to slant the result with occasional appeals.

If there is a long period between conventions, the same argument applies to all recent questions. Others will receive a dispassionate review depending on their remoteness. However, several problems counterbalance this advantage: If a legislature is determined to achieve an unconstitutional objective, they will not stop because their conduct might be censored in ten, fifteen, or twenty years. The negative effects of their abuses would often be completed before the scheduled convention. And if not completed, they would be of long-standing, taken deep root, and not easily corrected.

Pennsylvania: Branch Encroachment

3 When the Pennsylvania Council of Censors met in 1783 and 1784, one objective was to ask if "the constitution had been violated, and whether the legislative and executive branches had encroached on each other." Some facts about the Council of Censors will illustrate my reasoning about the current discussion.

Party Activists/Council Leaders

4 *First.* Some Council leaders were also activists in the parties that pre-existed in the State.

Some in Council Reviewed Own Work

5   *Second.* The council leaders had been active, influential members of the legislative and executive branches during the period reviewed.

Two members had been vice president of the Senate, several had been members of the executive council, one had been speaker and, several others, distinguished members of the legislature. As members of government, they supported or opposed the measures brought before the council for the constitutional test.

Passions Ruled Debates

6   *Third.* These facts effected their deliberations. The council split into two fixed and violent parties. No matter how unimportant or unconnected the issues, the same men stood on opposite sides of them. Every unbiased observer may think, without being judgmental, that *passion*, not *reason*, presided over the Council's decisions.

When men exercise their reason coolly and freely on a variety of distinct questions, inevitably they have different opinions on some of them. When a common passion guides people, their opinions, if they can be called "opinions," will be the same.

Some Constitutional Misinterpretations

7   *Fourth.* In several instances, the Council misconstrued the constitutional limits on the legislative and executive branches, increasing rather than limiting their power.

No Effect on Legislature's Behavior

8   *Fifth.* The Council's constitutional decisions, whether right or wrong, have not influenced the legislature. In one case, the current legislature denied the opinions of the council and actually prevailed.

Problems Exist, Council Didn't Cure

9   `A study of the council proves that the disease exists and the remedy doesn't work.

Crisis Doesn't Excuse Liabilities

10   Pennsylvania was at a crisis, fueled by partisan rage. There will never be a seven-year period free from partisanship. We cannot presume that any State, at any time, will be exempt from it. And we should never even desire no partisanship, because an extinction of parties implies either a massive threat of danger or an absolute extinction of liberty.

Excluding Government Officials

11   Even if every member of the government during the time being reviewed had been excluded from the Council, it wouldn't solve the prob-

lem. Less qualified men would have had to perform the task. Although they might not have been members of the government, they would probably have been associates of the parties connected with these measures and probably be elected under their sponsorship.

PUBLIUS

Number 51: Separation of Powers: Checks and Balances

The Constitution divides government power among three branches. The government must be designed so that the three branches—executive, legislative, and judiciary—can keep each other in their proper places. We will study the Constitution and decide whether it fulfills this goal.

Perfect Separation: People Appoint All Officials

2   To preserve liberty, government's powers must be separated. The first step towards the separation of powers is finding a way to appoint or elect people to each branch, without the appointee being overly dependent on people in another branch.

If we wanted total separation of powers, the people would elect every member of the executive, legislative, and judiciary branches. This would be difficult and expensive. Instead, each branch must have as little input as possible in appointing members of the other branches.

Judiciary: Specific Qualifications

Electing judges might not be very successful.

First, judges must have specific qualifications. There should be a way to choose judges that secures these qualifications.

Second, since judges are appointed for life, they will not feel obligated or dependent on the people who appoint them.

Compensation Creates Dependence

3   If executive and judicial branches depend on the legislature for their pay, they would not be independent. Therefore, members of each branch should depend—as little as possible—on other branches for their pay.

Resisting Usurpations

4   There needs to be a way to block a branch of government from getting more power than the constitution gives it. Each branch needs both constitutional tools and personal motives to block encroachments. Ambition must counteract ambition. The personal interests of the man must be connected with the constitutional rights of his office.

Government Reflects Human Nature; Angels Don't Need Government

Government is, after all, the greatest of all reflections on human nature. If men were angels, no government would be necessary. If angels governed men, no controls on government would be necessary. But men govern men. So, security measures are necessary to control the abuses of government.

In framing a government, the great difficulty lies in this:

> first, the government must control the governed, and
> second, it must be forced to control itself.

The primary control on the government is its dependency on the people. But experience teaches us that more precautions are necessary.

Checks, Balances in All Organizations

5   All organizations use rival interests to maintain a balance of power. To keep a balance of power, power is divided among lower-level offices. The goal is to structure the organization so that the offices become a check on each other. When the goal is met, the personal interest of the office-holder guards the public rights. This balanced structure is just as important when distributing the supreme powers of government.

Divide Legislative; Fortify Executive

6   But it is impossible to give each branch of government an equal power of self-defense. In a republic, the legislature always has the most power. To counteract this, (1) the legislature is divided into two houses, (2) the houses are elected in different ways, and (3) they have different constitutional powers.

The legislative houses are as little connected as their duties and dependence on society will allow. And more blocks to dangerous encroachments may be necessary.

The strength of the legislative power requires that it be divided. The executive is weak and may need strengthening. The executive should have the power to veto legislation. But veto power, alone, may not be enough. It might be dangerously abused or might not be used when it is needed. Is there a way to structure government so that the weaker side of the stronger legislative branch could support the constitutional rights of the weaker executive branch, without hurting the rights of its own branch?

Constitution and Separation of Powers

7   The federal Constitution does not do a perfect job of separating government's powers. However, the State constitutions do a worse job of separating powers.

8   Two things make America's federal system unique.

States Check on Federal Government

9   *First.* In a single republic, the people surrender some of their power to a single government. To block usurpations, the government is divided into separate branches.

America is a compound republic. The people surrender some power, which is divided between the State and federal governments. Then the powers given to each government is subdivided among the separate branches. This means that the rights of the people are doubly protected. The State and federal governments will control each other; at the same time, each will have internal controls.

Oppression from Society

10   *Second.* In a republic, society must be protected against the oppression of its rulers. And one part of the society must be guarded against the injustice of another part.

Different groups of citizens have different interests. If a majority is united by a common interest, the rights of the minority will be in danger. There are only two ways to remove this danger.

One, create a will in the community independent of the majority— that is, independent of the society itself. This method prevails in dictatorships. At best, it is a weak security. At worst, a dictator can turn against both the majority and minority interests.

Or two, make sure there are so many different types of citizens in the society that unjust majority alliances will be impossible or impractical. The federal republic of the United States is an example of this. All authority will come from and depend on the citizens. The citizens will have many different interests. And there will be so many different groups of citizens that individual rights and minority rights will be in little danger.

In a free government, the security for civil rights is the same as that for religious rights. A society with a wide variety of interests secures civil rights; a wide variety of religions secures religious rights. This security depends on the size and population of the country.

To all people who like republics, this recommends a proper federal system. As territories become States and join the Union, it will be easier for an oppressive majority group to grow. The security for the rights of every citizen will diminish. Therefore, some part of government must be more stable and independent.

Justice is the final goal of civil society and government. It will be pursued until it is obtained or until liberty is lost in the pursuit.

When a society is structured so that a strong faction can easily unite and oppress a weaker group, anarchy reigns. This happens in nature. A weak individual is not protected against the violence of the stronger. Yet even in nature, some stronger individuals form a "government" that may protect the weak as well as themselves just because they are unsure of what may happen.

In human society, a similar motive will encourage powerful factions or groups to want a government that will protect all groups, the weaker as well as the more powerful.

Let's suppose the State of Rhode Island was separated from the Confederacy and left to itself. Factious majorities would repeatedly oppress the people. Even the people within some of the majority faction would worry about losing their rights. They would call for a power that is independent of the people to help. The very factions, whose misrule had made it necessary, would look for outside help.

The United States is a large republic. It will include a great variety of interests, groups, and sects. A factious majority could seldom happen on any principles other than justice and the general good. There is less danger to a minority from the will of a majority party. There will also be fewer reasons to pass laws that secure minority goals but are not supported by a majority of society itself.

The larger the society, provided it lies within a practical size, the more capable it will be of self-government. And happily for people who want a *republic,* the practical size can be large by using judicious modifications and a mixture of the *federal principle*.

PUBLIUS

Legislative: House of Representatives

Number 52: Representatives: Candidates, Elections, Term

I will examine parts of the government, starting with the House of Representatives.

Voter Qualifications

2   In each State, the citizens who are qualified to vote for the State legislature will vote for members of the House of Representatives. Voting is a basic right of republican government. The Constitution defines and guarantees this right. The federal House of Representatives should depend on the people, not the State governments.

It would have been difficult for the convention to establish one rule for the entire country. And some of the States would have been dissatisfied. Therefore, the Constitution has the best solution. It satisfies every State, using the rule established by the State itself. The United States will be safe because, even though the State governments make the rule, it is based on the State constitutions and the State governments cannot change it. And the people will not change this part of the State constitutions to lose the rights secured to them by the federal Constitution.

Qualifications for Representative

3   This defines the qualifications of Representatives:
- A Representative of the United States must be 25 years old,
- must be a citizen of the United States for seven years,
- at the time of his election he must be an inhabitant of the State he is to represent, and
- while serving as a Representative, he must hold no other office under the United States.

These are reasonable qualifications. Good people of every description may become Representatives, whether native or adoptive, young or old, and without regard to poverty, wealth, or religion.

Representatives' Term in Office

4   The representatives' term is two years. We will consider two questions:
(1) Will biennial elections be safe?
(2) Are biennial elections necessary?

Frequent Elections

5   To maintain liberty, the government and the people must have a common interest. The House of Representatives needs to both depend on the people and sympathize with their constituents. Frequent elections se-

cure this dependence and sympathy. But it is impossible to figure out how frequent the elections need to be. Let us consult experience, the guide that should always be followed whenever it can be found.

Elections in Great Britain

6 We will look at a few examples that are similar to our case.

The first is the House of Commons in Great Britain. The earliest records say that parliaments were to *sit* every year, not *elected* every year. And some monarchs used excuses to stop the House of Commons from meeting for several years at a time. To fix this problem, a law passed during the reign of Charles II limited the intermissions to three years.

A revolution took place when William III became king. The subject was seriously studied. *Frequent* parliament sessions were declared a fundamental right of the people. A few years later, a statute defined the term "frequent." A new parliament must be called within three years after the previous parliament session is ended. Earlier this century, it was changed again. The time was extended from three to seven years.

Great Britain seems to believe that three years between elections is the shortest period needed to keep representatives dependent on voters. Even with elections every seven years and a limited constitution, Great Britain has some liberty. Therefore, if our federal Representatives are elected every two years, they should feel dependent on the voters.

Ireland's Elections Rare

7 Until recently, the monarch decided when Ireland would have elections and they were rare. One parliament started when King George II began his rule and continued throughout his 35-year reign. The representatives were dependent on the people only when there was an election to fill vacancies and the occasional general election.

The Irish parliament might have wanted to uphold citizens' rights. But the king controlled the subjects parliament could discuss. Recently, eight-year terms for parliament have been established. We will have to wait and see the effect of this partial reform.

We cannot learn much from Ireland's experience. However, the people of Ireland, even with these disadvantages, have some liberty. Therefore, biennial elections will secure the liberty that depends on a connection between representatives and the people.

Colonies: Elections 1 - 7 Years

8 The example of the States, when British colonies, is well known. At least one house of each State legislature follows the principle of representation. But the election periods varied from one to seven years.

192

Let's look at how the people's representatives behaved before the Revolution. Does their behavior give us any reason to think that biennial elections are dangerous to liberty? The fact that we were able to fight a revolution for independence proves that some liberty existed. This was as true for the colonies that had elections every seven years as well as those with annual elections.

Virginia was the first colony to resist the parliamentary usurpations of Great Britain. And it was the first to pass the resolution of independence. At the time, Virginia held elections every seven years. This proves that *biennial* elections will not endanger liberty.

Short Terms, Depend on People

9 Three things will strengthen the conclusions from these examples:

First, the federal House of Representatives will have only part of the supreme legislative authority. It is an important rule that, excluding all other circumstances, the greater the power, the shorter ought to be its duration. And conversely, the smaller the power, the more safely may its duration be lengthened.

Second, in addition to being dependent on the people, the House of Representatives will be watched and controlled by the State legislatures.

Third, we cannot compare the ability of the more permanent branches of the federal government to seduce, if they want to, the House of Representatives from their duty to the people, and the ability of the Senate to influence the House of Representatives. Therefore, with less power to abuse, the federal representatives will be less tempted on one side and doubly watched on the other.   PUBLIUS

Number 53: Biennial Elections Safe, Promote Quality

Some people say, "Where annual elections end, tyranny begins." Although clichés develop for a reason, people often use them for cases to which they do not apply. For proof, look at the case before us.

What was the original reason for this cliché? Of course, there is no scientific connection between how many times the earth goes around the sun and how long a man can remain virtuous and not be tempted by power.

Fortunately, liberty is not limited to any single amount of time. Under different circumstances, different lengths of time are appropriate. If it was important, elections could be held daily, weekly, monthly, or annually. But in some circumstances less frequent elections are needed.

The largest house of each State legislature has a variety of term lengths: six months in Connecticut and Rhode Island, two years in South Carolina, and yearly in the other States. But it would be hard to show that Connecti-

cut or Rhode Island is better governed or enjoys more liberty than South
Carolina.

No Constitution: Laws Change Government

2   I found only one reason for this cliché and it does not apply to our
case. Americans understand that the people create a Constitution. And it
is the supreme power. The government cannot alter the Constitution. On
the other hand, the government makes laws and the government can
change them. Other countries don't seem to understand this distinction.

When the legislature has supreme power, the legislature can change
government's structure. British citizens discuss political liberties, civil
liberties, and constitutional rights. But Parliament's authority is supreme.
Several times, Parliament has passed laws that fundamentally change the
government, specifically, the election period. On the last occasion, they
replaced three-year terms with seven-year terms. The people elected them
to a three-year term but they stayed in office seven years.

Free governments have frequent elections. Parliament's actions
alarmed the voters. The voters wanted to find a way to secure their liberty
against this danger. The United States has a Constitution. Other nations
don't have this security. Other security was sought. The length of time between elections became the way to measure the danger of changes. The
simplest length of time was a year. Hence, the annual-election doctrine
became a barrier against the gradual changes of an unlimited government.
And the approach of tyranny was measured by how far away from annual
elections.

But the Constitution will limit our federal government. Annual elections will not be needed. Constitutionally mandated biennial elections will
keep the liberties of the American people more secure than annual elections in other nations. Those nations can change the length of time between elections by simply   passing a law.

3   Several reasons show that biennial elections are necessary and useful.

Legislator Experience Important

4   A competent legislator has good intentions, sound judgment, and
some knowledge of legislative subjects. He gets some knowledge in private life. Another part can only be completely learned while serving as a
legislator. Therefore, the length of service should be somewhat proportional to how much the legislator must know to adequately serve.

In most States, the larger legislative house has annual elections. A federal congressman has more to learn than a State congressman. Is two years
long enough to learn the increased information? Can a federal congressman learn the greater knowledge needed for federal legislation in two
years?

Large Area, Diversified Laws

5   A State legislator needs to know existing laws, which are uniform throughout the State. Most citizens understand the general affairs of the State. State issues are not very diversified and everyone studies and discusses them.

Understanding national issues is different. The laws vary in every State. The country is large with diverse responsibilities. They are difficult to learn outside the federal capitol, where representatives of the entire nation bring knowledge of them.

All federal legislators need to know something about State issues and laws. To write national regulations for foreign trade, legislators need to know something about the commerce, ports, and regulations of the different States. To regulate trade between States, they need to know about their different situations. To fairly impose and effectively collect taxes, they need to know the laws and situations in the different States. To write national militia regulations, they need to know the issues that make the States different from each other.

Trade, taxes, and the militia are the important subjects of federal legislation. Federal representatives need a lot of information on these and other subjects.

Knowledge Will Increase

6   Starting the new government and creating the first federal code will be a difficult task. Improvements will become easier and fewer every year. New members can learn from what the federal government has done before. Citizens will discuss the Union's affairs. As commerce between the States increases, so will knowledge of State affairs. And the different State laws will become more similar.

But even with these changes, federal legislation will always be more difficult than the legislative business of a single State. Therefore, the longer term is justified.

Foreign Affairs Learned as Legislator

7   A federal representative also needs to understand foreign affairs, including commercial treaties and policies of the United States and other nations. He should have some knowledge of the law of nations. The House of Representatives will not directly participate in foreign negotiations. However, the different areas of public affairs are connected. And they will sometimes demand legislative sanction and cooperation.

A man may learn some of these things in his private life. But some things can only be learned from public sources of information. And the majority will be learned during the period of actual service in the legislature.

Representatives' Distance Traveled

8 Other considerations are less important, but are worth mentioning.

If terms are only one year, some qualified men will not serve because of the travel distance. Although the existing Congress is elected annually, most members are automatically reelected by the State legislatures. But Representatives will be elected by the people.

Some Members Will Serve Long Time

9 As happens in all such assemblies, a few members will have superior talents, be reelected and become members of long standing. They will be masters of public business. The more new members, the less information the assembly will have. And they will be more likely to fall into the snares laid for them. This is true for both the House and the Senate.

Investigating Irregular Elections

10 If elections are held every year, there wouldn't be enough time to investigate spurious elections. If election results need to be annulled, there wouldn't be enough time for the annulment to take effect. If an election is won, even if won illegally, the irregular member will hold his seat long enough time to fulfill his goals. This would encourage election fraud, particularly in the more distant States.

Each house judges the legality of member elections and qualifications. And even if the process is simplified and faster, a great part of a year would go by before an illegitimate member could be removed from his seat. The fear of being unseated would do little to stop unfair and fraudulent elections.

11 Biennial elections will be useful for handling public affairs and safe to the liberty.

PUBLIUS

Number 54: Representatives/Direct Taxes: Same Rule

The States use the same rule for direct taxes and appointing Representatives.

Representation/Population; Taxes/Wealth

2 Proportional representation should be based on State populations. The Constitution also uses population to determine each State's tax obligation. Using a State's population for both is based on two different principles.

In the case of the House of Representatives, proportional representation refers to the personal rights of the people.

In the case of taxes, it is proportional wealth. It is not an exact measure of wealth. In fact, it is very imperfect. However, it is the least objectionable method. And Americans recently agreed to use this method, so the convention selected it.

Counting Slaves In Population

3   Some people want slaves counted for taxation but not counted for proportional representation. They argue that slaves are considered property, not persons; therefore, they should be counted for taxation. But they should not be counted when determining representation, which is determined by a census of persons. This seems to be the objection. I will state the opposite side of the argument.

Change Law, Slaves Become Citizens

4   A Southern friend might say, "We agree representation relates more to persons and taxation more to property. But we deny that slaves are only property and in no way persons. They have both qualities. Our laws consider them, in some ways, persons and, in other ways, property.

"The slave is forced to labor for a master. The master can sell him. His liberty is limited. And his body is forced to do what another person tells him to do. For these reasons, the slave may not seem human. He may seem more like a farm animal, which is defined as property.

"However, the slave is protected against violence, even by his master. And if the slave hurts another person, he can be punished. Therefore, the law considers the slave a member of society, not an animal. He is seen as a moral person, not as a mere article of property.

"The federal Constitution, therefore, correctly looks at slaves as both persons and property. Non-slave States don't want to include slaves in the census. But the pretexts of laws, alone, have made Negroes property. And if laws restored the rights that have been taken away, the Negroes could not be refused an equal share of representation.

Condemn Slavery, Call Slaves Property

5   "We can look at this question in another way. Numbers measure wealth and taxation. And numbers measure representation. What if the convention had excluded slaves from the population when calculating representation, then inserted them to calculate taxes? Would the Southern States agree to a system that considered their slaves, in some degree, as men when the burden of tax is imposed, but refused to consider them in the same way when the advantage of representation is conferred?

"Some people reproach the Southern States for the barbarous policy of considering part of their human brethren as property. Now the same people say the federal government should consider this unfortunate race more completely in the unnatural light of property than the very laws they complain about.

Slaves: Computing Representation

6   "They may argue that, in the States with slaves, slaves are not included in computing the state representation. They neither vote nor increase the votes of their masters. If the Constitution didn't use them to compute representation, it would follow State laws.

Constitution Defines Number of Representatives

7   "One fact voids this objection. The number of representatives from each State is determined by a rule in the federal Constitution, based on population. However, each State decides who can vote for Representatives. Different States may have different voter qualifications. Some people in every State will not be allowed to vote. But they will be included in the federal census that determines the number of representatives. Southern States might argue that the Constitution doesn't require that all States have the same suffrage policy. Therefore, the full number of slaves should be included in the census, because other States count people who do not have all the rights of citizens.

"However, the southern States have waived a strict adherence to this principle. They want equal moderation on the other side. Let slaves be considered a specific case and the Constitutional compromise adopted. Slaves are people debased by servitude below the equal level of free people; the Constitution regards the *slave* as divested of 2/5 of the *man*.

Government Protects Property, People

8   "There is a better defense of this article of the Constitution. So far, we have assumed that representation relates only to persons and not to property. But is this valid?

"Government is established to protect both property and people. Therefore, government represents both property and people. In several States, one branch of government guards property and is elected by people most interested in this governmental objective.

"In the federal Constitution, the same hands protect both property and personal rights. Therefore, some attention ought to be paid to property when choosing those hands.

Influence of Wealth

9   "There is another reason federal representation should be somewhat proportional to the comparative wealth of the States. Wealthy States, unlike wealthy individuals, don't influence each other. Although a wealthy

citizen has only one vote, his wealth frequently influences other voters towards his choice. Through this invisible channel, property rights are conveyed into public representation.

"A State doesn't have this kind of influence over other States. The richest State will probably never influence the choice of a single representative in any other State. And the representatives of large, rich States will have no advantage in the federal legislature over the representatives of other States, except the advantage resulting from their superior number. Therefore, if their superior wealth entitles them to any advantage, they should get it through a larger share of representation.

"The new Constitution is very different from the existing Confederation and other confederacies where federal resolutions must be approved by the states before becoming laws. In those confederacies, each state has an equal vote in the federal councils. However, they have an unequal influence, depending on the subject of the resolutions.

"Under the proposed Constitution, the federal laws will take effect without the agreement of the individual States. They will depend only on the majority of votes in the federal legislature. Therefore, each vote, whether from a large or small State, or a State more or less wealthy or powerful, will have equal weight and efficacy. Any influence will come from the personal character of a representative rather than whether he comes from a wealthy district."

Arguments Favor Apportionment Plan

10   This is how an advocate for the Southern interests might discuss this subject. And although it may appear to be a little strained in some points, I believe it shows that the Constitution's rule for representation works.

States' Census Bias

11   In one respect, using one rule to calculate representation and taxation will have a very good effect. To a large degree, the accuracy of the federal census will depend on the disposition, if not on the cooperation, of the States. It is important that the States feel as little bias as possible to increase or reduce their numbers.

If the census was only used to determine proportional representation, the States would want to exaggerate their population. If the census was only used to determine proportional taxation, States would want a smaller number. By using the census to determine both, the States will have opposite interests, which will control and balance each other, and produce an impartial census.

PUBLIUS

Number 55: Total Number in House of Representatives

The number of members in the House of Representatives is an interesting topic. Some respected people argue against it. They say:

1) Such a small number of Representatives is unsafe.

2) With such a large number of constituents, Representatives will not know enough about the **local circumstances**.

3) Representatives will be from the **upper class** of citizens. They will not understand the feelings of the mass of the people and will aim at a permanent elevation of the few on the depression of the many.

4) As the population increases, the number of representatives **will become more disproportionate.** And it will be difficult to increase the number of representatives.

Constituent/Legislator Ratios

2   There is no formula to determine the correct size for a representative legislature. The State legislatures have many different representatives-to-population ratios.

Delaware has the smallest legislature. Its largest branch has 21 representatives.

Massachusetts, the largest State legislature, has 300-400 members. With nearly the same size population, Pennsylvania's legislature is 1/5 the size of Massachusetts with a representative for every 4 or 5,000 constituents.

New York's population is to that of South Carolina as 6:5, but it has about 1/3 the number of representatives.

There is also a great difference between Georgia and Delaware or Rhode Island. In Rhode Island, the proportion is 1:1,000. In Georgia, the proportion may be 1:10 voters, far exceeding the proportion in any other State.

Ratio Changes with Population

3   Very large and very small populations should have different representative to constituent ratios. If the Virginia ratio was the same as Rhode Island, Virginia would have 400-500 representatives. And 20 years from now, 1,000. And if Pennsylvania's ratio was used in Delaware, Delaware would have 7-8 representatives.

Political decisions cannot be based on arithmetic. Sixty men might be more trusted with power than six. But that doesn't mean 600 men would be even safer. And 6,000 men reverses the whole reasoning.

The number needs to be large enough for open discussion and to guard against conspiracies. But the number can be too large, creating confusion and an intolerant mob. In all very large assemblies, passion always overtakes reasoning. Even if every Athenian citizen had been a Socrates, every Athenian assembly would still have been a mob.

Representatives' Power Limited

4   Remember the discussion about biennial elections. The limited powers of the House justify less frequent elections than the public safety might otherwise require. For the same reasons, the number of representatives can be fewer than if there were no Senate.

Objection: Small Number, Too Much Power

5   With these ideas in mind, let's weigh the objections against the number of members proposed for the House of Representatives.

First, it is said that so small a number cannot be safely trusted with so much power.

Size of House will Quickly Grow

6   When the government begins, the number will be 65. A census will be taken within three years. Then the number may increase to one for every 30,000 inhabitants. A new census is to be taken every ten years. The House may continue to grow under the above limitation.

The first census will probably increase the number of representatives to at least 100. Using a 3/5 proportion for Negroes, the population will be three million, if it isn't already.

After 25 years, the number of representatives will probably be 200. In 50 years, 400. This should end fears that it is too small.

The number of representatives will increase from time to time. If the Constitution did not provide for this increase, the objection would be legitimate.

Number Won't Threaten Liberty

7   Will the temporary, small number be dangerous to liberty? There will be 65 members for a few years, then 100 or 200 for a few more. Is this number safe for the limited power of legislating for the United States?

To answer no, I would have to change my beliefs about the spirit of the State legislatures and the upright political character of our citizens.

I cannot imagine that Americans will elect—and every second year reelect—65 or 100 men who want to pursue tyranny. And I am unable to believe that any 65-100 elected Representatives will have the desire or ability, in only two years, to betray the solemn trust given to them.

I can't predict the future. But judging from our present circumstances and what may happen in the near future, American liberties will be safe in the number of hands proposed by the federal Constitution.

Small Congress During Revolution

8   From where will the dangers come? Are we afraid of foreign gold? If foreign gold could easily corrupt our federal rulers, enabling them to ensnare and betray their constituents, why are we currently free and independent?

A small congress led us through the Revolution. They were neither chosen by nor responsible to their fellow citizens. Though appointed from year to year and recallable at pleasure, before the Articles were ratified, they usually served for three years or more. They always held secret discussions. They had complete control of our affairs with foreign nations. During the war, they held the fate of their country in their hands. And from the greatness of the prize and Britain's desire to win, we can suppose that they would have used bribes. Yet the public trust was not betrayed. Nor has the purity of our public councils, in this area, ever suffered from even the whispers of slander.

Corruption of Representatives?

9   Should we fear the other branches of the federal government? How could the President or the Senate corrupt Representatives? Their salary will not be enough to be used to corrupt them, except if they are already corrupt. Their private fortunes, as American citizens, cannot be sources of danger. The only way they can corrupt Representatives will be through giving out government appointments. Is this where suspicion arises? Sometimes we are told that the President will use this source to corrupt the Senate. Now the fidelity of the other House is to be the victim.

Such a disloyal conspiracy by government officials is improbable. Officials will stand on as different foundations as republican principles will allow. And they will be accountable to the society they govern.

Fortunately, the Constitution has another safeguard. The members of Congress cannot hold any civil offices that were created or the pay increased during their term in Congress. Therefore, no offices can be given to existing members except when vacated by ordinary casualties. And to say this would be enough to purchase the guardians of the people, elected by the people, is to renounce every rule by which events are forecast and substitute an indiscriminate, illogical jealousy.

The sincere friends of liberty, who extravagate this danger, are injuring their own cause. Mankind does have a degree of depravity that requires carefulness and distrust. But human nature also has qualities that justify some esteem and confidence. Republican government assumes that these qualities exist.

Political jealousy influences the opinion of some people. If the way they see human character is accurate, then people are not virtuous enough for self-government. And the only way they can be stopped from destroying each other is to live under a dictator.

PUBLIUS

Number 56: Opposition: Too Few Representatives

The second charge against the House of Representatives is that it will be too small to understand the public's wide variety of interests.

Congress: Different Type of Legislature

2   The United States is very large. Our citizens have a wide variety of interests. However, the United States Congress will be different from other legislatures. A brief description will explain why the House of Representatives will be large enough.

Specific Knowledge Necessary

3   Of course, a representative should know about his constituents. However, he only needs to know about things that relate to his authority. He doesn't need to understand the wide variety of subjects that do not fall within the legislature's authority.

What subjects fall under the representatives' authority?

Commerce, Taxes, Militia

4   Commerce, taxation, and the militia are the areas of federal legislation that require local knowledge.

Regulate Commerce

5   The proper regulation of commerce requires a lot of information. However, only a few federal representatives need to know the State commercial laws and situations.

Union Tax Codes will Borrow From States

6   Duties on commerce will be the primary form of taxation. Therefore, the remark about commerce applies.

Internal tax collections may require more knowledge. However, a few intelligent men, elected from different areas, will have enough knowledge.

State tax laws will be guides. In many cases, the federal legislature could study the State laws, and then write the federal tax law. With the aid of local tax codes, one person could create a tax law for the whole country without any other information. And whenever internal taxes are necessary, particularly when they need to be uniform across the nation, the simplest objects will be preferred.

The House of Representatives will have another advantage. Many federal Representatives will have served in the State legislatures. They will bring the information into the federal legislature.

Within States, Militia Discipline Uniform

8   The comments on taxation apply to the militia. Although different States may have different rules of discipline, they are the same throughout each State.

Need to Acquire Wider Knowledge

9   I explained why a huge number of Representatives is not necessary. However, Representatives need a lot of information and the time needed to learn it. They must understand the different laws and circumstances within the States. This is difficult.

Within each State, laws are the same and there is only a small variety of interests. A few knowledgeable men can represent them. If each State had uniform laws and interests, which were perfectly simple and uniform, a single member taken from any part of the State could competently represent the whole State.

However, different States have very different laws. These differences will be the subject of federal legislation. And federal representatives should understand the differences. While representatives from each State bring information about their own State, every representative will need to learn about all the other States.

In time, there will be fewer differences between the States. The effect of time on the internal affairs of the individual States will have the opposite effect.

At present, some States are mostly farmers. A few States have some industry, which gives a variety and complexity to the affairs of a nation. As the States develop, they will need full representation. And as the population progresses, the representative branch of the government will also grow.

Great Britain: Citizens to Representative Ratio

10   In these Papers, we often refer to Great Britain's political and monetary systems. Great Britain's experience with representation agrees with what we have just said. The population of England and Scotland is at least eight million. The British House of Commons has 558 representatives, elected as follows:

364 people elect 11% of the representatives [62] and 5,723 people elect 50% of the members [279]. [The general population elects the rest.]

In other words, 0.7% of the population elects half the representatives.

These representatives do not live among the people. They do not add to the people's security against the government. And they do not represent the people's interests in the legislative councils. In fact, they more frequently help the monarch than guard and advocate for popular rights. Therefore, they cannot be considered "real" representatives of the nation. We might even deduct them from the number of "real" representatives.

However, we will not deduct the large number of representatives who do not live among their constituents, are very little connected with them, and have little knowledge of their affairs.

This leaves only 279 representatives to guard the safety, interest, and happiness of eight million. In other words, there is only one representative to maintain the rights and represent 28,670 constituents. At the same time, the House of Commons is exposed to the whole force of the monarch's influence, which extends his authority to every legislative subject. And Great Britain's interests are very diversified and complicated.

But most of the people's freedom has been preserved. And the defects in the British code are only partly because the representative do not understand the people's circumstances.

The House of Representatives will have one representative for every 30,000 inhabitants. When we compare this to Britain, we see that the House will be both a safe and a competent guardian of the interests entrusted to it.   PUBLIUS

* Burph's *Political Disquisitions.*—PUBLIUS

Number 57: Charge: Representatives from "Upper Class"

The *third* charge against the House of Representative is that members will come from the upper class of citizens, who have little in common with the mass of the people. And their ambition will sacrifice the many to the benefit of the few.

Elitist House, Republican Government

2   This objection to the Constitution suggests an oligarchy will develop. And it strikes at the root of republican government.

Want Rulers Pursuing Common Good

3   The first goal of every political constitution is finding men to rule who have the wisdom to understand and the virtue to pursue society's common good. Next, it needs a way to keep them virtuous while they are in office.

Republican governments elect rulers. Many things help to prevent their degeneracy. The most effective is limiting their term in office. Because they have to face reelection, they will feel responsible to the people.

House Based on Republican Principles

4   What in the Constitution about the House of Representatives violates the principles of republican government? How does it favor the election of an upper class of people?

Isn't the opposite true? Doesn't the Constitution strictly follow republican principles? Isn't it impartial to the rights of every class and description of citizens?

Voters, Candidates

5   Who will elect the federal Representatives? Not the rich more than the poor. Not the educated more than the ignorant. Not the haughty heirs

of famous names more than the humble sons of obscurity without a family fortune. The people of the United States will vote. They will be the same people who elect representatives to the State legislatures.

6   Who will be elected? The candidate will be a citizen whose merit recommends him to the esteem and confidence of his country. There are no qualifications of wealth, birth, religious faith, or civil profession.

Internal Securities

7   Several things assure us that the Representatives will be faithful to their constituents.

Because Elected, Have Good Qualities

8   First. Their fellow citizen will choose them. They will have some good qualities, including an understanding of their obligations as an elected official.

Representatives Feel Gratitude

9   Second. When they begin to serve, they will have at least a temporary affection for their constituents. When citizens honor a person, he responds positively. This guarantees some grateful and benevolent returns.

People often discuss ingratitude. And it does happen too frequently, both in public and private life. But the extreme anger the discussion of ingratitude inspires proves that most people feel grateful.

Politicians Court Voters' Favor

10   Third, the representative is also tied to his constituents for selfish reasons. Being an elected official flatters his pride and vanity. A large number of men advance politically because of their influence with the people. And they have more to gain from preserving the voters' favor, than from working to change the government in a way that subverts the people's authority.

Frequent Elections

11   Fourth. These securities would not be enough without the restraint of frequent elections. The bi-annual elections to the House of Representatives will remind members of their dependence on the people.

Before they have time to forget how they got the power of their high office, they will be forced to think about the next election, when their actions will be reviewed. They will be reminded that they will become a common citizen if they haven't faithfully discharged their trust and truly deserve to be reelected.

Must Live Under Laws They Pass

12   Fifth. Every law the House of Representatives passes will operate on the Representatives and their friends, as well as the society. This is another restraint on the power.

This creates a strong bond and common interests between rulers and the people. Few governments have this feature. And without it, every government degenerates into tyranny.

What stops the House of Representatives from making laws that favor themselves and a specific class of society? The whole system. The nature of just and constitutional laws. And, above all, the vigilant spirit of the people of America—a spirit which nourishes freedom and, in return, is nourished by it.

Laws that Presage Tyranny

13   If the people of America ever tolerate a law that does not apply to legislators, as well as on the people, the people will be prepared to tolerate anything but liberty.

Bonds Between Representatives/Citizens

14   Duty, gratitude, interest, and ambition will keep Representatives faithful to the people. However, these may not be enough to control the caprice and wickedness of man. But are these the only possible bonds? Aren't they the bonds that republican government provides for liberty and happiness? Doesn't every State government rely on the same bonds to get these important ends?

What can we say about the objection this paper refutes? What should we say to men who profess a love for republican government, yet boldly impeach the fundamental principle of it? What should we say about men who pretend to support the right and ability of the people to choose their own rulers, yet maintain voters will only elect people who will immediately betray the trust given to them?

Will Only Few Elite People Vote?

15   What if someone reads this objection but doesn't read the Constitution, which defines how representatives will be chosen? He would conclude that only people owning a large amount of property could vote. Or that only special families or wealthy people could vote. If nothing else, he would think that the election method in the federal Constitution is quite different from the State constitutions.

However, there are no property, family, or wealth qualifications for voters. The only difference between the States and federal Constitutions is the number of people who elect representatives. 5,000 or 6,000 citizens will elect each United States Representative. In the States, 500 or 600 citizens elect representatives. Does this difference mean that the State governments are good and the federal government is not? Let's examine this point.

5,000 vs. 500 Voters

16   Is this conclusion *logical*? No. Five or six thousand citizens can choose as capable a representative as 500 or 600 citizens. And the larger group is not more easily corrupted than the smaller.

Logic says that it will be easier to find a fit Representative in the larger group. And it will be harder for ambitious or rich people to corrupt the election.

17   Is the *consequence* from this doctrine admissible? If we say that only 500 or 600 citizens can vote, shouldn't we take away the peoples' right to choose public servants whenever the administration of the government does not require as many of them as will amount to one for that number of citizens?

US House V. British House of Commons

18   Do *facts* support this doctrine? The last paper showed that representation in the British House of Commons is one for every 30,000 inhabitants. And the United States Constitution does not have qualifications that favor the aristocracy and wealthy.

In Britain, a county representative must have real estate with the clear value of 600-pound sterling per year. City and borough representatives must have an estate of half that annual value. County voters must have a freehold estate with the annual value of more than 20 pounds sterling. In spite of these criteria and some unequal laws in the British code, we can't say that British representatives have elevated the few on the ruins of the many.

Populous Districts

19   But we don't have to look at Britain to learn about this subject. Our own experience is explicit and decisive.

New Hampshire's State senate districts are nearly as large as her federal Representatives' districts. The districts in Massachusetts and New York are larger. In fact, in Albany and New York City nearly as many voters elect state Assemblymen as will be entitled to a Representative in Congress, if there are only 65 members of the House of Representatives. Each voter votes for a number of representatives at the same time. They certainly will be able to choose one federal Representative.

Pennsylvania is another example. Some counties that elect State representatives are almost as large as the districts that will elect federal Representatives. Philadelphia has between 50,000 and 60,000 people. Therefore, it will form nearly two districts for the choice of federal Representatives. However, it forms only one county with one representative in the State legislature. And the whole city actually elects *a single member* for executive council. This is the case in all counties in the State.

Are Representatives Elected by Large Group Less Worthy?

20   Don't these facts disprove this argument against the House of Representatives? Do the senators of New Hampshire, Massachusetts, and New York, or the executive council of Pennsylvania, or the members of the Assembly in the two last States sacrifice the many to the few? Are they less worthy than the representatives and magistrates elected in other States by very small groups of the people?

Entire States Elect Governors

21   But there are more powerful examples than these. The entire State of Connecticut elects the members of one branch of the State legislature. So are the governors of that State, Massachusetts, and New York, and the president of New Hampshire.

Every man can decide whether these methods of choosing State officials tend to elevate traitors and undermine public liberty.

PUBLIUS

Number 58: Number of Representatives Will Grow

I will examine one more charge against the House of Representatives. It has been said that the number of members will not grow as population growth may demand.

Fear Unfounded

2   If true, this would be an important objection. However, it is like most objections against the Constitution. It is either the result of limited information about the subject or a jealousy that produces an irrational hatred towards all things.

Temporary Number; 10-Year Census Will Adjust Number

3   One. The number of Representatives stated in the Constitution is temporary, for only three years.

4   A census of inhabitants will be taken every ten years. The census has two objectives: First, to periodically adjust the ratio of representatives to inhabitants; the exception is that each State will have at least one representative. Second, to increase the number of representatives, but the whole number will not exceed one for every 30,000 inhabitants.

Some State constitutions have no regulations on this subject. Others are very similar to the federal Constitution. And the highest security in any of them is only a suggestion.

State Legislatures Have Increased

5   Two. The States have increased their representatives as the populations increased. When the citizens requested an increase, the representatives have agreed.

Large States Will Enforce House Increase

6   Three. Both the people and their representatives will carefully watch the growth in the number of federal Representatives.

The House of Representatives represents the citizens; the Senate represents the States. Consequently, in the House of Representatives, the larger States will have the most weight. The Senate favors the smaller States. We can assume that large States will want to increase the number of Representatives from their States and their influence will predominate.

The four largest States will have a majority of the votes in the House of Representatives. Therefore, if the nine smaller States oppose adding members, the four large States can overrule the opposition. Normally, rivalries and prejudices might prevent the States from agreeing to an issue. But they would join together to support their common interest and desire to uphold the equity and principals of the Constitution.

Senate Blocking Increase in House

7   It may be argued that the Senate might block efforts to increase the number of Representatives. Since the Senate's agreement is necessary, it could defeat the just, constitutional actions of the House.

This problem worries the jealous friends of a large representation. Fortunately, it is an illusion. It vanishes on close inspection.

House Will Prevail in This Situation

8   The House and Senate will have equal authority on all legislative subjects except money bills—the House originates all money bills. However, the House will have more members. When the more powerful/larger States follow the will of a majority of the people, they will support the House of Representatives. And the House will have an advantage over the Senate.

9   Logic and the Constitution make the House of Representatives even stronger. And opponents to increasing the size of the House will be fighting against the force of all these strong forces.

Senate Also Influenced By State Size

10   The States range in size from small to large. Several medium size States, are closer in size to the large than the small States. Therefore, those Sates will probably not oppose the larger States' just and legitimate claims. Therefore, it is not certain that a majority of votes, even in the Senate, would block the growth in the number of Representatives.

Reapportionment: New, Growing States

11   Also, the Senators from new States may agree to increase the House of Representatives. The population in the new States will increase rapidly. They will want frequent reapportionments to reflect their increased population.

The large States will have the most power in the House of Representatives. They will want both reapportionments and increased membership in the House. And the Senators from all the fastest growing States will fight for increasing House membership because of their States' interest in reapportionment.

Representatives, Alone, Hold the Purse

12   For these reasons, alone, there should be no fear that the House will not increase in size. However, the larger States will have another, constitutional remedy to increase the size.

The House of Representatives, alone, proposes the bills that provide the government with the supplies it needs. They hold the purse. This is a very important power. Britain has the monarchy, the House of Lords (run by the aristocracy), and the House of Commons, (the representative body of the people). Because it controls the money, the House of Commons has slowly increased its activity and importance. It is now the most powerful branch of British government.

Power over the purse is the best weapon any constitution can give the people's representatives. It can correct every problem and promote the people's wishes.

Will House Cave to Senate?

13   Won't the House of Representatives want to maintain the proper functions of the government? Will the House allow the Senate to determine its existence or reputation? Or if there was a trial of firmness between the two houses of Congress, would not either one be as likely as the other to yield first?

These are not difficult questions. When a small, visible group of people with long terms in office hold power, each person feels more personally responsible to fulfill their duties. Senators represent the dignity of their country in the eyes of other nations. They will be very sensitive to the possibility of public danger or dishonorable stagnation in public affairs.

The British House of Commons has more power than the other branches of the government when money bills are discussed. If the monarchy and House of Lords became absolutely inflexible, the government would have been thrown into confusion. However, this has never happened.

The federal Senate and President will never be able to completely resist the House. And the House will be supported by constitutional and patriotic principles.

Danger of Large Governing Body

14   Some people might want to temporarily lower the number of representatives to save money. This subject could have been used as an objection to the Constitution. And under the present circumstances, it might be
difficult to have as many people in the federal government as the people
will probably elect.

I must add one observation, however, because it is very important. The
larger the number of members in any assembly or legislature, the fewer the
number of men who will, in fact, direct their proceedings. This is the result of several factors.

First, as the number of people in an assembly grows, the rule of passion
over reason also grows.

Second, as the size of a group grows, so does the proportion of members with limited information and less ability. A few eloquent leaders can
sway people with these personality types. In the ancient republics, where
the whole population assembled in person, a single orator or an artful
statesman generally ruled as if he was a king or dictator.

Third, on the same principle, the bigger a representative assembly becomes, the more it will take on the problems that accompany collective
meetings of the people. Ignorance will be the dupe of cunning. Passion
the slave of sophistry and declamation.

People may think that the bigger the assembly, the stronger the barrier
against government by the few. However, this is a big mistake. Experience shows the opposite. *After an assembly is large enough to secure
safety, to understand local information, and to be sympathetic to society*,
every additional representative will defeat this purpose. The government
may look more democratic, but it will actually be more oligarchic. The
assembly will be larger, but fewer people—often in secret—will direct its
actions.

Super Majorities Lead to Minority Rule

15   This is a good place to discuss how many members are needed for
legislative business. It has been said that a quorum should be more than a
majority. And in particular cases more than a majority should be required
for a decision.

This precaution may have some advantages. It might be an additional
shield against some special interests. And it could be another obstacle to
hasty and partial measures. But these considerations are outweighed by
the inconveniences on the opposite side.

Whenever justice or the general good might require new laws or active
measures, a quorum of more than a majority would reverse the fundamental principle of free government. The majority would no longer rule. The
power would be transferred to the minority.

If a super majority was limited to specific cases, an interested minority might take advantage of it. They could protect themselves from equitable sacrifices or, in emergencies, to extort unreasonable indulgences.

Lastly, it would facilitate and foster a bad practice that goes against all principles of good government. This would lead more directly to public tumult and the ruin of popular government—secessions.

PUBLIUS

Legislative: Congress

Number 59: Congress Can Regulate Federal Elections

The Constitution authorizes Congress to regulate elections. It says: "The *times, places,* and *manner* of holding elections for Senators and Representatives shall be prescribed in each State by the legislature thereof; but the Congress may at any time by law make or alter *such regulations,* except as to the *places* of choosing Senators."

Many people criticize this provision. Some critics condemn the whole Constitution. Other critics have fewer objections. One gentleman agrees with every other part of the Constitution, but objects to this clause.

Government Preserves Itself

2   However, it is the easiest clause in the Constitution to defend. It is proper because *every government should have the ability and means to preserve itself.*

The convention followed this rule. Every logical person will agree with the convention. And he will disapprove of every deviation from it. If the government cannot protect itself, it could become weak and, in the future, may turn into anarchy.

3   The Constitution cannot have an election law that applies to every possible future situation.   There must be a flexible power over elections. There are three ways to modify this power: completely by the national legislature, or completely by the State legislatures, or primarily by the States and ultimately by the national. The convention chose the last way.

Initially, local governments will regulate federal elections. This will usually be both convenient and satisfactory. But the national legislature may intervene when it feels it is necessary for its safety.

States Effect Federal Government

4   If the States had complete power to regulate national elections, the Union's existence would be entirely at their mercy. At any time, they could end the nation by not having an election. There would be no one to administer the national government.

It is pointless to say that this probably would not happen. Saying something is constitutionally possible but there is no risk of it happening, is an unanswerable objection. And there is no reason for taking that risk.

The conclusion that the federal government will abuse its power is based on jealousy. It is as easy for a local government to abuse power as a national government. Therefore, it is just as fair to assume that the State governments will abuse their power as the national government. And it is more logical to trust the Union with the care of its own existence, than to give that care to State governments.

5   Suppose the Constitution gave the national government the power to regulate State elections. Everyone would condemn it. It should be a State, not federal, power. And the federal government could use it to destroy the State governments.

It is just as clear that the existence of the national government should not be left to the States. As far as possible, each government should be able to preserve itself.

State Control of Federal Elections

6   If State legislatures had total power to regulate federal elections, the national Senate might be in danger. By not appointing Senators, State legislatures could give a fatal blow to the Union. The national Senate depends on the States.

Each State has an interest in maintaining its representation in the national councils. It could be argued that this would provide complete security against an abuse of the trust.

7   Although it sounds good, this argument is not valid. If the State legislatures refused to appoint Senators, the national government might be destroyed. But just because the States have the power to not appoint Senators, it does not mean that they should also have the power to not elect Representatives. The States can do more harm with the power to regulate congressional elections than with their power to appoint Senators. And there is no counter-balancing reason for taking the risk.

The Constitution establishes the organization of the national government. If the Constitutional organization of the national government is exposed to injury from States, it is an evil. But this evil could not be completely avoided. The States, as political units, need to be part of the national government. Therefore, the State legislatures appoint Senators.

Under the federal principle, the States need to be included in the national government. And it gives the State governments a safeguard. Although it is inconvenient, States need to appoint Senators. However, we cannot infer from this that the States should control all federal elections when it is not necessary or when it doesn't fulfill a greater good.

8   There is a greater risk to the national government if the States control the elections of Representatives than from their power to appoint Senators. Senators will serve for six years. Their terms will rotate. Elections for a third of the Senate seats will be held every two years. And no State is entitled to more than two senators. A Senate quorum will be sixteen members. Therefore, even if a few States stopped appointing senators, the Senate would not disappear and it could keep functioning. And we have nothing to fear from a widespread, permanent conspiracy of the States.

Sinister plots by leaders in a few State legislatures might start a conspiracy. To be permanent, it would require support by the general population. However, it will probably never happen. If a widespread conspiracy

does develop, it will probably be because the national government becomes inept at advancing the people's happiness. And if this happens, no
good citizen will want it to continue.

Possibility of National Crisis

9   But members of the federal House of Representatives will be elected
every two years. If the State legislatures had exclusive power to regulate
these elections and if the leaders of a few important States conspired to
prevent an election, every election would create a crisis that could result in
the Union dissolving.

Public Interests v. Ambition

10   Some people say that each State will have federal Representatives.
And this will provide some security against the States using federal elections to abuse their power. This argument is somewhat valid.

But it will not provide complete security. There is a difference between
the people's interest in public happiness and their local rulers' interest in
power. The American people may like the federal government at the same
time that some State rulers—supported by strong factions—want power
and personal aggrandizement. There is already a conflict in some States
between a majority of the people and powerful government officials.

If the nation was divided into several separate confederacies, the
chance of this conflict multiplies. It will be a constant temptation to State
politicians to increase their own benefits instead of advancing the public
welfare.

If the States had exclusive power to regulate national elections, a few
men from influential States might destroy the Union. They could use
some little dissatisfaction among the people (that they may have promoted)
to stop choosing Representatives.

European nations will be jealous of a firm Union with an efficient government. Sometimes foreign powers will try to subvert our government.
And they will support internal intrigues. Therefore, when possible, the
government's preservation should be guarded by people with an immediate interest in faithful and vigilant performances of the trust.

PUBLIUS

Number 60: Dangers of Union Regulating Its Own Elections

Giving State legislatures total control over federal elections would be
dangerous. What are the dangers from the Union regulating its own elections?

No State would ever be excluded from its share in representation. In
this respect, the interest of all would be the security of all.

But some people say that the federal government might use the power to regulate the "time and manner" of elections to make sure people from a favorite class will be elected. They say that the national government could exclude some voters by locating polling places in areas that are difficult for some voters to reach. Of all the unbelievable ideas, this seems to be the most unbelievable.

It's impossible to imagine that such dangerous men would ever be part of the national government. However, if men who wanted to create an aristocracy held national offices, they would act more directly than just making polling places difficult to get to.

No Voting Rights will lead to Revolt

2   Such an attempt is improbable because the State governments would immediately revolt.

During turbulent and factious times, a majority might deny a specific group of people the fundamental right of freedom—suffrage. However, if the government tried to take away the voting rights of the great mass of people, the people would revolt.

3   Let's look at a few facts that will wipe out all fears on the subject. Each part of the national government will be structured differently and will behave differently. The different branches will block election conspiracies.

People in different parts of the Union have different behaviors and habits. Representatives will bring a wide range of feelings to the national government. As they work closely together, they will begin to think more alike. But physical and moral causes may nourish their different propensities and inclinations.

But here is the main reason that the parts of the federal government will probably not conspire to control who is elected: each part will be elected in a different way. The House of Representatives will be elected directly by the people. The Senate by the State legislatures. The president by electors who are chosen for that purpose by the people.

Representatives, Senators and the President are chosen in very different ways. Therefore, they probably won't have a reason to prefer one specific class of electors.

4   The national government will be limited to regulating the "time and manner" of elections. This can't influence the choice of Senators. Entire State legislatures can't be influenced by this regulation. This fact, alone, should satisfy us that the feared discrimination would never be attempted.

What could induce the Senate to concur in a preference in which it would not share? Or what would be the purpose if it could be established in one federal legislative house but not the other? In this case, the composition of one would counteract the other.

We can never assume the House would agree with Senate appointments, unless we can also assume that the State legislatures will cooperate. If we assume that the State legislatures can be corrupted, then it doesn't matter where the power in the question is placed—whether in their hands or in the Union.

5   What would be the objective of this unpredictable favoritism in national councils? Who would be discriminated against? Would it be different industries, different kinds of property or different amounts of property? Will property owners, merchants, or manufacturers be favored?

Or, to talk like the opponents of the Constitution, will it encourage the elevation of the "wealthy and the well-born" to the exclusion and debasement of all the rest of society?

6   If favoritism is shown, I assume the competition will be between property owners and merchants. And it is more likely either would have excessive influence in local rather than national councils.

Agricultural Interests

7   To various degrees, the States are addicted to agriculture and commerce. In most, if not all, agriculture is predominant. However, commerce is very important in a few States and it has a lot of influence in most of them.

Agriculture and commerce will also influence the national legislature. And there will be a wider variety of interests than found in any single State. Therefore, the national legislature will be less likely to be partial to either interest than in a single State.

8   When a country is mostly farmers and has equal representation, farm interests will usually predominate in the government. As long as farm interests prevail in State legislatures, they will also prevail in the national Senate. The Senate will usually be a copy of the majorities in the State legislatures. Therefore, we can't assume that farmers will be sacrificed to the benefit of merchants in the federal Senate.

People who strongly support State power cannot believe that outside influences will sway State legislatures from their duty. The same situation will have the same effect on the federal House of Representatives. An improper bias in favor of merchants isn't expected.

Importance of Merchants

9   Will the national government have an opposite bias? Will federal officials tend to become a monopoly of property owners? Such a bias probably won't worry people who would be immediately injured by it. So an elaborate answer isn't needed.

First, for reasons stated elsewhere, citizens are more likely to favor State rather than Union councils.

Second, there won't be a temptation to violate the Constitution in favor of property owners because that group will have as much influence and power as it will want.

And third, commerce is very important to both public prosperity and revenue to government. Merchants understand managing business. And if they were excluded, it would wound the national government. Commerce is so important that Congress will not make merchants angry. As public needs become apparent, Congress will need their help.

"Wealthy, Well-Born" Representatives

10   Critics talk about another kind of favoritism. They warn us about "wealthy and the well-born" politicians. I will briefly discuss the probability that specific industries and property owners will be preferred.

Critics say that "wealthy and well-born" politicians will be raised to a status above their fellow citizens. However, first critics claim this is the natural consequence of having a small representative body. Then they say it is the result of not allowing citizens to vote.

Federal Election Power Restricted

11   But where can an election be held to create a preference? Are "the wealthy and the well-born," confined to specific geographic locations in the States? Have they, by some miraculous instinct or foresight, set apart in each State a common place of residence? Are they only in towns or cities? Or are they scattered over the face of the country as avarice or chance has cast their lot or that of their ancestors? The latter is the case, as every intelligent man knows. Therefore, the policy of confining the places of election to specific districts would subvert its aim.

The only way rich people could take over control is if there were property qualifications for either voters or nominees. But the national government doesn't have this power. Its can only regulate the *times*, the *places*, and the *manner* of elections. The qualifications of voters or nominees are defined in the Constitution and Congress can't change them.

12   However, let's assume, for argument's sake, that selfish interests prevail. Let's also assume that the national rulers overcame all the scruples arising from a sense of duty or fear of the experiment. It still couldn't be carried out without the help of a military force large enough to subdue the resistance of the population. We've already discussed that raising a big enough force is improbable. But let's pretend that such a force exists and the national government has it. What would happen?

If the rulers wanted to invade the rights of the community and had the ability to do it, would they amuse themselves with the ridiculous task of changing election laws to secure that a favorite class of men be elected?

Wouldn't they do something to immediately gain personal power? Wouldn't they boldly take power with one act of usurpation, rather than trust to precarious expedients that might end in their dismissal, disgrace, and ruin? Wouldn't they fear that citizens would travel great distances to election places, overthrow their tyrants and substitute men who would want to avenge the violated majesty of the people?

PUBLIUS

Number 61: Regulation of Federal Congressional Elections

Some critics of the election provision in the Constitution agree that it is proper, but needs one addition. They want it to say that all elections should be in the counties where the voters live to protect against an abuse of the power.

This would be harmless. If it quieted fears, it might be desirable. But it would give little security against the feared danger. And an impartial examiner will never consider the lack of it as a serious objection to the Constitution.

If liberty is ever the victim of ambitious national rulers, it can not be blamed on the election provision.

Voter Apathy: Distance Reduces Turnout

2   The State constitutions have provisions about State elections. If we study them, it will remove any negative feelings about this clause in the federal Constitution. I will limit myself to the example of New York.

The New York constitution says members of the Assembly are elected in the *counties,* and members of the State Senate are elected in the State districts. Currently, there are four Senate districts. Each district has two to six counties. Obviously, New York could defeat the voting rights of her citizens by limiting the places where people can vote.

Suppose the city of Albany was the only place to vote in its county and district. The people who live in Albany would quickly become the only electors of both the Senate and Assembly for that county and district. Would the voters who live in the remote areas travel to Albany to vote for State officials quicker than they would travel to New York City to vote for members of the federal House of Representatives?

Voting is a privilege. Yet people seem indifferent about voting. We have seen that when the voting place is at an *inconvenient distance* from the voter, it doesn't matter whether the distance is 20 miles or 20,000 miles. Therefore, objections to the federal power of regulating elections also apply to the same power in the New York constitution. It is impossible to find one satisfactory and condemn the other.

If we look at most State constitutions, we'll come to the same conclusion.

"Problem" Ignored in State Constitutions

3   If someone says, "The defects in the State constitutions don't excuse defects in the proposed federal Constitution," I answer, "No one has said that the State constitutions don't secure liberty. But the complaints thrown at the federal Constitution apply to them also."

Therefore, we must assume that these trivial accusations have been created to support a predetermined opposition to the Constitution. They are not logical conclusions from an honest search for the truth.

To people who believe that this is an unforgivable error in the federal Constitution and it is only an innocent omission in the State constitutions, nothing can be said. Or we must ask them, "Why can State representatives resist the lust of power better than federal representatives?"

They should prove that it is easier to subvert the liberties of the entire country than a single State. The country has three million people. Their local governments will support them if they must oppose a tyrannical federal government. 200,000 citizens of a State don't have that advantage.

They should also prove that a strong faction in a single State will be less likely to promote a specific class of electors than the representatives of thirteen States, spread over a vast region, with a diversity of local circumstances, prejudices, and interests.

Uniform Elections to House

4   I have shown that the election clause is theoretically proper. It would be dangerous to place the power elsewhere. And putting it in the proposed Constitution is safe. The federal elections clause also has an advantage that could not have been as effectively gotten in any other way.

I'm talking about a uniform time for the election of federal Representatives. This uniformity may prove important to the public welfare. It can be a security against continuing an unhealthy spirit in the body and a cure for the diseases of faction.

If each State could choose its own time for elections, there could be as many different times as there are months in the year. Currently, States hold elections at different times between March and November. If the House elections are held at different times, it would never be totally dissolved and remade. If an improper spirit took over the House of Representatives, as new members joined, they would probably be infected by the improper spirit. The mass would likely hold onto the improper spirit and gradually assimilate new members into itself. The older members would have an influence that few new members would have enough willpower to resist.

The entire House of Representatives will be dissolved every two years. This means there will be less danger to liberty than a shorter term with gradual changes.

Uniform Senate Elections

5   Uniform election times for Senators seem no less required. The legislature can assemble at a specific time each year.

Election Time Unnecessary

6   Why couldn't an election time be in the Constitution? The zealous adversaries of the federal Constitution in New York are, in general, zealous admirers of our New York State constitution. We could ask them, why wasn't an election time put in the State constitution?

The best answer is that it is safe for the legislature to decide. If a time had been fixed in the Constitution, once implemented it might have been found less convenient than some other time.

The same answer applies to the federal Constitution. The possible danger of a gradual change is speculative. Therefore, it would not have been a good idea to establish a time for elections in the Constitution. It would have deprived States of the convenience of having State and national elections at the same time.

PUBLIUS

Legislative: Senate

Number 62: Senators: Qualifications, Reasons Necessary

Next, I will examine the Senate. The subjects to be considered are:
- The qualification of Senators.
- The appointment of them by the State legislatures.
- The equality of representation in the Senate.
- The reasons a Senate is needed. The number of Senators and their term in office.
- The powers vested in the Senate.

I Qualifications of Senators

2   A Senator must be at least thirty years old and a citizen for nine years. A Representative must be 25 years old and a citizen for 7 years.

A Senator needs more knowledge and a stable character. The Senator should be old enough to have these advantages.

Senators are involved with foreign policy. They should be weaned from attitudes and habits resulting from a foreign birth and education. Nine years is a good compromise.   Adopted citizens, who may have talents and earned public confidence, are not totally excluded. But they can't immediately become Senators, which might create a channel for foreign influence in the national council.

II State Legislatures Appoint Senators

3   There is no need to discuss the appointment of senators by the State legislatures. Public opinion seems to want this method of appointment. It has two advantages. The State government plays a role in the forming the federal government. And it secures the States' authority and links the two systems.

III. Equal Representation in Senate

4   Equal representation in the Senate doesn't need much discussion. It is a compromise between the opposite demands of the large and small States.

When **people** join to become one nation, every district should have a *proportional* share in the government.

When sovereign **states** form a league, the states, however unequal in size, should have an *equal* share in common councils.

If these principles are true, in a compound republic, with characteristics of both a national and a federal government, that government should have a mixture of proportional and equal representation.

We don't need to evaluate this part of the Constitution. Everyone agrees that it is the result "of a spirit of amity, and the mutual deference and concession that our special political situation made indispensable."

The United States needs a government with the powers necessary to meet its objectives. The smaller States won't agree to a government that favors the large States. Therefore, the large States can either accept the proposed government or one that is more objectionable. Let's look at why it may be a good idea to not have proportional representation in the Senate.

Equality Protects State Sovereignty

5   Equal votes in the Senate constitutionally preserve the sovereignty that remains in the States. Both large and small States want to guard against an improper consolidation of the States into one simple republic. Therefore, the large States should accept this equality.

Block against Bad Legislation

6   Equality in the Senate also helps block improper legislative acts. No law or resolution will pass without a majority of the people [House of Representatives] and then a majority of the States [Senate] agreeing to it.

This check on legislation can be both injurious and beneficial. Small States will need this defense when they have interests that are different from those of the large States and those interests might be exposed to danger. The larger States will always have more power over supplies than the small States. Therefore, the larger States will always be able to defeat unreasonable laws proposed by small States.

The ease and excess of law-making are the diseases to which our governments are most liable. This part of the Constitution may be more convenient in practice than it appears in contemplation.

IV. The reasons a Senate is needed. Number of Members, Term in Office

7   The number of senators and their term in office are considered next. To judge these points, we will look at the purposes of the Senate. What problems would the republic have if it didn't have a Senate?

Differences Thwart Conspiracies

8   *First.* Administrators of the republic may forget their obligations to the people and betray their important trust. A senate as a second house of legislature is a good check on the government. It doubles the people's security. Two separate bodies will have to agree to schemes of usurpation or perfidy. Without it, one corrupt body would be enough.

There are clear principles for this precaution. Sinister conspiracies are less probable as the difference between the geniuses of the two legislative bodies grows. Therefore, making them as different as possible, within the principles of republican government, is prudent.

Passions Sway Large Assemblies

9   *Second.* All single, large assemblies tend to give in to sudden, violent passions; they can be seduced by factious leaders into extreme and harmful resolutions. Therefore, a Senate is necessary.

Numerous examples on this subject could be cited. But no one will contradict this point. A body formed to correct this problem should be, itself, free from it. Consequently, it should be smaller with longer terms in office to make it more stable.

Familiarity with Objectives, Principles

10   *Third.* Senators will be familiar with the objectives and principles of legislation.

Most members of the House of Representatives will be men with jobs in the private sector. They will have a short term in office with no reason to devote their time while serving as Representatives to the study of laws and all the interests of their country. If the House was the only legislative assembly, it would make a variety of important errors.

Many of America's present embarrassments can be charged on the blunders of our governments. These blunders have come from the heads rather than the hearts of most of the authors of them.

Indeed, acts that repeal, explain, and amend laws fill and disgrace our huge codes. They are monuments to a lack of wisdom. Each legislative session discredits the preceding session. A Senate will be very helpful.

Good Government→ Happiness

11   A good government implies two things. First, it is faithful to government's objective—the happiness of the people. Second, it knows how to reach this objective.

Some governments don't have either of these qualities. Most governments don't have the first. In American governments, too little attention has been paid to the last. The federal Constitution avoids this error. And it provides for the last in a way to increase the security for the first.

Frequent Turnover Hampers Success

12   *Fourth.* Frequent changes in public councils, however qualified the new members may be, shows why a stable institution in the government is necessary.

Every election changes half the representatives. This turnover creates a change of opinions and a change of legislation. But continual change, even if it is good legislation, is inconsistent with every rule of prudence and every hope of success. Private life verifies this observation. And it becomes more just and more important in national transactions.

Frequent Legislative Changes Harmful

13   A history of the harmful effects of a mutable government would fill a volume. I will list a few, each of which is a source of others.

Mutable Government Forfeits Respect

14   A mutable government forfeits the respect and confidence of other nations, and all the advantages connected with national character.

All prudent people know that a person who frequently changes his plans or lives his life without any plan at all will quickly fall victim to his own unsteadiness and folly. His friendly neighbors may pity him, but all will decline to connect their fortunes with his. And more than a few people will seize the opportunity to make their fortunes out of his.

One nation is to another as one individual is to another, with one sad difference. Nations have fewer benevolent emotions than people. They feel fewer restraints from taking advantage of each other. Every nation that shows a lack of wisdom and stability may expect every possible loss to the more systematic policy of their wiser neighbors.

Unfortunately, the best example is America. She is ridiculed by her enemies. And she is prey to every nation that wants to speculate about her changing councils and embarrassed affairs.

Often Changing Laws Threatens Liberty

15   The domestic effects of a mutable policy are even worse. It poisons the blessings of liberty itself.

It won't benefit the people that the laws are made by men of their own choice, if the laws are so voluminous that they cannot be read or so incoherent that they cannot be understood. Or if they are repealed or revised before they are promulgated or are changed so frequently that no man who knows what the law is today can guess what it will be tomorrow.

Law is defined to be a rule of action. But how can it be a rule when it is little known and less fixed?

Laws Benefiting Only a Few Citizens

16   There is another effect of having laws that are not stable. It gives the few perceptive, enterprising, and wealthy citizens an advantage over the industrious and uninformed mass of people.

Every new regulation about commerce or revenue or that affects property value is a new opportunity to those people who watch the change and can predict its consequences. They don't create this opportunity. It is created by the toils and cares of the great body of their fellow citizens. When this happens, it may truthfully be said that laws are made for the *few*, not for the *many*.

Discourages Business, Commerce

17 An unstable government also hurts the economy. When people don't know what actions the government might take, projects where success and profit may depend on the existing laws continuing will be discouraged.

What prudent merchant will jeopardize his fortunes in a new area of commerce when he doesn't know if his plans may be made unlawful before they can be executed? What farmer or manufacturer will commit himself to a specific cultivation or project when he can't be sure that his preparations and investment will not make him a victim to an inconstant government?

In a word, if an improvement or praiseworthy enterprise needs the protection or security of a consistent national policy, it will not be pursued.

Mutability Damages Respect

18 But the worst effect is that the people will feel less attachment and reverence to the government. No government will be respected without being truly respectable. And it will not be respectable if it doesn't have some order and stability.

PUBLIUS

Number 63   IV. (continued) Number Senators, 6-Year Term

I will continue discussing why a Senate is useful.

A *fifth* aim is national reputation. The government needs a stable part. Without it, our policies will change frequently and we will lose the respect of foreign nations. And the national government will not be sensitive to the opinion of the world, which is necessary to obtain its respect and confidence.

2 The judgment of other nations is important for two reasons:

1) Independent of the merits of any specific plan or measure, it is desirable that other nations see it as coming from a wise and honorable policy.

2) In doubtful cases, particularly when some strong passion or momentary concern warps the national government, the opinion of the impartial world may be the best guide.

How has America's poor reputation with foreign nations hurt us? And how many errors would she have avoided, if she had first looked at how her policies appeared to unbiased observers?

Size, Term Effect Responsibility

3   A large legislature that has members with only a short term in office cannot create a good national reputation. In a small legislature, each member shares the praise and blame for laws. And when a legislator has a long term in office, his pride becomes part of the reputation and prosperity of the community.

Representatives in Rhode Island serve for six months. When they discussed grossly unjust laws, the opinion of foreign nations or the other States probably had little effect. What if a second, stable legislative body had to agree to the laws? Its members would want national respect. This would have prevented the calamities under which the people now live.

Frequent Elections → Responsibility

4   S*ixth* aim: Less frequent elections increase the government's responsibility to the people. This comment may seem both new and paradoxical. However, it is true and important.

Long Term Governmental Goals, Policy

5   Responsibility must be **reasonable** and **effective**.

To be **reasonable**, it must be limited to objects within the power of the responsible party.

To be **effective**, constituents must be able to see and judge the operations of that power.

There are two types of legislation. Some legislation takes immediate effect. Other legislation is part of a chain of measures that have a gradual and, perhaps, unobserved operation.

The latter type of legislation is important to the welfare of every country. A legislature with a short term can provide only one or two links in a chain of measures. But they cannot be held responsible for the final result. This is the same as a building project that takes six years. A carpenter employed for one year is not responsible for the final result.

When a legislature is elected every year and is working towards a long-term goal, the people don't know how to judge the influence of each annual assembly. And in a very large legislature, it is also hard to make each representative feel personally responsible.

Senate: Long Term Objectives

6   The remedy is a second legislative body. The members should have long enough terms to meet objectives that require constant attention and a series of measures. They can be responsible for meeting those objectives.

Slowness Blocks Bad Legislation

7   Sometimes a Senate protects the people from their own errors and delusions.

In all governments, the community's objectives should prevail over the objectives of its rulers. And it will prevail in all free governments.

However, inappropriate passions sometimes influence citizens. Ambitious and clever men may mislead them. Then citizens may ask for laws that they will later lament and condemn.

If a second, temperate legislative body made up of respectable citizens must agree to the laws, it could block misguided laws. It can stop the blow planned by the people against themselves until reason, justice, and truth can be restored to the public mind.

The Athenians would have escaped bitter pain if their government had such a safeguard against the tyranny of their own passions. We might not now blame liberty for decreeing, to the same citizens, hemlock on one day and statues on the next.

Size No Protection from Mass Hysteria

8   Someone might say that when people are spread over a large area they cannot, like the crowded inhabitants of a city, be infected by violent passions or conspire to pursue unjust measures. This is important. In a former paper, I explained that this is one of the important advantages of a confederated republic.

However, this advantage doesn't mean that other precautions are unnecessary. The large area will exempt Americans from some of the dangers seen in smaller republics. But it also means that we will live for a longer time under the influence of the misrepresentations.

Senates in All Long-Lived Republics

9   History shows us no long-lived republic without a senate. Sparta and Rome had a senate for life. The senate in Carthage is less known. It probably also had a senate for life. It certainly had some quality that made it an anchor against popular fluctuations. A smaller council, drawn out of the senate, was both appointed for life and filled up vacancies itself.

We should not imitate these examples. They are repugnant to the American spirit. However, when we compare them to other short-lived and turbulent ancient republics, they prove that an institution that blends stability and liberty is necessary.

The American government is different from other ancient and modern popular governments. When comparing governments, we must be very careful. But after noting their differences, their similarities make these examples worth our attention.

A senate corrects some of the defects caused by a large legislature. The people can never willfully betray their own interests, but their representatives may betray them. The danger is greater when one group of men has the whole legislative trust. There is less danger when two dissimilar groups must agree to every public act.

Ancient Republics had Representatives

10   There is a difference between America and other republics. The difference is the principle of representation. Representation is essential to the American republic. Apparently, ancient republics didn't know about representation. This difference is important. However, ancient governments did have some representation.

Greece had Representative Executives

11   In the most pure democracies of Greece, many executive functions were not performed by the people. They were performed by elected officers, *representing* the people in their *executive* capacity.

Representation in Athens, Carthage

12   Prior to the reform of Solon, nine Archons governed Athens. *The people at large elected them annually.* We are not sure how much power they had.

After that period, an assembly of 400 to 600 members was annually *elected by the people* and *partially* represented them as legislators. They made laws and proposed legislation to the people.

The senate of Carthage, whatever its power or term in office, appears to have been *elected* by the people. Similar examples might be found in most, if not all, the popular governments of antiquity.

Representatives in Sparta, Rome, Crete

13   Lastly, Sparta had the Ephori, and Rome had the Tribunes. These two bodies were small. The *whole body of the people elected them annually* and they were considered the *representatives* of the people with almost full power.

The Cosmi of Crete were also annually *elected by the people.* Some authors say it was similar to the institutions of Sparta and Rome. However, the representative body of Crete was elected by only a part of the people.

Large Size, United States Advantage

14   Clearly, some ancient governments used representatives. The true difference between the ancient governments and the American governments is that *the people, in their collective capacity, are totally excluded* from any part in the *American governments*. It is not the *total exclusion of representatives* from the administration of the *ancient governments.*

However, after noting this difference, the United States has an advantage. To take full effect of this advantage, we can't separate it from the advantage of being a large country. No form of republican government could have succeeded within the tiny area occupied by the democracies of Greece.

Senate Becoming Aristocracy

15   These arguments support having a Senate. However, jealous opponents of the Constitution will disagree. They will probably say that a senate that is not elected directly by the people and with six-year terms will slowly become powerful. And it will eventually turn into a tyrannical aristocracy.

Abuse of Liberty Endangers Liberty

16   Liberty can be endangered by the abuses of liberty as well as by the abuses of power. There are many examples of both. And the former, rather than the latter, are apparently most to be feared by the United States.

Tyranny: Too Many People Involved

17   Before transforming into a tyrannical aristocracy, the Senate must first corrupt itself. Next it must corrupt the State legislatures. It must then corrupt the House of Representatives. And, finally, corrupt the people at large.

The Senate must be corrupted first before it can try to establish a tyranny. To do this, it must corrupt the State legislatures; if not corrupted, the States would elect new members to the Senate, changing the whole body.

If the House of Representatives wasn't corrupted, it would inevitably defeat the attempt.

And without corrupting the people, new representatives would quickly restore all things to their perfect order.

Can any man seriously believe that the proposed Senate can achieve the objectives of lawless ambition through all these obstructions?

Maryland's Senate Alleviates Fears

18   Reason condemns this fear and so does experience.

The Maryland constitution is the best example. That senate is elected, as the federal Senate will be, indirectly by the people and for a term of five years. It can even fill its own vacancies. And it doesn't have rotating terms as provided for the federal Senate.

The Maryland senate has some other differences that expose it to objections that do not apply to the federal Senate. Therefore, if the federal Senate is dangerous, we should be seeing symptoms of a similar danger in the Maryland senate. But no symptoms have appeared. On the contrary, the fears of skeptics have slowly disappeared.   And the Maryland constitution has a great reputation.

House of Commons v. Aristocracy

19   But if anything could silence the fears on this subject, it should be the British example.

The British senate [House of Lords] is a hereditary legislature of rich nobles. Instead of six years, they have a lifetime term. And only special families can be members.

The British house of representatives is the House of Commons. The representatives are elected for seven years instead of two years. And only a very small proportion of the people are allowed to vote.

We should see the aristocratic usurpations and tyranny in Great Britain that are expected to happen in the United States. However, the British House of Lords has not been able to defend itself against the continual encroachments of the House of Commons. First the House of Lords lost the support of the monarch, than it was crushed by the weight of the popular branch.

People's Representatives Stronger House

20   From the little we know about ancient republics, they support our reasoning.

In Sparta, the Ephori, the annually elected representatives of the people, were an overmatch for the senate for life. It encroached on the senate's authority until it had all the power.

The Tribunes of Rome, the representatives of the people, won almost every contest with the senate for life. In the end, the people's representatives triumphed over it. This fact is even more amazing since unanimity was required in every act of the Tribunes, even after their number was increased by ten. This proves that the branch of a free government that has the people on its side is the most powerful branch.

We can add Carthage to these examples. Polynius says that instead of becoming all-powerful, at the start of the second Punic War, its senate had lost almost all of its power.

Senate must Gain People's Support

21   These facts show that the federal Senate will never be able to transform itself, by gradual usurpations, into an independent, aristocratic body.

Additionally, we believe that if the Senate does evolve into an aristocratic body—for a reason that we can't predict—the House of Representatives with the people on their side will restore the Constitution to its original form and principles. Against the force of the people's representatives, the only way the Senate will be able to maintain even its constitutional authority will be enlightened policy and an attachment to the public good. Then the Senate will regain the affections and support of the entire population.

PUBLIUS

Number 64: President, with Senate, Makes Treaties

Some people condemn the entire proposed Constitution. They even severely criticize some of its most harmless articles. Why do they condemn every part of the Constitution? The only explanation is that enemies of specific persons and measures rarely limit their censures to the parts worthy of blame.

Senate Must Ratify Treaties

2   Article 2, section two gives power to the President, *"by and with the advice and consent of the Senate, to make treaties,* PROVIDED TWO THIRDS OF THE SENATORS PRESENT CONCUR."

Indirect Election of President, Senate

3   The power to make treaties is important. It relates to war, peace, and commerce. Qualified men should make treaties, in the manner most conducive to the public good.

In the Constitution, electors, selected by the people for that purpose, will choose the President. And the State legislatures appoint the senators.

This system has a great advantage over direct elections by the people. Party zeal has a great influence in direct elections. It can take advantage of indifference, ignorance, and the hopes and fears of the unwary and uninterested people. And men are often elected by a small proportion of the electors.

Most Qualified Men will be Chosen

4   Electors will choose the President. State legislatures will appoint the senators. They will usually be enlightened and respectable citizens. We can presume that they will vote for able and virtuous men, who have the people's confidence.

The Constitution supports this objective. The President must be at least 35 and Senators 30 years old. The people will have time to judge the candidates. Sometimes a candidate can briefly appear brilliant and patriotic, misleading and dazzling the public. But the electors and legislators will not be deceived.

The electors will have extensive and accurate information about men and their characters. Their appointments should be made with discretion and discernment.

We can infer that the President and Senators, so chosen, will understand our national interests, whether as related to the States or foreign nations. They will promote those interests. They will have reputation for integrity that inspires confidence. The power of making treaties may be given to such men.

Term, Rotating Elections => Stability

5   We know that any business requires systems. But most people don't realize how important they are to national affairs.

Some people want the House of Representatives to make treaties. However, House membership changes too quickly. Two years is not long enough for Representatives to study all the issues required to make treaties. Therefore, the convention wisely gave the Senate the power to make treaties.

Senators will have six-year terms. Able and honest Senators will be in office long enough to understand national concerns and create a system to manage them. While in office, they can increase their political information. Their total experience will benefit their country.

The Constitution has another good feature. If the entire Senate was elected every six years, all great affairs could be totally transferred to new men. By leaving a lot of the members in place, uniformity and order, and the succession of official information, will be preserved.

Maintains Conformity in Trade

6   Trade and navigation regulations should be cautiously formed and steadily pursued. Both treaties and laws should support trade and navigation. Conformity should be carefully maintained. This is supported by making the Senate agree to both treaties and laws.

Treaties Drafted Secretly, Quickly

7   Frequently, treaties must be negotiated in *secrecy* and require immediate *execution*. Sometimes the most useful intelligence can be obtained if the people who have it can be free from the fear of discovery. This fear effects people whether they have mercenary or friendly motives. Many people with either mercenary or friendly motives would rely on the secrecy of the President. Yet they wouldn't want to talk to the Senate, let alone the larger House of Representatives.

The convention has divided the power to make treaties so that the President can manage intelligence as prudence suggests. Then he will form the treaties with the advice and consent of the Senate.

President: Quick Reactions

8   There are cycles in the affairs of men. The cycles are very irregular in their duration, strength, and direction. And they seldom run twice exactly in the same manner or measure.

People who preside over national affairs must understand and profit by these cycles. Experienced men say that there are times when days, or even hours, are precious. The loss of a battle, the death of a prince, the removal of a minister, or other events changes the posture and appearance of affairs. Sometimes they turn the most favorable cycle into a negative one.

As in the field, so in the cabinet. There are moments to seize as they pass. And people presiding in either should have the capacity to improve them.

Until now, we have not had secrecy and speed. The Constitution needed to address those objectives. Secrecy and speed are needed to facilitate attaining the objectives of the negotiation. The President will be able to provide these. And if anything occurs that requires the advice and consent of the Senate, he may at any time convene them.

The Constitution provides treaty negotiations with the advantages of talents, information, integrity, and deliberate investigations on the one hand. On the other hand, it provides for secrecy and dispatch.

Objections Contrived

9   Objections to this plan are contrived.

Objection: Treaty has Force of Law

10   Some people object because ratified treaties will have the force of laws. They say that only the legislature should make treaties.

The legislature has the power to make laws. However, other acts also have the force of laws. Judgments from our courts and constitutional commissions given by our governor are as valid and binding as the laws passed by our legislature. All constitutional acts of power are as legally valid as those from the legislature. Therefore, the power of making treaties may be given to the executive or judicial branch.

It doesn't follow that just because the power of making laws is given to the legislature that, therefore, they must have every sovereign power by which the citizens are bound and affected.

Objection: Treaty is Supreme Law

11   Other critics are averse to treaties being the *supreme* laws of the land. They insist, and say they believe, that treaties, like legislative acts, should be repealable at pleasure. This idea seems to be new and specific to this country. But new errors, as well as new truths, often appear.

Remember that a treaty is only another name for a contract. And no nation would make any contract with us that would be binding on them *absolutely*, but on us only so long and as far as we may think.

People who make laws may, without doubt, amend or repeal them. And people who make treaties may alter or cancel them. But let us not forget that two contracting parties make treaties. Consequently, since the consent of both was essential to their formation, both must agree to alter or cancel them.

The proposed Constitution, therefore, hasn't extended the authority of treaties. They are currently binding and beyond the lawful reach of the legislature. They will be the same in the future, under any form of government.

Fear: Treaties Bad for Some States

12   Jealousy is useful in republics, just like bile is useful in the human body. But when too much jealousy infects politics, people are easily deceived by delusional appearances. This causes some people to fear that the President and Senate may make treaties without an equal eye to the interests of all the States.

Others suspect two thirds of the Senate will oppress the remaining third. They ask whether those gentlemen are made sufficiently responsible for their conduct. Whether, if they act corruptly, they can be punished. And if they make disadvantageous treaties, how are we to get rid of those treaties?

Promote Good of Whole Nation

13   All the States are equally represented in the Senate. Senators will promote the interests of their constituents. They will have an equal degree of influence, especially while the proper people are carefully appointed and their punctual attendance is demanded.

As the United States assumes a national form and character, the good of the whole will get more attention. If the national government forgets that the good of the whole can only be promoted by advancing the good of each of the parts, it will be very weak.

Neither the President nor the Senate will have the power to make treaties by which they and their families and estates will not be equally bound and affected with the rest of the community. And having no private interests distinct from those of the nation, they will be under no temptations to neglect the latter.

Corruption Voids Treaty

14   The problem of corruption is not imaginable. Anyone who thinks that the President and two-thirds of the Senate will ever be capable of such unworthy conduct, must either have been very unfortunate in his interactions with the world or has a heart very susceptible to such impressions.

The idea is too gross and too invidious to be entertained. But if it should ever happen, the treaty so obtained from us would, like all other fraudulent contracts, be null and void by the law of nations.

Integrity, Fear Guarantee Responsibility

15   It is difficult to imagine how their responsibility could be increased. The influences of honor, oaths, reputations, conscience, love of country, and family affections and attachments afford security for their fidelity. The Constitution has been careful that they shall be men of talents and in-

tegrity. We believe that the treaties they make will be as advantageous as could be made, all circumstances considered.

And so far as the fear of punishment and disgrace can operate, the motive for good behavior is supplied by the article on the subject of impeachments.

PUBLIUS

Number 65: Senate as Court for Trial of Impeachments

The Constitution gives the Senate two more powers:

(1) The Senate participates with the executive in the appointment to offices.

(2) The Senate acts as a court for the trial of impeachments.

Since the executive branch makes appointments, appointments will be discussed when we examine that branch. We will now study the judicial character of the Senate.

Political Passions → Biased Opinions

2   An elected government needs a court for the trial of impeachments. The court will judge the misconduct of public men. It will judge abuses or violations of public trust. The offenses are called POLITICAL because they usually relate to injuries done to society. Therefore, the prosecution of them will usually bring out the passions of the whole community. Citizens will feel either friendly or hostile to the accused, depending on preexisting factions or political parties. All their anger and interests will line up on one side or on the other. Because of this, there will always be the danger that the stronger party will make the decision. The decision may not be an objective decision about innocence or guilt.

Political Reputations

3   Every public official worries about his political reputation. In an elected government, it is difficult to place trust correctly. The most conspicuous government officials will often be the leaders or the tools of the most cunning or the biggest faction. They probably will not be able to impartially judge impeached officials.

Senate as Court of Impeachment

4   The Constitutional Convention thought that the Senate was the best place to place this important trust. If you understand the intrinsic difficulty of the problem, you will not hastily condemn this decision. Let's look at why they chose the Senate.

House Impeaches, Senate Tries

5   What is an impeachment court? It is a NATIONAL INQUEST into the conduct of public men. The proper inquisitors are the representatives of the nation.

If one house of the legislature starts the inquiry by impeaching the official, shouldn't the other house be part of the inquiry?

The convention used the British model. The House of Commons prefers the impeachment; the House of Lords decides it.

Several State constitutions follow the example. Those States and Great Britain see impeachment as a bridle in the hands of the legislature on the people in the executive branch of government. Isn't this the proper view?

Senators: Independent Judges

6   The Senate is dignified and independent. What other group of people would feel *enough confidence* to not be awed and influenced? What other group could feel impartial towards both the accused *individual* and the *representatives of the people—the House of Representatives*—his accuser?

Need Large Impeachment Court

7   Does the Supreme Court fit this description? Some Supreme Court justices will probably not have the courage needed for such a difficult task. Sometimes the impeachment court will not convict the person who has been accused by the people's representatives. Supreme Court justices probably will not have the authority needed for the people to accept their decision.

A deficiency in courage would be fatal to the accused; a deficiency in credibility would be dangerous to the public tranquility. These problems could only be avoided, if at all, by making the Supreme Court so large that it would be very expensive.

An impeachment trial requires a very large court. In common cases, the discretion of courts is limited in favor of personal security. There can never be strict rules for impeachment trials. There can never be a specific list of prosecutable offenses. Nor can there be strict rules for how the judges will construe the offenses. There will be no jury. The judges will pronounce the sentence of the law. A court of impeachments has the awful discretion to doom to honor or infamy the most trusted and distinguished people of the community. Therefore, the responsibility must not be held by a small number of persons.

Separate Court for Prosecution

8   For these reasons, alone, the Supreme Court should not be an impeachment court.

Another consideration strengthens this conclusion. If an impeached official is found guilty, his punishment is perpetual ostracism from the esteem, confidence, honors, and emoluments of his country. But he can also be prosecuted and punished in the ordinary course of law. Would it be proper for the same judges, who had already found him guilty, judge the case where the accused life and fortune could be forfeited?

Wouldn't an error in the first trial be carried over to the second? Wouldn't the strong bias of the first decision overrule the influence of any new information that might change the second? Those who know anything about human nature will say "yes." If the same people judge both cases, the accused would lose the double security intended by a double trial.

When an official is impeached and found guilty, his punishment is dismissal from his current office and disqualification from future offices. If the same judges preside in both trials, the loss of life and property would often be virtually included with this punishment.

Requiring a jury at the second trial might cancel the danger. But judges frequently influence juries. Juries are sometimes encouraged to find verdicts that the judge wants. Who would be willing to stake his life and his estate on the verdict of a jury acting under the authority of judges who have already decided he is guilty?

Chief Justice, Senate: Compromise

9   Would uniting the Supreme Court with the Senate to form the court of impeachment improve the plan? This union would have several advantages. But they would be overbalanced by the important disadvantage caused by having the same judges preside in the double prosecution of the accused.

The Constitution makes the chief justice of the Supreme Court the president of the court of impeachment. This will have some of the benefits of uniting the Supreme Court and the Senate. At the same time, the inconveniences of combining the entire Supreme Court with the Senate will be substantially avoided. This was, perhaps, the prudent compromise.

Also, if the Constitution gave the power to try impeachments to the Supreme Court, it would have increased the authority of the judiciary. This would have given opponents another pretext to talk against the judiciary.

Court of "Outsiders"

10   Should the court for the trial of impeachments be composed of persons who are completely distinct from the other departments of the government? There are strong arguments in favor and against such a plan.

One objection is that it would increase the complexity of the political machine. It would add a new department to the government with little usefulness.

But there are objections that are more important. This type of court would be very expensive and/or very inconvenient. It would have permanent officers based in the capitol, officers that have to be paid. Or it would be made up of specific officers of the State governments who would be called upon whenever an impeachment was actually pending. It isn't easy to imagine any other way it could be organized.

Since it would be a large court, anyone who compares the amount of things that the public wants with the ability of the government to pay for them will reject the first plan.

The second plan will receive only cautious support after the following problems are seriously considered. It will be difficult for men who live throughout the nation to gather together. This would delay decision and injure an innocent person. However, the delay could be an advantage to a guilty person, with its opportunities for intrigue and corruption. And, in some cases, the delay could hurt the government. A designing majority in the House of Representatives could impeach a faithful official, stopping him from performing his duties and exposing him to persecution. This suggestion may seem harsh and it might rarely happen. But we should never forget that the demon of faction will sometimes affect all numerous bodies of men.

Government Will Not Be Perfect

11   But even if there is a better way to set up the court for the trial of im-peachments, this is not a reason to reject the entire Constitution. If no government could be set up until every part of it is perfect, society would soon become an anarchy and the world a desert. Adversaries to the Con-stitution should prove, not merely that certain provisions are not the best possible, but that the whole plan is bad and very harmful.

PUBLIUS

Number 66: Objections to Senate as Impeachment Court

There are several objections to the way the court for the trial of impeachments is setup in the Constitution. We will review them.

Objection: Legislature Gets Judicial Power

2   The *first* objection: It violates the separation of powers maxim because the Senate will have both legislative and judicial authority.

Our discussion of the separation of powers showed that the powers can be partially mixed for special purposes. Sometimes a small mixing of powers is proper and necessary. Each branch of government needs to be able to defend itself against the other branches. The president can use the veto to block legislative encroachments on the executive. Impeachment powers give the legislature a check on executive encroachments.

Impeachment powers are divided between the two houses of the legislature. The House accuses and the Senate judges. Therefore, the same persons are not both accusers and judges. This guards against the danger of prosecution from a majority faction in either house. Two-thirds of the Senate is needed to find a person guilty, providing security to the innocent.

Senate Acts as Supreme Court in NY

3   The same men that admire New York's constitution oppose this part of the proposed Constitution, using the separation of powers argument. The New York constitution combines the Senate and the Supreme Court for an impeachment court; it is also the highest court in the State in all civil and criminal cases. New York's Supreme Court is small. In fact, New York's judicial authority resides in its Senate.

If the proposed Constitution violates the separation of powers rule, how much worse is the constitution of New York?*

Objection: Makes Senate Too Powerful

4   *Second* objection: If the Senate is the impeachment court, it will have too much power. And it will be too much like an aristocracy.

The Senate will have concurrent authority with the Executive in forming treaties and appointing to offices. The objectors say that if it is also the court for the trial of impeachments, Senators will have too much influence.

This is an imprecise objection. Therefore, a precise answer is difficult. How can we measure if the Senate has too much, too little, or the proper degree of influence? Won't it be safer and simpler to dismiss

---

* In the New Jersey constitution, also, the final judiciary authority is in a branch of the legislature. In New Hampshire, Massachusetts, Pennsylvania, and South Carolina, one branch of the legislature is the court for the trial of impeachments.—PUBLIUS

vague arguments? Shouldn't we examine each power then decide which branch should have it.

Treaties, Appointments, Impeachments

5 The power to make treaties is justified by the reasons stated in a former paper and in others to come. Future papers will explain why joining the Senate with the Executive in the power of appointing to offices is a good idea. And Paper #65 showed that this is the most practical way to form an impeachment court.

If these statements are true, than we shouldn't worry about the Senate having "too much" influence.

House is Stronger Legislative Body

6 The comments about the senators' term in office also refute this worry. The House of Representatives, elected by the people, will have more influence than any other part of the government.

House Powers that Senate Won't Have

7 And the Constitution gives the House several important powers that counterbalance the Senate's additional authorities.
It originates money bills. And it will institute impeachments. Isn't this a complete counterbalance to judging them?

Sometimes, no presidential candidate will get a majority of electors. The House will decide those elections. This could be a source of influence for that body. As an influence, this will outweigh all the Senate's powers.

Critics: Senate Approves Appointments

8 A *third* objection to the Senate as an impeachment court is based on the Senate's role in the appointments to office. Since the Senate participates in an appointment, it is imagined that the Senate would be too indulgent when judging the office holder's conduct.

This objection would condemn a practice seen in all the State governments, if not in all governments. I'm talking about the practice of making people who hold offices during pleasure dependent on the pleasure of those who appoint them. The objectors seem to be saying that when political appointees misbehave, the people who appointed them will protect them from punishment.

However, the people who make appointments will feel responsible for the fitness and ability of the people they appoint. They will want a respectable administration of affairs. And they will want to remove anyone whose conduct proves them unworthy of the trust. This is a basically sound presumption.

The Senate only approves executive choices. This will not blind them to such extraordinary evidence of guilt that the Representatives of the nation accuse him.

Senate's Minor Role in Appointments

9   The Senate will probably not feel a favorable bias towards an impeached official who was appointed by the President. If further arguments are necessary, let's look at the Senate's role in appointments.

The President will *nominate* and, with the advice and consent of the Senate, *appoint*. Of course, the Senate will have no part in the *choice*. The Senate may defeat one person that the President has chosen, but they cannot *choose*. The Senate can only ratify or reject the choice of the President.

The Senate might prefer someone else, but confirm the appointment because it has no grounds to oppose him. And what if the Senate didn't approve the nomination? It would have no way of knowing who the next nominee would be. It might not even be a person who—in their estimation—was more meritorious than the one rejected.

Thus, the majority of the Senate would not be more biased towards the appointee than appearances of merit might inspire and the lack of proof will destroy.

Objection: Senate Ratifies Treaties

10   A *fourth* objection comes from the Senate's union with the Executive in making treaties. The objectors say that when a corrupt or perfidious treaty is made, the Senators would have to judge themselves. If they conspired with the Executive to betray the interests of the nation in a ruinous treaty, would they get the punishment they deserved if they were the impeachment court? Would they find themselves guilty of the accusation brought against them for the treachery?

Argument Based on False Foundation

11   This is the most earnest and reasonable objection against this part of the Constitution. But it rests on an erroneous foundation.

No Punishment for Acts Done as Bodies

12   The Constitution provides security against corruption and treachery when forming treaties. This security comes from the numbers and characters of the people who are to make them. Both the President and two-thirds of the Senate, a body carefully selected by each State legislature, must approve treaties. This assures fidelity in forming treaties.

When writing the Constitution, the convention might have included a punishment for the President if he doesn't follow the Senate's instructions or doesn't act with integrity during treaty negotiations. They might also have suggested how a few of the leading individuals in the Senate might be punished, if they used their influence in the Senate for foreign corruption. But the convention could not suggest impeaching and punishing two-thirds of the Senate, if the Senate agreed to an improper treaty.

The Constitution does not include a method for punishing a majority of the Senate or the House for passing a very harmful or unconstitutional law. I don't believe any government has ever done this.

How could a majority in the House of Representatives impeach themselves? This idea is no better than two thirds of the Senate putting themselves on trial. If the House of Representatives can pass an unjust and tyrannical law and not be punished, why should more than two thirds of the Senate be punished for approving an injurious treaty with a foreign power?

The Senate and House of Representatives need to feel free and independent to discuss issues. The members must be exempt from punishment for acts done in a collective capacity. Society's security depends on the care taken to put the trust in proper hands, people who want to execute it with fidelity. It should be as difficult as possible for them to conspire in any interest opposite to that of the public good.

Senate Will Punish Abusers of Power

13   If the Executive misbehaves by perverting the instructions or contravening the views of the Senate, the Senate will want to punish the abuser and defend their authority. For this, we can count on their pride, if not their virtue.

What will happen if leading Senators influence the majority into measures the community doesn't like? If corruption can be proved, the psychology of human nature says that the other Senators will want to divert the public resentment from themselves. They will sacrifice the authors of their mismanagement and disgrace.

PUBLIUS

Executive

Number 67: Deceptive Arguments Against Proposed Executive

2 Framing the executive branch was probably the most difficult part of the Constitution. Yet the vehement criticism isn't based on sound judgment.

Critics Magnify President into Monarch

3 When they write about the executive branch, opponents of the Constitution have showed their talent for misrepresentation. The people hate and fear the monarchy. Building on this fear, opponents of the Constitution claim the President will be just another form of a monarchy. To prove this, they have even drawn arguments from fiction.

They claim he will have more dignity and splendor than a British king. He has been pictured with a sparkling crown, wearing imperial robes, sitting on a throne. We've seen images of murdering guards and a mysteries future palace.

Accurate Description Needed

4 The attempts to morph the president into a king make it necessary to look at its real nature and form.

Deceit Used to Pervert Public Opinion

5 Opponents use false arguments to pervert public opinion on the subject. They exceed the usual unjustified license of party artifice. It's difficult to treat them seriously. Opponents are deliberately using fraud and deception.

President and Senate Vacancies

6 For example, they have had the nerve to say that the President of the United States will have a power that the proposed Constitution *expressly* gives to the State Executives. I'm talking about the power to fill Senate vacancies.

False Conclusion Built on False Premise

7 This has been argued by a writer who (whatever may be his real merit) has often been applauded by his party. He has built a series of observations. Each is based on this false, unfounded suggestion. Let him now see the evidence. And let him, if he is able, justify the shameful outrage he has offered to the dictates of truth and the rule of fair dealing.

Constitution: Executive Appointments

8   Article 2, section 2, clause 2 gives the President of the United States the power "to nominate, and by and with the advice and consent of the Senate, to appoint ambassadors, other public ministers, and consuls, judges of the Supreme Court, and all other *officers* of the United States whose appointments are *not* in the Constitution *otherwise provided for,* and *which shall be established by law.*"

Opponents use the next sentence to say the President has a power that the Constitution does not give him. It says, "The President shall have power to fill up all *vacancies,* that may happen *during the recess of the Senate,* by granting commissions which shall *expire at the end of their next session.*"

The obvious meaning of the clauses shows that the deduction is not even plausible.

President Appoints Non-Constitutional Officers

9   The first clause provides a way to appoint officers, "whose appointments are *not otherwise provided for* in the Constitution, and which *shall be established by law.*" Based on this clause, the President cannot appoint senators. The appointment of Senators is *otherwise provided for* in the Constitution and are *established by the Constitution.* The appointment of Senators is a Constitutional power and cannot be changed by law.

President Never Appoints Senators

10   Clearly, the second clause does not include the power to fill vacancies in the Senate, for the following reasons.

First. The relationship of the clauses shows that the second clause is only a supplement to the first clause. Since the President and Senate *jointly* make appointments, without the second clause, appointments could only be made while the Senate is in session. However, vacancies might happen *in their recess.* These offices may need to be filled without delay. The second clause authorizes the President, *by himself,* to make temporary appointments "during the recess of the Senate, by granting commissions which shall expire at the end of their next session."

Second. The *vacancies* mentioned in the second clause refer to the "officers" described in the preceding clause. This excludes members of the Senate.

Third. The power is to operate "during the recess of the Senate" and the appointments will last until "to the end of the next session." These phrases further clarify the provision. If it included senators, the clause would have referred to the State legislatures, not the national Senate. The State legislatures appoint Senators. If the clause referred to Senate vacancies, it would mention the recess of State legislatures. And the temporary senators would stay in office until the next session of the State legislature, instead of making it expire at the end of the next session of the national Senate. The clause mentions only the national Senate. Therefore, the clause must be talking about vacancies in offices to which the President and Senate, jointly, make permanent appointments.

Lastly. Article 1, section 3, clauses 1 and 2 destroys all doubt and misconceptions. The former provides that "the Senate of the United States shall be composed of two Senators from each State, chosen *by the legislature thereof* for six years." And the latter directs that "if vacancies in that body should happen by resignation or otherwise, *during the recess of the legislature of* ANY STATE, the Executive THEREOF may make temporary appointments until the *next meeting of the legislature,* which shall then fill such vacancies."

The State Executives will fill vacancies in the Senate by temporary appointments. The President will not have the power to fill vacancies in the national Senate. This proves that the opponents' arguments are deceptive. The deception is obvious. And it is too atrocious to be excused by hypocrisy.

Example Proof of Misrepresentations

11   This misrepresentation proves the inexcusable cunning used by opponents of the Constitution. They want to prevent a fair, impartial judgment based on the real merits of the Constitution. I ask any honest opponent of the new Constitution: Does language give us severe enough denouncements for this shameless attempt to defraud the citizens of America?

PUBLIUS

Number 68: Method of Electing President

Opponents of the Constitution have slightly approved the method of appointing the chief Executive of the United States. If the method isn't perfect, it is at least excellent. It clearly unites all the advantages wished for.

Electing Presidential Electors

2   The President will hold an important trust. The will of the people should be included in the choice. To achieve this objective, the people will choose the men [electors] who make the decision. The electors will be chosen at the appropriate time for this specific purpose, rather than having any pre-established body make the decision.

Small Group, Higher Qualifications

3   The men electing the President will study the important qualities. They should make a thoughtful decision. Reason should govern their

choice. A small number of people, selected by their fellow citizens, will probably have the information and the judgment needed for a thorough investigation.

Electors Vote in Home State

4　The President of the United States will administer the government. When electing an executive to such an important job, tumult and discord are feared evils. But the Constitution has security against these evils.

The people will choose *several* men to form a group of electors. By choosing several, riots within the community are less likely to happen than if only *one* person was elected.

The electors are to assemble and vote in the State that chose them. This detached, divided situation will expose them to less heat and turmoil than if they were all to be convened at one time in one place.

Foreign Influence, Presidential Elections

5　Every practical block to conspiracies and corruption must be erected. These are deadly adversaries of republican government. They can come from several places. But they will most likely come from foreign powers that want an improper influence in our government. The best way to influence our government is to promote a person they want as President of the Union.

But the convention carefully guarded against all danger. The appointment of the President doesn't depend on a pre-existing group of men who might be tampered with beforehand to sell their votes.

Instead, the people of America will choose electors for the temporary and sole purpose of making the appointment. Any people who are too devoted to the President in office are not eligible to be electors. No Senator, Representative, or other person holding a place of trust or profit under the United States can be an elector. Thus, without corrupting all citizens, the presidential electors will at least begin the task free from any sinister bias. Because of their brief existence and detached situation, they should be unbiased. To corrupt such a large number of people requires time and funds.

And it would not be easy to suddenly start a corrupt conspiracy. The spread of electors over thirteen States is another protection. Between the appointment of electors and their election of the President, it won't be easy for them to conspire for motives that might not be corrupt, but might mislead them from their duty.

President Elected by People

6　There is another goal. The President should depend on the people, alone, for reelection. Otherwise, he might be tempted to sacrifice his duty to ingratiate himself with people whose favor was necessary to stay in office. His reelection will depend on electors, picked for the single purpose of electing the President.

Constitution Includes All Safeguards

7   The Constitution combines all these advantages. The people of each State will choose a number of electors, equal to the number of senators and representatives of each State in the national government. The electors will assemble within the State and vote for some fit person as President. Their votes will be sent to the seat of the national government. The person with a majority of the whole number of votes will be the President.

One man might not receive a majority of the votes. And it might be unsafe to permit less than a majority to be conclusive. Therefore, the Constitution says that, if this happens, the House of Representatives will select the man they feel is best qualified for the office from the five candidates with the highest numbers of votes.

Election Method Assures Highest Quality

8   This method of electing the President makes sure that no man who doesn't have the qualifications will hold the office of President.

A man who is talented in low intrigues and who is popular and charming may be able to become a State governor. But he will need other talents and a different kind of merit to get the esteem and confidence of the whole Union. He'll need enough talents and merits to become a successful candidate for the distinguished office of President of the United States. We can say that men known for their ability and virtue will fill the office.

This will highly recommend the Constitution to people who understand that the executive in every government is largely responsible for its good or ill administration. We cannot agree in the political heresy that says:

> For forms of government let fools contest—
> That which is best administered is best—

But we can say that the true test of a good government is its aptitude and tendency to produce a good administration.

Vice President Chosen Same Way

9   The Vice President is to be chosen in the same manner with the President, with one difference. The Senate is to do, in respect to the former, what is to be done by the House of Representatives, in respect to the latter.

V-P Senate's President, May Be President

10   The appointment of a second person as Vice President has been objected to as superfluous, if not mischievous. Some people have suggested that the Senate elect a Senator to fill the office.

But two reasons seem to justify the convention's decision. First, so that the Senate will never have a tie vote, the President of the Senate should have only a casting vote. If a Senator from any State was taken from his seat and made President of the Senate, his home State would lose a vote in the Senate.

Second, the Vice President may occasionally become President. So, all the reasons that recommend the way the President is elected, apply to the election of the Vice President.

This objection could be made against the constitution of New York. We have a Lieutenant-Governor, who is chosen by the people at large. He presides in the senate. And New York's Lieutenant-Governor becomes Governor under the same circumstances that would authorize the Vice President to exercise the authorities and discharge the duties of the President.

PUBLIUS

Number 69: President's Constitutional Authority

I will now discuss the authorities of the Executive branch of the federal government, as defined in the proposed Constitution. They have been misrepresented.

One Person Has Executive Authority

2   One person will hold most of the Executive authority, the President. This feature doesn't help us decide if the Executive authority, as defined in the Constitution, is appropriate. Because it is one person, it may look like the king of Great Britain. However, it also looks like the Grand Seignior, the Khan of Tartary, the Man of the Seven Mountains, and the governor of New York.

Four-Year Term

3   The President will be elected for *four* years. He is re-eligible as often as the people of the United States think him worth their confidence.

This is totally different than a British king, who is a *hereditary* monarch. His crown is passed down to his heirs forever.

However, the President and a New York governor are similar. The governor is elected for *three* years and is re-eligible without limitation. It would be quicker to establish a dangerous influence in a single State than establishing a similar influence throughout the nation. We must conclude that the President's *four*-year term is less dangerous than a *three*-year term for the governor in a single State.

President Liable for Misdeeds

4   The President can be impeached, tried, and if convicted of treason, bribery, or other high crimes or misdemeanors, removed from office. Afterwards he can be prosecuted and punished in the ordinary course of law.

The king of Great Britain is sacred and inviolable. He is not accountable to any constitutional tribunal. And a national revolution is the only way he can be punished.

In the delicate and important area of personal responsibility, the President of the United States will be like the governor of New York. And he will have more personal liability than the governors of Massachusetts and Delaware.

President's Qualified Negative: Veto

5   The President will have the power to return a bill that has passed the two houses of Congress for reconsideration. If the bill is later passed by two thirds in both the Senate and House, it will become law.

The king of Great Britain has an absolute negative on the acts of the two houses of Parliament. Although the power hasn't been used for a long time, it still exists. In fact, the only reason it hasn't been used is because the king has used his influence rather than his authority. If the monarch used his authority to permanently veto laws passed by Parliament, there would be some degree of agitation in the nation. Instead, he has learned to gain a majority in one of the two houses of Parliament.

The qualified negative of the President is very different than the king's absolute negative. However, it matches the authority of the Council of Revision of New York, of which the governor is a member. In this respect, the power of the President exceeds that of the governor of New York. The President will have, himself, what the governor shares with the chancellor and judges. But it is the same power as the governor of Massachusetts. This article seems to have been copied from the Massachusetts constitution.

Commander-in-Chief, Pardons

6   The President is to be the "commander-in-chief of the army and navy of the United States, and of the militia of the several States, when called into the actual service of the United States;

"He is to have power to grant reprieves and pardons for offenses against the United States, *except in cases of impeachment;*

"to recommend to the consideration of Congress such measures as he shall judge necessary and expedient;

"he may, on extraordinary occasions, convene both houses of the legislature, or either of them, and, in case of disagreement between them *with respect to the time of adjournment,* to adjourn them to such time as he shall think proper;

"to take care that the laws be faithfully executed;

"and to commission all officers of the United States."

In most of these, the President's power resembles both the British king and the governor of New York with these differences:

First. The President will only occasionally command the nation's militia. Congress must first call the militia into service.

The king of Great Britain and the governor of New York are always in command of all the militia within their jurisdictions. In this authority, the power of the President is inferior to that of either the monarch or the governor.

Second. The President is to be commander-in-chief of the army and navy of the United States.

Both the President and the British king have the title "commander-in-chief." But the President's authority is far more limited than the king's. The President is only the supreme commander of the military and naval forces. He is first general and admiral of the Union.

The British king has far more power. He can *declare* war, and he can *raise* and *regulate* fleets and armies. Under the proposed Constitution, Congress will have this authority.

The governor of New York can only command the militia and navy. The constitutions of several other States expressly declare their governors can also be commander-in-chief of the army. New Hampshire and Massachusetts, in this respect, may give their governors more power than a President of the United States.

Third. The power of the President, in respect to pardons, would extend to all cases *except impeachment.*

The governor of New York can pardon even impeachment, except for treason and murder. Isn't the power of the governor, as far as political clout in this area, greater than that of the President? A group of people could conspire against the State government. If their plot is discovered before they take treasonous actions, the governor can pardon them. They won't be punished. If a governor of New York led a conspiracy, until the hostilities actually started, he could insure his accomplices entire impunity.

On the other hand, the President of the United States can pardon treason when prosecuted in the ordinary course of law. But he could not shelter an offender from the effects of impeachment and conviction.

If the governor of New York led a conspiracy against public liberty and if the plan was discovered before it was carried out, New York's governor could pardon his coconspirators, something the President could not do. If the plan was carried out, the President might be able to pardon his coconspirators. However, if the coconspirators realized that the President might be impeached and convicted, they would also realize that he would be unable to pardon them during any stage of planning or execution of the plan. There would be a greater temptation to continue a conspiracy with the governor of New York than the President.

The proposed Constitution limits the offense of treason "to levying war upon the United States, and adhering to their enemies, giving them aid and comfort." The laws of New York have a similar definition.

Fourth. The President can only adjourn Congress in the single case of disagreement about the time of adjournment.

The British monarch can adjourn or even dissolve the Parliament. The governor of New York can also adjourn the State legislature for a limited time. This power may be employed to very important purposes.

Senate Must Approve Treaties

7 The President will, with the advice and consent of the Senate, make treaties, provided two-thirds of the senators present concur.

The king of Great Britain is the only representative of the nation in all foreign transactions. On his own, he can make treaties of peace, commerce, alliances, and of every other description. Some people have said that his treaties with foreign powers are subject to the revision and ratification of Parliament. But I believe this doctrine was never heard of until it was broached on the present occasion. Every jurist[5] in Britain and every man acquainted with its constitution knows that the monarch makes all treaties. And they are legal and valid.

Sometimes Parliament changes existing laws so that they conform to a new treaty. This may be where the idea that Parliament needs to approve treaties came from. But this parliamentary action comes from a different cause—the need to adjust an artificial, intricate system of revenue and commercial laws to conform to the treaty.

In the making of treaties, there is no comparison between the limited presidential power and the actual power of the British sovereign. The British king can do alone what the President can only do with the concurrence of a branch of the legislature.

In this area, the President's power exceeds that of any State executive. But this arises naturally from the sovereign power relating to treaties. The question of whether governors have this important power would only come up if the Confederacy was dissolved.

Greeting Ambassadors, Ministers

8 The President will also receive ambassadors and other public ministers. Many speeches have been given on this topic. But this is more a matter of dignity than of authority. It will have no effect on the administration of the government. And this will be far easier than if the legislature or one of its houses had to meet every time a foreign minister arrived, even though he was only replacing a departing minister.

Appoints Ambassadors, Judges, Etc.

9 The President is to nominate and, *with the advise and consent of the Senate*, appoint ambassadors and other public ministers, Supreme Court

---

[5] *Vide* Blackstone's *Commentaries*, vol. I. p.257. –PUBLIUS

judges, and all officers of the United States established by law and whose appointments are not otherwise provided for by the Constitution.

The king of Great Britain is called the fountain of honors. He not only appoints to all offices, but can create offices. He can confer titles of nobility and give out an immense number of church honors.

In this area, the President has less power than the British king. Nor is it equal to that of the governor of New York. The governor and four people chosen from the Senate make up the appointment council. The governor *claims,* and has frequently *exercised,* the right of nomination and is *entitled* to a casting vote in the appointment. If he really has the right of nominating, in this respect his authority is equal to that of the President, and he exceeds it with the casting vote.

In the national government, if the Senate is divided, no appointment could be made. In New York, if the council is divided, the governor can vote and confirm his own nomination.[6]

The New York governor, in private with an appointment council of two to four people, appoints State officials. Presidential appointments will receive a lot of publicity, and it needs a Senate confirmation. It would be much easier to influence the small number of people in an appointment council than the large number in the national Senate. Therefore, the governor's power to appoint State officers is greatly superior to that of the President of the Union.

President: Far Less Power than King

10   With the exception of the President's authority in making treaties, it is difficult to determine whether he would have more or less power than the governor of New York.

It is very clear that there is no reason for the parallel that some people have attempted to make between him and the king of Great Britain. But to highlight the difference, we will take a closer look at the dissimilarities.

President vs. Monarch's Authorities

11   The President of the United States would be elected every *four* years; the King of Great Britain is a perpetual and *hereditary* prince.
The one could face personal punishment and disgrace; the other is sacred and inviolable.

The one would have a *qualified* negative on the acts of the legislative body; the other has an *absolute* negative.

---

[6] Candor, however, demands an acknowledgment that I do not think the governor has the right of nomination. Yet it is always justifiable to reason from the practice of a government, until its propriety has been constitutionally questioned. And independent of this claim, when we take into view the other considerations, and pursue them through all their consequences, we shall be inclined to draw much the same conclusion.—PUBLIUS

The one would have a right to command the military and naval forces of the nation; the other also has the authority to *declare* war, and *raise* and *regulate* fleets by his own authority.

The one would have a concurrent power with a branch of the legislature in the formation of treaties; the other is the *sole possessor* of the power to make treaties.

The one can confer no privileges whatever; the other can make citizens of aliens, noblemen of commoners, can erect corporations with all the rights of corporate bodies.

The one cannot regulate the commerce or currency of the nation; the other can regulate commerce, establish markets and fairs, regulate weights and measures, lay embargoes for a limited time, coin money, authorize or prohibit the circulation of foreign coin. The one has no religious jurisdiction; the other is the supreme head of the national church!

What should we say to people who try to tell us that things so dissimilar resemble each other? The same answer that should be given to people who tell us that a government, with the whole power in the hands of the elective and periodical servants of the people, is an aristocracy, a monarchy, and a despotism.   PUBLIUS

Number 70: One Person Holds Executive Authority

Some people say that a republic cannot have an energetic Executive. People who understand and support this type government must hope that there is no foundation for this idea. If it were true, it would condemn their belief in the principles of good government.

The executive branch of government must have the powers to fulfill its duties. Energy in the executive is an important characteristic of good government.

The community must be protected against foreign attacks. Property must be protected against conspiracies that block justice. And liberty must be protected from the negative effects of ambition, faction, and anarchy. The republic of Rome often had to give all executive power to a single man with the title of Dictator. He stopped internal conspiracies, led by ambitious and tyrannical people who threatened the government. And he blocked invasions by external enemies who tried to conquer and destroy Rome.

Feeble Executive => Bad Government

2   A feeble executive implies a feeble execution of government. A feeble execution is another way to say a bad execution. And a badly executed government is a bad government.

Safe Republic, Energetic Executive

3   Therefore, let's agree that an energetic executive is necessary. What ingredients create this energy? How can they be combined with the ingredients that keep the republic safe from a dictator? And how well does the proposed Constitution combine an energetic executive with republican safety?

Qualities of Energetic Executive

4   To have energy, the executive needs:

        (1) unity,
        (2) duration,
        (3) guaranteed compensation,
        (4) and enough powers.

Qualities of Republican Safety

5   The ingredients that constitute safety, in the republican sense, are: (1) due dependence on the people, (2) due responsibility.

One Executive; Numerous Legislature

6   Respected statesmen say that there should be a single executive and a large legislature. They say that energy is the most important quality of the executive branch of government. And this is achieved when one person holds the executive power.

A large legislature is best for deliberation and wisdom. It will have the people's confidence and secure their privileges and interests.

Benefits of Unified Executive

7   Unity promotes energy. One man can be more decisive, keep secrets, and act faster than any greater number of people. And as the number of people increases, these qualities diminish.

Executive Unity Destroyed

8   Unity may be destroyed in two ways. Executive power can be given to two or more people with equal status and authority. Or it can be given ostensibly to one man who is subject, in whole or part, to the control and cooperation of other people who act as counselors to him.

The two consuls of Rome are an example of the first. We find examples of the second in several State constitutions. New York and New Jersey, I think, are the only States that give one man the entire executive authority.[1]

There are supporters of both ways of destroying the unity of the executive, but more people want an executive council. The two types of plural

---

[1] New York only has a council for appointing to offices. New Jersey's governor may consult a council. But I don't think their resolutions bind him.—PUBLIUS

executive are different. However, objections to them are similar and can be examined together.

History: Plural Executives

9   History teaches us little about this topic. Looking at the experiences of other nations, we learn that a plural executive is not a good idea. The Achaeans tried having two Praetors, but they were forced to get rid of one.

Roman history records the problems that arose from arguments between the Consuls and the military Tribunes, who were at times substituted for the Consuls.

But history gives us no examples of any real advantages of a plural executive. We might be surprised that disagreements between Consuls were not more frequent or more fatal, until we remember the Roman republic's almost constant situation. The government was divided between the Consuls, who were usually chosen from the aristocrats. The aristocrats constantly fought with the common people to keep their ancient authorities. The Consuls often united to defend the privileges of their class.

After the military increased the size of the republican empire, the Consuls divided the administration of the empire between themselves by lot. One Consul remained at Rome to govern the city and surrounding area. The other took command of the distant areas of the country. This probably prevented rivalries that might have threatened the peace of the republic.

Logic Rejects Plural Executive

10   If we leave the lessons of history and use only logic and good sense, we discover more reasons to reject the idea of a plural Executive of any kind.

Plural Executive: Animosity Inevitable

11   Wherever two or more persons are engaged in a common pursuit, there is always danger of differences of opinion. If it is a public trust or office, where they have equal rank and authority, there is a real danger of personal envy and even animosity. Envy and animosity often cause bitter disagreements. The people who disagree lose some respect and authority. And they distract from the plans and operations needed to attain the goal.

Let's say that two or more people must serve as the top executives of a country. During an emergency, envy and animosity could slow down or even block important government actions. And worse, they might split the community into violent and irreconcilable factions that support the different individuals who compose the executive.

Envy, Pride Motivate Opposition

12   Men often oppose a thing just because they had no part in planning it, or because people they dislike may have planned it. But if they have been

consulted and have disapproved, their opposition becomes an absolute duty of self-love. They feel bound in honor and personal infallibility to defeat a plan that is contrary to their beliefs.

This psychological reaction can lead men to take desperate actions. And men often have enough followers to sacrifice the interests of society to their vanity, conceit, and obstinacy.

Perhaps the consequences of the question now before the public may give us sad proofs of the effects of this despicable frailty, or detestable vice, in the human character.

Legislature Designed to Act Slowly

13   In a free government, these inconveniences must be tolerated from the legislature. But it is unnecessary and unwise to introduce them into the executive branch. And they can be the most harmful in the executive.

In the legislature, fast decisions are more often evil than good. Although different opinions and party haggling can sometimes obstruct good plans, they often promote deliberation and careful analysis. They block excesses by the majority. Also, when a law is passed, the opposition must end. And breaking the law is punishable.

But there are no advantages to disagreements in the executive branch. There are only disadvantages. There is no point at which they cease to operate.

Disagreements about a specific plan would weaken the execution of the plan, from the first step to the end. Vigor and expedition are necessary executive qualities. Disagreements among the executives would block these, without any counterbalancing good.

During war, when national security depends on a strong executive, everything would be feared from a plural executive.

Council Also Weakens Executive

14   These comments principally apply to the first case, a plural executive where each person has equal authority. Few people want this type of executive.

But if the ostensible executive needs the approval of an executive council before he can act, most of the same comments apply. An artful cabal in the council could distract and weaken the whole system of administration. If no such cabal existed, the diversity of views and opinions, alone, would make the executive feeble and slow to act.

Plurality Hides Faults, Responsibility

15   But one of the strongest objections to both types of plural executive is that it tends to conceal faults and destroy responsibility.

There are two types of responsibility: moral and legal. Irresponsibility leads to censure and to punishment. Censure is the more important, especially in an elective office. An irresponsible man in public office will more often act in a way that makes him unworthy of trust than in a way that makes him subject to legal punishment.

But when more than one person holds the position of Executive, it is difficult to figure out who is morally or legally responsible. The people in the executive will accuse each other. It often becomes impossible to determine who to blame or punish for a harmful act. Blame is shifted from one to another with so much dexterity that the public doesn't know who made the decision.

The circumstances leading to any national misfortune can be extremely complicated. We could clearly see that there has been mismanagement. But if several people were involved in making the decision, it may be impossible to say who is truly responsible for the evil.

Can't Determine Individual Responsibility

16   "I was overruled by my council."

"The council was so divided in their opinions that it was impossible to obtain any better resolution on the point."

These and similar pretexts are always available, whether true or false. And who will take the trouble or incur the odium of a strict scrutiny into the secret discussions of the council? If a zealous citizen wants to take on the task and if there is collusion between the parties involved, it would be easy to make each participant's part in the plan so ambiguous that no one could discover the precise conduct of each member of the council.

New York's Disastrous Experience

17   The governor of New York is coupled with a council for one duty, appointing to offices. And we have seen the mischiefs described. Scandalous appointments to important offices. Some cases, indeed, have been so flagrant that EVERYONE agrees they are improper. When asked about them, the governor has blamed the members of the council who blamed it on his nomination.

Meanwhile, the people have no idea who picked such unqualified and improper people.

Accountability, Plural Executive

18   The people have two securities that public officials will use their delegated powers faithfully. A plural Executive tends to deprive the people of these securities.

First. The restraints of public opinion lose their effectiveness because it is difficult to divide censure among a number of people.

Second. It will be difficult to discover which public official is responsible for misconduct, so they can be removed from office or punished, if appropriate.

King Unaccountable, Perpetual Executive

19 In England, the king is the lifetime executive. For the sake of public peace, he is unaccountable for his administration and his person is sacred. Therefore, giving the king a constitutional council means that someone will be responsible to the nation for the advice they give. Without this, there would be no responsibility whatever in the executive branch—an idea inadmissible in a free government.

But the king is not bound by the resolutions of his council, though they are answerable for the advice they give. He is the absolute master of his own conduct as the nation's executive. He can use or disregard the advice given to him.

Council Would Damage U. S. Executive

20 But in a republic, every executive should be held personally responsible for his behavior in office. The reason for the British council doesn't apply. And an executive council might decrease the executive's perceived responsibility. In the American republic, a council would greatly diminish the responsibility of the Chief Executive himself.

The monarch of Great Britain, who is the chief executive, cannot be held responsible. To some degree, the monarch is a hostage to the national justice for his good behavior.

One Executive Safer

21 Many State constitutions include a council to the Executive. They have developed from the maxim of republican jealousy, which considers power as safer in the hands of a number of men than of a single man. In this case, I think the disadvantages outweigh this possible advantage.

But I do not think the rule applies to the national executive power. I agree that to be "deep, solid, and ingenious, the executive power is more easily confined when it is ONE."[2] It is far safer for the people to watch one person. And a plural Executive is more dangerous than friendly to liberty.

Easier for Group to Usurp Power

22 The kind of security sought for in a plural EXECUTIVE is unattainable. The number has to be so great that conspiracy is difficult; otherwise conspiracies become a source of danger rather than security.

When power is placed in a small number of men, a talented leader can easily get them to agree to a common enterprise. A small group is easier to abuse and more dangerous when abused, than a single man. One man can be closely watched and more easily suspected.

The Decemvirs of Rome, whose name denotes their number,[7] could more easily usurp power than any ONE of them, alone.

---

[2] DeLolme.—PUBLIUS

[7] Ten.—PUBLIUS

No one would think of proposing an executive much larger than the Decemvirs. From six to a dozen have been suggested for the number of the council. The largest number isn't too great for an easy conspiracy. America would have more to fear from such a conspiracy than from the ambition of any single individual.

A council to an executive, who is responsible for what he does, clogs his good intentions, becomes accomplices of his bad deeds, and almost always is a cloak to his faults.

Plural Executive Expensive

23 I won't dwell on the subject of expense. However, a council, which is large enough to fulfill the goal aimed at by instituting it, would be very expensive.

Prior to the discussion about the proposed Constitution, nearly every intelligent man I met said that the UNITY of the New York executive is one of the best features of our State constitution.

PUBLIUS

Number 71: Duration: President's Term in Office

The second requirement for energy in the Executive is duration in office. Duration includes:

1) the executive's personal firmness in the employment of his constitutional powers and

2) stable system of administration adopted under his sponsorship.

First. The longer the time in office, the greater is the probability of getting this advantage. It is a principle of human nature that a man is interested in something he possesses in proportion to the firmness or precariousness by which he holds it. He will be less attached to something he holds for a short time. And he will be willing to risk more for something he firmly holds than for the something he precariously holds.

This remark applies to a political office just as to any article of property. We can infer that a chief executive who knows he *must* leave his office may have little interest in it. He might not take the chance of censure or entanglement from the independent use of his powers. He won't act if he might encounter ill-humors from either a large part of society or a large faction in the legislative body.

Instead, if he only *might* leave office unless reelected, and if he wants to be reelected, his wishes, conspiring with his fears, would tend still more powerfully to corrupt his integrity or debase his fortitude.

In either case, the executive would become feeble and irresolute.

Leaders Ignore Bad Fads

2   Some people think that a pliant Executive, who acts as the community or legislature seems to want, is good. But these people have crude ideas about the purpose of government and the true way to promote public happiness.

The republican principle demands that the will of the community should govern the conduct of those people who are entrusted with management of their affairs. But it does not require absolute compliance to every sudden passion or impulse aroused within the people by clever men who flatter the community's prejudices to betray their interests.

It is true that the people commonly *intend* the PUBLIC GOOD. This often applies even to their errors. But the people's good sense would hate the adulator who pretends that they always *reason right* about the *means* of promoting it.

They know from experience that they sometimes err. It is amazing that they make so few mistakes. They are constantly bombarded by the wiles of parasites and sycophants, by the snares of the ambitious, the avaricious, the desperate, by the artifices of men who have more confidence than they deserve, and of those who seek to possess rather than to deserve it. When the interests of the people are different than what they may want, it is the government's duty to guard those interests, to withstand the temporary delusion and give them time for cooler, sedate reflection.

We can show examples of when leaders saved the people from fatal consequences of their own mistakes. The people are thankful to the leaders who had courage to serve them at the peril of their displeasure.

Executive Should Act Independently

3   But even if we insist that the Executive always comply with the will of the people, we can not argue that the legislature must comply in the same way. Sometimes the legislature may oppose the executive. At other times, the people may be neutral. In either case, it is certainly desirable that the Executive should act on his own opinion with vigor and decision.

Separation Avoids Legislative Dominance

4   Separation of power between the branches of power is very important. Each branch should be independent of the others. Why separate the executive or the judiciary from the legislative, if the legislative can void the acts of both the executive and the judiciary? Such a separation would be in name only. And it couldn't produce the result for which it was established.

Being subordinate to the laws is different from being dependent on the legislative body. The first agrees with and the last violates the fundamental principles of good government. And despite the Constitution, it unites all power in the same hands.

Executive: Number 71

As shown in earlier papers, the legislative branch tends of absorb every other branch. In a republic, this tendency is almost irresistible. The representatives of the people sometimes seem to believe that they are the people themselves. They become impatient when the executive or judiciary exercise their rights. They act like it is a breach of legislative privilege and an outrage to the representatives' dignity.

The legislature often seems to want imperial control over the other branches. And since they commonly have the people on their side, they act with a force that makes it very difficult for the other branches of the government to keep the constitutional balance.

Term Effects Executive Independence

5   How can a short term in office affect the independence of the Executive on the legislature, unless the one has the power of appointing or displacing the other?

One answer comes from the principle already mentioned. A man is apt to have less interest in an office he holds for a short term. And he will have little reason to expose himself to inconvenience or hazard. Another answer is that the legislature influences voters. Their influence might be used to prevent the re-election of a man who, by resisting a sinister legislative project, makes himself the target of its resentment.

6   Is four years the proper term in office? If not, should it be a shorter period because it provides a greater security against ambitious designs. Or a longer period that is too short to inspire the desired firmness and independence of the executive.

4-Year Term Seems Best

7   We don't know for sure that four years is the correct period of time. But it would influence the spirit and character of the government. Between the beginning and end of a four-year term, there would be a long time before the thought of having to get reelected would have an improper effect on the conduct of a man with enough fortitude. He could promise himself that there was enough time to make the community aware that the measures he wishes to pursue are proper.

As reelection approaches, his confidence might decline. But it will increase if he has established himself in the esteem and good will of his constituents during his time in office. So he might take a chance, if he has proven his wisdom and integrity, and become respected by his fellow citizens.

A four-year term contributes to the firmness of the Executive. But it is not long enough to justify any alarm for the public liberty.

The British House of Commons has *the small power to agree or disagree to new taxes.* Using this one power, from its beginning the House of Commons has been able to reduce the monarch's choices and the nobility's privileges. They have set limits to each that they feel are compatible with the principles of a free government. At the same time, the House of Commons has raised itself to the rank of co-equal branch of the legislature. In one instance, they abolished both the royalty and the aristocracy, and overturned all the ancient establishments, in the Church as well as the State. On a recent occasion, it made the monarch tremble at the idea of an innovation attempted by them. (This refers to Mr. Fox's India bill in the House of Commons, and rejected in the House of Lords, to the satisfaction, as it is said, of the people.--PUBLIUS)

Therefore, what would be feared from an elected executive with a four-year term and the limited authorities of a President of the United States? What, but that he might be unequal to the task assigned him by the Constitution?

I will only add that if a term of four years leaves a doubt of his firmness, that doubt is inconsistent with the worry about his encroachments.

PUBLIUS

Number 72:   Presidential Term Limits

In its largest sense, the administration of government includes all government operations. But in its most precise definition, it is limited to executive duties.

Government administration includes conducting foreign negotiations, preparing financial plans, asking for and spending public money as appropriated by the legislature, directing the army, navy and operations of war, and other similar duties. Therefore, the people who manage these areas should be considered assistants or deputies of the chief executive. The President should appoint them or, at least, nominate and supervise them. This suggests the close connection between the President's term in office and a stable administration.

To prove his worth, a new office-holder often reverses his predecessor's actions. When the change is because of an election, the new person can assume that his predecessor lost the election because people disliked his measures. And the less he acts like his predecessor, the more his constituents will like him. For these reasons and the influence of friends, every new President will probably change the men filling offices.

For these reasons, the government's administration can become dangerously mutable.

Reelection of Good Administrator

2   The President will serve for four years and will be eligible to be reelected [no term limits].

The four-year term gives the president the desire to do a good job. And it gives the community time to see his measures and form an opinion of their merits. Without term limits, the people may reelect him. He can continue using his talents and virtues. The government will have the advantage of continuing a wise system of administration.

Presidential Term Limit Bad Idea

3   Some respected people want presidential term limits. It appears like a good idea. But close inspection shows that it is not a good idea. Term limits mean that a president continues in office for a certain period of time and then is excluded from that office either for a limited period or forever.

Whether temporary or forever, excluding a man from running for President would have almost the same effects. And these effects would be more harmful than beneficial.

Possible Reelection Effects Behavior

4   One bad effect: Term limits would reduce the reasons for good behavior. Most men feel less zeal to perform a duty when they know that the advantages connected with their office must be given up at a predetermined time. They have more zeal when there is a hope of *obtaining*, by *meriting,* a continuance in office.

The desire for a reward motivates human conduct. And the best security for fidelity is to make a man's interest coincide with his duty.

The love of fame is the strongest passion of the noblest minds. A man might undertake difficult tasks for the public benefit that require a long time to finish, if he feels he might be reelected and be able to finish what he started. However, the desire for fame would stop him from starting the project if he knows he must leave before finishing the work. He wouldn't want to give the project and his reputation to a successor who might be unequal or unfriendly to the task. The most we can expect of men who cannot be reelected is the negative merit of doing no harm, instead of the positive merit of doing good.

Effect on Avaricious Office Holder

5   Second bad effect: The man would be tempted to evil thoughts, embezzlement, and usurpation. An avaricious man, who knows when he must give up the benefits of his office, would be tempted to make the best use of his limited opportunity. He might use corrupt methods to make his harvest as large as it was transitory.

If the same man felt he might be reelected, he might be content with the regular benefits of his office. He might not want to risk the consequences of abusing his opportunities. His avarice might be a guard on his avarice.

Perhaps he is vain or ambitious, as well as avaricious. And if he expected to be reelected if he behaved properly, he might hesitate to sacrifice his desire to be reelected to his desire for gain. But if he is forced to leave office, his avarice would probably win over his caution, his vanity, or his ambition.

Effect on Ambitious Office Holder

6   Also, let's say an ambitious man held his country's highest position of honor. If term limits were going to force him to descend from the exalted eminence forever and if he knows that no merit on his part could save him, he would be tempted to find a way to prolong his power. He will risk every personal hazard to maintain his position.

Effect of Living Ex-Presidents

7   Would the community be more peaceful or the government more stable if a half-dozen former presidents were wandering among the people like discontented ghosts, sighing for a place they are destined never more to possess?

Experience Parent of Wisdom

8   Third bad effect: The community could not use the experience gained by a president.

Experience is the parent of wisdom. Experience is the most desirable and essential quality in the head of a nation. Is it wise to constitutionally ban this desirable and essential quality? This is what term limits would do.

Effect of Changing During Crisis

9   Fourth bad effect: Men who might be needed during emergencies could not be President. Every nation has needed, at one time or another, the services of specific men in specific situations, perhaps even to save the nation. Therefore, term limits prohibit a nation from using its own citizens during emergencies!

Even if a man weren't essential, changing Presidents as a war breaks out or during any similar crisis, even for a man of equal merit, would always be detrimental to the community. It would substitute inexperience for experience. And it would tend to unhinge and set afloat the already settled administration.

Effect of Policy Changes

10   Fifth bad effect: Term limits would create a constitutional ban on a stable administration. By *requiring* a change of President, it would guarantee mutable measures. When the man holding an office changes, policies will also change. And we need not worry about too much stability when there is the option of changing.

We should not prohibit citizens from reelecting someone they trust. And where they may prevent the inconveniences of changing councils and policy.

Partial/Perpetual Term Limits

11   These are some of the disadvantages of term limits, especially life-time exclusion. And a partial exclusion would make reelecting a former President a remote possibility. Therefore they apply nearly as fully to both cases.

Advantages of Term Limits

12   What are the promised advantages of term limits? They are (1) great-er independence in the executive and (2) greater security to the people.

The first advantage can only be inferred if the exclusion is permanent. Couldn't he sacrifice his presidential independence to a future objective? Won't he have friends for whom he may sacrifice it? Might he be less willing to take decisive actions that could make personal enemies, when he knows that very soon he will be just a citizen? And he will be exposed to their resentments on an equal, even an inferior, footing?

It is hard to say whether he would be more or less independent in such a situation.

Term Limits: People's Security

13   There is a greater reason to doubt the second supposed advantage.

Let's say a man was excluded from the office for the rest of his life. A man of irregular ambition would reluctantly leave the office forever, an office where he had acquired a passion for power and pre-eminence. If he had been fortunate or adroit enough to become a favorite of the people, he might get them to reconsider the effects of term limits. He could show that term limits are an odious and unjustifiable restraint on the people because it takes away their right to give a fresh proof of their attachment to a favor-ite.

We can imagine the people becoming disgusted because they can't reelect a favorite man. Liberty could be in more danger than could be feared from the possibility of continuing in office by the voluntary votes of the community.

Disadvantages Outweigh Advantages

14   The idea of stopping the people from voting to continue in office men who they admire is too much refinement. The advantages are at best speculative and equivocal. And they are overbalanced by certain and deci-sive disadvantages.

PUBLIUS

Number 73: Executive Salary; Executive Powers, Veto

The third ingredient for an energetic President is the provision for its support. Without this, there really would be no separation between the executive and the legislative branch.

If the legislature could change the salary and benefits of the Chief Executive, he would have to do what the legislature wanted him to do. They might pay him nothing or tempt him with a lot of money. There are men who would never sacrifice their duty for money. But this stern virtue is rare. Generally, power over a man's support is power over his will.

There are plenty of examples that confirm this truth, even in this country. Executives have been either intimidated or seduced by the legislature that is paying their salary.

Presidential Compensation Unalterable

2   Therefore, the proposed Constitution pays close attention to this subject. It provides that "The President of the United States shall, at stated times, receive for his service a compensation *which shall neither be increased nor diminished during the period for which he shall have been elected;* and he *shall not receive within that period any other emolument* from the United States, or any of them."

This is an appropriate provision. When a President is elected, the legislature will state the compensation for his services during his term in office. Once done, they cannot change his salary. It will not increase or decrease until the next presidential election.

They cannot refuse to pay the President, which could weaken his courage. And they cannot bribe him and corrupt his integrity with more money. Neither the Union nor any State can give him more money. And he cannot accept any other benefits. He can have no monetary reason to not be independent.

Appropriate Presidential Powers

3   An effective executive needs to have the appropriate powers. Let us consider the proposed presidential powers.

Qualified Negative: Presidential Veto

4   The first power is the qualified negative [veto] of the President on the acts or resolutions of the two houses of the legislature. He will have the power to return bills to congress with his objections. The bills will only become law if two-thirds of each house of the legislature ratifies them.

Defense against Legislative Plundering

5   I've discussed how the legislative branch of government tends to intrude on the rights and absorb the powers of the other branches. And

words on paper are not enough to maintain the boundaries. The Constitution must provide a way for each branch to defend itself.

The Executive needs either an absolute or qualified negative [veto] on legislative acts. Without the veto power, the President could not defend himself against Congress. The legislature could pass a series of resolutions which take away the President's powers. Or it could vote to take away all the President's powers. Congress could quickly hold both the legislative and executive powers.

Even if the legislative body never wanted to invade the rights of the Executive, no branch of government should be left to the mercy of another branch. Each branch should have a constitutional way to defend itself.

Veto Defends against Bad Laws

6   But the veto has another use. It shields the Executive and is another security against improper laws. It is a check on the legislature. It guards the community against the effects of faction, haste, or any impulse unfriendly to the public good that could influence a majority of congress.

Critics: Improper Control over Legislature

7   Some people say a presidential veto is not proper because it assumes that one man has more virtue and wisdom than a group of men. If this was true, it would be improper to give the executive any type of control over the legislative body.

Closely Examine Laws Passed in Haste

8   When examined, this observation will be seen as specious. The veto power isn't proper because the Executive has superior wisdom or virtue. The veto is proper because the legislature won't be infallible. The love of power may sometimes cause the legislature to encroach on other branches of the government. A faction may pervert its deliberation. Passions may hurry it into passing laws that it would condemn after careful reflection.

The primary reason to give the Executive the veto is to enable him to defend himself.

The secondary reason is to decrease the possibility that bad laws, passed through haste or on purpose, will take effect. The more often a law or regulation is examined by different types of people, the less the danger of errors. Errors can happen from a lack of deliberation or from the corruption of some common passion. The same dangerous views will probably not infect all parts of the government at the same moment and about same subject.

Restraint on Excess Law-making

9   The power of preventing bad laws includes the power to prevent good ones. It can be used for both purposes. But this objection will not be very

important to anyone who knows that mutable laws hurt the character of our governments. Every power that restrains the excess of law making is more likely to do good than harm, because it favors greater stability in legislation. Preventing bad laws will make up for defeating a few good laws.

Veto Rarely Used against People's Will

10 Nor is this all. In a free government, the legislature has superior weight and influence. In a trial of strength with the legislature, the Executive can lose some of its authority. This gives security that the veto will be used with great caution. The Executive is more likely to be charged with not using the veto often enough than using it too frequently.

The British king has sovereign powers and great influence. But he doesn't like to veto resolutions passed by the two houses of Parliament. Instead, he uses his influence to stop bills he doesn't like as they work their way through Parliament. He doesn't want to risk the displeasure of the nation by opposing the will of the legislative body.

The king only uses his veto when it is absolutely proper or necessary. All informed men in that kingdom will agree that this remark is truthful. It has been a very long time since he has used the veto.

Cautious Use of Veto Power

11 If the powerful British king has scruples about using this power, a President of the United States will be even more cautious. A President has the executive authority for only four years.

Rare, But Used When Needed

12 Clearly, there is greater danger that the President will not use the veto when it in necessary than using it too often. Indeed, an argument against its usefulness has been drawn from this very source. Some people have said that it is a power odious in appearance, useless in practice. But just because a power may be rarely used, doesn't mean it would never be used.

The veto power is chiefly designed to stop an attack on the constitutional rights of the Executive. It is also designed to be used when the public good is clearly sacrificed. In these cases, a man with some firmness would use this constitutional defense. He will be responsible and do his duty. When he sees an attack on the Executive, he will want to secure the power of his office. If the public good is being sacrificed, he will act because his constituents, who would normally agree with the legislative body, would probably support the veto. I speak now of a President with only a normal amount of courage. There are men who, under any circumstances, will have the courage to do their duty at every hazard.

Qualified Veto, Legislature Concurrence

13   But the convention chose a qualified veto. The executive might use this type of veto more often than an absolute veto. The qualified veto will only take effect if a large part of the legislative body agrees with him.

A man might be afraid to defeat a law by his single VETO. But he might not hesitate to return it for reconsideration by congress if it would only be rejected if more than one-third of each house agrees with his objections. He would be encouraged. His opposition would prevail only if it was supported by a very large part of congress. Public opinion would support his conduct.

An absolute negative appears harsher than the stating of objections to be approved or disapproved by those to whom they are addressed. The less it might offend, the more apt it is to be used. For this reason, in practice it may be more effective than an absolute negative. It is hoped that improper views will not often govern two-thirds of both branches of the legislature at the same time, in spite of the counterbalancing weight of the Executive. At any rate, it is less probable than that such views would taint the resolutions and conduct of a bare majority.

The executive veto will often have an unperceived, though strong, operation. When men are pursuing unjustifiable goals and they know that obstructions may come from a person they cannot control, the possibility of opposition often restrains them from doing what they would eagerly rush into, if no such external controls were feared.

New York's Veto Successful

14   The qualified negative in New York is vested in a council, consisting of the governor with the chancellor and judges of the Supreme Court, or any two of them. It has been used, frequently with success. Its usefulness has become apparent. People who were opponents of it when the constitution was being written have become admirers.[*]

Maintaining Independent Judiciary

15   When forming this part of the Constitution, the convention followed the Massachusetts' constitution rather than New York's.

There are two probable reasons for this preference. One is that judges, who are interpreters of the law, might be improperly biased because they have a previous opinion. The other is that judges are often associated with the Executive, so they might be too vested in the political views of that executive. Eventually, the executive and judiciary branches might become dangerously close.

---

[*] Mr. Abraham Yate, an opponent of the Constitution, is of this number.—PUBLIUS

Judges cannot be too separate from every other avocation than that of expounding the laws. It is very dangerous to place them in a situation where they could be either corrupted or influenced by the Executive.

PUBLIUS

Number 74: Commander-in-Chief, Reprieves, Pardons

The President of the United States is to be "commander-in-chief of the army and navy of the United States, and the militia of the several States *when called into the actual service* of the United States."

This provision is proper and consistent with the State constitutions. Little need be said to explain or enforce it. Most of the people, who want an executive council in other areas of power, agree that the President, alone, should have the military authority.

The direction of war is a governmental concern that demands that one person have the power. The direction of war implies the direction of the common strength. And the power of directing the common strength is an essential part of the executive authority.

Reports from Executive Departments

2   "The President may require the opinion, in writing, of the principal officer in each of the executive departments, upon any subject relating to the duties of their respective officers."

I consider this a redundancy in the Constitution. The right it provides would result, anyway, from the office.

Reprieves, Pardons

3   He is authorized to grant "reprieves and pardons for offenses against the United States, except in cases of impeachment."

Humanity and good policy dictate that the pardoning power should be available. Every country's criminal code is very severe. Without the power to pardon cases of unfortunate guilt, justice would be too cruel.

Feelings of responsibility are stronger as fewer people are involved. Therefore, we may infer that a single man would most carefully study the motives that might plead for a mitigation of the rigor of the law. And one man is less likely to shelter a proper target of its vengeance. When the fate of a person depended on his *sole fiat,* he would be scrupulous and cautious. Equal caution, though of a different kind, would come from the dread of being accused of weakness or connivance.

On the other hand, men generally derive confidence from a group. A group of men with this power might often encourage each other's inflexibility. A group might be less attuned to suspicious apprehensions or censure for an injudicious or affected clemency. For these reasons, one man is a better dispenser of the government's mercy than a group.

Pardons for Treason

4   The Presidential power of pardoning has only been questioned in relation to the crime of treason. It has been urged that pardons for treason should depend on one or both houses of the legislature agreeing.

There are strong reasons for requiring this concurrence. Treason is a crime against the society. When an offender has been found guilty, it seems like the legislature should decide if he should be pardoned. And the Chief Executive ought not to be entirely excluded.

But there are also strong objections to such a plan. A single man of prudence and good sense is better fitted to balance the motives that may plead for and against a pardon, than any group of people.

It is important to remember that treason will often be connected with seditious acts by a group of people in the community, as recently happened in Massachusetts. In these cases, the people's representatives may feel the same spirit that motivated the offense. And when parties are equally matched, the secret sympathy of friends of the condemned person might bestow impunity where the terror of an example was necessary.

Expedited pardons

5   On the other hand, when the causes of the sedition inflame the resentments of the majority party, they might be obstinate and inexorable when policy demands clemency.

But the principal argument for giving the power of pardoning in this case to the Chief Executive is this: during times of insurrection or rebellion, there are often critical moments when a well-timed offer of pardon to the insurgents or rebels may restore the tranquility of the nation. And if the time passed with no action, it may never be possible afterwards to recall. It takes time to convene the legislature or one of its houses. The golden opportunity could be lost. The loss of a week, a day, or an hour may sometimes be fatal.

It may be suggested that the President could be given the power to pardon in such a situation. There are two problems with this suggestion. First, in a limited Constitution, the power could probably not be delegated by law. Second, it would be unwise to take any step before hand that might hold out the possibility of impunity. Giving the President this power, out of the usual course, could be seen as timidity or weakness. And it would have a tendency to embolden guilt.

PUBLIUS

Number 75: President, with Senate Approval, Makes Treaties

The President will have the power, "by and with consent of the Senate, to make treaties, provided two thirds of the senators present concur."

This provision has been strongly attacked. However, it is one of the most unexceptional parts of the Constitution.

One objection says it mixes powers. Some people say the President alone should make treaties. Others, the Senate.

Others object to the small number of people who can make a treaty. Some want the House of Representatives involved. Others think that two thirds of *all* Senators should have to agree rather than two thirds of the members *present*. An earlier Paper covered this subject. I will make a few more remarks.

Treaty Roles, Separation Rule

2   Other Papers explained the separation of powers rule. The union of the President with the Senate when forming treaties does not break that rule. And because of the nature of treaties, the union is particularly proper.

Several people say making treaties is an executive authority. However, this is an arbitrary classification. If we look at how treaties operate, they have more legislative than executive characteristics. But they don't fall strictly within the definition of either.

The legislature makes laws. It makes the rules that regulate society. The executive enforces laws and employs the common strength.

The power to make treaties is not one or the other. Treaties don't enforce existing laws or make new ones. And they don't have anything to do with using the common strength.

Treaties are CONTRACTS with foreign nations. They have the force of law, but they are enforced through good faith. They are not laws prescribed by the sovereign to the subjects, but agreements between sovereign governments. Therefore, this power forms a separate category; it is neither a legislative nor executive power.

The qualities needed for foreign negotiations are listed in another Paper. They show that the Executive is the best agent in those transactions. But treaties are an important trust and operate like laws. The legislative body should have some role in making them.

Foreign Influence, President Acted Alone

3   It may be proper and safe to give a monarch, who is chief executive, the entire power to make treaties. But it would be improper and unsafe to give that power to an elected President with a four-year term.

A monarch often oppresses his people. But he has personally too much stake in the government to be in any danger of being corrupted by foreign powers.

But a private citizen will become President, with a moderate or small fortune. And in a short time he will be a private citizen again. He will be tempted to sacrifice his duty to his personal interest. He would need great virtue to not give in to the temptation. An avaricious man might betray the nation to acquire wealth. A foreign power might help an ambitious man make his own aggrandizement the price of his treachery to his constituents.

The nation's dealings with the rest of the world are delicate and very important. If the President was solely responsible for foreign negotiations, he would have to be very virtuous. And the history of human conduct doesn't justify the opinion that people have that much virtue.

Advantages of President's Involvement

4   If the Senate, alone, made treaties, the benefits of the President's participation in foreign negotiations would be lost. The Senate could employ a person to do the negotiations. But the Senate would have the option of not doing this. Animosity or cabal might cause them to do the latter rather than the former.

Besides this, if the Senate employed a person to negotiate, he would not get the same respect from foreign nation as the President. And he would not have the same influence or efficacy. The Union would lose an important advantage in foreign negotiations. And the people would lose the additional security from the President's involvement.

It would not be wise to give such an important trust to the Executive, alone. But his participation would add to society's safety.

The President and Senate will have the joint power to make treaties. This provides more security than if either of them have the whole power. Also, anyone who has seriously studied how the President will be elected knows that men of wisdom and integrity will fill the office. The President's participation in forming treaties will be very desirable.

House Too Inexperienced, Large

5   An earlier Paper showed why the House of Representatives shouldn't have a role in making treaties. House membership will change frequently. And the House will grow very big. Therefore, we can't expect it to have the qualities essential to properly execute such a trust.

The people involved in treaty negotiations need several characteristics: knowledge of foreign politics, stable views of the national character, decisiveness, *secrecy*, and speed. House membership changes too often and is too large to have these characteristics.

Needing so many different people to agree is an objection. Also, the House would need more and longer sessions to agree to each new part of the treaty. This would be inconvenient and expensive, and should condemn the idea.

Two-Thirds Ratification, Minority Rule

6   The last objection is to require two thirds of all Senators to agree, rather than two thirds of the members *present*.

When more than the majority is required to pass resolutions, it hurts governmental operations. And the will of the majority is subject to the minority. This is important. The convention has secured the advantage of numbers in the formation of treaties. And it will support the majority will of the community.

If two thirds of all Senators were required, some Senators could simply not attend the session. To pass, every Senator present might need to agree to the treaty. The history of every political body using this principle is a history of impotence, perplexity, and disorder. Proof comes from the examples of the Roman Tribune, the Polish Diet, and the Netherlands' States-General. However, an example at home makes other examples unnecessary.

Proposed Senate, Current Congress

7   What if a fixed proportion of the whole Senate was required to approve treaties? This would probably not add to the advantage of requiring two thirds of the attending members.

When a specific number of votes are needed to pass every resolution, there is less reason for members to attend the sessions. But when a resolution can be passed based on a proportion of the members who are present, it has the opposite effect. The absence or presence of a single member can be very important. This promotes punctuality. And the members tend to show up. As many members will probably decide Senate resolutions as if two thirds of all members were required, with fewer reasons for delay.

Under the existing Confederation two members *may*, and usually *do*, represent a State. Consequently, Congress, which holds *all the powers* of the Union, rarely has more members than the proposed Senate. Members vote by States. When only one member from a State is present, a State vote is lost. In the proposed Senate, members will vote individually. There will rarely be fewer active members than in the existing Congress.

When we include the President of the Senate, we will have more security against an improper use of the power to make treaties under the new Constitution than under the Confederation. And the Senate will get larger as new States are added. There will be enough members to entrust the power. A body larger than the Senate will become would not be fit for the proper discharge of the trust.

PUBLIUS

Number 76: President, with Senate, Makes Appointments

The President is "to *nominate*, and, by and with the advice and consent of the Senate, to appoint ambassadors, other public ministers and consuls, judges of the Supreme Court, and all other officers of the United States whose appointments are not otherwise provided for in the Constitution. But the Congress may by law vest the appointment of such inferior officers as they think proper in the President alone, or in the courts of law, or in the heads of departments. The President shall have the power to fill up *all vacancies* which may happen *during the recess of the Senate,* by granting commissions which shall *expire* at the end of their next session."

Best Method of Appointing Officers

2   Paper #68 said, "The true test of a good government is its aptitude and tendency to produce a good administration." If true, the method of appointing the national officers is very good. It will promote a judicious choice of men. And the character of government administration depends on having good men in national offices.

Possible Appointment Methods

3   Of course, having the public make appointments is impractical. If nothing else, they would have little time to do anything else. Therefore, appointments can be made in one of three ways: by a one man, by a moderate sized group of people, or by a single man with the approval of a moderate sized, select group.

People are spread out across the nation. If the people made the appointments, they could not be coerced by cabals and intrigue. The fear of coercion is the main objection to giving the power to a smaller group of men.

One Man Best Judge

4   Because of the method for electing the President, he will probably be a man of abilities, at least respectable. Based on this, I'll state this rule: One man of discernment does a better job analyzing the qualities needed for specific offices than a group of men of equal, or even superior, discernment.

Reasons Group Decision Bad

5   One man will feel the full responsibility and a sense of duty. He will feel obligated to investigate the qualities required to fill the offices. And he will impartially prefer the persons who have the most qualifications.

He will have *fewer* personal attachments than a group of men, who each may have an equal number. He will be less likely to be misled by friendship. A group's decision can be warped by diverse views, feelings, and interests. A single, well-directed man does not have as many distractions.

People become very passionate when they have to choose a person. Deep personal feelings can influence the choice. When a group of men appoint people to offices, all private and party friendships and animosities felt by the people in the group effects the choice. The choice will be a victory of one party over the other or a compromise between parties. The candidate's merit will often not be considered.

The ability to unite the party's votes will be more important than the person's job qualifications. The choice will often be a compromise: "Give us the man we wish for this office and you can have the one you wish for that." This will usually be the bargain. Public good will rarely be the primary objective of either party victories or party negotiations.

Nominate vs. No Approval Needed

6   The intelligent people who don't like this provision know this is true. They say the President, alone, should appoint federal officers. But the power of *nomination* will have nearly all the same advantages. And several disadvantages will be avoided.

The President will use his judgment when he nominates a candidate. With the Senate's approval, the man he nominates will fill an office. Therefore, the President will be responsible for the choice. In this respect, there is no difference between nominating and appointing. The same motives will influence the choice. No man could be appointed without being nominated, so every man appointed will be the President's choice.

Senate Rejections Rare

7   His nomination might be overruled. But he will make the next nomination. The person ultimately appointed will be his choice, though perhaps not his first. And his nomination will probably not be overruled very often.

The Senate might prefer a different person. But they won't be tempted to reject the nomination because they couldn't be sure that the person they wanted would be the second or any other nomination. A future nomination might not be a more acceptable candidate. And since their rejection might stigmatize the nominee and reflect badly on the President's judgment, they will rarely reject a nominee except when there are strong reasons.

Senate Restraint on President

8   Why require the Senate's approval? Needing their approval will have a powerful though, often, silent operation. It will be a check on presidential favoritism. And it will tend to prevent the appointment of unfit people from State prejudice, family connection, personal attachment, or from a desire to be popular. It will also make the administration more stable.

Thoughtful Nomination

9   When a man has the sole power to appoint people to offices, his private desires and interests will often guide his choice. When a house of the legislature must agree, he will be more careful. The possibility of rejection is a strong motive to be careful when nominating.

The Senate will study the choice. And the Senate's opinion influences public opinion. He will not want to show favoritism or pursue popularity because the Senate's reaction could hurt his reputation or political life. Federal offices are distinguished and lucrative. He would be afraid to nominate candidates with no other merit than coming from the same State, or being a personal ally, or being so pliant that they will always agree with him.

Executive Influence on Senate

10   Some people say that the President's nomination power will influence the Senate to approve the nomination. Assuming that human nature is universally weak is as wrong as assuming universal integrity.

Delegated power implies that some people have virtue and honor. And experience justifies the theory. Virtue and honor exists even during the most corrupt periods of the most corrupt governments.

The British House of Commons has long been accused of accepting bribes. And many members have been bribed. But many members are independent, public-spirited men who influence the nation's councils. Even during the present reign, it often controls the monarch, both with regard to men and to measures.

The President may influence some Senators. But he probably could not buy the integrity of the entire Senate. A man with a realistic view of human nature, who doesn't exaggerate its virtues or vices, will be confident of the Senate's integrity. Corrupting and seducing a majority of the Senate would be impractical. And he will need the Senate's approval. This will restrain the President's conduct.

We don't have to rely on the Senate's integrity, alone. The Constitution has important guards against the danger of executive influence on the legislative body. The Constitution says it that "no senator or representative shall, during the time *for which he was elected*, be appointed to any civil office under the United States which shall have been created, or the emoluments whereof shall have been increased, during such time; and no person, holding any office under the United States, shall be a member of either house during his continuance in office."

PUBLIUS

Number 77: Executive Appoints Administration Officers

The Senate's role in appointments will help create a stable government. The Senate must consent to displacing as well as appointing. When a new President is elected, fewer government officers will change than if he, alone, appointed officers. When a man is doing a good job, a new President will be less likely to replace him with his choice. He will worry that the Senate might block the attempt, bringing some discredit on himself.

People who believe a steady administration is important will like this provision. It connects government officers with the approval or disapproval of the Senate, which will probably be the most stable part of the government.

Balanced Plan

2   The Senate and the President will each have a role in appointments. Some people say the President has too much influence over the Senate. Others say it will have an opposite effect—a strong proof that neither suggestion is true.

No Improper Influence over Senate

3   The first argument says the President will improperly *influence* the Senate because the Senate will have the power to *restrain* him.

This is absurd. If the President had the entire power of appointment, he might establish a dangerous empire over the Senate. But he only has the power of nomination, subject to the Senate's control.

Senate Influencing Appointments

4   The opposite idea is that "the Senate will influence the Executive." This objection is imprecise. And there is no precise answer. How will the Senate influence the President?

As used here, the power to influence a person implies a power of giving him a benefit. How could the Senate benefit the President? It can only reject his nomination. Sometimes the Senate might agree to the President's choice when public opinion disagrees with it. However, the President will be too rarely interested in the result to be materially affected by the Senate's decision.

The person or group with the POWER to *originate* the disposition of honors and salary is more likely to attract than be attracted to the POWER that can only block them.

If "influencing" the President means *restraining* him, this is the intention. The restraint will have a good effect. But it will not destroy the advantages of the President making the appointments. Nomination produces all the good of an appointment and avoids most of its evils.

Public Evaluates Appointments

5   We can compare the plan for appointing officers in the Constitution with New York's constitution. The United States Constitution is better. In New York, the Executive has the total power of nomination.

The US Constitution makes it necessary to submit each nomination to the judgment of an entire house of the legislature. Because of this, the appointment process becomes a public issue. And the public can determine what part was performed by the different actors. The President will be blamed for a bad nomination. The Senate will probably be blamed for rejecting a good nomination. If a bad appointment is made, the Executive, for nominating, and the Senate, for approving, will share the blame.

NY Appointments Veiled in Secrecy

6   The reverse of all this characterizes the manner of appointment in New York. The appointment council has three to five people, including the governor. This small group makes appointments in secret.

The governor claims the right of nomination based on some ambiguous clauses in the constitution. But no one knows when he actually nominates someone or when he is contradicted or opposed.

Each person's role is uncertain. The censure of a bad appointment is neither strong nor long lasting. And when there is an open opportunity of conspiracy, all responsibility is lost. The public only knows that the governor claims the right of nomination. *Two* out of the small number of *four* men can too often be influenced without much difficulty. If some of the members of the council don't want to go along with the plan, the council can meet at times when it is inconvenient for them to attend. Whatever the cause, a great number of very improper appointments are made.

Does a governor of New York use his power in this important part of the administration? Or does he appoint people, whose chief merit is their devotion to his will? This would support a despicable and dangerous system of personal influence. Unfortunately, we can only speculate about the answers to these questions.

Appointment Counsel

7   No matter how it is put together, every appointment council will support cabal and intrigue. Without an unacceptable increased expense, it cannot be large enough to exclude easy conspiracy.

Each member would have friends and connections to provide for. Members of the council would scandalously barter for votes. The private attachments of one man might easily be satisfied. But to satisfy the private attachments of a dozen, or of twenty men, a few families might end up holding a monopoly of government offices. This would lead directly to an aristocracy or an oligarchy.

The council members could change frequently, to avoid this problem. However, this would create all the problems of a mutable administration.

An appointment council would be more likely to influence the executive than the Senate. It would be smaller than the Senate and its actions would get less public scrutiny. A council would be expensive. It would multiply the evils of favoritism and intrigue in giving out public honors. The government would be less stable and diminish the security against an improper influence of the Executive. And yet some people want an amendment to the proposed Constitution, creating such a council.

House: No Part in Appointments

8   A few people have said that the House of Representatives should have a role in appointments. I can't imagine that many people think this is a good idea. The House is large and frequently changes membership. It can never be deemed proper for the exercise of that power. Remember that in only fifty years it may have three or four hundred members. All the advantages of stability, both of the Executive and of the Senate, would be defeated by including the House of Representatives. And infinite delays and embarrassments would happen. The example of most of the States encourages us to reject the idea.

Other Executive Powers

9   The only remaining powers of the Executive include:
- giving information to Congress on the state of the Union,
- recommending to their consideration measures he thinks expedient,
- convening Congress or either house on extraordinary occasions,
- adjourning them when they cannot themselves agree on the time of adjournment,
- receiving ambassadors and other public ministers,
- faithfully executing the laws, and
- commissioning all the officers of the United States.

Convene Congress; Receive Ambassadors

10   There have been some trivial objections to the power of convening *either* house of the legislature and receiving ambassadors. No other objections have been made to this group of authorities. Nor could there be any. Indeed, it required an unlimited enthusiasm for disapproval to invent objections we have seen.

The President can convene either house of the legislature on extraordinary occasions. In respect to the Senate, we can quickly discover a good reason for it. The Senate has a role with the Executive in making treaties. It might be necessary to convene the Senate. But it would not be necessary to convene the House of Representatives.

As to receiving ambassadors, I answered this in an earlier Paper.

Safety of Executive

11   We have studied the structure and powers of the executive department. It has all the requirements for energy, as far as republican principles will permit.

Does it also have the required safeties, in a republican sense? Does it depend on the people? Is it responsible?

As we studied the characteristics of the executive, we got the answer. Remember, the President is elected every four years by persons immediately chosen by the people for that purpose. He can be impeached, tried, dismissed from office, and banned from serving in any other. And he can then be prosecuted and could lose his life and estate.

But these are not the only strong precautions for public security in the Constitution. In the only areas where abuse of executive authority may be feared, the President will be subjected to the control of the Senate. What more could an enlightened and reasonable people want?

PUBLIUS

Judiciary

Number 78: Federal Judiciary: Term: *Good Behavior*

We will now examine the judiciary branch of the proposed government.

Federal Judiciary Necessary

2   We have studied the defects in the existing Confederation. It is clear that a federal judiciary is needed. Everyone agrees with this conclusion. We will discuss its structure and its extent.

Structure of Federal Judiciary

3   The structure of the federal judiciary includes:
      1) the method of appointing judges,
      2) their tenure in office, and
      3) the judicial authority of the different courts and their relationship to each other.

1. Appointing Judges

4   Judges will be appointed using the same method as other officers of the Union. This was fully discussed in the last two papers.

2. Tenure

5   The tenure of judges concerns how long they stay in office, how they will be paid, and precautions for their responsibility.

Duration in Office: Good Behavior

6   All federal judges will hold their offices *during good behavior*. This conforms to the most approved State constitutions, including New York's.

Adversaries of the Constitution question whether this is proper. This criticism shows us that opponents of the Constitution are so determined to find objections that their judgment is impaired. Lifetime judicial appointments, during good behavior, are a great improvement in government.

In a monarchy, it is a barrier to a king's tyranny. In a republic, it helps block encroachments and oppressions by the legislature. In any government, it is the best way to secure an impartial administration of the laws.

Least Threat to Constitutional Rights

7   When the government's powers are separated into three branches, the judiciary is the least dangerous to constitutional rights. It will be least able to injure them.

The executive decides who will have government jobs and holds the community's sword. The legislature commands the purse and creates the laws that regulate every citizen.

The judiciary, however, doesn't have a sword or a purse. It can take no actions. The judiciary has neither FORCE nor WILL, merely judgment. It even depends on the executive to enforce its judgments.

Permanency in Office: Independence

8   The judiciary is the weakest of the three branches of power.[1] It can never successfully attack the other two. And it must be able to defend itself against their attacks.

The courts of justice might oppress a single person. However, if the judiciary is separate from the legislature and the executive branches, it will not be dangerous to the general liberty of the people. "There is no liberty, if the power of judging is not separated from the legislative and executive powers."[2]

Liberty has nothing to fear from the judiciary alone. But if the judiciary unites with either of the other branches, liberty will be in danger. If the judiciary had to depend on the other branches, we would see the negative effects.

The judiciary is weak. It is always in danger of being overpowered or influenced by the legislature or executive. A lifetime appointment makes it more firm and independent. Therefore, it is indispensable. And it is important to public justice and public security.

Enforce Limited Legislative Authority

9   In a limited Constitution, courts must be completely independent. A "limited" Constitution has specific exceptions to the legislative authority. For example, the legislature cannot pass bills of attainder or *ex post facto* laws. Courts of justice preserve these limitations. They declare all acts contrary to the meaning of the Constitution void. Without this, all Constitutional rights and privileges would mean nothing.

Power to Void Unconstitutional Laws

10   If laws are contrary to the Constitution, the courts will declare them void. Some people argue that since judges can declare laws void, the judicial power must be superior to the legislature's power.

This is an important doctrine in all the American constitutions. A brief discussion of it is appropriate.

Congress: Actions Limited

11   The Constitution defines the legislature's authorities. No legislative act contrary to the Constitution is valid. Denying this would mean that the

---

[1] Montesquieu says: "Of the three powers above mentioned, the judiciary is next to nothing." *Spirit of Laws,* Vol. I, page 186.—PUBLIUS

[2] *Idem,* page 181.

representatives of the people are superior to the people themselves. Or that a man may do both what he has the authority to do and what he is forbidden from doing.

Authority: Constitution vs. Legislature

12   It may be argued that the legislature decides what its constitutional powers are. And the other branches have to accept the legislature's interpretation. But this is not a logical conclusion from any part of the Constitution.

The Constitution does not say that the people's representatives can substitute their *will* for the people's will. The courts stand between the people and the legislature. Among other things, the courts keep the legislature within their constitutional limits.

Courts interpret law. A constitution is a fundamental law. Therefore, the courts determine its meaning, as well as the meaning of legislative acts. If the two conflict, the superior one should be preferred.

Therefore, the Constitution is preferred over the statute; the intention of the people is preferred to the intention of their agents.

People's Constitution Superior to Both

13   This doesn't mean that judicial power is superior to the legislative power. It only means that the power of the people is superior to both.

When the will of the legislature, as seen in the laws it passes, opposes the will of the people, as declared in the Constitution, judges should be governed by the Constitution. Their decision should be based on fundamental laws.

Decide Validity of Contradictory Laws

14   When two laws contradict each other and neither has a repealing clause, the courts decide which is superior. The courts have the authority and duty to clarify the laws' meaning and operation. When this is impractical, one law takes effect and the other law does not.

The courts usually decide that the most recent law is the more valid law. But no law created this "rule." It just seems logical. The courts don't have to follow this rule, but it seems proper that it should direct their conduct as interpreters of the law. It seems reasonable that between conflicting acts of an *equal* authority, the last indication of its will should have preference.

Constitution Superior to Laws

15   The legislature is a lower authority. It was created by the people's Constitution. The Constitution is the superior, original authority. When the legislature passes a law that conflicts with the Constitution, the opposite of the "rule" must be followed. The earlier act of a superior authority, the Constitution, is preferred to the later act of a lower authority.

Therefore, when a law contradicts the Constitution, judicial courts must follow the Constitution and disregard the law.

Courts Negating Legislative Will

16   Some people argue that if the courts find a law repugnant, they may substitute their own will for the constitutional intentions of the legislature. This could happen when two laws contradict each other or during the adjudication of a single law.

This argument carries no weight. The courts must declare the meaning of the law. And if they exercise their WILL instead of JUDGMENT, their will would be substituted for the will of the legislative body.

Permanent/Lifetime Tenure

17   Courts of justice guard a limited Constitution against encroachments by the legislature. This duty is a strong argument for the lifetime tenure. Judges will feel independent. Independence is essential to do this difficult duty.

Independent Judges Protect Liberty

18   Independent judges guard both the Constitution and the rights of individuals. People need protection from bad ideas. Bad ideas can come from designing men. Or they can simply spread through the community. As the people get better information, bad ideas quickly go away. However, before they do, the government can make dangerous changes and seriously oppress the minority in the community.

The people can alter or abolish the constitution if it is not consistent with their happiness. This is the fundamental principle of republican government. Friends of the proposed Constitution will never agree with its enemies[3] and question that fundamental principle.

But let's say a majority of the people don't like a provision in the existing constitution. They tell their representatives. Then the representatives pass an unconstitutional law based on the people's wishes. The courts could not uphold the unconstitutional law. Until the people have changed or abolished the Constitution, through an authoritative act, it is binding on them collectively and individually. No presumption or knowledge of the people's wishes gives representatives the authority to depart from the Constitution. Judges need great fortitude. They must faithfully guard the Constitution after legislative invasions of it are started by the majority voice of the community.

Restraint on Bad Legislation

19   Independent judges are an essential safeguard against bad laws, not

---

[3] *Vide* "Protest of the Minority of the Convention of Pennsylvania," Martin's Speech, etc.—PUBLIUS

just Constitutional infractions. Sometimes these involve an injury to the rights of specific citizens by unjust laws.

The lifetime appointment of judges lessens the severity of such laws. It both moderates the problems caused by laws that have been passed and it operates as a check on the legislative body in passing them. The legislature will realize that the courts will block their unjust actions. And it will be more careful about the laws it passes.

This restraint on bad legislation will influence the character of our governments. Several States have already felt the benefits of an honest and moderate judiciary. The courts may displease people with sinister motives. But virtuous people praise them.

Everyone should prize whatever will tend to create or fortify that temper in the courts. No man can be sure that he may not be tomorrow the victim of a spirit of injustice by which he gains today. Injustice saps the foundations of public and private confidence, replacing it with distrust and distress.

Owe Allegiance Only to Constitution

20 Courts of justice must strictly enforce Constitutional and individual rights. But judges with a temporary tenure cannot be expected to have this strength.

Temporary appointments would be fatal to judicial independence. If the president or legislature appointed judges, judges might give in to the branch making the appointment.

If the president and legislature jointly made the appointment, judges would not want to displease either. If the people appointed judges or if a special council appointed judges, popularity would be more important than knowledge of the Constitution and the laws.

Limited Number of Qualified People

21 There is another, more important reason for the permanency of judges. It comes from the qualifications they need.

A huge number of laws is a necessary inconvenience of a free government. To avoid arbitrary decisions, the courts should follow strict rules and precedents that define their duty in every case that comes before them. A variety of controversies grow out of the folly and wickedness of mankind. Therefore, precedents will swell to a very large bulk. Long and laborious study will be needed to acquire a competent knowledge of them. Hence, only a few men in the society will have enough knowledge of laws to qualify them for the office of judge.

Some people will be disqualified for the ordinary depravity of human nature. The number of people with both the integrity and knowledge to become judges is still smaller.

The government has limited choices between people of fit character. A temporary time in office would discourage qualified people from quitting a lucrative practice to accept a seat on the bench. Temporary tenure would tend to throw the administration of justice into hands less able and less well qualified.

Temporary tenure would have great disadvantages.

Good Behavior Important Inclusion

22   The convention acted wisely in copying from the constitutions that have established *good behavior* as the tenure for judges.

Rather than being blamed for including this, their plan would have been inexcusably defective if it didn't include this important feature of good government. The experience of Great Britain illustrates the excellence of the institution.

PUBLIUS

Number 79: Judiciary: Independence, Salary, Impeachment

After permanency in office, nothing assures independent judges more than a fixed provision for their support. The comment made about the President applies equally here: *a power over a man's subsistence amounts to a power over his will.*

The complete separation of the judicial from the legislative power will never happen if judges depend on the legislature for their pay.

Some State constitutions don't have instructions about paying judges. And friends of good government lament this omission.

Some State constitutions say that *permanent** salaries should be established for judges. But, in practice, the wording is not precise and legislatures can evade paying judges.

An unambiguous provision is required. Therefore, the Constitution provides that the judges of the United States "shall at *stated times* receive for their services a compensation which shall not be *diminished* during their continuance in office."

Judicial Salary Can't Be Reduced

2   This is the best provision possible. The value of money and the payment rate for jobs changes. Therefore, the Constitution couldn't state a fixed salary. An amount that might be extravagant today could be totally inadequate in half a century. Therefore, the legislature must be able to change the salary as circumstances change. However, the legislature cannot lower a judge's pay. A judge cannot be deterred from his duty by fears that his salary will be diminished.

---

* Vide *Constitution of Massachusetts,* chapter 2, section 1, article 13. –PUBLIUS

The clause has two advantages. When necessary, the salaries of judicial officers may be changed. But the pay of a specific judge can never be lower than when he was appointed.

The convention set up the compensation for the President and for judges differently. The President's pay cannot be increased or decreased. Judges' pay can only not be decreased. This difference probably arose from the difference in the terms in office. The President is elected for no more than four years. Therefore, an adequate salary, fixed at the time he enters office, will almost always be adequate until the end of the four years.

Judges, if they behave properly, will have a lifetime job. It may happen, especially in the early years of the government, that a salary that is enough when they are appointed will become too small over the time they serve.

Judicial Independence

3   This provision for the support of the judges is wise and effective. Together with lifetime tenure, it makes federal judges more independent than any of the State judges.

Judges Can Be Impeached

4   To assure that judges will act responsibly, they can be impeached by the House of Representatives and tried by the Senate. If convicted, a judge may be dismissed from office and disqualified for holding any other. This is the only provision that could be made that is consistent with judicial independence. It is also in the New York State constitution.

Judges Mental Ability

5   There is no provision for removing judges because they are unable to do their job. People have complained about this. However, such a provision would either not be used or it would be more often abused than used properly.

Science hasn't found a way to measure the abilities of the mind. If someone tried to define the line between mental ability and inability, personal and party attachments and animosities would probably influence them more than the interests of justice. The result, except in the case of insanity, would be mostly arbitrary. And insanity, without an express provision in the Constitution, is a virtual disqualification to become a judge.

No Forced Retirement

6   The New York constitution, to avoid vague and dangerous investigations, has selected a specific age as the criterion of inability. No man can be a judge beyond age sixty. Most people disapprove of this provision. Age doesn't change a person's qualifications to be a judge. The mental

facilities needed to deliberate remain strong far beyond the age of sixty. Few men outlive their time of intellectual vigor. And few people over sixty will be on the bench at any given time. Therefore, age limitations have little to recommend them.

In a republic, judges will probably not be wealthy. They will depend on their job for subsistence. When a man has served his country long and usefully, there should be a better reason for dismissing him from office when he is too old to start a new occupation to support himself than the imaginary danger of a superannuated bench.

PUBLIUS

Number 80:   Extent of Federal Judicial Authority

To judge the proper extent of the federal judiciary, we must consider its objectives.

Cases Heard in Federal Court

2   The judicial authority of the Union should extend to several types of cases:

1.   Cases that concern the execution of the provisions in the Constitution.
2.   Cases that come from the laws of the United States passed through the constitutional power of legislation.
3.   Cases in which the United States is a party.
4.   Cases involving the PEACE of the CONFEDERACY, whether they relate to the relationship between the United States and foreign nations or between the States themselves.
5.   Cases that originate on the high seas and are of admiralty or maritime jurisdiction;
6.   Cases in which the State courts cannot be expected to be impartial and unbiased.

1. Constitutional Provisions

3   The first seems obvious. There should be a way to enforce constitutional provisions.

For example, the Constitution limits State authority. The States are prohibited from doing several things. Some are incompatible with the interests of the Union. Others are incompatible with the principles of good government. There must be a way to enforce the restrictions.

For example, the States cannot tax imported articles. And they cannot issue paper money. State prohibitions would not be obeyed if the federal government didn't have the power to stop or correct the infractions of them. The federal government needs either the power to veto State laws or an authority in the federal courts to overrule any violation of the Union's Constitution. The convention preferred the latter.

2. Federal Legislation

4   The government's judicial power should be as extensive as its legislative power.

National laws must be interpreted uniformly. If each State had an independent court of final jurisdiction over the same cases, arising out of the same laws, it would create a hydra in government. The State courts would contradict each other and their decisions would be confusing.

3. Nation vs. States or Citizens

5   Even less needs to be said about the third type. Only national courts can decide controversies between the nation and its States or citizens. Any other plan would be contrary to reason, precedent, and decorum.

4. U.S. vs. Foreign Nations, Citizens

6   The fourth type rests on the idea that the peace of the WHOLE should never depend on a PART. The Union will answer to foreign powers for the conduct of its States. And the responsibility for an injury should always be accompanied with the ability to prevent it.

If a citizen of another country is denied justice or is wrongfully convicted, it can become a **just cause for war** [Number 3]. Therefore, the federal judiciary should have jurisdiction in all cases concerning the citizens of other countries. This is essential to both public faith and tranquility.

Treaties and the laws of nations may seem different than municipal laws. Treaties and the laws of nations may seem proper for federal jurisdiction and municipal laws for State jurisdiction. However, let's say a foreign citizen gets an unjust sentence solely because of the location in our country where he is tried. If the unjust sentence is not corrected, his native country could see it as an aggression. It could also be seen as a violation of a treaty stipulation or the general laws of nations.

And it would be very difficult, if not impossible, to decide if a case falls under federal or municipal jurisdiction. Many cases in which foreigners are parties involve national questions. It is safer and faster to refer them to national courts.

Between States, Citizens of Different States

7   To keep the Union peaceful, the federal government must have the power to determine causes between two States, between one State and the citizens of another, and between the citizens of different States.

Wars between Germanic states devastated Germany before Maximilian created the Imperial Chamber in the 15th century. This court made the final decision in differences among the Germanic states. And it created peace in the empire.

Territorial Disputes

8   Until now, the federal government has been able to decide territorial disputes between the States. But there are many other sources of bickering and anger between States, besides territorial claims.

We have seen some already. I am talking about the fraudulent laws that have been passed in many of the States. The proposed Constitution establishes specific guards against repeating those cases. But we should worry that the same spirit that produced them will assume a new shape, which can not be foreseen nor specifically provided against.

It is proper for the federal government to control things that disturb the harmony between the States.

Universal Citizenship

9   It is the foundation of the Union that "the citizens of each State shall be entitled to all the privileges and immunities of citizens of the several States." Every government *should have the ability to execute its own provisions by its own authority.* Therefore, to keep the equality of privileges and immunities, the national judiciary should preside in all cases where one State or its citizens are opposed by another State or its citizens.

This fundamental provision can be effective only in a court that has no local attachments. The court will probably be impartial between the different States and their citizens because it is a federal court. Therefore, its only bias will probably be towards the principles on which it is founded.

5. Maritime Jurisdiction

10   There will be little criticism of the fifth type. Even the most bigoted idolizers of State authority say the national courts have jurisdiction of maritime causes. These are often based on the laws of nations and often affect the rights of foreigners. They relate to the public peace. Under the present Confederation, the federal courts determine the most important cases.

6. When State Courts Can't Be Impartial

11   The national courts should decide cases where the State courts cannot be impartial.

No man should be a judge in his own cause or in any cause in which he has an interest or bias. The federal courts are the proper tribunals for determining controversies between different States and their citizens. And it should have the same operation in regard to some cases between citizens of the same State.

Claims to land under grants of different States are of this description. The courts of neither State could be expected to be unbiased. The laws may have even prejudged the question. The courts may be forced to rule in favor to the grants of the State to which they belong. And even where this had not been done, it would be natural that the judges, as men, would feel partial to the claims of their own government.

Federal Judicial Authority

12   These principles should regulate the federal judiciary. Using these principles, we will test its powers, according to the Constitution.

The federal judiciary is to decide "all cases in law and equity arising under the Constitution, the laws of the United States,

"and treaties made, or which shall be made, under their authority;

"to all cases affecting ambassadors, other public ministers, and consuls;

"to all cases of admiralty and maritime jurisdiction;

"to controversies to which the United States shall be a party;

"to controversies between two or more States; between a State and citizens of another State; between citizens of different States;

"between citizens of the same State claiming lands and grants of different States;

"and between a State or the citizens thereof and foreign states, citizens, and subjects."

This is the entire judicial authority of the Union, as stated in the Constitution. Let us now review it.

Constitutional, Federal Law Cases

13   *First.* To all cases in law and equity *arising under the Constitution* and *the laws of the United States.* This corresponds with the first two types of cases, discussed above. And it is proper jurisdictions of the United States.

How are "cases arising under the Constitution," different from cases "arising under the laws of the United States"?

The difference has been already explained. For example, Constitution restricts the authority of the State legislatures. They are not to emit paper money. This restriction comes from the Constitution. It is not connected with any law of the United States. If paper money is emitted, the controversies concerning it would be cases arising under the Constitution and not the laws of the United States.

"Equitable" Jurisdiction

14   It has been asked why the word "equity" is needed. What equitable causes can grow out of the Constitution and laws of the United States?

Almost every subject of litigation that doesn't involve *fraud, accident, trust,* or *hardship* could be an object of equitable rather than legal jurisdiction as the distinction is known and established in the States.

For example, it is the duty of an equity court to relieve against what are called hard bargains. These contracts may not involve direct fraud or deceit sufficient to invalidate them in a court of law. But it may take advantage of the needs or misfortunes of one of the parties that a court of equity would not tolerate. When foreigners are concerned on either side of such cases, it would be impossible for the federal courts to do justice without equitable as well as legal jurisdiction.

Agreements to convey lands claimed under the grants of different States are another example of the need for an equitable jurisdiction in the federal courts. This reasoning may not be as obvious in the States where the formal and technical distinction between LAW and EQUITY is not maintained. Unlike in New York where it is used every day.

Treaties, Ambassadors

15, 16   *Second.* To treaties made, or which shall be made, under the authority of the United States, and to all cases affecting ambassadors, other public ministers, and consuls. These belong to the fourth class of cases; they have a clear connection with the preservation of the national peace.

Admiralty, Maritime

17   *Third.* Admiralty and maritime cases are the fifth class of causes proper for national jurisdiction.

United States a Party

18   *Fourth.* To controversies to which the United States shall be a party. These constitute the third class.

Between States

19   *Fifth.* To controversies between two or more States; between a State and citizens of another State; between citizens of different States. These belong to the fourth class and partake, in some measure, of the nature of the last.

Land Disputes, Citizens of the Same State

20   *Sixth.* To cases between the citizens of the same State, claiming lands under grants of different States. These fall within the last class. And they are the only instances in which the proposed Constitution directly contemplates the jurisdiction of disputes between the citizens of the same State.

State, Citizen vs. Foreign Country, Citizen

21   *Seventh.* To cases between a State and the citizens thereof and foreign countries, citizens or subjects. These belong to the fourth class. They are the proper subject of the national judicature.

Federal Judiciary Conforms to Principles

22   The specific powers of the federal judiciary, as stated in the Constitution, seem to conform to the principles that govern the structure of the judiciary. And they are necessary. If some seem inconvenient, the national

legislature will have the authority to make *exceptions*. Congress can make any regulations that are needed to prevent or remove these inconveniences.

There is a possibility of specific mischiefs. However, this is not a solid objection. The principle avoids most problems and produces many advantages.

PUBLIUS

Number 81: Authorities of Supreme, Inferior Federal Courts

The judicial authority will be divided between different courts.

Supreme Court, Inferior Courts

2   "The judicial power of the United States is" (by the Constitution) "to be vested in one Supreme Court, and in such inferior courts as the Congress may, from time to time, ordain and establish."[81]

Supreme Court as Part of Legislature

3   There should be one supreme court of final jurisdiction. I stated the reasons for this in another place. They don't need to be repeated.

One question has been asked: Should the Supreme Court be a separate body or one house of the legislature?

Some men object to the Senate acting as the impeachment court, saying it improperly mixes powers. Now the same men seem to want to give the ultimate decision of all causes, in the whole or in a part, to the Senate.

Supreme Court as Legislative Body

4   This seems to be their argument:

"The proposed Supreme Court will be a separate, independent body. The Supreme Court will interpret laws, according to the *spirit* of the Constitution. It will be able to mold laws into any shape it thinks proper. Therefore, its authority will be superior to the legislature because the legislature cannot correct its decisions. This is unprecedented and dangerous.

"In Britain, the House of Lords, part of the legislature (Parliament), has the judicial power of last resort. The State constitutions imitate this. Both Parliament and the State legislatures can correct, by law, court decisions they object to. But there will be no way to correct the errors and usurpations of the Supreme Court of the United States."

On examination, this will be found to be false reasoning based on misconceived fact.

---

[1] Article 3, Section 1. –PUBLIUS

Judging Constitutionality of Laws

5   Nothing in the new Constitution *directly* give the national courts the power to interpret laws according to the spirit of the Constitution. In this respect, it has no more power than the courts of every State.

The Constitution should be the standard for the construction of laws. When laws conflict with the Constitution, the Constitution takes precedence over the laws. But this doctrine is not in the proposed Constitution. It comes from the general theory of a limited constitution. And, as far as this doctrine is true, it also applies to the State governments.

Therefore, this objection could be made against local courts. And it will not help to condemn every constitution that tries to limit legislative actions.

Legislators, Judges: Different Talents

6   But perhaps the objection is to the specific organization of the Supreme Court.

The Supreme Court will be a separate body of judges. It will not be one of the legislative houses as in Great Britain and New York.

If the authors of the objection insist that the Supreme Court must be part of the legislature, they must renounce the meaning of the separation of powers maxim.

These Papers explain the separation of powers maxim. It is not violated by giving the ultimate power of judging to *part* of the legislature. But it is close to violating it. And the structure in the Constitution fulfills the maxim better than making the federal judiciary part of the legislature.

Even if the legislature was only partly responsible for passing bad laws, the same branch would rarely want to change them. The same spirit that made the laws would probably interpret them. The same legislators, who infringed on the Constitution when they made the laws, would not feel like repairing the breach when they act as judges.

Nor is this all. There are good reasons for judges to have a lifetime tenure, during good behavior. The same reasons argue against giving the judiciary power, in the last resort, in a body of men, who serve for a limited period. Federal judges with lifetime tenure would hear the cause first. Then the final appeal would be heard by judges who are temporarily in office. This would be absurd.

The lower-court federal judges will be selected for their knowledge of the laws, learned through long and laborious study. Then the final appeal would be made to legislators who don't have the same knowledge. It is even more absurd. Legislators will rarely be chosen because they have the qualifications of a judge. We could expect all the bad consequences that come from not having the right information.

Legislatures naturally divide by party. Therefore, faction may poison the fountains of justice. Out of habit, Senators are on the opposites sides of issues. The voices of law and equity will probably not be heard.

Separate Supreme Court, Legislature

7   In some States, the judicial court of last appeals is an independent body of men, separate from the legislature. This is wise.

In this respect, the Constitution copies the constitutions of New Hampshire, Massachusetts, Pennsylvania, Delaware, Maryland, Virginia, North Carolina, South Carolina, and Georgia. We applaud following those models.

Changing Supreme Court's Ruling

8   There is another point. The future United States Congress can over-rule objectionable decisions just like the Parliament of Great Britain and the State legislatures. This theory authorizes the legislature to revise the judicial ruling by passing a new law. It is not forbidden in the proposed Constitution. The impropriety of the thing, on the general principles of law and reason, is the only obstacle.

A legislature, without exceeding its authority, cannot reverse a deter-mination once made in a specific case. But it can make a new rule for fu-ture cases. This is the principle. It applies to the State governments. And it applies to the national government under consideration. Not the least difference can be pointed out in any view of the subject.

Legislature can Impeach Judges

9   Lastly, the danger of judiciary encroachments on the legislative au-thority is often mentioned. This will not happen. Now and then, specific laws may be misconstrued. Or, occasionally the will of the legislature may be blocked. But they can never be extensive enough to inconvenience or change the political system.

This is inferred from several things: the nature of judicial power, its objects, the way it is exercised, its weakness, and its inability to support its usurpations by force.

This conclusion is strengthened by the important constitutional check on the judiciary. One part of the legislative body can impeach judges and the other tries them.

This is complete security. Judges will not want to usurp the legisla-ture's authority while the legislature has the power to punish them and re-move them from office.

This should remove all worries on the subject. It also is a good argu-ment for making the Senate the court for the trial of impeachments.

Inferior Federal Courts

10   I trust that these points have removed the objections to an independent Supreme Court. I will now show that the power of creating inferior courts is proper.[2] And I will show the relationship between these and the Supreme Court.

11   With inferior federal courts, every case of federal jurisdiction will not need to go to the Supreme Court. The national government can *authorize* inferior courts in each State or district. Those courts can decide matters of national jurisdiction within their limits.

State Courts Hearing Federal Cases

12   Could State courts fill this role? This has several answers.

Even if the State courts are competent to handle federal cases, this constitutional power is necessary. Before the State courts could try federal cases, the national legislature would have to give them jurisdiction over causes arising out of the national Constitution. Congress might give the State courts the power to decide federal cases. That action would perhaps fulfill the requirement "to constitute tribunals."

But should the Constitution say that State courts should be used? There are good reasons why it shouldn't.

Local attitudes and opinions may disqualify local courts from hearing federal cases.

And the structures of some of the State judiciary systems are improper channels of the Union's judicial authority.

Some State judges hold their offices during pleasure or from year to year. They will not be independent enough to objectively execute national laws. If the United States Constitution said that State courts must be the first court to hear federal cases, the door for appeals would need to be as wide as possible. Appeals should be easy or difficult in proportion to the grounds of confidence in or distrust of the subordinate tribunals. I believe the appellate jurisdiction, as defined by the Constitution, is proper. However, anything that allows *unlimited* appeals is a source of inconvenience.

Federal Court Districts

13   The United States might be divided into four, five or six districts. Each district could have a federal court instead of putting one in every State. The district court judges, with the help of State judges, may hold circuits to try cases in their district. Justice can be administered with ease and dispatch. And appeals may be safely limited.

---

[2] Some people claim this power abolishes all the county courts in the States, which are often called inferior courts. But the Constitution says: to constitute "tribunals INFERIOR TO THE SUPREME COURT." This means that local courts, subordinate to the Supreme Court, can be created either in States or larger districts. It is ridiculous to say it abolishes county courts. –PUBLIUS

This plan appears to me the best that could be adopted. The power of creating inferior courts should be in the Constitution.

Inferior Federal Courts Imperative

14   The Constitution gives Congress the power to create inferior federal courts. Without this power, the Constitution would be defective.

Let us examine how the judicial authority will be divided between the Supreme and the inferior courts of the Union.

Ambassadors, Consuls, States

15   The Supreme Court will have original jurisdiction only "in cases affecting ambassadors, other public ministers, and consuls, and those in which a STATE shall be a party."

Public ministers are representatives of their sovereigns. All cases involving them are directly connected with the public peace. To keep the public peace and out of respect to the countries they represent, the highest court in the nation should hear their cases.

Consuls are not strictly diplomatic, but they are the public agents of their nations. So the same observation applies to them.

Cases that involve a State shouldn't be turned over to an inferior tribunal.

Citizens Suing State for Debt

16   Although it is not part of the subject of this paper, I will mention a mistaken idea that has alarmed some people.

Some people say that if public securities of one State are assigned to citizens of another State, the citizens could sue the State in the federal courts for the amount of those securities. This assumption has no foundation.

Idea Conflicts with State Sovereignty

17   A sovereign nation or state cannot be sued by an individual *without its consent.* Every State has this exemption. Therefore, unless the Constitution gives up this immunity, the States will keep it.

And the danger intimated must be merely ideal. The circumstances needed to remove State sovereignty were discussed when taxation was discussed. They need not be repeated here. By adopting the Constitution, the State governments would not lose the privilege of paying their own debts in their own way. Their only constraint will be the obligations of good faith.

The contracts between a nation and individuals are only binding on the conscience of the sovereign. A nation cannot be forced to comply. They confer no right of action independent of the sovereign will.

What would be the purpose of authorizing suits against States for the debts they owe? How could recoveries be enforced? Clearly, it couldn't be done by waging war against the State. And to give federal courts the ability to destroy a pre-existing right of the State governments would not be justified.

Supreme Court Hears 2 Types of Causes

18   Let us resume studying the subject of this paper.

The Supreme Court will have original jurisdiction in only two classes of causes. And they rarely happen.

All other federal cases will be heard by the inferior courts. The Supreme Court will have only appellate jurisdiction "with such *exceptions* and under such *regulations* as the Congress shall make."

Appeals Based on Law, Facts

19   The propriety of this appellate jurisdiction has been rarely questioned. But the clamors have been loud against it as applied to matters of fact.

Some well-intentioned men in New York have gotten ideas from the language and forms that apply to New York courts. They believe that "appellate jurisdiction" implies that trial by jury will be replaced by the civil-law mode of trial that is used in the New York courts of admiralty, probate, and chancery. New York State uses a technical meaning to the term "appellate." It often refers to appeals in the course of civil law.

However, I don't believe any part of New England would give it the same meaning. In New England, an appeal from one jury to another is familiar. It is a matter of course until there have been two verdicts on one side.

Therefore, the word "appellate" will not have the same meaning in New England as in New York. This shows it is improper to use a technical interpretation from the jurisprudence of only one State.

The expression means that one tribunal reviews the proceedings of another, either as to the law or fact, or both. The method used for appeals depends on ancient customs or legislative provision. (In a new government it must depend on the latter.) And the appeals court may or may not use juries.

Therefore, if the proposed Constitution allows the reexamination of a fact once determined by a jury, it may be regulated to be heard by a second jury. It could be remanded to the court below for a second trial of the fact or directed immediately out of the Supreme Court.

Reexamination of Facts Not Imperative

20   But it does not mean that the reexamination of a fact, once determined by a jury, will be permitted in the Supreme Court.

When a writ of error is brought from an inferior to a superior court of law in New York, does the latter have jurisdiction of the fact as well as the law? It cannot start a new inquiry concerning the fact. But it takes jurisdiction of it as it appears on the record. And it pronounces the law arising on it.[3] This is jurisdiction of both fact and law.

They cannot be separated. Juries in the common-law courts of New York State determine disputed facts. They have jurisdiction of both fact and law. When the facts are agreed in the pleadings, there is no need for a jury and they proceed at once to judgment. Therefore, the expression, "appellate jurisdiction, both as to law and fact," does not necessarily mean that the Supreme Court will reexamine facts decided by juries in the inferior courts.

Appellate Court May Review Facts

21 The following ideas could have influenced the convention in relation to this provision.

The appellate jurisdiction of the Supreme Court (they may have argued) will extend to causes determined in different modes. Some may be determined in the course of the COMMON LAW and others in the course of the CIVIL LAW. In the former, the proper role of the Supreme Court will be the revision of the law. In the latter, the reexamination of the fact is agreeable to usage. And in some cases (prize causes, for example), determining the fact might be essential to preserve the public peace. The appellate jurisdiction should sometimes extend in the broadest sense to matters of fact.

Cases originally tried by jury cannot be completely excluded because in some States *all causes* are tried by jury.[4] And matters of fact could not be reviewed, when proper.

The Supreme Court will have appellate jurisdiction both as to law and *fact*. And this jurisdiction will be subject to *exceptions* and regulations written by the national legislature. The government can modify it so it serves public justice and security.

Trial by Jury Not Abolished

22 Some people have said this provision *abolishes* trial by jury. This is fallacious and untrue. The United States Congress will have full power to say that in appeals to the Supreme Court facts cannot be reexamined if juries tried the original causes. This would be an authorized exception. But if it is thought too extensive, it might be limited to causes determined at common law by jury trials.

---

[3] This word is composed of JUS and DICTO, *juris, dictio,* or a speaking or pronouncing of the law.—PUBLIUS

[4] I believe States will have concurrent jurisdiction with the inferior federal courts in many cases of federal jurisdiction. This is explained in my next paper. –PUBLIUS

Summary: Judicial Branch

23   These are the observations made about the authority of the judicial branch:

It is restricted to causes that are proper for the national judicature.

The authority is divided. A small part of original jurisdiction is given to the Supreme Court. The rest is given to the inferior tribunals.

The Supreme Court will have an appellate jurisdiction both as to law and fact in all the cases referred to them, both subject to any *exceptions* and *regulations* that may be thought advisable.

This appellate jurisdiction does not *abolish* the trial by jury.

And an ordinary degree of prudence and integrity in the national councils will insure that we have the advantages of the proposed judiciary without exposing us to the inconveniences that have been predicted.

PUBLIUS

Number 82: Federal-State Judiciary

A new government can be carefully and wisely created. But there still will be questions. This is especially true when a country's new constitution incorporates a number of distinct sovereignties. This type of compound system needs time to mature and become perfect. Time will clarify the meaning of the parts and they will come together into a harmonious WHOLE.

State Court Jurisdiction

2   There have been questions about the proposed Constitution, especially the judiciary branch. What is the role of State courts in causes that fall under federal jurisdiction? Is the federal jurisdiction to be exclusive? Or will the State courts have a concurrent jurisdiction? If the latter, what will be their relationship to national courts?

Wise men ask these questions. And they certainly deserve attention.

Federal Authorities Defined

3   An earlier Paper explained that the States will keep all *preexisting* authorities not exclusively given to the federal government. There are three types of exclusive federal authority:

1) where the Constitution says that the federal government will have exclusive authority,

2) where the Constitution gives the federal government a specific authority and the States are prohibited from having a similar authority,

3) or where the Constitution gives the federal government an authority and a similar authority in the States would be incompatible.

These principles apply to both judiciary and legislative power. Therefore, the State courts will *keep* the jurisdiction they now have, unless one of the three ways takes it away.

Concurrent State/Federal Jurisdiction

4   One statement in the Constitution confines the causes of federal jurisdiction to the federal courts: "The JUDICIAL POWER of the United States *shall be vested* in one Supreme Court and in *such* inferior courts as the Congress shall from time to time ordain and establish."

This might be interpreted in two ways. It could mean that the supreme and inferior courts of the Union should have all the power to decide federal causes. Or it could mean that the national judiciary should be one Supreme Court and as many lower courts as Congress appoints. In other words, the United States should exercise its judicial power through one supreme tribunal and a number of inferior ones.

The first excludes, the last includes, the concurrent jurisdiction of the State tribunals. The first would alienate State power by implication. But the last appears to be the most natural and the most defensible interpretation.

Limited Concurrent Jurisdiction

5   Concurrent jurisdiction applies only to cases where the State courts have jurisdiction before adopting the Constitution. It does not apply to cases that are *specific* to the Constitution. Not allowing State jurisdiction in these cases would not limit preexisting authority.

The United States Congress may pass legislation that gives the decision of cases arising from a specific law to the federal courts alone, if it seems expedient. But State courts will not lose any of their original jurisdictions further than an appeal. When States are not expressly excluded by the future acts of the national legislature, they will take jurisdiction of the cases to which those acts may give birth.

I infer this from the nature of judicial power. The judicial power of every government looks beyond local or municipal laws. And in civil cases, it looks at all subjects of litigation between parties within its jurisdiction, even if the disputes deal with laws in the most distant part of the globe. Those of Japan, not less than of New York, may furnish the objects of legal discussion in our courts.

The State and national governments are parts of ONE WHOLE. The State courts have a concurrent jurisdiction in all cases arising under the Union's laws when not prohibited.

Final Appeal to Supreme Court

6   Another question arises. What relationship would exist between the national and State courts in cases with concurrent jurisdiction?

An appeal could be made to the Supreme Court of the United States.

The Constitution gives the Supreme Court appellate jurisdiction in all the cases of federal jurisdiction where it doesn't have original jurisdiction. It doesn't confine its operation to the inferior federal courts.

The objects of appeal, not the courts from which it is made, are alone considered. Therefore, it extends to State courts. Either this is true or the local courts must be excluded from a concurrent jurisdiction in matters of national concern. If this was not true, the judicial authority of the Union could be avoided by every plaintiff or prosecutor. Neither of these consequences should be involved without clear necessity. The latter would be entirely wrong because it would defeat some of the most important purposes of the proposed government and would embarrass its measures. Nor do I see any foundation for such an assumption.

The national and State systems are to be regarded as ONE WHOLE. The State courts will be natural auxiliaries to the execution of the laws of the Union. And an appeal from State courts will naturally be to the federal judiciary. The federal judiciary will unite and assimilate the principles of national justice.

The Constitution lists specific causes that will receive their original or final determination in the federal courts. There are important public reasons for this.

If the appellate jurisdiction of the Supreme Court were confined to appeals from inferior federal courts instead of allowing their extension to the State courts, it would abridge the latitude of the terms in subversion of the intent, contrary to every sound rule of interpretation.

Appeal to Lower Federal Courts

7   Could an appeal be made from the State courts to an inferior federal court? This question is more difficult than the former. The following considerations suggest an affirmative answer.

First, the Constitution authorizes the national legislature "to constitute tribunals inferior to the Supreme Court."*

Next, it says, "the JUDICIAL POWER of the United States *shall be vested* in one Supreme Court, and in such inferior courts as Congress shall ordain and establish."

It then lists the cases to which this judicial power extends.

Afterwards, it divides the jurisdiction of the Supreme Court into original and appellate. But it doesn't define the jurisdiction of the subordinate courts. They are only described as "inferior to the Supreme Court." And they won't exceed the limits of the federal judiciary.

Whether the lower courts' authority is original or appellate or both is not defined. This seems left to the discretion of the legislature. I can see no reason why there can't be an appeal from the State courts to the inferior

---

* Section 8, article 1. –PUBLIUS

national courts. And there could be many advantages. There would be fewer reasons to have multiple federal courts. The State courts could hear federal cases and most appeals. And appeals to State court decisions could be made to district federal courts.

PUBLIUS

Number 83: Trial by Jury

Some people object to the Constitution because it doesn't have a *constitutional provision* for the trial by jury in civil causes. This objection is disingenuous.

The proposed Constitution says nothing about *civil causes.* Opponents claim this means that trial by jury is being abolished. They say that trials by jury are being abolished in all civil and *criminal causes.*

To argue that trial by jury is being abolished in criminal cases is vain and fruitless.

Silence Doesn't Imply Prohibition

2   Regarding civil causes, opponents argue that since trial by jury *isn't mentioned,* it is *abolished.* However, there is a big difference between *silence* and *abolition.*

The inventors of this fallacy try to support it by perverting the true meaning of *legal maxims* of law interpretation. Therefore, let's look at their arguments.

Legal Maxim Cited

3   They base their arguments on maxims like this: "A specification of particulars is an exclusion of generals;" or "The expression of one thing is the exclusion of another."

They say, the Constitution establishes trial by jury in criminal cases and is silent about civil cases. Therefore, this silence is an implied prohibition of trial by jury in civil cases.

Interpretation of Laws: Common Sense

4   The rules of legal interpretation are rules of *common sense* adopted by the courts in the interpretation of the laws. Therefore, the true interpretation is whether it conforms to the source from which it is derived.

If a provision says that criminal cases must be tried by juries, does that mean that the legislature cannot permit trial by jury in other cases? Is this common sense? It isn't rational to say that requiring trial by jury in certain cases is a ban of it in others.

Create Courts → Determine Trial Mode

5   The legislature has the power to create courts, which includes the power to impose the mode of trial. Therefore, if the Constitution said nothing about juries, the legislature could either adopt trial by jury or not.

The Constitution says all criminal cases must be tried by jury but it doesn't mention civil cases. There is no obligation to use juries in civil cases. But the legislature has the power to decide the proper mode of trial. Therefore, to say the national legislature could not require that federal civil cases be heard by juries is a lie.

Maxim Used Incorrectly

6   Trial by jury in civil cases would not be abolished. And using the maxims in this way is contrary to reason and common sense.

Even if these maxims were being used correctly in this case, which they are not, they never apply to a government's constitution. Constitutional provisions are to be interpreted using their obvious meaning, not technical rules.

Restricts Legislative/Judicial Authority

7   I will show how the maxims are used properly by examples.

The Constitution declares that the *national legislature's* power will extend to specific cases. This list of specific authorities excludes a general legislative authority. If a general authority was intended, a list of special powers would be absurd and useless.

8   The Constitution lists the cases within federal jurisdiction. Federal courts can't extend their jurisdiction beyond these limits. A more extensive authority is excluded.

9   These examples show how the maxims should be used. Here is another example.

10   Suppose a New York law says that a married woman cannot convey her property. So the legislature makes a law that says she can dispose of her property by deed executed in the presence of a judge. In this case, the specific rule excludes all other methods because the woman had no previous power to dispose of her property.

Now let us say that later in the same law it says that no woman can dispose of property of a **specific value** without the consent of three of her nearest relatives and they must sign the deed. Could we infer from this regulation that a married woman could not get the approval of her relatives when conveying property of inferior value? This is absurd. Yet this is the reasoning of people who say that trial by jury in civil cases is abolished because it is required in criminal cases.

Civil Causes: State Jurisdiction

11   Clearly, the Constitution doesn't abolish trial by jury.

And in civil cases between individuals, trial by jury will be the same as provided in the State constitutions. It will not change by the adoption of the Constitution. The national judiciary will not have jurisdiction. They will continue to be heard in State courts, according to the State constitutions and laws.

All land causes, except those involving claims from different States, will belong to the jurisdiction of State courts. And all other controversies between the citizens of the same State, unless they involve violations of the US Constitution by acts of the State legislatures, will also be under State court jurisdiction.

Admiralty cases and most equity cases are decided by our government without a jury.

State jurisdiction of civil cases will not be greatly affected by the proposed change in our system of government.

Trial by Jury Valuable

12   Friends and adversaries of the Constitution agree that trial by jury is valuable. But there may be a small difference between them. Friends of the Constitution regard it as a valuable safeguard to liberty. Adversaries represent it as the only safeguard.

I hold trial by jury in high esteem. It is essential in a representative republic. It is even more important as a defense against the oppression of a hereditary monarch. Trial by jury is useful and friendly towards liberty. But I cannot see the inseparable connection between the existence of liberty and the trial by jury in civil cases.

Judicial despotism comes from arbitrary impeachments, arbitrary methods of prosecuting pretended offenses, and arbitrary punishments on arbitrary convictions. These all relate to criminal trials. Therefore, trial by jury in criminal cases, aided by *habeas-corpus*, is important. The Constitution provides for both.

Safeguard Against Oppressive Taxes

13   It is said that trial by jury is a safeguard against oppressive taxation. This idea deserves to be studied.

14   Trial by jury can not influence the legislature, which decides the *amount* of taxes, the *objects* of taxation, and the tax apportionment *rule*. Therefore, trial by jury can only influence how taxes are collected and the conduct of the revenue officers.

Recover Taxes: Jury Inappropriate

15   In New York, trial by jury is rarely used for tax collection. Taxes are usually levied by the summary proceeding of distress and sale. And everyone agrees that this is essential to the efficacy of the revenue laws. The delay of a trial to recover the taxes imposed on individuals would not fulfill public needs. And it would often cost more than the original tax.

Officers' Conduct Criminal Offense

16   Revenue officers who abuse public authority or extort citizens commit criminal offenses against the government. Trial by jury in criminal cases will give complete security. Officers can be indicted and punished.

Corrupting Officers of the Court

17   The importance of trial by jury in civil cases depends on circumstances other than the preservation of liberty. Security against corruption is the strongest argument in its favor.

There is more time to tamper with a judge than with a jury summoned for one trial. Perhaps a judge could more easily be corrupted than a jury. This argument is, however, diminished by other considerations.

The sheriff summons ordinary juries. The clerks of courts nominate special juries. Both are standing officers. It might be easier to corrupt them than judges. Those officers could select corrupt jurors.

It might be easier to corrupt jurors, who are randomly chosen, than to corrupt judges, who are chosen for their good character.

Despite these considerations, trial by jury is a valuable check on corruption.

Currently, both the judge and the jury would have to be corrupted. When the jury is clearly wrong, the judge will generally grant a new trial. In most cases, it would be useless to corrupt the jury unless the judge is also corrupted. This is a double security.

Judges will be less tempted when it is necessary to also corrupt the jury than if they exclusively determined all causes.

Constitutional Definition Difficult

18   I doubt that trial by jury in civil cases is essential to liberty. However, it is an excellent way to determine property questions. Because of this alone it would be entitled to a constitutional provision if it were possible to define the limits within which it should be used.

However, this is difficult. In a federal government that is composed of societies whose ideas and institutions vary from each other that difficulty increases. I believe that real obstacles prevented including this subject in the Constitution.

Judiciary in State Constitutions

19   Within the States, the use of the jury trial varies widely. An explanation of the differences is necessary before we make a judgment about its omission from the Constitution.

The New York judicial system resembles Great Britain's. New York has courts of common law, courts of probates (similar to the spiritual courts in England), a court of admiralty, and a court of chancery. The trial by jury prevails only in the courts of common law and there are exceptions. In all the others, a single judge presides without a jury, following either canon or civil law.[1]

In New Jersey, a court of chancery is like New York's. But it doesn't have courts of admiralty nor of probates, like the New York courts. The New Jersey courts of common law have the jurisdiction in cases that in New York are determined in the courts of admiralty and of probates. And the jury trial is more extensive in New Jersey than in New York.

Pennsylvania doesn't have a court of chancery, and its common-law courts have equity jurisdiction. It has a court of admiralty, but none of probates, at least like New York's.

Delaware is like Pennsylvania.

Maryland and Virginia are like New York, except that Virginia has many chancellors.

North Carolina is most like Pennsylvania; South Carolina is like Virginia.

I believe, however, that some States with admiralty courts use jury trials for those cases.

Georgia has only common-law courts. An appeal, of course, lies from the verdict of one jury to another, called a special jury, which has a specific mode of appointment.

In Connecticut, they have no separate courts of chancery or admiralty. Their probate courts have no jurisdiction of causes. Their common-law courts have admiralty and some equity jurisdiction. In important cases, their General Assembly is the only court of chancery. In Connecticut, therefore, the trial by jury extends in *practice* further than in any other State yet mentioned.

The situation in Rhode Island is, I believe, much the same as Connecticut. Massachusetts and New Hampshire, in regard to the blending of law, equity, and admiralty jurisdictions, are similar. In the four Eastern States, trial by jury has a broader foundation than in the other States. And they have a function that is not seen in the other States. There is an appeal from one jury to another, until there have been two verdicts out of three on one side.

State Standard Couldn't Be Used

20   The use of trial by jury in civil cases in the States is diverse. From this fact we see that:

First, the convention couldn't make a general rule that corresponded with the use of trial by jury in civil cases in all the States.

---

[1] It has been erroneously said that the Chancery Court tries disputed facts by a jury. The truth is, juries in that court are rare and not necessary except where the validity of a devise of land comes into question.—PUBLIUS

Second, the convention might have adopted the rule of one State. But that would have caused more problems than omitting any provision and leaving the matter, as has been done, to legislative regulation.

Federal Judiciary New Institution

21   People have suggested how to correct the omission. However, the suggestions illustrate the problem, they don't correct it. The minority of Pennsylvania proposed that "Trial by jury shall be as heretofore." This would be senseless and worthless.

All provisions in the proposed Constitution refer to the United States, in their united or collective capacity. Although each State uses jury trials, in the United States, *as such*, it is unknown. The present federal government has no judiciary power. Therefore, there is nothing to which the term *heretofore* could relate. It has no meaning. It is too uncertain to be used.

22   On the one hand, this provision would not fulfill the intent of the people proposing it. On the other, it would be inexpedient.

I presume that what they mean to say is this: Inferior federal courts will be located in the States. And these inferior federal courts should use the same mode of trial as the States in which they sit. Therefore, if a State where the federal court is located uses trial by jury in a specific type of case, then the federal court should use trial by jury. For example, admiralty cases should be tried by a jury in Connecticut, but without one in New York.

Using different modes of trial for similar cases under the same government is capricious. Cases would be tried with or without a jury, depending on the accidental situation of where the court and the parties to the case are located. This is a really bad idea.

Technical Knowledge Important

23   But this is not the greatest objection. I believe that trial by jury is not appropriate for all cases. This is particularly true in cases that concern the public peace with foreign nations. Those cases usually involve the laws of nations.

All prize causes are this type of case. Juries would need a thorough knowledge of laws and usages of nations. We can't assume that juries will have this knowledge. And they will sometimes be influenced by considerations other than public policy. The rights of other nations might be infringed by their decisions, giving reasons for reprisal and war.

Although juries are supposed to determine matters of fact, in most cases, legal consequences are complicated with fact. It may be impossible to separate the two.

Treaties Often Specify Trial Types

24 Also, treaties often state the method of determining prize causes. By treaty, in Great Britain the king, in his privy council, determines them. The fact and the law are reexamined.

This shows why putting a provision in the Constitution, making the State systems a standard for the national government is a bad idea. And it shows why it is dangerous to put provisions in the Constitution that are not absolutely proper.

Separating Equity, Law Jurisdictions

25 Separating equity from law jurisdiction has advantages. It is improper to give juries cases that belong in equity courts.

The primary use of equity courts is to give relief *in extraordinary cases*, which are *exceptions*[2] to general rules. If the jurisdiction of such cases was united with the ordinary jurisdiction, every case would need a *special* determination. Separating them has the opposite effect. One will be a sentinel over the other. And each stays within its limits.

Equity cases are often very complicated. They often require long and deliberate investigation. Therefore, they are incompatible with jury trials. It would be impractical to call men from their jobs and force them to decide the case before they could return to their jobs.

Trial by jury requires that the matter to be decided should be reduced to a single, obvious point. Chancery trials often include many tiny and independent facts.

26 The separation of the equity from the legal jurisdiction is unique to the English system of justice. Several States follow this model.

But trial by jury has not been used in cases where they are united. The separation is essential. It preserves trial by jury.

An equity court can easily extend its jurisdiction to matters of law. But extending the jurisdiction of the courts of law to equity causes will change the nature of the courts of law. It will undermine trial by jury by introducing questions too complicated for a decision in that mode.

Pennsylvania Suggestion Rejected

27 For these reasons, the national judiciary should not use the system proposed by the Pennsylvania minority.

Massachusetts Suggests Tiny Change

28 Let's examine the suggestion from Massachusetts. It says: "In civil actions between citizens of different States, every issue of fact, arising in

---

[2] The principles governing that relief are now reduced to a regular system. But it is no less true that they are usually applicable to SPECIAL circumstances that form exceptions to general rules.—PUBLIUS

actions at common law, may be tried by a jury if the parties, or either of them, request it."

29   This defines one type of cause. We can infer one of two things. Either they thought it is the only class of federal causes proper for trial by jury. Or they may have wanted a more extensive provision, but they found it impractical to devise one.

If the first, the omission of such a minor point is not a material imperfection in the Constitution. If the last, it corroborates the extreme difficulty of the thing.

What cases entitled to jury trial?

30   But this is not all. Let's look at the State courts again and their different powers. Some have vague descriptions of when trial by jury is allowed.

In New York, the line between common law and equitable jurisdiction follow the rules in England. In many of the other States, the boundaries are less precise.

In some, every cause is tried in a court of common law. Every action may be considered an action at common law to be determined by a jury, if any of the involved parties choose it. Therefore, this would create the same confusion that I mentioned as resulting from the regulation proposed by Pennsylvania.

In one State, a cause would be determined by a jury, if any of the parties requested it. But in another, the same cause must be decided without a jury, because the State judicatories vary as to common-law jurisdiction.

Same Jurisdictions Among States

31   Before the Massachusetts suggestion can be used, all the States must adopt one plan that sets the limits of common-law and equitable jurisdictions. This is a difficult task. It might even be impossible to create a regulation acceptable to all the States or that would perfectly conform to the State institutions.

Choosing One State System Won't Work

32   Why couldn't the constitution of New York be used as a standard for the United States? Other States probably don't have the same opinion of our institutions as we do. They probably like their own systems more.

If the convention used one State as a model, its adoption would be difficult. Each representative would favor his own government. And it is uncertain which State would have been the model. It has been shown that many of them would be improper ones.

If the convention had selected one State's system, the other States might be jealous. And the enemies of the Constitution would have many pretexts for raising prejudices against it that might endanger its ratification.

Trial by Jury in All Cases

33   Defining which cases should be tried by juries would be difficult. To avoid these problems, men have suggested a constitutional provision establishing it in all cases. I don't believe any State has a precedent for this. And the establishment of the trial by jury in *all* cases would have been an unforgivable error in the plan.

34   In short, any provision would say too much or too little. Or it might have opened other sources of opposition to the essential objective of introducing a firm national government.

Conclusions of This Discussion

35   The different views of the subject in this paper will remove most worries on the point. They have shown the following:

Trial by jury in criminal cases, alone, is necessary to secure liberty. This is provided for in the Constitution.

Most civil cases will use trial by jury. This is established in the State constitutions, untouched and unaffected by the Constitution.

Trial by jury is not abolished[3] by the Constitution.

And there are great, if not insurmountable, difficulties to making a proper provision for it in a Constitution for the United States.

Trial by Jury May Be Over-used

36   Wise people will not want a constitutional provision for jury trials in civil cases. They know that society continually changes. In many cases, a different method to determine property cases is preferred.

I believe it could be extended to some cases in New York to which it does not currently apply. And it might be limited in others.

All reasonable men agree that it should not be used in all cases. The examples in these States as well as in Great Britain show that it should be limited. Future experience may discover that other exceptions may be proper and useful. I suspect it is impossible, because of its nature, to fix the exact point where the operation of the institution should stop. This is a strong argument for leaving the matter to the discretion of the legislature.

Constitution: General Principles

37   This is now the case in Great Britain and Connecticut.

More encroachments have been made on the trial by jury in New York since the Revolution than in Connecticut and Great Britain. The men who make these encroachments often tell the people that they are great

---

[3] *Vide* Number 81 refutes the idea that it is abolished by the appellate jurisdiction in matters of fact being vested in the Supreme Court.—PUBLIUS

defenders of liberty. Then they ignore any constitutional obstacles to their career.

Truthfully, only the general GENIUS of a government can be relied on for permanent effects. Specific provisions, although not useless, have less virtue than commonly ascribed to them.

Criticism Extremely Harsh

38   It is both harsh and extraordinary to say that there is no security for liberty in a Constitution that establishes the trial by jury in criminal cases, because it does not do it in civil also. Connecticut, which is always regarded as the most popular State in the Union, has no constitutional provision for either.

PUBLIUS

Number 84: Bill of Rights; Capital; Debts due Union; Expenses

In this review of the Constitution, I have tried to answer most of the objections against it. However, a few objections either did not fall naturally under a specific topic or were forgotten in their proper places. These will now be discussed. Because the discussion has been quite long, I will put all my thoughts on these miscellaneous points in a single paper.

Bill of Rights

2   The most important of the remaining objections is that the new Constitution contains no bill of rights. Some of the State constitutions also have no bill of rights.

New York has no bill of rights. Yet people who oppose the new Constitution, people in New York who profess an unlimited admiration for New York's constitution, are demanding a bill of rights. To justify their zeal, they allege two things:

1) The New York constitution has provisions in favor of specific privileges and rights that, in substance, amount to the same thing.

2) New York's constitution includes the common and statute law of Great Britain. Many rights, not expressed in it, are secured.

Many Rights within Constitution

3   To the first, I answer that the proposed Constitution, like the New York constitution, contains a number of such provisions.

Clauses Assuring Rights

4   Besides clauses that relate to the structure of the government, we find the following:

Article 1, section 3, clause 7: "Judgment in cases of impeachment shall not extend further than to removal from office, and disqualification to hold and enjoy any office of honor, trust, or profit under the United States; but the party convicted shall, nevertheless, be liable and subject to indictment, trial, judgment, and punishment according to law."

Section 9, clause 2: "The privilege of the writ of *habeas corpus* shall not be suspended, unless when in cases of rebellion or invasion the public safety may require it."

Clause 3: "No bill of attainder or *ex-post-facto* law shall be passed."

Clause 7: "No title of nobility shall be granted by the United States; and no person holding any office of profit or trust under them, shall, without the consent of the Congress, accept of any present, emolument, office, or title of any kind whatever, from any king, prince, or foreign state."

Article 3, section 2, clause 3: "The trial of all crimes, except in cases of impeachment, shall be by jury; and such trial shall be held in the State where the said crimes shall have been committed; but when not committed within any State, the trial shall be at such place or places as the Congress may by law have directed."

Article 3, section 3: "Treason against the United States shall consist only in levying war against them, or in adhering to their enemies, giving them aid and comfort. No person shall be convicted of treason, unless on the testimony of two witnesses to the same overt act, or on confession in open court."

Article 3, section 3, clause 3: "The Congress shall have power to declare the punishment of treason; but no attainder of treason shall work corruption of blood, or forfeiture, except during the life of the person attainted."

Habeas Corpus, Ex-Post-Facto Laws

5   Are these not of equal importance with any found in the constitution of New York?

The proposed Constitution establishes the writ of *habeas corpus*, prohibits *ex-post-facto* laws and TITLES OF NOBILITY, *a provision not in the New York constitution.* These secure liberty and the republic better than anything in the New York constitution.

Tyrants love using *ex-post-facto* laws. These laws create crimes after someone has done something. In other words, men are punished for actions that, when they were done, broke no law. The tyrant can put anyone in prison by using this method.

Blackstone is worth quoting: "To bereave a man of life, (says he) or by violence to confiscate his estate, without accusation or trial, would be so gross and notorious an act of despotism, as must at once convey the alarm of tyranny throughout the whole nation; but confinement of the person, by secretly hurrying him to jail, where his sufferings are unknown or forgotten, is a less public, a less striking, and therefore *a more dangerous engine* of arbitrary government." [1]

To remedy this fatal evil, Blackstone praises the *habeas corpus* act. He calls it "the BULWARK of the British Constitution." [2]

Prohibits Titles

6   Prohibiting titles of nobility is important. This is the cornerstone of republican government. As long as titles are excluded, there can never be serious danger that the government will be any other than that of the people.

"Bills of Rights" Limit Government

7   The second is the pretended establishment of the common and statute law by the constitution. They are subject "to such alterations and provi-

---

[1] *Vide* Blackstone's *Commentaries*, vol. 1., p. 136. –PUBLIUS

[2] *Vide* Blackston's *Commentaries*, vol. Iv., p. 438. –PUBLIUS

sions as the legislature shall from time to time make concerning the same."
Therefore, the legislature can repeal them. And they have no constitutional sanction.

The declaration only recognizes ancient law and removes doubts that
the Revolution might have caused. Consequently, this is not a declaration
of rights that limits the power of the government.

Constitution: People Retain All Power

8   Bills of rights are agreements between kings and their subjects. They
reserve to citizens the rights not surrendered to the king.

The MAGNA CHARTA is an example. Barons with swords in their
hands made King John sign. Succeeding princes confirmed the Magna
Charta. The *Petition of Right* agreed to by Charles the First is an example.
So is the Declaration of Rights presented to the Prince of Orange in 1688.
Parliament then made it the "Bill of Rights."

The proposed Constitution is founded on the power of the people.
The people's representatives will execute it. Therefore, a bill of rights
doesn't belong in the Constitution. The people surrender nothing. And
they keep everything. Specific reservations are not needed.

"We, THE PEOPLE of the United States, to secure the blessings of liberty to ourselves and our posterity, do *ordain* and *establish* this Constitution for the United States of America."

This recognizes popular rights. And it is more effective than the large
number of aphorisms that make up our State bills of rights, which would
sound much better in a treatise on ethics than in a constitution of government.

Constitution: General Structure

9   A specific list of rights is even less applicable to a Constitution like
the one under consideration. It only regulates the general political interests
of the nation. It does not regulate every type of personal and private concern. Therefore, if people use this point to oppose the new Constitution,
the constitution of New York must be condemned. However, both constitutions meet their objectives.

Stating Rights Might Imply a Power

10   A bill of rights is not only unnecessary in the proposed Constitution,
but would be dangerous. It would contain exceptions to powers not granted. This would give the government a good pretext to claim more powers
than were granted. Why declare that things shall not be done when there is
no power to do it?

For instance, why say that the liberty of the press shall not be restrained when no power is given to impose restrictions? Such a provision
would not confer a regulating power. However, men who want to usurp
power could use it to claim that power. They might argue—with some

logic—that it is absurd to say there is no authority when the Constitution has a provision against the abuse of that authority. They could say that the provision against restraining the liberty of the press clearly implies that the national government has a power to regulate it.

This is an example of the many handles that would be given to the doctrine of constructive powers by the indulgence of an injudicious zeal for bills of rights.

Liberty of the Press

11 I cannot help adding a remark or two about liberty of the press.

In the first place, New York's constitution says nothing about it.

In the next, the provisions in other State constitutions amount to nothing. What does it mean that "liberty of the press shall be inviolably preserved"? What is liberty of the press? Who can define it in a way that would not leave wide latitude for evasion?

I believe it is impractical. Whatever any constitution might say, security must depend on public opinion and the spirit of the people and the government.[3] This is, after all, where we must look for the only basis of all our rights.

Constitution as Bill of Rights

12 The Constitution is, in every rational sense and to every useful purpose, A BILL OF RIGHTS.

The several bills of rights in Great Britain form the British constitution. Conversely, the constitution of each State is its bill of rights. And the proposed Constitution, if adopted, will be the bill of rights of the Union.

Does a bill of rights list the political privileges of the citizens in the structure and administration of the government? The new Constitution does this. And it includes precautions for public security that are not found in any of the State constitutions.

---

[3] The power of taxation has been used to show there is a constitutional power to affect liberty of the press. It is said that high taxes could be the same as a prohibition. Would the statement in the State constitutions in favor of the freedom of the press block the State legislatures from taxing publications? No amount of taxes, however low, would limit the liberty of the press.

Newspapers are taxed in Great Britain. But the British press enjoys great liberty. If any tax can be laid without violating liberty, the amount must depend on legislature, regulated by public opinion. Statements about liberty of the press will not add security. Some State constitutions declare liberty of the press. Yet they can use taxation to limit freedom of the press. The same thing can happen under the proposed Constitution. Saying that the government should be free or that taxes should not be excessive would have the same significance as saying that the liberty of the press should not be restrained.—PUBLIUS

Should a bill of rights define certain immunities and modes of proceeding in personal and private concerns? This is also included, in many cases, in the Constitution.

Therefore, referring to what is meant by a bill of rights, it is absurd to say that it is not in the proposed Constitution. It may be said that it does not go far enough, though it is hard to make this point. It is immaterial what method is used to declare the rights of citizens in the constitution that establishes the government. Therefore, many comments on this subject rest on verbal distinctions, entirely foreign from the substance of the thing.

Capital too Far from States

13   Objectors also say, "It is improper to give such large powers to the national government, because the capital will be too far away from many of the States. The citizens won't know the conduct of the representative body."

If this argument proves anything, it proves there should be no federal government. For the powers that everyone seems to agree should be vested in the Union cannot be safely entrusted to a body that is not under every requisite control.

But the objection is baseless. Most of the arguments about distance are imaginary.

How do people in Montgomery County, New York, receive the information they use to judge the conduct of their representatives in the State legislature? Not by personal observation. They must depend on information from men who they trust. And how do these men get their information? They get it from the type of public measures passed, from press reports, from correspondences with their representatives and with other persons who live in the state capital.

This applies to all the counties that are far from the seat of government.

Information about National Government

14   The same sources will be used for information about the federal government.

The State governments will carefully watch it. This, alone, will overbalance the distance problem. The executive and legislative bodies of each State will watch every part of the national government. They will use a regular and effective system of intelligence. Therefore, they will know the behavior of national representatives. And they can easily communicate their knowledge to the people. They will tell the community about anything that may prejudice its interests, if only because of jealousy of a rival power.

The people may know more about the conduct of their national representatives than their State representatives.

Capital Citizens Inform Distant Ones

15   The citizens who live in or near the capital will, in all questions that affect general liberty and prosperity, have the same interest with those who are at a distance. They will sound the alarm when necessary. And they will point out the actors in any harmful project.

Newspapers will quickly spread information to the most remote areas of the Union.

Debts due to United States

16   The oddest objection against the Constitution is that it lacks a provision about the debts due to the United States.

This has been represented as both an implied relinquishment of those debts and a wicked way to protect public defaulters. The newspapers have teemed with the most inflammatory railings on this subject. But the suggestion is entirely void of foundation. It shows either extreme ignorance or extreme dishonesty. I've talked about this before. I will now just say that it is a dictate of common-sense and an established doctrine of political law, that "*States neither lose any of their rights, nor are discharged from any of their obligations, by a change in the form of their civil government.*"[4]

Expense of Federal Government

17   The last major objection, that I presently remember, is expense. However, even if adopting the proposed government meant a large increase in expense, it would not be an objection against the Constitution.

Division of Powers Necessary

18   Most Americans believe that their political happiness depends on staying united in one Union. Most men with good judgment agree that the Union cannot be preserved under the present system without very big changes. They agree that the national government needs new and extensive powers. And these powers require a different organization of the federal government because it would be unsafe to give a single body such wide authorities.

In conceding all this, the question of expense must be given up. It is impossible, with any degree of safety, to narrow the foundation on which the system is to stand.

In the beginning, the two houses of the legislature will have only sixty-five people, the same number as the Congress under the existing Confederation. This number will increase as the population and resources of the country increase. Clearly, a smaller number would be unsafe. And

---

[4] *Vide* Rutherford's *Institutes,* vol. ii, book II, chap. x., sects, xiv, and xv. *Vide* also Grotius, book 11, chap. ix., sects. Viii. And ix.--PUBLIUS

keeping the present number as the population grows would inadequately represent the people.

Expense of New Offices

19   From where is the dreaded increase of expense to come? One source mentioned is the multiplication of offices under the new government. Let us examine this a little.

Federal Employees

20   The main departments of the present government are the same as those required under the new.

There is now a Secretary of War, a Secretary of Foreign Affairs, a Secretary for Domestic Affairs, a Board of Treasury—consisting of three persons—a Treasurer, assistants, clerks, etc. These officers are indispensable under any system. And they will work under the new as well as the old.

We will continue to have ambassadors and ministers in foreign countries under the proposed Constitution. The only difference will be the increased respectability of the country they represent, making their services more useful.

There will be a large increase in the number of federal revenue collectors. However, it does not follow that this will increase public expense. It will mostly be an exchange of State for national officers. For instance, in the collection of all duties, the persons employed will be totally of this description. The States will not need any revenue agents for this purpose. What is the difference in the expense to pay customs officers appointed by the State or by the United States? There is no good reason to suppose that either the number or the salaries of the latter will be greater than those of the former.

Federal Judges

21   Where do we look, then, for the additional, enormous expense?

The chief item that occurs to me is the support of the judges of the United States.

I do not add the President because there is now a president of Congress. The expenses of the President of the United States may not be much more than the current president of Congress.

The support of the judges will be an extra expense. The amount will depend on the specific plan adopted. But in no reasonable plan can it amount to a huge sum.

Congress Less Expensive

22   Let's see what counterbalances any extra expenses accompanying the establishment of the proposed government.

First, the President will handle much of the business that now keeps Congress sitting through the year. Even the management of foreign negotiations will devolve on him, cooperating with the Senate and subject to their final agreement. Hence, both the Senate and the House of Representatives will need to be in session for only part of the year. We may suppose about a fourth for the latter and a third, or perhaps half, for the former. The extra business of treaties and appointments may make the Senate sessions longer.

Until the House of Representatives is increased greatly beyond its present number, there will be a large saving of expense from the difference between the constant session of the present and the temporary session of the future Congress.

Less Burden on State Legislatures

23 But there is another circumstance of great importance in the view of economy. Up until now, the business of the United States has occupied the State legislatures as well as Congress. Congress has made requisitions that the State legislatures have had to fulfill. Therefore, the State legislative sessions have been much longer than necessary for the local business of the States. Much of their time is employed in matters that relate to the United States.

There are now more than two thousand members of the State legislatures. And they preformed the same duties that, under the new system, will be done, initially, by sixty-five people. And, in the future, the number will probably not grow to more than 400 or 500 people.

The Congress under the proposed government will do all the business of the United States. Henceforth, State legislatures will attend only to the affairs of their specific States. They will not have to sit nearly as long as they have done until now. The shorter sessions of the State legislatures may be a saving equivalent to any additional expense from adopting the new system.

Expenses Balanced by Savings

24 These observations show that the additional expense from the establishment of the proposed Constitution are much fewer than may be imagined. They are counterbalanced by considerable saving. And while it is questionable on which side the scale will preponderate, it is certain that a government less expensive would be incompetent to the purposes of the Union.

PUBLIUS

Number 85: In Conclusion, Ratify Now, Amend Later

I listed the subjects to be discussed in the first paper. Two points remain: "A comparison of the proposed Constitution to the New York constitution," and "How the Constitution will preserve liberty, property and the republican form of government."

However, these topics have been discussed in these Papers. Now I can only repeat, in a diluted form, what has been already said.

Same "Defects" in NY Constitution

2   The proposed Constitution resembles New York's constitution. The New York constitution has many of the same imagined defects, as well as the real excellences.

Among the imagined defects are:

>no term limits for the Executive,
>no executive council,
>no formal bill of rights, and
>no provision for the liberty of the press.

New York's constitution doesn't have these provisions. And it doesn't have several others. If a man bitterly complains about the proposed Constitution but easily excuses the New York constitution, he isn't consistent.

Some people who admire the New York state government have furiously attacked the new Constitution for provisions that are also in New York's constitution. This proves that their attacks on the Constitution are insincere.

New Constitutional Securities

3   If we adopt the Constitution, our republic, our liberty, and our property will be more secure.

Keeping the Union will restrain local factions and insurrections. And it will restrain the ambition of powerful people in single States who could become despots.

Breaking up the Confederacy would invite foreign intrigue. Keeping the Union will limit foreign influence.

If the States disunited, they would find reasons to fight each other. By staying united, fewer military forts and bases will be needed.

It will guarantee a republican form of government in each State.

It will exclude all titles of nobility.

And it will guard against the States repeating acts that have hurt property and credit, planted mutual distrust between citizens, and caused an almost universal decrease of morals.

Presented Rational Arguments

4   I have finished the task I assigned to myself. With what success, your ratification vote must determine.

I hope, at least, that I have addressed myself purely to your judgments. And I hope I avoided the harshness that often disgraces political disputes and has been seen in the language and conduct of the opponents of the Constitution.

Supporters of the new Constitution have been indiscriminately charged with conspiracy against liberty. This charge is wanton and malignant. Everyone who knows it is a lie is angry. The lies keep citizens from hearing the truth. All honest men must demand reprobation. Because of these circumstances, I may have used some intemperate expressions that I did not intend. I often struggled between emotional responses and moderation. If the former sometimes prevailed, my excuse is that it has not been often or much.

Every Man Must Now Decide

5   Have these Papers vindicated the Constitution from the aspersions thrown on it? Is the Constitution worthy of approval? And is the Constitution necessary for public safety and prosperity?

Every man must answer these questions, according to his conscience and understanding. And he must vote as his judgment demands. This is a duty without dispensation. As a member of society, he is obligated to vote sincerely and honestly. No special interests, temporary passions or prejudices, or partial motives should sway his vote. They will not justify to himself, to his country, or to his posterity, an improper vote.

Every man must beware of stubbornly voting the way his party wants him to vote. He must remember that his vote to ratify the Constitution will effect more than just his community. It will determine the very existence of the nation. And let him remember that a majority of America has already ratified the plan that he is to approve or reject.

Constitution Best Solution for Us

6   I am confident of the arguments that recommend the Constitution to your adoption. And I believe that the opposing arguments are not persuasive. I believe it is the best for our political situation, habits, and opinions. And the Constitution is superior to any plan that the revolution has produced.

Constitution Admittedly Imperfect

7   The friends of the new Constitution have said that it isn't absolutely perfect. Its enemies see this as a small triumph. They ask, "Why should we adopt an imperfect plan? Why not amend it and make it perfect before it is irrevocably established?"

This may be plausible, but it is only plausible. In the first place, they have exaggerated the concessions. They are stated as if they are an admission that the Constitution is very defective. And that it needs some big changes before the rights and the interests of the community can be safely confided to it.

Although the Constitution may not be perfect, it is a good plan. It is the best that the present views and circumstances of the country will permit. And it promises every type of security that a reasonable people can desire.

Group Decisions Never Perfect

8   It is unwise to prolong the dangerous state of our national affairs. We should not expose the Union to the jeopardy of more experiments in the effort to find a perfect plan.

Imperfect men can never create a perfect plan. Group discussions always include errors and prejudices, as well as good sense and wisdom, just like the people in the groups. The agreement that will make thirteen States into a union must be a compromise of many different interests. How can a perfect plan come from such materials?

New Convention Not Good Idea

9   An excellent pamphlet was recently published in New York City.[1] It gives the reasons why a new convention probably couldn't be assembled under circumstances as favorable to producing a good constitution as those in which the late convention met, deliberated, and concluded. I will not repeat the arguments. I assume a lot of people have seen it. Every friend to his country should read it.

However, one view of amendments hasn't been discussed. I will discuss it now.

Amend After Ratification

10   The Constitution can be amended after it is ratified. This will be much easier than doing it before the ratification process is finished. Why do I say this?

If the Constitution is altered before it is ratified, it immediately becomes a new constitution. And it must be ratified again in each State. All thirteen States would have to agree to the new constitution.

However, if all the States ratify the Constitution, nine States can change it at any time. The chances are as thirteen to nine[2] in favor of an amendment after ratification over adoption of an entire governmental system.

Issues, States Multiply Difficulty

11   This is not all. Every Constitution for the United States must include the interests of thirteen independent States. In any group given the duty to

---

[1] Entitled "An Address to the People of the State of New York."—PUBLIUS

[2] It is actually TEN. Two thirds may propose the measure, but three fourths must ratify.—PUBLIUS

write it, we will see different people agreeing on different points. People in the majority on one question may become the minority on a second. And a different group may be the majority on a third.

The document must be written to satisfy all the States. Therefore, the difficulties of getting every State to agree multiply. And the multiplication must be a ratio of the number of issues and the number of States.

Amendment: One Issue Each

12   However, once the Constitution is established, each amendment would be brought forward separately. Compromises on other points would not be necessary. The will of the required number would decide the issue. Whenever ten States want an amendment, that amendment will become part of the Constitution.

Therefore, there is no comparison between the ease of adding an amendment and of establishing a complete Constitution.

National Rulers Must Allow Amendments

13   Opponents argue that it may be impossible to amend the Constitution after it is ratified. They argue that the people administrating the national government will not want to give up any of their authority once they have it.

When people carefully consider an amendment and decide that it should pass, I believe it will deal with the organization of the government, not to the extent of its powers. For this reason alone, people serving in the national government will not oppose it.

Also, governing THIRTEEN STATES will be difficult. I believe national rulers will need to fulfill the reasonable expectations of their constituents.

But there is another consideration that proves the observation is wrong. It is this: the national rulers, whenever nine States concur, will have no option on the subject. By the fifth article of the Constitution, the Congress will be *obliged* "on the application of the legislatures of two thirds of the States (currently, nine), to call a convention for proposing amendments, which *shall be valid*, to all intents and purposes, as part of the Constitution, when ratified by the legislatures of three fourths of the States, or by conventions in three fourths thereof."

The words of this article are peremptory. The Congress "*shall* call a convention." Nothing is left to the discretion of Congress. Consequently, all the arguments about the disinclination to a change vanish.

It may be difficult to unite two thirds or three fourths of the States in amendments that affect local interests. However, such a difficulty cannot be feared on issues that effect the general liberty or security of the people. The State legislatures will block encroachments by the national government.

Ratification Before Amending

14   If the forgoing argument is a fallacy, then I am deceived by it. It is one of those rare cases where a political truth can be mathematically tested. People who zealously want amendments must agree that the Constitution must be ratified first.

Delicate Balance of Creating Constitution

15   The people who want to amend the Constitution before it is established must stop if they agree with the following observations of a writer equally solid and ingenious.[3]

"To balance a large state or society (says he), whether monarchical or republican, on general laws, is a work of so great difficulty, that no human genius, however comprehensive, is able, by using only reason and reflection, to do it. The judgments of many must unite in the work; EXPERIENCE must guide their labor; TIME must bring it to perfection, and the FEELING of inconveniences must correct the mistakes which *inevitably* are seen during their first trials and experiments."

These wise thoughts contain a lesson of moderation to all the sincere lovers of the Union. They should guard against hazarding anarchy, civil war, a perpetual alienation of the States from each other, and perhaps the military despotism of a victorious demagogue, while they pursue what they can only learn from TIME and EXPERIENCE. I may lack political fortitude, but I believe that it is dangerous to continue in our present situation.

A NATION without a NATIONAL GOVERNMENT is an awful spectacle. The establishment of a Constitution, during peacetime, by the voluntary consent of a whole people, is an EXTRAORDINARY ACCOMPLISHMENT. I look forward to its completion with trembling anxiety.

I can think of no reason to let go of the hold we now have on this arduous an enterprise. Seven out of the thirteen States have ratified the Constitution. There is no reason to start over again. I dread the consequences of new attempts because I know that POWERFUL INDIVIDUALS, in this and in other States, are enemies of any national government.

PUBLIUS

---

[3] Hume's *Essays*, vol. I, page 128: "The Rise of Arts and Sciences."—PUBLIUS

Glossary

Abbe, title of clergyman, monk

abolish, abolition, remove, get rid of

abridge, abridging, diminish, curtail, decrease

abroad, outside the country

absolute, not limited

absurd, illogical, untrue, goes against common sense

abuse of power wrong, improper or harmful use of power

abyss, very deep crack in the earth, situation that seems so bad that it doesn't have a solution

accuracy, inaccuracy

adjudication, settle an issue judicially

admiralty, court with jurisdiction over civil and criminal maritime offenses

admonition caution against something; counsel against a fault, oversight

advantage benefit arising from some course of action

adventurer

adverse unfavorable; opposed to one's interests

advocate person who speaks or writes in support of a cause

affirm assert positively; declare

afford furnish; supply

agency means of accomplishing something

agitate emotionally arouse public interest

ambiguity doubtfulness; uncertainty

agriculture

ambition, wants to get or earn money, power, and/or goal

amend, repair; correct

amity, peaceful relationships

Amphictyonic council, federal council that governed Greek city-states

Amphictyony, an association/ confederacy of ancient Greek republics

annihilation nonexistence; destroy utterly

aphorism concise statement of general truth

appellate authority to review and affirm, reverse, or modify judgment or decision of another tribunal

appointment vested power of a person or the state to use the property subject to that power. e.g. government's right to take and use tax money

apportion allocate proportionally

arbitrary convenient, not necessarily rational; characterized by absolute authority

arraign accuse of wrong, inadequacy, imperfection; find fault

artifice trickery; guile; cleverness; ingenuity

ascribe credit to a source; attribute

Athenian, citizen of Athens

Athens, ancient Greek city-state

attainder (noun) loss of all civil rights upon being sentenced to death or being convicted of treason or a felony

aulic court hall

axiom self-evident truth requiring no proof

basis foundation

bill of credit issued by a state, circulated like money on the state's credit

breach infraction or violation, as a law

bulwark defense wall; protection against external danger

cabal small group of secret plotters against a government

candor impartial, honest, sincere

cantons small territorial district, especially one of the states of Switzerland

capacity legal qualification

capricious lacking predictable pattern, erratic, whimsical

casting vote casting voice, vote cast by a presiding officer or judge to break a tie or sometimes to create a tie

censure strong disapproval, criticize harshly

century Roman voting unit with property being the qualification

cessions ceding; surrender formally; transfer

character good reputation; composite of good moral qualities; moral excellence and firmness blended with resolution, self-discipline, high ethics, and judgment.

civil service nonmilitary government administration

claim demand as a right; assert as a fact

code system of laws, rules, regulations

commence begin; start

commission authority granted for a particular action or function

compact formal agreement

competent appropriate or suitable to certain position or rank; pertinent to

conclusive settles or decides a debate

concurrence acting in conjunction

conduce contribute to a result

confirm establish or attest to validity

conjecture opinion formed without sufficient evidence

connivance cooperate secretly; conspire

conspiracy a group plan to commit an unlawful or evil act

constituent component defined by the constitution; having power to frame or alter a political constitution

constitute will be; will form

construct structure; put together; build

construction construing, interpreting, explaining a declaration or fact

contiguous touching

corruption dishonest behavior

culpable meriting condemnation or censure

debase to lower the quality, character, dignity of

demagogue gains power by arousing people's emotion and prejudices

denounce condemn; censure publicly

derive receive or obtain from a source

despoil take possessions, rob, plunder

despot tyrant or oppressor

determination settling and ending of controversy by judicial decision

devolve pass from one to another, as estate or responsibility; change

dictator a ruler or tyrant exercising absolute power

diet formal public assembly of governing body of realm or confederation

discernment intelligence

disingenuous lacks candor, sincerity; insincere; give false appearance of simple frankness

dispassionate calm in judgment; uninfluenced by prejudice, favoritism, partisanship, passions or emotions

dispatch dispose of rapidly (as piece of business), execute quickly

dispose of settle; bestow; distribute; apportion; allot

disposition power to settle or control; prevailing tendency, inclination, propensity

disquisition formal discourse or treatise; systematic inquiry into a subject; elaborate analytical essay

dominion sovereign authority; realm

due proper, adequate according to excepted norms of what is reasonable, fitting, or necessary

dupe easily deceived or fooled

duty sum paid as tax on import, export, manufacture, or consumption of goods

effect cause to happen; result produced by cause, influence

efficacy effective; has desired result

elector voter

eligible suitable, preferable

elude avoid; evade

embarrass hamper, impede

emit issue formally, as paper money

emolument compensation for employment; recompense; benefit; advantage

encroach gradually or stealthily trespass on the rights, domain, or property of another

energy effective force, vitality; capacity to act or operate effectively, inherent power

engagements debts; obligations

enlightened understanding free of ignorance, false beliefs, prejudices

enmity bitter hatred; overt or concealed ill will; absence of any friendly spirit

ensnare to take in as if in a snare; entrap

entertain take into consideration

entrust give to for protection

equitable fair, just, proper

equivocal deliberately ambiguous; uncertain, doubtful; questionable

erroneous having an error; incorrect

esteem respect

event outcome or consequence

evince make evident; manifest

excises internal, indirect tax on commodity within a country

exigencies urgencies; something needed, required; emergency

ex officio all people who hold one job or position automatically hold a second position

expedient governed or marked by self-interest, temporarily advantageous, separate from what is just or right

ex post facto law adds punishment to act after the fact

fabrics framework, structure

in the face of in opposition to, in defiance of, despite

faction a party or clique (within a government or association) often contentious, self-serving, or reckless to the common good

factious form parties or factions in organization and raise dissension, sometimes seditious

faculty powers of the mind; inherent capability of the body; resources

fallacious deceptive, not true, misleading

felicity state of happiness

forbear to bear with, endure; refrain from; abstain; be patient or self-controlled

force moral or mental strength, especially manifested as power of effective action

fortunes turns and courses of luck accompanying the progress of a person through life or towards success

genius distinctive inherent characteristic, roots, history

good faith justice trustworthiness

grade rank; class of persons or things

guarantee responsible for the fulfillment of agreement of another; assume suretyship

hazard take a chance that could have a bad outcome

heretofore before this; up until now

honors title, high public office or rank

ill hostile; unfavorable, adverse

illicit unlawful

imbecility weakness; incapacity; inability

impair make worse, weaken, damage

impeachment a calling into question or discrediting

impose deceive, defraud, cheat; to thrust intrusively upon others

imposition deception

imposts tax; duty; generic term for tax

impunity exemption from punishment or detrimental effects

inconstant likely to change, often without apparent reason; change character, purpose

indefinite having no fixed limits

indue provide, supply; invest; transfuse

inexpedient not likely to achieve a purpose or success

infamy vicious, detestable action

inflammatory

ingenious free from deceit or disguise; innocent

insult attack, assault, unexpected military attack; treat with insolence, indignity or contempt by word or action

insurrection revolting against civil or political authority or against an established government, rebellious

intemperate exceeding reasonable limits

intimate make known indirectly, suggested

invade encroach, intrude, infringe

inviolable secure from destruction, infringement, or desecration

irregular haven't satisfied requirements of the group

irregulars combatants not part of a regular military force

judicature jurisdiction of judge or court

just true; correct

kindred similar

Lacedaemonia Sparta, ancient Greek city-state

landed class people who own real property (land)

late recent

latitude range or variety of action or opinions that is permitted or tolerated

lay to devise, as a plan

letters of marque written authority granted by a government to seize the subjects of a foreign state or their goods to retaliate for injuries. Government grants license to a private person to arm a vessel, cruise the sea and plunder the enemy

levies conscription of troops

liable subject or susceptible, likely or apt

magazine room to keep explosives; military depot for arms, provisions

magistracy check forms of this word in text collective body exercising governmental powers

magistrate public official entrusted with administration of laws

marque reprisal, retaliation (see *letters of marque*)

mass aggregate, whole

maxim concise saying embodying a general truth

measure legislative bill or enactment might want to change in text

medium intervening or surrounding conditions; means of conveyance

misconstrue misinterpret the meaning or intention of

mutable prone or liable to change, inconstant; being changed in form, quality, or nature

mutual reciprocal; having same relation toward each other

notwithstanding (prep.) in spite of; (adv.) nevertheless; (conj.) although

novelties state or quality of being novel (new kind)

332

object objective, mission

obnoxious subject to the authority or power of another

obscurity not readily seen

obstinacy unreasonable adherence to an opinion

obtain become recognized or established; prevalent or general

occasion to cause; bring about

odious hateful

odium intense hatred; reproach, discredit some action

oligarchy despotic power exercised by a privileged, exclusive group

oracle expert; person of great authority or wisdom whose opinions are respected

ordinary judge of probate in some States

ostensibly to all outward appearances

overrule decide or determine because of superior authority

partisan supporter of person or cause

patrician aristocrat

peremptory leave no opportunity for denial or refund; dictatorial

perfection quality or state of being finished, complete, whole

perfidy being dishonest or disloyal, deceit; act of betrayal

perplexity entanglement

perverse turned away from what is right or good; contrary to accepted standard, incorrect, inaccurate

phocian, person who lives in the Greek state of Phocis

pleasure "holding their offices during pleasure" (people's will)

plebeian common person (not an aristocrat)

politic shrewd or prudent in practical matters; expedient

political concerned with government

populous heavily populated; crowded

posse comitatus power of a county, a sheriff may summon help from citizens to preserve public peace or execute laws

preside exercise management/ control

pretend assert, claim; represent or assert falsely

pretense pretending; feigning; false claim; justification

pretension claim to something, often unwarranted or false; claim recognition of right or privilege

pretermit to let pass without mentioning, omit, leave unpaid; break off, interrupt, suspend

pretext appearance assumed in order to cloak the real intention or state of affairs

privilege fundamental rights considered guaranteed and secured to all persons by modern constitutional governments

propriety quality or state of being proper or fitting; suitability

prosperity success

prove to ascertain the genuineness of, verify. "acts, records, and proceedings shall be *proved*" United States Constitution

province sphere of authority

provision arrangement made beforehand; legal or formal stipulation

prudence, prudent judicious in practical affairs; caution

quarters place where people sleep

quorum number of members required to be present to conduct business

railings uttering bitter complaints

reasonable within the bounds of reason, being logical

reciprocal given or felt by each toward the other, mutual

redress setting right what is wrong; remedy; compensate

refine subtle reasoning; small change that is intended to improve something

regard feeling of approval, appreciation, respect based on attractive characteristics

regular characterized by fixed principle or procedure

representation a statement made to influence opinion

reproach express disapproval of; censure; blame

reprobation wicked; condemn

resistance work to counteract or defeat, striving against, opposing

rule method prescribed for performing a mathematical operation

sacred regarded with reverence

sanction authoritative permission or approval; makes oath binding; punishment or withholding a reward to coerce obedience

saving clause a clause in an instrument or law exempting something from its operation or providing that the rest of it will stand if part is held invalid

scruple moral or ethical consideration that inhibits action

sedition incitement of discontent or rebellion against government; conduct tending to treason but without an overt act

select judicious or restrictive when choosing; superior value or excellence

singular extraordinary, exceptional; unique

sovereignty supreme authority of the state

specious seems true but lacking real merit

stadholder viceroy in province of the Netherlands or chief executive of United Provinces of the Netherlands

subscribe approve; give support to

subvert to undermine the principles of ; corrupt; overthrow

suffrages opinion in favor of; approval; vote, right to vote

supremacy supreme authority/ power

susceptible of of such a nature, character, or constitution as to permit; capable of submitting successfully to action or process

suspend make inactive

sympathy affinity, association, or relationship between persons or things; loyalty

thebans, people who lived in ancient Greek state of Thebes

temper state of mind or feelings

temperate moderate; restrained

tempered even-temper; moderate feelings

tenure conditions that apply to holding something like property or office

thereafter from that time forward

title describes office or status

tyranny arbitrary or unrestrained exercise of power; oppressive or unjust government

tyrant a ruler or person in authority who exercises power oppressively or despotically; an absolute ruler

usurpation seize power without authority or legal right

utility useful

utopian ideal place; perfect society

vassals persons granted use of land in return for homage and fealty to a lord

venial can be forgiven

vice shortcoming

viceroy person appointed to rule a country or province as the deputy of the sovereign

want lack, have deficiency in

Index

This index refers to the Paper Number [paragraph in that paper] rather than page number. The paragraphs are the same in most editions of *The Federalist Papers*. However, the paragraphs in the Avalon Project edition of *The Federalist Papers* (found on the internet) are often different. Therefore, the paragraph numbers in this index will often be off (usually by one paragraph).

Paper Number [paragraph in that paper]

335

336

24[7-8], 25[4,9], 45[11]; money, value, coin, 42[14], 44[4]; naturalization,
42[17]; piracy, laws of nations, 42[5];
representatives, 75[7]; taxation,
45[11], *see* **quotas and requisitions**; territorial disputes, 80[8]; treaties, 42[3-4], 44[2-3]; war, declare,
41[8]; weights and measures, 42[16]
States under Articles of Confederation
-new, 43[10]; military requisitions,
15[6]; repeal by, 22[19]; sovereignty, 42[17], 44[12-13]

Articles of Confederation, defects,
1[1], 6[19], 14[12], 15[2-3,5-7,15], 21-
22, 37[5], 38[5,7,9,10], 40[9,16], 42[3-
4,14], 80[8], 85[3]
bill of rights, none, 38[9]
commerce, can't regulate, 22[1-4], 42[11-
13]
Congress, 22[17-18], 38[10-11], 44[20],
53[8], 62[10]
guaranty for States, none 21[3-5]
judicial branch, none, 21[2], 22[14], 78[2],
83[21]
laws, unenforceable, 21[2-3], *see* **legislation for states**
mutable policies, *see* **energy in government**
quotas/requisitions to raise money and
armies, *see* **quotas and requisitions**, no limit on, 38[10]
ratification, 22[18], 38[5], 43[30], 55[8]
separation of powers, lacks, 84[18]
States, equal suffrage, 22[7-9]
States' rights clause, 21[2], 42[13]
supreme court, none, 22[14-16]
Asia, **Europe dominates,** 11[14]; trade
with, 4[6]

attachments, 2[11], 76[5,8], 77[7]
to foreign nations, 5[10]; to liberty, 8[4]; to
party, 79[5]; to republican government, 49[1], 57[10]; to States and/or
Union, 2[9,14], 28[3], 36[14], 41[15],
46[2-3,6,9], 57[15], 59[10], 80[9],
83[32]
levels of, 17[4-5,7-8], 27[4], 64[15], 71[1]
mutable government loses, 62[18]

representatives to constituents, 10[19],
71[7], 72[1,13]
war, reason for, 6[3]
attainder, bills of, *see* **bills of attainder**
authority, governmental, *see* **powers**

balance of power, *see* **separation of
powers**
bankruptcy, *Ar* 1 *Sec* 8, 42[10,18]
bases, military *see* **defense, bases**
bear arms, *see* **arms**
behavior, *see* **human behavior**
bias, bigotry, prejudice, 1[5], 6[6], 22[16],
41[4], 49[6], 84[14]
influences behavior, decisions, 1[2,4],
10[8], 15[14], 38[4], 50[6], 54[11],
65[2,8], 66[8-9],68[5], 73[15],
80[2,9,11], 85[5,8]
leads to oppression, 27[2]
local, 10[21], 13[2], 17[4-5], 19[10],
22[15], 46[2-3,6], 58[6], 61[3], 76[8]
opponents, used by Constitution's, 1[4],
14[1], 29[9], 31[1,3-4], 35[5], 37[2],
83[32]
ruler's, legislature's, 1[5], 10[16], 15[13],
60[8-9], 71[2]
Bible, language causes ambiguity, 37[10]
bicameral congress, *see* **Congress**
bill of rights, Amendments 1-10, 38[7,9],
84[2-12], 85[2]
Constitution is bill of rights, 84[8,12]
Great Britain, *see* **Great Britain**
press, freedom, Amendment 1, 41[24],
84[10-11], 85[2]
Second amendment, Amendment 2,
8[10], 28[5-10], 46[9]
State constitutions, 24[6], 25[9],
84[2,8,12], 85[2]
bills of attainder, *Ar* 1 *Sec* 9, *Ar* 1 *Sec*
10, prohibited, 44[3,6], 78[9], 84[4]
bills of credit, *Ar* 1 *Sec* 10, 38[9], 44[2,5]
Blackstone, William, 69[6], 84[5]
border, **defined by peace treaty,** 14[6];
defense, 24[11-13]; neighbors, 3[6],
4[8]

337

smuggling, **6**[16-17], **12**[8-10], **13**[4], **35**[2]

States, *Ar* 1, Sec 9, **11**[1,12-13], **14**[10], **22**[2-4], **23**[3], **41**[20], **42**[9-12,17-18,20], **60**[7]; restrictions on, **23**[3], **44**[7]; Representatives' knowledge of, **53**[5], **56**[4-6]

taxation, *see* **taxation**, creates monopoly, **35**[2]

war, **4**[4-9], **6**[3,8-17], **7**[5-6], **11**[6-7], **34**[4]

wealth, **8**[8], **12**, **15**[3], **21**[7], **41**[20], **60**[9], **62**[16-17]

confederacies, *see* **disunited States, federal government, confederate republic**

American confederacy, *see* **Articles of Confederation, Articles of Confederation, defects**

historical, **16**[1,6], **17**[10,14], **18-20**, **37**[5], **43**[15], **45**[4], **54**[9], see **Greek republics, Germany, Poland, Switzerland, United Netherlands**

States can't join other **44**[2-3]

confederate republic, **6**[20], **9**, **39**, *see* **Montesquieu**

Congress 59-61, *Ar* 1 *Sec* 1, *see* **legislative branch, Senate, House of Representatives**

abuse of power, see **abuse of power**

adjourn, *Ar* 1 *Sec* 5; President adjourns, **69**[6], **77**[9], *Ar* 2 *Sec* 3; effects presidential veto, *Ar* 1 *Sec* 7

appointments, *see* **appointments**

authority, limited, **52**[9]; House vs. Senate, **58**[8], **62**[8], **66**[6-7]

compromise, **22**[9]

constitution limits actions, **50, 71**[4], **78**[9-13], **83**[7]

election to: executive, election role, **39**[12]; irregular elections, **53**[10]; regulate elections of members, **59-60;** *see* **House of Representatives, Senators**

emergencies, response to, **22**[9-10]

expense, **34**[6], **75**[5], **77**[7], **84**[22]

governs federal capital, territories, *Ar* 1 *Sec* 8, **32**[2], **43**[4-5], *see* **territories**

House stronger than Senate, **66**[6]

impeachment, *see* **impeachment**

as judiciary, **81**[3-8]

members: not punished for collective acts, **66**[12]; number ratio to constituents/wealth, **10**[19], **54**[3,9-10], **55**[2], **56**[9]; represent people/States, **58**[6]; restrictions on holding offices, *Ar* 1 *Sec* 6, **55**[9], **76**[10], *see* **Representatives, Senators**

partisanship, natural, see partisan politics, factions

powers, see legislative branch, powers

quorum, *Ar* 1 *Sec* 5

sessions shorter, **84**[22]

States influence Congress **46**[6]

terms in office, **63**[3-5]

turnover, frequent, harmful, **62**[12-13]

veto, *see* **executive branch,** veto

Congress of 1774, **2**[11-13], **46**[3], **55**[8]

Congressional Meeting, Feb 1787, **40**[2,4-5]

congressmen, *see* **Representatives, Senators**

Connecticut, **7**[3,4,9], **13**[2], **21**[4,6], **22**[7], **40**[11]; commerce, **7**[6]; executive, **57**[21]; judiciary, **83**[19, 22, 37, 38]; legislature, **53**[1], **57**[21]; separation of powers, **47**[11]

conspiracies, collusion, cabal, **10**[20], **63**[8], *see* **abuse of power, usurpations**

election, **60**[3-4], **68**[5-6]

House, Senate differences thwart, **62**[8]

judicial, **16**[10], **83**[17]

by legislature, **55**[3,7,9], **78**[18], **26**[11], **62**[8]

Presidential, **25**[6,11], **69**[6]
  -plural executive, **70**[14-16,22], **76**[3], **77**[6-7]

property, **70**[1]

by States, **59**[8-9], **60**[3-4]

in State, **43**[16-17], **69**[6]

war, leads to, **6**[6],

Constitution, *see* **Constitutional Convention 1787**

amending, *Ar* 5, 37[5], 38[1,4-5], 39[15-16], 43[25-26], 49[4], 85[9-end]

arguments against, *see* **opponents … Constitution**

authors of, 2[10], 3[9], 37[14], 38[1-4], 40[5], 85[8,15]

authority from people, *see* **powers**, people source of

is bill of rights, *see* **bill of rights**

compromises, 37[12-15], 54[7], 62[2-4], 65[9], 73[13], 85[7-11]

enforcing, 16[5], **50**
  -by judiciary, 78[9-11,13,18], 78[10-15], 81[5]

federal vs. national character, 10[19], **39**

imperfect, 16[11], 37[3-6], 38[5-7], 41[4], 59[7], 65[11], 85[7-8,15], *see* **opponents … Constitution**

interpretation, 32[5], 41[24], 44[12]
  -only "the people" can, 49[3], *see* **power**
  -rule, 32[5]

law, fundamental, 53[2], 78[12-15], *see* **supreme law**

liberty, *see* **liberty**, Constitution

limited, defined, 78[9,11]

means what it says, 83[6]

oath to support, *Ar* 6, 44[24-26]

opposition to, *see* **opponents … Constitution**

outline only, 83[37], 84[9]

parchment, paper, only, 40[15]

people guardian of, 16[10]

people's right to change, 78[18]

popular government, rescues, 10[11]

power from people, Preamble, *see* **powers**, people source

ratification, *see* **ratification**

republic established, **39**

see **separation of powers**

study Constitution, **1**, 2[1]

"supreme law of the land," *see* **supreme law**

unconstitutional, 16[10], 32[4], 33[7], 44[17], 50[2], 66[12], 78[9-10,17-21]

weak, leads to tyranny, 20[18]

Constitutional Convention 1787, 2,
  3[9], 13[1], 14[8], 12, 32[5], 33[5-7],

34[10-11], **37**, 38[8], **40**, 41[1, 26], 42[4], 43[7-8,25-26], 44[6,13-14,16], 45[4], 51[1], 52[2], 54[5,10], 56[8], 59[2-3,7], 64[3,5,7], 65[4-5], 66[12], 68[5,10], 69[5], 73[13,15], 75[6], 78[22], 79[2], 80[3], 81[21], 83[20,32]

authority, 39[7-8], **40**

delegates, 2[10], 38[1-4], 40[5], 85[8,15]
  God's influence on 37[14]

didn't sacrifice substance to form, 37[12], 40[8-9,17]

drafting difficulties, **37**

objectives, 40[6]

constitutional convention, future, **49, 50, 85**[9]

constructive powers, 84[10]

consumption tax, *see* **taxation, taxes**

"contributions," *see* **taxation, taxes**

copyright, 43[2-3], *Ar* 1 *Sec* 8

corruption, *see* **abuse of power**

counterfeiting, 42[10,15], *Ar* 1, *Sec* 8

courts, *see* **judicial branch**

credit, consumer, 15[3]

credit, public, 30[10], 44[2,5], **85**[3]

crisis, *see* **emergencies**

crown lands, United States territory, 7[2]

currency,
  counterfeiting, *Ar* 1 *Sec* 8, 42[10,15]
  paper, 10[22], 44[5]
  no State currency, 44[2, 5], 80[3,13]
  value, 42[10, 14-15], 69[11]; foreign, regulate value of, *Ar* 1 *Sec* 8, 42[10, 14]

cycles, in human affairs, 41[22], 64[8]

danger, 2[11], 8[14]; can't guard against all, 16[11]; excuse to usurp power, 25[6]

debts, national, 7[7-8], 25[4], 29[11], 30[1,6, 8,10], 38[9-10], 41[6,22-23], 43[22-24], *Ar* 1 *Sec* 8, *Sec* 10, *Ar* 6, Amendment 14

causes hostilities between States, 7[7-8]; in Holland, 6[13]; in Germany, 12[3]

defense, 34[6-10]

Revolutionary War, 15[3], 34[8]

Declaration of Independence, 40[16]

defendant's rights, 65[7]

defense, 3-4, 14[11-12], 23-29, 41[5-26], 45[10], Preamble, *Ar* 1 *Sec* 8; *see Articles* of Confederation

appropriations, *see* **appropriations**

borders, 24[11-13]

see **commander-in-chief**

best defense, 4[10]; bases, forts, ports, arsenals, 8[2,5], 13[4], 14[1], 24[7-9,12-13], 25[2-3], 26[3,6-7], 28[5], 29[7], 41[12-14], 43[4-6], 45[2], 46[9], 85[3], *Ar* 1 *Sec* 8, 9

emergencies, power must equal, *see* **powers**

Europe, dangers from, *see* **Europe**

expense, 12[10], 14[11], 22[5], 23[10], 24[11], 29[6], 30[1-9], 34[6-7], 36[16], 41[26]; vs. executive, 34[7]; largest , 34[6-8]

Indians, danger from, *see* **Indian Nations**

federal duty, 3, 4, 23, 25, 41[7], 42[5]

frontier States, 14[11]

legislative authority, 26

liberty, effect on, *see* **liberty**

military, *see* **military**

militia, *see* **militia**

Montesquieu, 9[9-13]

nations take advantage of weakness, *see* **weakness**

navy, *see* **navy**

neutral nation needs, 11[6]

offensive war, none, 34[5]

peacetime, see military, standing army

powers needed for, 23-26, 31[6]

President, *see* **commander-in-chief**

raising armies, State quotas, *see* **quotas and requisitions**

revenue for, 16[5], 30[8], 34[4-8], 41[22] -from disunited States, 4[15-16]

standing army, *see* **military**, standing army

States, *see* **disunited States**

best men, 4[12]; disproportionately burdened, 22[6]; legislatures raise military, 26[6]; military dangerous to liberty, 25[3-4]; protected, 43[15]; requisi-

tioned, 23[7]; restrictions, *Ar* 1 *Sec* 10; strongest army, 4[12]; united, 4

strong, importance of, 11[6-7]; reduces risk of war, 46[10]

Union, 14[11-12], [12-13,17], 41[14-15]

usurpation, *see* **usurpation**

war, *see* **war**

Delaware

constitution, 47 [15]; separation of powers, 47[15]

governor, 39[5], 47[15], 69[4]; executive vice president, 47[15]

jury trial, 83[19]

legislature, state, smallest, 55[2-3]

military, peacetime, 24[6]

supreme court, State, 47[15], 81[7]

democracy, pure, 21[5], 26[11], 39[3] 48[5], 58[14], *see* **republic**

dangers, 49[6-7]

definition, 10[13], 14[3]

factions, problems with, 10[11-13]

v. republic, 10[14-22], 14[1-6]

includes representatives, 63[10-12]

dictators, *see* **tyranny, tyrants**

diplomats, *see* **ambassadors**

distance effects voters' interest, 17[4-5,8], 27[4]; Europe example 17[10]

District of Columbia, *see* **capital, federal**

disunited States, 9[3-4], 14[12]

alliances, 1[3], 5[9,10-12], 15[9, 13-14]; with foreign nations, 5[10-12], 7[10], 11[7]

commerce, 6[8-16], 7[5-6], 11[6,8-9,13], 12[9,12], 13[2,4]

confederacies, States form several, 1[8], 2[2-3,14], 3[7,9], 4[1,12,15-17], 5-8, 11[11], 12[8,11], 13, 16-17, 23[11], 41[18], 59[10];vs. consolidation of States, 9[3,15], 32[2], 39[7], 62[5]

dangers, 2[3], 3-8, 9[5], 11[14], 38[12], 41[14-15]; to public peace, 28[4]

expensive, 13

government employees, large number needed, 13[4]

judicial systems, different, 3[9]

military expansion, 8, 26[14], 41[14-15,18], 85[3,15]

reasons to stay united, *see* **Union**

domestic policy, 62[15-18]

violence, Union protection, 9[1],
43[13,16-21]

duties, *see* **taxation**

duty, 76[5,6]

v. ambition/greed, 22[13], 27[6], 60[12],
68[6], 70[12], 72[4,6], 73[1,12], 75[3]

citizens re: Constitution, 85[5]

of courts, 78[9,14,15,17,18,21], 79[2]

defense, 31[6]

of delegates at Constitutional Convention, 2[12], 39[8], 40[14]

of electoral college, 68[5]

of government, 48[9], 52[9], 57[14],
65[10], 71[1]

of militia, 24[11], 28[2], 29[13]

of States to Union, 23[7]

economic issues, 62[17]

Egypt, ally of ancient Greece, 18[18]

elections, 39[12], 53, 59-61, *see* **Great
Britain, House of Representatives,
Senators, President, voters**

agricultural interests, 60[7-9]

in colonies, 52[8]

fraud, 10[18]

frequency, 52[4-end], 53, 55[4], 57[11];
effects responsibility, 52[5], 63[4];
policy -changes, 37[6], 62[12]

impeachment, 65[3]

irregular, 53[10]

in Ireland, 52[7]

location of polls, 60[1-3,5,10-11], 61[1-3]

modes, different, 51[6]

regulation of, 38[7], 59-61

in States, 39[5], 45[7], 52[2-3], 53[1-
5,10], 59[5], 61, 63[18]

Vice President, 68[9-1 0]

voters, *see* **voters**

electoral college, *see* **President**

emergencies, calamities, crisis, 23[4],
25[10], 28[1-3], 30[11], 36[16], 45[9-
10], 58[15]

action/speed important 22[9], 26[9],
70[11]

defense 23[4,10], 26[9,13], 28[2-3], 29[3],
30[8], 43[16-17,20]; military (takes
over city/country because of an
emergency), 8[9], 25[6], 29[3]; power
must equal, 26[5]

effect on civil laws, 8[9]

money needed, 30[8-9], 34[4], 36[16]

Netherlands, congress over steps authority, 20[18]

States disunite, more, 8[3,9]

tyranny, leads to, 20[18], 25[6], 48[5],
59[10]

weak government, 18[9], 20[18], 22[9],
62[15], 70[11], 72[9]

employees, federal, 30[1], 84[20]

more people work for States, 45[8], 46[2]

energy (efficiency) in government, 1[5],
3[4,8], 4[12,17], 11[5], 13[1], 23, 26[2],
30[7], 36[17], 37[1-6], 41[18], 59[10]

*Article*s of Confederation, lack of, 15[5],
21[4-5], 22[9,17]

executive, 70[1-7,13], 71[1], 77[11]; feeble, bad, 70[2]

v. mutable government, 37[6], 62[13-18],
72[1,10], 73[9], 77[7]

equality/unequal, 1[3], 6[3], 31[1]

of citizens' abilities, 10[6]; of property,
10[6-7,22]; of wealth, 21[8];
basis of commerce in America, 7[5]

of government branches, 51[6], 58[8],
63[17], 71[7]; political, 10[13]

human plan can't guarantee, 5[5]

passions, 10[4,6]

people to run for office, 36[1]

power = emergency, 26[5], 30[6], 31[5],
41[11], 70[1]

of protection, Amendment 14

of public burdens, 21[8]

States' suffrage, 37[12], 38[7]; confederacy vs. consolidation, 9[15]; in *Article*s of Confederation, 21[6], 22[6-8],
54[9]; in Senate, *Ar* 5, 38[7], 39[12],
43[25-26], 62[1,4-6], 64[13]

suffrage, 60[8]; Greece, 18[2,13]; Netherlands, 20[2]

tax, authority, 32[3], 34[1,3]; burden,
21[9], 23[10], 35[1,3,4]

344

63[5], *see* **power equal to, happiness, general welfare, public good**

faction, control, *see* **factions**

justice 51[10]

passions, control, **13**[1], **15**[12], **16**[7], **49**[10], **71**[2]

primary function, **10**[6]

protect people/property, **54**[8]

safety/security of citizens, *see* **safety**

self-preservation, **16**[10], **28**[6], **41**[12], **43**[30], **59**[2-3,5]

Great Britain, **5**[1,3,10], **13**[1], **17**[12], *see* Europe

American territory, **3**[6,15], **4**[8], **7**[2], **11**[2,4,5], **24**[10-12], **25**[2,6], **52**[8]

Bill of Rights, **26**[4,6], **84**[2,12]

bribes Swedish officials, **22**[13]

commerce, **3**[6], **4**[4-5,8], **6**[14,17], **11**[3-4, 9], **12**[5,10], **22**[2-3], **69**[7,11]

constitution, **41**[16-17], **47**[5-7]

Montesquieu respects, **47**[4-7]

copyright, **43**[2-3]

corruption, **8**[12], **41**[17], **75**[3]

defense, *see* military (below)

executive, **6**[5,15], **34**[7], **47**[6-7], **48**[4-5];vs. U.S. President powers, **47**[7], **67**[3,5], **69, 70**[19-20], **73**[10]

House of Commons, **6**[15], **56**[9], **57**[18], **58**[13]; elections, term, **41**[17], **52**[6], **63**[19]; blocks aristocratic tyranny, **63**[19], **71**[7], **76**[10];vs. House of Representatives, **57**[18], **63**[19], **65**[5]

House of Lords vs. US Senate, **63**[19] -supreme court, **22**[14-15], **47**[6], **81**[4,6,8]

impeachment, **47**[6-7], **65**[5]

judiciary, **37**[10], **47**[6-7], **78**[22], **83**[19,26,36-37] -common law, "felony" defined, **42**[5]

legislative branch, parliament, **14**[6], **39**[3], **47**[6], **53**[2], **56**[9], **81**[8], *see* House of Commons (above)

liberty, **52**[8], **56**[9]

Magna Charta, **52**[6], **84**[8]

merchants, **6**[17]

military, **4**[13-14], **8**[11-12], **26**[3-4], **34**[5-7], **41**[14,16-17,19]; expense, **34**[7],

41[16-17]; island nation, **5**[3], **41**[14,18]

Norman Conquest, **26**[4]

Petition of Right, **84**[8]

republic, not one, **39**[3]

separation of powers, **47**[5-7]

suffrage, **57**[18]

taxation, **12**[5,11], **21**[11], **71**[7]

treaties with U.S., **3**[6,10], **7**[2], **11**[3]

usurpation, *see* **usurpation**

wealth, national, **34**[7]

Cardinal Wolsey, **6**[5]

Greek republics, ancient, 18, **38**[2-4], **43**[14], **45**[4]

alliances, **4**[15], **18**[13,18]; Achaean league, **16**[1], **18**[11-19], **38**[2,4], **70**[9]

Amphityonic council, **18**[1-12,14,18], **38**[2], **43**[13-14]; Athens, **6**[4,10], **18**[4-5,7-8,18], **25**[10] **38**[2-4], **55**[3], **63**[12]; Lacedaemonia, Sparta, **18**[4-8,14,18],] **25**[10], **38**[2-4,8]; Ephori, representatives, **63**[13,20]; senate, **63**[9]

anarchy, tyranny, **9**[1], **18**[19], **63**[7]

confederacy weak, doomed, **18**

Crete, republic, **38**[2], **63**[13]

democracies, **63**[14]; with representatives, **63**[11-12]

executive, **9**[17], **63**[11]

internal strife, **9**[1-3], **14**[3]

judges, appointments of, **9**[17]

laws, tyrannical, **9**[1], **18**[18], **63**[7]

military, **8**[8]

Peloponnesian War, **6**[4], **18**[8], **25**[10]

Grotius, 20[12], **84**[16]

group behavior, **10**[1], **76**[4-5], **85**[8,11]

faction, *see* **factions, human behavior**

discord within, **15**[14], **19**[9], **38**[4]

group acts worse than individuals, **15**[12], **74**[3]

"group think," **15**[12-15], **61**[4]

large groups swayed by passions, become a "mob," **6**[9], **27**[3], **55**[3], **58**[14], **62**[9], **63**[2,9], **65**[10]

group plan can never be perfect, **37**[3]

representatives think they are "the people," **71**[4]

small group, **68**[3]

usurp power, **70**[22], *see* **usurpation**

habeas corpus, *Ar* 1 *Sec* 9, **83**[12], **84**[4-5]

happiness, **1**[6], **2**[3], **5**[1], **9**[5,12-13], **14**[12], **15**[1,11], **20**[23], **22**[15], **24**[8], **28**[2], **31**[10], **37**[2], **38**[5], **40**[16,17,19], **41**[4], **46**[6], **56**[9], **57**[14], **59**[8], **71**[2], **84**[18]

v. *Article*s of Confederation, **40**[9]

good government promotes, **62**[11]

government's objective, **30**[3,7], **40**[16-17], **43**[30], **45**[2], **62**[11], **78**[18]

history, inattention to, *see* **experience**

Holland, **6**[13], **20**[15-16, 19], **39**[3], **43**[13-14]

House of Representatives 52-58, 59-61, *Ar* 1, *see* **Representatives, Congress**

abuse of power, *see* **abuse of power**

agricultural interests, **60**[5-9]

appointment, presidential, no role, **77**[8]

apportionment rule, **54**, **55**[6], **58**[4,11]

appropriations, *see* **appropriations**

corruption of, **22**[12-13], **26**[11], **38**[7], **55**[8-9], **57**[16-17]

elections, *see* **Representatives**

foreign nations, deal with, **53**[7], **75**

impeachment, *see* **impeachment**

influenced by passions **62**[9]

members, *see* **Representatives**

opponents (critics), *see* **opponents** ...

    Constitution, House of Representatives

power, limited, **52**[9], **55**[4]; *see* **power**

Presidential: elections determined, *Ar* 2 *Sec* 1, Amendment 12, **66**[7]; influencing, **55**[9]

quorum, **58**[15]

Senate, relationship to, **52**[9], **53**[9], **55**[9], **58**[7-13], **63**[17-21]; different than, **62**[8], **63**[20], **66**[7]

size, number of members, **55-58**, **62**[9]

human behavior, motivated by:

see **abuse of power**

ability, talent, **33**[3], **70**[22]; judges, **81**[6]; mental, **79**[5]; national candidates/ representatives, **3**[8], **4**[12], **35**[7], **53**[9], **62**[2], **64**[5,815], **68**[8], **72**[2], **81**[6]

-for misinformation, **67**[3],

admiration, *see* respect (below)

advice, **2**[11-14], **15**[11], **18**[13], **38**[6,7], **40**[18], **70**[19]

affection/attachment to, **5**[1,4], **14**[12], **17**[4-5,8,10], **27**[1,4], **43**[19], **57**[9], **64**[15], **76**[5]

aggrandizement, **1**[3], **4**[3], **6**[20], **16**[3], **22**[17], **46**[6], **49**[8], **57**[1],**59**[10], **60**[12], **75**[3]

ambition, *see* **ambition**

angels don't need government, **51**[4]

animosity, **1**[4], **7**[7], **10**[7], **22**[4], **33**[6], **70**[11], **75**[4]

avarice, **1**[4], **6**[9,15], **12**[2], **15**[1], **30**[10], **42**[11], **60**[11], **72**[5], **73**[2], **75**[3], *see* **temptations**; controls behavior, **72**[5]; leads to smuggling, **12**[8]; effects tax policy, **42**[11]

attachments, *see* **attachments**

aversions, **6**[9], **67**[3]

bellicosity, **6**[2-3], **10**[7,11], **34**[5]

benefits, *see* **powers**, **7**[2,5-6], **11**[4], **14**[11], **15**[8], **17**[7,8], **28**[9], **30**[9], **59**[10], **62**[15-16], **73**[2];vs. evil **70**[13]

bias, *see* **bias**

bigotry, *see* **bias**

cabal, *see* **conspiracies**

capriciousness of human mind, **15**[7], **57**[14]

character, *see* **character**

common/good sense, **5**[3], **14**[12], **22**[7], **29**[9], **30**[6], **31**[1,2,3], **32**[1], **35**[6], **37**[3], **70**[10], **71**[2], **74**[4], **80**[3], **83**[4,6], **84**[16], **85**[8]

conspiracy, *see* **conspiracies**

contempt, **4**[17], **9**[5], **22**[9], **27**[2], **83**[2]

corruption, *see* **abuse of power**

courage, **18**[8], **28**[6], **71**[1], **73**[12]

danger, *see* **danger**

deceptions, **14**[12], *see* misrepresentation (below)

human nature

Hume's *Essays,* "Rise of Arts and Sciences," 85[15]

impeachment, 64[15], 65-66, *see* **Great Britain**
House of Representatives impeach, *Ar* 1 *Sec* 2
judges, federal, 79[4], 81[9]
judicial despotism, 83[12]
jury trial, none, *Ar* 3 *Sec* 2
legislators, can't impeach for laws, 66[12]
offenses, impeachable, *Ar* 2 *Sec* 4
opponents, 65[2], *see* **opponents ... new Constitution**
President, 39[5], 69[4], 77[11]
New York governor pardons, 69[6]
no power to pardon, *Ar* 2 *Sec* 2, 69[6], 74[3]
punishment limited, *Ar* 1 *Sec* 3, 84[4]
safety, republican 77[11]
Senate tries, 38[7], 65-66, 79[4], 81[3,9], *Ar* 1 *Sec* 3
States, 39[5], 47[9-15], 66[3]

import duties, *see* **taxation**

India, commerce, 4[6]

Indian Nations (tribes), 7[2]
commerce, 24[12], 40[11], 42[10, 13]
defense against, 3[13-14], 24[10-11], 25[2, 6]
living in, but not citizens of, State, 42[13]

industrialists, *see* **merchants**

Internal Revenue Service (IRS)
-number of tax collectors, 45[8]

interstate commerce, *see* **commerce, States**

Ireland, elections, 52[7]

Italian states, 3[18], 14[3], 6[12], 9[1-3], 39[3], 48[8], *see* **Rome**

Jefferson, Thomas
block/correct usurpation of powers 49
legislative usurpation of power, Virginia 48[7-8]; "Notes On ... Virginia," 48[8], 49[1]
people source of power 49[3]

judges, 49[8]

appointing, *Ar* 2 *Sec* 2, 39[5], 51[2], 67[8], 69[9], 76-77, 78[3-4], *see* **appointments**; Greece, 9[17]; States, 3[9], 47[9-20]
bound by US Constitution, *Ar* 6, 44[18-26]
compensation, 79[1-3], 84[21]
corrupt, 73[15], 83[17]
impeachable, 79[4], 81[9]
jury, influences, 65[8]
interprets laws, 73[15]
knowledge needed, 81[6]
opinion, 73[15]
qualities of, 3[8], 51[2], 78[21], 79[5]
tenure, good behavior, *Ar* 3 *Sec* 1, 9[3], 39[5], 51[2], 78-79, 81[6-7]; no forced retirement, 79[6]

judicial branch, federal, *Ar* 3, 3[8], 36[17], 64[10], 78-83, *see* **judges, jury trial, Supreme Court, Germany, Great Britain, Switzerland**
see **Article**s of Confederation, defects
conspiracies by, *see* **conspiracies**
Constitution, enforce, interprets, 32[5], 78[9-15,18-20]
despotism, 83[12]; blocks legislative, 78[6]
districts, federal court, 81[13]
in disunited States, 3[9]
expense, 34[6], 84[21]
impeachment, *see* **impeachment**
independence, 16[7], 22[14], 47[8,9], 51[3], 71[4], 73[15], 78, 79[1-4], 81[6-7]
inferior courts, 81[10-14]
jurisdiction, 14[8], 37[10], 80, 81[23], 82; limited, 83[8-11]
laws: decide constitutionality of, 78[10,15], 81[5]; enforces, 14[8], 15[11], 16[7,10-11]; interprets, 22[14-15], 44[17], 73[15], 78[12-16,19], 81[6]
legislative authority, 78[9-18], 81[4]; encroachment on, 81[9]
legislature: affecting, 48[13], 81[9]; changing ruling, 81[8]; regulates judiciary, 80[22], 81[2,11,18,21], 82[4]
as oppressor, 78[8], 83[12]

powers, *Ar* 3, *Sec* 1, *Sec* 2, Amendment 11, **16**[7], **21**[2-3], **42**[10], *see* jurisdiction (above)

-too powerful, **38**[7]

-weakest branch, **48**[6], **78**[7-8], **81**[9]

rights, guardian **78**[7,18-19], **80**[9]

State vs. federal, **17**[7], **45**[8], **80**[2,7-9,11], **81**[2,12,21], **82**, **83**[3-7,19,27,30,33], *see* **New York**

see **usurpation**

jury trial, **48**[11], **81**[19-23], **83**, **84**[4], *Ar* 3, *Sec* 2, Amendment 5, Amendment 6, Amendment 7

Grand Jury, Amendment 5

impeachment, **65**[7-8]

judge influences jury, **65**[8]

justice, Preamble, *see* **passions**

administration of, influences affection and reverence towards government, **17**[7], **81**[6]

executive branch, **70**[1]

faction/passions more powerful motivator than, **6**[9], **10**[1,8,12], **15**[8,12]

-wars **4**[3], **6**[9], **80**[6]

government's goal, **51**[10]

independent courts promote, **78**[8-9], **79**[5]

injustice, **51**[10], **78**[19]

-of faction kills popular government, **10**[1]

-local government more often unjust, **3**[10-11], **10**[21], **27**[2]

-morals, alone, don't control, **10**[12]

majority rule, **58**[15]

representation aids, **10**[16,21]

Senate's role, **63**[7]

unconstitutional laws voided, **78**[9,17-21]

wars started because of, **7**[9]

knowledge important, **62**[11]

citizens', **84**[13-4]

judges, **78**[21], **81**[6], **83**[23]

legislator, **53**[4-7], **55**[1], **56**[1,3-9], **75**[5]

Lacedaemonia, *see* **Greek republics, Lacedaemonia**

land grants, *Ar* 3 *Sec* 2, **7**[2,4], **40**[11], **80**[11-12,14,20]

language, inherent problems when conveying a concept, **37**[10-11]

law of nations, *Ar* 1 *Sec* 8, **42**[1,5], **53**[7], **64**[14], *see* **laws of nations**

laws, legislation, **35**[10], **78**[20]

bad, "evil," **37**[10], **62**[10], **66**[12], **70**[13], **73**[6], **81**[6]; benefit a few/hurt many, **62**[16]; business, hurts, **62**[17]; citizens want, **63**[7]; contradictory, **78**[14]; mutable laws, **37**[6], **62**[10-17]; quick decisions, **70**[13], **73**[8]; short term in office, **63**[3]; too many, **62**[6,12-18], **73**[9], **78**[21]; Senate blocks, **62**[6], **63**[7]

change/abolish government, **53**[2], **64**[11]

classes of, **63**[5]

commerce, regulate, *see* **commerce**

constitutionality of, decide, **33**[6,7], **44**[17], **66**[12], **78**[9-16], **81**[4-5]

Constitution, fundamental law, **53**[2], **78**[12-15]

defined, rules that regulate society, **75**[2]

District of Columbia, **32**[2], **43**[4-5]

effect, as judicial determinations, **10**[8]

enforced by courts, military, executive, **15**[7,11-12], **16**[2-7,11], **27**, **28**[1], **29**[4], **37**[6], **69**[6], **80**[2-4,12-13], **81**[12], *see* **executive**

no federal law enforcement under *AofC*, **21**[2]

federal **23**[9], **33**[2-3], **44**[9-24]; uniform nationally, **80**[4]

act on individuals, **16**[7], **23**[8] [see federal government authority over citizens]

foreign laws, *see* **law of nations,** **3**[7,9-14], **11**[7], **42**[1,5], **53**[7], **64**[14], **80**[6,10], **83**[23]

ignoring weakens government, **25**[10]

interpreted, **37**[10], **83**[2-4]; by executive branches, **44**[17]; by judiciary, **22**[13], **44**[17], **73**[15], **78**[12-16], **81**[4-5]

judiciary/executive "laws," **64**[10]

judiciary restraint on bad, **78**[19]; equity, *Ar* 3 *Sec* 2, **37**[10], **80**[12-14], **81**[6], **83**[11,19,25-26]; limited jurisdiction,

353

judicial system, **83**[19]; supreme court, **81**[7]

state senate, **39**[5], **63**[18]

Massachusetts, **7**[4]

constitution, separation of powers, **47**[10]

governor, **57**[21], **69**[4-6]; veto, **69**[5], **73**[15]

judicial system, **81**[19]; jury trial, **83**[28-31]; supreme court, **81**[7]; judges' salary, **79**[1]

legislature, **47**[10], **55**[2], **57**[19-20]

impeachment court, **66**[3]

military, **28**[3]; peace time, **24**[6], **25**[9]

Shays rebellion, **6**[7,19], **21**[4], **25**[9], **28**[3], **74**[4]

mathematical theorems

compared to truths in behavioral sciences, **31**[1-3]

merchants, **4**[7], **11**[8,12], **12**[2]

"class" of people, **10**[7]

as representatives, **35**[6,9], **36**[1-2], **60**[5-9]

taxes, effect of, **35**[2-3]

unstable government, effect of, **62**[17]

military, *Ar* 1 *Sec* 8, *Ar* 2 *Sec* 2; Amendment 2, Amendment 5, Amendment 14, **4**[15-16], **8**, **19**[9-12], **23**[4-9], **24-29**, **41**[5-21], **43**[18], **45**[11], **46**[9], **60**[12], *see* **defense**

see **appropriations**

army, **23**[6-8], **24**[4], **25**[3], **28**[10], **29**, **46**[9], *see* standing army (below); addition to militia, **25**[8], **28**[3], **41**[9]; enforce Constitution, **16**[5]; executive using, **8**[10], **25**[6], **26**[10-13]; Revolution, during, **22**[5]

bases, forts, ports, arsenals, *see* **defense**

see **commander-in-chief**

commerce, **12**[9-10], **13**[4], **14**[1]

courts-martial, **40**[11]

enlistment, forced, incentives, **22**[5]

expansion, **26**

expense, **30**[1-9], **34**[6-7], **36**[16]

federal authority over, **43**[4,6]

historically, **4**[14], **6**[10-11], **8**[12], **19**[16], **20**[4, 8-11, 15-16], **38**[4], **41**[13], **46**[9], **70**[9]

laws, enforced by, **15**[11], **16, 27-28**

legislature, **26**[2,6,11]

see **liberty, liberty endangered**

militia, *see* **militia**

navy, *see* **navy**

peacetime, *see* standing army (below)

people control, **28**[5]

power, **4**[9,12,16], **8**[11], **11**[2,5-6], **16**[11]

raise military, **20**[4], **22**[5], **23**[4], **26**[6], **41**[9-10]

revenue needed, **30**[1], *see* **appropriations**

standing army, **8**[2-14], **16**[3-5], **20**[10], **24**, **25**[5-9], **26**, **28**[5-6], **29**[3,7], **41**[11-14,18], **46**[9]

-endangers liberty, **24**[6], **25**[9], **26**[13]

-State, **8**[11], **25**[2-4,9], **26**[6-7], **28**[9-10], **45**[8], **47**[19]

-if States disunite, **4**[15]

taxes, **20**[15-16], **30**[1], **41**[14]

military, peacetime, *see* **military, standing army**

militia, **28, 29, 41**[6,21], **43**[8], **56**[4,7], *see* **defense,** *Ar* 1 *Sec* 8, *Ar* 2 *Sec* 2; Amendment 2, Amendment 5

citizen-soldiers, must leave work, **29**[6]

commander-in-chief, **4**[12-13], **69**[6], **74**[1]

defense, strengthens Union's, **4**[12-13,17], **41**[6]

enforce laws, **28**[2-4]

liberty, defends, **26**[14], **29, 46**[9], *see* **liberty, endangered**

professional army, **8**[12], **24**[11], **25**[8], **26**[12-14], **29**[3,7]

national regulation of, **29, 53**[5], **56**[4,7]

officers appointed by States, **29**[2,9], **45**[8], **46**[9], **56**[7]

opponents, *see* **opponents ... Constitution,** militia

Milot, Abbe'18[8]

ministers, public, **42**[1-4], **64**[4], **80**[12,16], **81**[15], **84**[20]; tenure, **39**[5]

President appoints, receives, *Ar* 2 *Sec* 2, *Sec* 3, **67**[8], **69**[8-9], **76**[1], **77**[9]

minority, **43**[16-17], **43**18], **85**[11], *see* **faction, majority vs. supermajority**

corruption easier, **22**[10]

opinions, influence, 10[6-7,11], 48[5], 58[14], 62[9], 63[2,7-8], 65[2,10], 70[11-12], 76[5]
  political, 49[7], 65[2]
  more powerful than reasoning, 6[9], 10[1], 20[21], 41[4], 49[10], 50[6], 55[3], 58[14], 63[7-9], 73[8]
  ruler's, 6[9]
  wars, leads to, 3[13-14], 6[3], 16[3], 34[5]
  within republic, 6[9]

patent, *Ar* 1 *Sec* 8, **43**[2-3]

patriots, patriotism, 1[2], 2[10], 10[16], 40[17], 46[9], 63[3], 64[4,15], *see* **Founding Fathers**

peace, 21[5], 28[2-4], 34[4], 80[6]
  government's duty to secure, 31[6]
  worldwide, "deceitful dream," 6[18]

peacetime military, *see* **military, standing army**

Peloponnesian War, 6[4], 18[8], 25[10]

Pennsylvania, 6[19], 7[3], 13[2]
  constitution: violated, Council of Censors, 48[9-15], 50[3-11]; right to alter, abolish, 78[18]; separation of powers, 47[14], 48[9]
  defense, 25[9], 28[3]; peace time military, 24[6], 26[2,8]
  executive, 47[14], 48[15]
  impeachment court, 66[3]
  judicial system, 83[19,21]; supreme court, 47[14], 81[7]
  legislature, 57[19-20]; ratio constituents/legislator, 55[2-3]
  wealth, measuring, 21[6]

people, American, *see* **social classes**
  armed and trained, need to be, 29[6], 46[9]
  character 3[1], 44[6], 55[7], 63[7], 60[3]: discernment, 29[12]; enterprising spirit, 7[5], 11[2,8]; intelligent, 2[9], 3[1], 14[12], 15[4], 26[5], 32[1], 41[4], 49[7]
  citizens equal, 3[7]
  stop congressional usurpation, 44[17]
  Constitution
    -guardians of, 16[10], 31[12], 49[3]
    -only paper until ratified by, 40[15-17]

culturally united, 2[5], 3[5-6], 14[12], 15[1]
  divide against themselves, 4[17]
  enterprising spirit, 7[5]
  freedom, spirit of, 57[12]
  government
    -confident of good government, 27[1], 37[2-4,6]
    -right to alter/abolish, 40[16]
  local government, feel more loyalty to, 21[5], 25[3], 26[10], 27[4], 28[10], 46[1-5,9]
  see **powers,** people source of
  republic, want, 39[2]
  taxes, won't tolerate high, 12[6]

Petition of Right, 84[8]

piracies, *Ar* 1 *Sec* 8, **42**[1, 5]

Plato, 49[6]

Poland, confederacy, 14[6], 19[14]
  legislature, 22[9], 75[6]; not republic, 39[3]

policy, national government, *see* **stable government**

political science, *see* **abuse of power, partisan politics, separation of powers,** 9[3], 18[15], 55[2]
  axioms, 31[1-7], 44[16], 47[2-5], 53[1], 59[4], 80[3]
  discussions rarely objective, 37[2]
  ethics, 31[1-3]
  difficulties when studying, 37[9-11]

politics, all local, *see* **"local" politics**

politicians, *see* **partisan politics**
  corruption of, 22[10-13]
  court voters' favor, 57[9-10]
  all not motivated by public good, 10[9], 62[8]

poll taxes, 36[12,16], Amendment 24

popular government , 9, 12[4], 14[12], 18[16], 36[4], 63[12], 83[12], *see* **democracy, government, republic**
  administration problems, 21[5]
  American unique, 63[9]
  area, large, 9[3]
  Constitution rescues, 10[11]
  democracy, 14[4]
  executive, 70[1-5,18]
  factions flourish, *see* **factions**

destroyed by: faction, **51**[10]; super majority, **58**[15]

implies people have virtue, **76**[10]

larger society more capable of self-government, **51**[10]

passions sway, **6**[9]

people not virtuous enough for, **9**[2], **55**[9]

people source of all, *see* **powers**, people source of

people stop federal usurpation, **46**[10]

public interest vs. rulers' ambition, *see* **public good**

republic, **14**[4], **39**[2-5]

wars, start, **6**[15]

population, 55[6]

future growth, **55**[3-7], **58**[4-11], **84**[19-20]

ports, naval, *see* **defense**, bases

Portugal, commercial treaty, **3**[6]

posse comitatus, 29[4]

post offices, *Ar 1 Sec 8,* **42**[10,20]

power, 13[1], **15**[12-13], **22**[13], **26**[1], **39**[4], **41**[4], **48**[2-3], *see* **Articles** of **Confederation** defects, **usurpation, abuse of power**

aristocracy, **17**[11-12], **63**[19]

compensation, **79**[1]

controlled ... enemy of power doing the controlling, **15**[13]

defined, **33**[2-4], **82**[3]

equal to objectives, emergencies, **3**[1], **23**[9,11], **26**[5], **30**[6], **31**, **34**[3-4], **36**[16], **38**[11], **41**[2-5], **44**[16], **62**[4], **70**[1]

federal, *see* **federal powers**

government's, *see* **federal powers, State vs. federal, House of Representatives, judicial branch, legislative branch, military, President, "necessary and proper" clause, separation of powers, States, 25**[3]

impeachment, *see* **impeachment**, House jealousy of, **7**[4]

limits on, **9**[3], **17**[1], **25**[9], **26**[13], **48**, **57**[3], **62**[6], **63**[7], **70**[1-3], **78**[9,16],

81[5], **84**[7], *see* **separation of powers**

love of *(motivates behavior),* **1**[3], **2**[10-11], **6**[3,9], **17**[1], **22**[7], **25**[3], **53**[1], **61**[1], **72**[13]

not necessarily used, **36**[16]

people source of government's powers, Preamble, **2**[2], **16**[10], **21**[5], **22**[18], **23**[11], **26**[2,11], **28**[5,7], **33**[6], **37**[6], **39**[4,10,12], **40**[16] **46**[1,6], **49**[3], **50**[1], **51**[4,9], **52**[2,4], **57**[4-6], **61**[3], **63**[7,12,21], **70**[18], **76**[10], **77**[11], **78**[13,18], **84**[8,10]

-term in office, **57**[3]

-in Holland, no power from people, **39**[3]

political, effects opinions, **1**[3,5], **2**[10]

v. power, **28**[7], **51**[4], **59**[10]

"sweeping clause", *see* **"necessary and proper" clause**

see **taxation**

v. term in office, **51**[9], **63**[12]

preamble of Constitution, 84[8]

President, 67-77, *see* **executive branch**

censure, **70**[15,18], **71**[1]

character of, **58**[13], **64**[3-4,15], **67**[5], **68**[6-8], **70**[1,7], **71**, **72**[8], **73**[2], **75**[2,4], **76**[4]

Congress, adjourn, *Ar 2 Sec 3,* **69**[6], **77**[9]

compensation, *Ar 2 Sec 1,* **48**[8], **51**[3], **70**[4], **73**[1-2], **79**[1-2], **84**[20]

election of, *Ar 2 Sec 1,* Amendment 12, Amendment 24, **64**[3-4], 68; electoral college, electors, *Ar 2 Sec 1,* Amendment 12, Amendment 14, **39**[5,12], **60**[3], **64**[3-4], 68, **77**[11]; House final arbiter, **66**[7], **68**[7]; State role, **39**[12], **44**[26], **45**[7]

-conspiracies blocked, **68**[5-6]

-electors, D.C., Amendment 23

-legislature sinister influence, **71**[5]

foreign influence, **68**[5-6], **75**[3]

impeachment, *see* **impeachment, 39**[5]

intelligence, secret, **64**[7-8]

leaves office, dies, *Ar 2 Sec 1,* Amendment 25

oath, *Ar* 2 *Sec* 1

opposition to, *see* **opponents … Constitution,** President

powers/authority, *Ar* 2 *Sec* 1, **44**[27], **69**, **70**, **73**[3-14], **74-77**, **78**[7], **84**[22], *see* **abuse of power, administration, appointments, pardons, Commander-in-chief, treaties**

v. governor's power, **69**

increased by emergency, crisis, **8**[5], **48**[5]

laws, recommends, **69**[6], **77**[9]

legislation, **71**[3], *Ar* 1 *Sec* 7

v. monarch's power, **67**[3-5], **69**, **70**[19-20], **73**[10]

source of, **39**[12]

veto power, *see* **executive branch**, veto

qualifications, *Ar* 2 *Sec* 1, age, **64**[4]

Representatives, coercing, **55**[9]

responsibility, **64**[14-15], **69**[4], **70**[1,5,15-22] **71**[1], **73**[12], **74**[3,5,6], **77**[11]; lost **70**[15,19], **77**[6]

Senators, never appoints, **67**[6-11]

state-of-the-union, **77**[9]

term 4 years, *Ar* 2 *Sec* 1, Amendment 20, **39**[5], **69**[3] **71**, **79**[2];vs. judicial term, pay, **79**[1-2]; no term limits, **68**[5], **71**[1], **72**, **85**[2]; term limits, Amendment 22

press

freedom, **41**[24], **84**[10-11], **85**[2]

State constitutions, **84**[11]

influences national discussion, **2**[11]

information about government, **84**[14]

private rights, **44**[6], **78**[19]

"privileges and immunities," **80**[9]

property, Amendments 5, Amendment 14

ability to acquire, **10**[6]

bankruptcy laws, **42**[18]

claims, **80**[11-12,14,15-20], **83**[11,18,36]

equal/unequal division of, **10**[6-7, 22]

federal government takes, **43**[4-6,10-12]

inheritance, **29**[4]

laws/regulations effect, **10**[7], **62**[16], **70**[1]

legislators as property owners, **10**[8], **35**[8-9], **36**[1], **60**[5-9]

owners/non-owners,**10**[6,7,8],**35**[8-9],**60**[5-10]

protection of, **1**[7], **5**[1], **8**[4], **10**[6], **11**[6], **17**[7], **25**[7], **41**[18, 20], **54**[8], **70**[1], **85**[1,3]

rights, **10**[6,13], **54**[9], **60**[5]

slaves, **54**[3-5, 8]

State responsibility, **45**[9]

tax, **10**[8], **12**[6,12], **21**[11], **34**[10], **36**[3,7,11], **35**[8], **54**[3-4]

value, **12**[2,6], **21**[6, 11], **36**[3]

-bad government decreases, **15**[3]

-increased value invites invasion/attack, **4**[9]

-laws effecting, **62**[16]

voters, federal, no property qualifications, **57**[15], **60**[11]

prosperity, **1**[7], **2**[12], **6**[9], **28**[2], **84**[15], *see* **commerce, wealth**

bills of credit, prohibition, **44**[5]

promoted by commerce, Constitution, union, **2**[3,12,14], **5**[6], **11**[3], **12**[1-2], **13**[4], **15**[3-4], **26**[2], **30**[7], **40**[16], **60**[9], **85**[5]

in States **45**[9], **46**[6]

prudence, **25**[9], **38**[6], **40**[18], **41**[11,16], **43**[3], **44**[6], **57**[14], **62**[17], **65**[9], **85**[8]

citizens', **31**[12], **33**[6]

good government has, **3**[15], **5**[5], **17**[2], **24**[11-12], **27**[6], **32**[4], **38**[4], **41**[14], **43**[31], **81**[23]

political virtue **23**[9], **62**[4,12], **64**[7], **74**[4]

psychology, *see* **human behavior**

public good, public welfare, public interest, pubic trust, common good, common interest, *see* **justice** **10**[8], **13**[1], **14**[1,4], **22**[9], **31**[5], **34**[9], **37**[2], **38**[11], **43**[2-3,31], **45**[2], **46**[6], **52**[5], **60**[3], **61**[4], **63**[21], **76**[5]

capital, **43**[4-5]

commerce, **11**[7-8]

defense, **4**[16], **24**[10], **64**[3], **66**[12]

government's objective, **30**[7], **36**[15], **41**[4], **45**[2]

government's power, **41**[4]

guided the Convention, **37**[15]

judges **3**[9], **78**[5], **79**[4]

laws equal, **57**[13], **64**[10]

v. money, **22**[13]

moral, **7**[9], **15**[8], **17**[8], **27**[6], **43**[23-24], **81**[17], **85**[5]

must be reasonable and effectual, **63**[5]

personal vs. group, **48**[15], **70**[15-18], **77**[5-6]

political, **62**[8], **63**[3-5],**77**[11], **79**[4]

power must equal **31**[5]

representatives', **62**[8]

rulers' to people, **38**[3], **55**[8], **57**[3], **63**[3-5], **64**[15], **66**[8], **70**[5,19-20], **70**[5], **77**[11]

State governments, *see* **States**

treaties, **64**[11], **69**[7], **75**[2]

two types: moral, legal **70**[15]

revenue, government's, **12, 21**[9], **23**[7-8], **30**

bills start in House of Representatives, *Ar 1 Sec 7*, **58**[8,12-13], **66**[7]

borrow money, **41**[6,22], *Ar 1 Sec 8*

decreased by: high taxes, **12**[4], **21**[10], **35**[2-4,11]; smuggling, **12**[8-10]

defense/war, relationship to, **6**[13], **8**[8] **16**[5], **23**[9], **30**[8], **31**[6-77], **34**[4-8], **41**[11,16-17,22,26], **45**[11], *see* **taxation** limits, **appropriations**

increased by: commerce, **12**[6,11-12]; money turnover, **12**[2-3]; staying united, **12**

for "general welfare," **23**[7], **41**[23-end], **45**[11], Preamble, *Ar 1 Sec 8*

limiting revenue limits power, **21**[10]

nation/States need, **7**[6], **12**[12], **13, 21**[9], **23**[8], **30, 31**[7-8], **32**[1], **34**[4-5,7-10], **41**[14,22]

State requisitions, *see* **quotas and requisitions**

taxation/taxes, *see* **taxation**

United States area will double soon, **38**[10]

revolt, *see* **sedition**

civil war, **16**[11]

denial of suffrage, **60**[2,12]

"scourge of republics," **28**[3]

Shay's, **6**[7,19], **21**[4], **25**[9], **28**[3], **74**[4]

Union barrier against, **9**[1,12-14]; pardons, **74**[4]; force to control, *Ar 1 Sec 8, Sec 9*, **8**[10], **16**[11], **26**[13], **28, 29**[1,13], **43**[16-17,20-21], **84**[4], **85**[3];

Revolutionary War, American, **2**[5,7-8,10], **14**[12], **22**[5-6], **23**[10], **25**[8], **45**[2], **46**[9], **55**[8], **84**[7]

fought to establish republic, **39**[2]

land grants at time of, **7**[2]

Pennsylvania executive violated constitution, **48**[15]

expense, **34**[8]

God's help, **37**[14], *see* **God**

Rhode Island, **7**[4,9]

constitution, separation of power, **47**[11]

disproportionate power, **22**[7-9]

judiciary, **83**[19]

legislature: elections, **40**[11], **53**[1], **63**[3]; ratio constituents/legislators, **55**[2-3]

rights, 1, 10[1], **43**[31], **84,** *see* **bill of rights**

civil rights, **1**[5], **8**[11], **9**[2], **10**[1,12], **51**[10]

American idea, **14**[12]

citizen, **36**[16], **54**[2], **56**[9]; bear arms, **46**[9]

-cede some rights to government, **2**[2]

-judicial branch, guardian, **78**[19-20]

defendant's rights, **65**[8]

endangered from least suspected source, **35**[3]

judiciary guards, **78**[18-20]

laws diminished, **44**[6]

liberty, *see* **liberty**

press, **41**[24], **84**[10-11], **85**[2]

privacy rights, **44**[6]

property, **10**[6,13], **54**[2-6,8-11]

religious, **51**[10]

slaves, rights, denied, **54**[4]

threat from military, **8, 25**[3]

State "legislative appeal," **22**[8]

States', **21**[2,5], **38**[7]

voter, **60**

rivalry

commercial, **4**[4-5], **6**[3,9], **11**[6], **12**[2], **35**[9], **36**[2]

disunited States, **14**[12], **15**[9], **18**[8]

363

defense, strong, **4-5**, **8**[13], **9**[1], **41**[14-16,18,26], **45**[2],

geographically united, **2**[4]

happiness, promotes, **45**[2]

purposes of union, **23**[3], **39**[14]

size, large, **9**[9-14], **10**

United Nations, *see* **group behavior, allies, alliances**

psychology of league of nations, **15**

non-compliance by members, **15**[14]

United Netherlands, confederacy, **20**

ambassadors, **28**[4,7]

authority, none from people, **39**[3]

commerce, **11**[3], **20**[14], **42**[12]

congress (States-General), **20**[2-4], **54**[9]

constitutional organization, **37**[15], **43**[14]

   -theoretically, **20**[2-11]

   -executive (stadholder), **20**[5-10,19]

   -in reality, **20**[12-24]

   -weakness leads to tyranny, **20**[18], **38**[11]

fatal flaw, government over government, **20**[13-18] *see* **legislature for states**

foreign nations, effect of **20**[20]

minority rule **75**[6]

taxes, federal **20**[14-16,22]

United States debts to **29**[11]

war, role in **6**[13]

wealth **21**[6]

United States of America, **53**[5]

adding States **14**[9]

affection for, **27**[1,4], **41**[15], **46**[2], **53**[6], **59**[10], **64**[15]

area will double soon **38**[10]

borders defined by peace treaty **14**[6]

capital **32**[2], **43**[4-6], **84**[13-15]

citizenship **42**[10, 17], **80**[9]

coin, security regulation **42**[10, 14]

consuls, ministers **42**[1, 3, 4]

culture **2**[5]

description of **1**[1]

example for other nations **1**[1], **9**[2], **20**[23]

Europe's relationship with, *see* **Europe**

federal government important, **1**[7]

federal vs. national, features of **39**

formation of United States **2**[8]

geography **2**[4]

-isolated **8**[13], **11**[14], **12**[10], **24**[10], **41**[14]

international reputation **11**[14], **63**[1-3]

officials

   -oath to support federal Constitution, *Ar* 6, **44**[24-26]

   -no religious test, *Ar* 6, **44**[24], **52**[2], **57**[6]

unique "American" spirit **14**[12]; negative **11**[14]

usurpation, **46**[1], *see* **abuse of power, tyranny**

by aristocracy **63**[19,21]

Bill of Rights **84**[10]

block/correct usurpation **49-50**; citizens **60**[12]; congress, two houses of **62**[8]; good constitution **41**[12], **42**[4], **51**[4]; States **28**, **46**[7-10], **51**[9]; union **9**[11]; *see* **impeachment**

Constitutional Convention **40**[11,17]

constitution, weak **20**[18], **38**[11]

Council of Censors **48**[9,12,15], **50**[3,5]

executive **48**[4-6,12,15], **71**[6]

   -executive council **70**[22]

   -republic limits **48**[5-6]

   -term limits **72**[5]

federal usurp State authority **17**, **31**, **33**[7-8]

Great Britain **52**[8]

by group **70**[22]

judicial **48**[6], **81**[4,9]

by legislature **44**[17], **48**[4-6,10], **49-50**

military/militia, **25**[6], **60**[12]

   --supports **8**[11], **26**[11], **28**[6], **29**[12]

in States **16**[10], **21**[4-5], **28**[6-9], **48**[7-9,12]

Venice, *see* **Italian states**

Vermont, dispute over territory, **7**[4]

veto, *see* **executive branch, veto power**

Vice President, *Ar* 1 *Sec* 3, *Ar* 2, *Sec* 1, *Sec* 4, Amendments 12, Amendment 14, Amendment 20, Amendment 23, Amendment 24, Amendment 25

election of, President of Senate, **68**[9-10]

Virginia

amendment proposed **40**[16]

constitution **47**[17], **48**[11]; separation of powers **47**[17]

elections **52**[8]

governor impeachable after term **39**[5]

Great Britain, resist usurpations **52**[8]

Jefferson, Thomas, **48**[8], **49**

judiciary **83**[19]; supreme court, **81**[7]

legislature, members/constituents, **55**[2-3]

   -senate term 4 years **39**[5]

   -usurped powers **48**[7-8]

seacoast vulnerable **41**[20]

wealth in **21**[6]

virtue, **2**[10], **6**[18], **15**[12],**49**[7], **53**[1], **55**[9], **57**[3], **64**[4], **66**[13], **68**[8], **72**[2], **73**[1,7,8], **75**[3], **76**[10]

voters, **53**[2], **54**[9], **57**, **60-61**

character of **64**[3-4]; apathy **61**[2]; corrupted **41**[17]

conspiracy **60**[3-4]

decide qualifications **10**[18], **35**[5-11]

indirectly elect President, Senate **64**[3-4], **68**[2-4]

national, more choices **27**[2]

qualifications **35**[8], **52**[2], **54**[7], **57**[5,15-18], **60**[11], **68**

in Rome **34**[2]

representatives listen, **52**[5,9],**55**[2],**57**[9-11]

representative/voter ratio **10**[19]

"Wag the Dog" scenario **6**[4]

war, **6**, **25**[7-8], **29**[2], **41**[12], **70**[13], *see* **Revolutionary War, defense, military, allies, alliance**

causes of, **3**[5-7, 12-16], **4**[1-3,8], **6-8**, **41**[12], **80**[6], **83**[23]

   -civil war in America, **5-8**, **16**, **85**[3,15]

   -commerce, **4**[4-9], **5**[10-11], **6**, **7**[5-6], **34**[4]

   -jealousy, **4**[9-10,15]

   -weak nation, **18**[9], **62**[14]

crimes during, Amendment 5

declare, *Ar* 1, *Sec* 8, **25**[7], **41**[6,8], enemy, **22**[11]

funding, *see* **appropriations,** **30**[8], **34**[4-6]

history of, **80**[7]

offensive, none **34**[5]

of parchment, **7**[9]

peace rare, **34**[5]

prevention of, **4**[10-12]

secretary of, **84**[20]

soldier quarters, Amendment 3

State prohibition, *Ar* 1 *Sec* 10

treason, *Ar* 3 *Sec* 3, **84**[4]

union provides *security* from, **3**, **5**[4]

Washington, D.C. *see* **capital, federal**

weakness in government. **6**[18,20], **15**[3], **17**[10], **19**[7], **20**[10], **23**[10], **25**[7], **30**[7], **38**[11], **62**[14-18], **70**[2], **71**[1-2], **75**[6]

anarchy, **20**[20], **22**[9], **26**[2], **70**[1]

emergencies, **18**[9], **20**[18], **22**[9], **62**[15], **70**[11], **72**[9]

Greek republics doomed by, **18**

ignoring laws creates, **25**[10]

invites foreign danger, **5**[2], **19**[13,17], **22**[12],

   -disunited States, **8**[5], **11**[6], **41**[14], **43**[15]

tyranny, leads to, **20**[18], **38**[11]

war, **18**[9], **62**[14]

wealth

abuse of wealthy people, **85**[4]

candidates, no __ qualification, **52**[3], **57**[6,18], **60**[5,10-11]

influence of, **54**[9]

laws, regulations favor, **62**[16]

love of **6**[9], *see* **money**

unequal State wealth, **21**[8], **37**[12]

wealth, national, **12**, **21**[6-7], *see* **prosperity, taxation**

commerce increases, **11**[8],**12**[1-3],**15**[3], **60**[9]

financing war, **30**[8-10]

Great Britain, **34**[7]

Holland, **20**[15-16]

measuring, **21**[6-7,11], **54**[2,5]

money turnover increases, **12**[3]

western territory will increase, **38**[10]

weights and measures, *Ar* 1 *Sec* 8, **18**[14], **40**[11], **42**[10,16], **69**[11]

welfare, *see* **general welfare**

of citizens, **1**[1,6], **18**[2], **26**[2], **45**[2]

Made in the USA
San Bernardino, CA
02 January 2020